The Immigrant's Way

For All Immigrants, By An Immigrant

Margaret W. Wong, Esq.

4th Edition

ISBN Number appears on Back Cover

ILW.COM, P O Box 1830, New York, NY 10156

IMPORTANT NOTICE:

This book is not intended to provide legal advice to any person. Each immigration situation, immigration administrative action, litigation in immigration court or federal action can be different and you may wish to consult with an immigration lawyer concerning specific issues in your particular case. This book provides an overview of common scenarios encountered by immigrants with practical pointers on how to tackle those situations but in no way are these to be construed as legal advice to any person. Nothing in this book should be taken as a substitute for the services of qualified legal counsel.

TABLE OF CONTENTS

<u>SECTION II</u>: IMMIGRATION PAPERWORK AND LEGAL PROCESS

PREFACE

Swedish Immigrant 1902;
In America they gave you good land for nothing, and in two years you could be a rich man; and no one had to go in the army unless they wanted to. That was what my uncle told us.

Italian Immigrant 1902;
Now and then I had heard things about America that it was a far off country where everybody was rich and where Italians went and made plenty of money so that they could return to Italy and live in pleasure. One day I met a young man who pulled out a handful of gold and told me he had made that in America in only a few days.

Chinese Immigrant 1902;
The Americans would not dare to treat Germans, English, Italians or even Japanese as they treat the Chinese, because if they did there would be a war.

Controversy has surrounded immigration topics in times of war, want, and need. As America's economic and political supremacy has begun to wane, there are cries for stricter regulation on immigration. Amidst the deliberations of politicians and pundits, immigrants have continued to come to our soil to work and to build. These are our foreign borns.

The Immigrant's Way begins with the history of immigrants from all parts of the globe coming to America over the course of the past millennium, along with the geopolitical, social, and economic factors which inspired people to seek opportunity in a new land. Margaret Wong describes and connects the legacy of immigration to the United States with concurrent shifts in legislative policy during different eras of American history, while relating her own story and allowing readers to more fully understand the context behind American immigration policy and reform.

In the second portion of the book, Margaret Wong guides readers through different nuances and changes in immigration law and provides an overview of what it takes to become an American in the 21st century.

While of interest to the American reader seeking to become better informed about U.S. immigration law and history, this book also provides current, prospective, and future immigrants with practical information on how to obtain a visa to visit the United States, secure a green card, decide whether to become a U.S. citizen, and ultimately achieve the goal of citizenship.

DEDICATION

To my parents, who sent me to America and made all this possible.

ALIEN

alien – noun

1. A person of another family, race or nation
2. A foreign-born resident who has not been naturalized and is still a subject or citizen of a foreign country; *broadly*: a foreign-born citizen
3. Extraterrestrial
4. Exotic

[Merriam Webster's Online Dictionary]

"For weak ye are, outcasts on stranger lands,
And forward talk beseems not strengthless hands."
[Aeschylus, *The Suppliants* -- Translated by E.D.A. Morshead]

This line from Aeschylus captures the difficult predicament of being an alien in a foreign land. The line is delivered by a father, Danaus, to his daughters, whose cousins were attempting to force them to marry. The father and daughters are now at the mercy of the king whose land, Argos, they are living in. They are fleeing injustice and seeking refuge. The author of this play, Aeschylus, was a famous playwright from ancient Greece, and one of the great tragedians. *The Suppliants* centers on those fleeing persecution, and so much from this ancient drama translates into trends in our current American media. It focuses on this one aspect of immigration, drawing public attention to the immigrants who are refugees. This could be one of the reasons why many Americans have begun to look at immigrants as supplicants asking for help, rather than people who can contribute to society. America today is a land comprised almost entirely of immigrants and the near-generational descendants of immigrants. When did we stop believing in the brave pioneers looking to build the country and create a new life for themselves through hard work and perseverance? When did they begin to see immigrants only as beggars - as supplicants?

King Pelasgus hesitates to grant Danaus and his daughters refuge because he fears starting a war. He only relents when his people vote to let the people stay. Think about this image, this powerful microcosm of modern day democracy and politics set two and a half millennia ago. This story closely parallels 20th century America.

As Danaus repeats to his daughters the Argive people's oath to protect them, it should be noted that the travelers are referred to as "stranger-guests," a much more polite and welcoming term than the one Danaus himself uses (weak… outcasts on stranger lands).

When I searched Yahoo and Google for the definition of aliens, a few words repeatedly came up. Foreign, exotic, different, outsider, estranged, excluded, not belonging, belonging to another place, another society, another family, another race. We need the image of people like us to change. Maybe we need to get rid of the words "alien" and "alienage," and use "foreign-born" or "immigrant." In this book I use "foreign born" rather than "aliens" to refer to immigrants and would-be immigrants.

ACKNOWLEDGEMENTS

I could not have written this book without the support of my husband, children, extended family, partners, colleagues, friends, clients, summer interns, externs and the newbie lawyers who deserve applause for suffering the indignity of being called in by this senior partner to help, research, add footnotes and observe sessions of books. Special thanks to friends, sisters, and brothers who pushed me to finish this project: Kam Chan, Steven Chan, Allison Chan, Cecilia Wong, Michael Fungsang, Francis Fungsang, Joseph Fungsang, Stephanie Fungsang, Rose Wong, Bernard Lee, Theresa Lee, Catherine Lee, George Hwang, Lily Yao Hwang, Jacqueline Hwang, Vincent Hwang, Alex Machaskee, Bill and Marianne Miller, George Veras, Mike Rogers, Gerald Seipp, Alan Carol, Dean Mutua, Thrity Umrigar, Judy Ruggie, Jerry Wareham, Sam Udani, Alan Ying, Esther Fridman, Scott Bratton, Lori Pinjuh, Larry Hadfield, Jason Lorenzon, Deborah Lee, Debu Gandhi, Brian Marek, Jackie Tong, Jilan Zhang, Arty Wynieski, Nathan Hsu, Audrey Jian, Leo Shipcka, Noli Delos Reyes, Alex Strmac, Lily Ying, Joyce Graham, Fabiola Cini, Annie Zheng, Cosmina Pop, Craig Schaefer, Jian Tang, Juliessa Roman, Kathy Hill, Vicky Ko, Vitali Pikus, Angela Ballou, Karim Berdiev, Luz Merced, Arianne Delos Reyes, Kim Lynce, Mahima Rao, Ilona Fleszar, Marian Kim, Steve Szabo, Qi Che, Lin Lin Huang, Chunli Wu, Judy Wong, Renee Holcomb, Danja Therecka, George Pop, Jared Glasbrenner, Andrew Bramante, Weronika Kowalczyk. Thanks to Green Street Studio and the photographer Crickett Karson for the photo on the backcover.

PROLOGUE

This book is meant to be read by all foreign borns, whether you aspire to come to America or are already here, whether you have legal status or not. You may feel disappointed in life and have not accomplished what you set out to do. I asked myself why I have this burning desire to write this manuscript and to give you my wisdom and lessons learnt from mistakes in my 40 years living in America. You and your parents have helped me build my immigration law practice. Without you, I really would not be here. So, to return your faith in me, and to thank you for allowing me the opportunity to work with you for all these years - helping you get permanent residency (Green Cards), fighting deportation, and obtaining U.S. citizenship - I am writing this book.

I understand how disappointed and sad you can get when you work so hard in this country for so long but cannot get a Green Card, the indicator of permanent residency and acceptance into the American system. Having experienced the same difficulties with the process of immigration to the United States, I wanted to help others along the way, which is why I chose to become an immigration lawyer. Now, looking back on these past four decades, I want to write down what I have learned so that other immigrants can benefit from my experiences, and more importantly, from my mistakes.

I think back to my own journey: leaving Hong Kong when I was only 19, a naïve school girl from an all-girl Catholic school; being fired from waitress jobs during college for not being able to distinguish between a Rob Roy with olive, a Manhattan with cherry, and a martini with a double twist; and now being a nationally known immigration attorney with offices in five cities, counseling thousands of foreign-borns on how to obtain and maintain legal status in the United States. I am living the American dream.

A lot of people probably wonder why we still want to come to America, with its high crime rate, interracial issues, highly publicized corruption, and shaky economic conditions, when the rising powers in India, China and Russia are starting to equalize the power structure of global markets. Yet it is my firm belief that the United States is still the best country in which to live, thrive, and become somebody.

Along my journey, I have become one of the honorees of the Ohio Women Hall of Fame, co-chair of the NAPABA District Immigration Law Committee, an honoree of the Ellis Island medal of honor, a life member of the 6th Federal Judicial District and the 8th Ohio Judicial District, and a board member of the United Way and Ohio Notre Dame College. For philanthropy I received the Margaret Ireland Award from the Cleveland Women's City Club and the 1997 Creative Philanthropy Award from the Women's Community Foundation. I am also named in Crain's Cleveland Business's "Women of Influence" list and Cleveland Magazine's list of "Most Interesting People." As the first Asian-American president of the Cleveland Chapter of the Federal Bar Association, the Cleveland chapter won the coveted Chapter Activity Award. I was also appointed by the Ohio Supreme Court as a charter member of the Continuing Legal Education Commission for attorneys, and I served as a member of its Ohio Supreme Court Racial Task Force.

While I have had many successes, there have been setbacks as well. My divorce was so painful that I have had to shut it out from my mind. After being physically and emotionally abused by my first husband, I was rendered so insecure that I believed even spending money on a Starbucks coffee would render me penniless when I grew old, with nobody to care for me. I still do not buy an ice cream cone or a nice mechanical pencil without thinking about it. In spite of my numerous awards and board memberships, that feeling of impotence, and of being an outsider, has driven me to write this book for all of us foreign-borns. There is hope for people like us, and dreams still waiting to be realized in America. I hope some of the experiences in this book will resonate with other zero-generation immigrants, who like me may often feel out of place both in the lands of our birth and our adopted homeland. (I use the term zero-generation to refer to those like me, who are immigrants to the U.S. and not born here. My children are first-generation Americans, although it is also valid to say I am a first generation immigrant, they are second generation).

How can more foreign-borns survive and thrive in this land and become truly a part of it, helping to make history along the way? How do we become what we are destined to be and make our parents, as well as our makers, proud?

First, there are certain things that most foreign-borns, or at least that I, may never understand: the New Yorker cartoons, and for that matter, most American jokes. Despite this, most foreign-borns in the United States are tenacious survivors. We work hard to save and to bring our families to America to enjoy a better life—in living standards, personal freedoms, and environmental conditions. We also tend to be stoic, do not voice our opinions often, and are generally more accepting and accommodating to the not-so-great things that happen to us or around us, while being thankful for the good things that do happen.

Please do not lose faith in yourself! Just because you were not born in this country and do not sound mainstream does not mean that you cannot become successful here. I have summarized my tactics toward success in 22 rules:

1. Learn to speak English.

I know it is difficult, especially when you work three jobs a day and are just trying to survive. Take an English language class at the library, or ask your neighbor to record a story on a tape for you. Whenever you are working, if it does not require answering phones, keep listening to it and repeating the words.

Try to learn twenty new words a day. Be sure you learn how to speak proper English (as opposed to slang words or the "F" word). Do not use swear words, or at least use them very rarely.

Keep in mind that most American women do not like to be called "baby," "darling," "young woman," or "honey." When in doubt, address Americans as Mr. or Ms. Suchandsuch, sir, or ma'am. It is always better to be humble than snobbish.

2. Become a good communicator.

We are not like natives in this land that we have made our home. They were born here and have spoken and written English their entire lives. However, expressing ourselves clearly is crucial for success in America.

Why did my bosses give me a raise and appreciate me as myself, and not just as a nondescript worker? It was because I knew how to express myself and worked hard on my job. I may speak with an accent, but if I am a good worker, my bosses will be able to tell. How do they know I am a good worker? They know because I can express my understanding of job, customers, co-workers and supervisors. Communicate your ideas. There are two ways to exert leadership: writing and speaking skills. At least be good at one of these skills.

3. Save your money, pay taxes, and file annual tax returns.

From where many of us come, our governments do not do enough good for our people. Bureaucrats may take our tax money and use it to buy things for themselves. In the United States, the system is different. The more money that we report we make, the more we can borrow and establish credit.

We should learn not to be too commercialized. We should remember to be more frugal, because most of us do not have a lot of friends or relatives in the United States who can help us on a rainy day. Buying many clothes, expensive clothes, or designer handbags is not worth it in the United States most of the time. Unlike our countries of birth, where wearing brand name clothes can impress others, in the United States, smart people will not feel differently as long as you are neat and clean while less smart people will only become jealous of you. So why bother?

4. Make friends.

Learn from those around you. Everyone has a different set of strengths and specialties in knowledge. You do not have to be inside a classroom to learn. Many of your native-born American friends can teach you a lot about American and Western history, culture, and language. Some of the knowledge they take for granted can be very helpful for you, who are lacking in this department.

Teach native-born Americans that you are not better or worse than those who are born in the United States, just different. You are an ambassador from your native culture, so help them understand you, and in doing so, they may get rid of some misconceptions about immigrants and foreigners. Show them that although you may be less practiced at English grammar and spelling than they, it does not mean you are stupider or less competent than those who were born in this country.

5. Smile often. Show gratitude, and remember to write thank you notes. Always be polite.

We want the best of both worlds, so we need to be accepted and fit into both worlds. Proper manners can help in this respect. Remember to knock on the door before you enter a private room. Westerners treasure their privacy in many cases more than the rest of the world. Remember to hold the door open for the next person going into the same door behind you. Do not spit or throw gum or cigarette butts out the window or on the streets. Also, remember not to squat on the ground; it is considered uncouth in the Western world.

I still remember when I first came to the United States in 1969. That day I was with my host family, and I opened the window on the highway to enjoy some fresh air. While I thought the air was fresher than that of Hong Kong, my hosts almost died from the wind because the car was going sixty-five miles per hour.

6. Keep your dreams. Visualize them, and make them happen.

Do not let the toughness of life in the United States wear you down. It is difficult when we do not have a permanent home and when we have to worry about our spouse divorcing us and causing us to lose our legal status, social security number, driver's license, bank accounts, etc. Remember that our status does not represent or define who we are. We are who we are from our side. In taking an intelligent choice and calculated risk to come to the United States to start a new life, we are the trailblazers from our countries of birth and for our families. We have to remember to keep our faith.

You and I are not here in America to be nobodies. We came to the United States for a better chance at becoming a "somebody" and living a good life – something we may not have the opportunity for in our countries of birth.

7. Be positive, think positive, act positive.

I was denied my foreign student visa three times before I was finally approved. That was only after my parents had begged one of their rich friends to sign for me, guaranteeing my living expenses in the United States in spite of my scholarship to the university. I am still friends with my sponsor to this day. In fact, their granddaughter, Karen Chang, is now in law school and clerked for our firm prior to returning to school. She also contributed to this book. Hopefully, she will become a lawyer at my firm one day.

Some people may view us with suspicion or even hostility, but that is mostly because of their ignorance and assumptions based on our looks and accents. Once we show them who we really are, they will "learn" to look past appearances and may even be less prejudiced when looking at other immigrants.

As foreign countries become wealthier, America will have fewer foreigners like us who have no status and are willing to work hard for very little money. If we leave, who will do our work here? Of course, I am only day dreaming, because the thought of me leaving this beloved country of mine is ridiculous.

8. Read, meditate, think, and manage your thoughts.

Just because we do not have permanent status does not mean that we should lose ourselves to the panic and depression and forget to live our lives. If we are constantly worried about the federal government picking us up and jailing us even though we may never have been ordered deported, or about some overzealous police officer calling ICE, we will lose sight of who we really are and where we want to go from here.

We need to clear our minds to focus on what will empower us so that we can improve ourselves and become stronger. We need to control our minds and our attitudes. We are not going to leave our home here anyway, so why drive ourselves nuts just thinking about it?

We are all scared of something. As foreign-borns in this country, we are always scared of the police, and because of this we often forget why we are here in this beautiful country in the first place – to raise our children and give them the dignity that they would never get in our countries of birth; to learn English; to be able to walk into a beautiful hotel and have tea in their restaurants like everyone else, which is often not possible in our countries of origin; to be free from harassment and kidnapping; to become the best we can be; and for some, to be the first in our families who came to America, and be the trailblazer.

Of course, we love this country even if some of the locally-born residents harbor resentment towards us. All we want is to stay here, make a quiet living, and live here to support our families.

9. Do not get on government support, even if those around us think it is free. Nothing is free in life.

Once we get Medicaid, Medicare, or Welfare, it is very hard to get green cards or to become United States Citizens. The more we do this, the more we play into the American stereotype of immigrants wanting something for free and living off "real" Americans' money. We are strong and good people. We can work for what we are entitled to in the United States. Although we may be poor in legal status, we should try very hard to avoid government support.

10. Do not drink alcohol before driving. Do not try illegal drugs. Do not get into fights.

Do not get violent no matter how angry you are at work, with friends, family, or strangers. Do not raise a knife to threaten people when you are angry. We have laws in America, and disobeying them can result in criminal charges. They can put us in jail even if we are just expressing anger since we do not speak English.

Do not hit your spouse or shout too loudly at them. It is a criminal offense in America to hit your spouse. Remember that in this country, just because she married you for life does not mean that she has to sleep with you. No means no. You cannot force a spouse to do things with you that she does not want to do.

Also, do not buy or carry a gun if you are not yet an American citizen. We are in a foreign land. We need to honor their rules just as we expect them to pay us fair wages because we work for them.

11. Children belong in schools. Education is their way toward greatness.

We do not want our children to be like us, doing menial and often smelly work with very little pay and no respect. We want them to be just like our picture of the other Americans - big, handsome, beautiful, and doing office work. They will be able to earn the big bucks so they don't have to depend on their children like we do when we get old. We see American kids as different. They have a lot of choices. We think they can do anything they want - buy 100 dollar Nike shoes (the real ones), buy beautiful bags that never in my life time I dared to dream of owning, and spoil themselves with little fear of retribution.

Being successful now, I try to help more people who are less fortunate in the world. So many people in your country of birth need our aid in U.S. dollars to help buy their food, build their huts, and buy medicine. America encourages its citizens to share their wealth with others.

12. Push yourself to keep up with the times – learn how to use computers and the internet.

I still remember when I first applied for my visa to come to the United States in 1969. We were at the height of the Vietnam War, and even though the youngsters in the U.S. were against it, and there were protests against it in Europe frequently, the western world respected America for sticking to its promises and its policies to fight the communists. The world was not as rich and the internet didn't exist back then. Now, you can find just about anything on the internet. Knowledge is king. We need to flow with it.

We need to push ourselves to learn how to use computers and other modern technology. We need to push our children to learn, as well. Then, they can be somebody one day. Our children can do anything they want to, provided they work hard for it.

13. Focus on your goals. See a good immigration lawyer at least once a year.

Everyone needs legal status in the United States. Remember to do a change of address by filling out the AR-11 form with the government whenever you move (until you become a U.S.C, when you can stop filling this out). It is really easy. To tell the truth, it is easier this way, because then we don't have to keep remembering who and what we said when. Always go to court when it is ordered, because the laws have changed since the '80s. If we do not go when we are told to, we will get an in absentia deportation order which is very difficult to reopen when you want to get a green card.

When you see an immigration lawyer each year, only see qualified help. Do not just go to anybody that your friend recommends. Immigration fraud is a big business, because the people know that we are desperate to stay here, and so they charge big bucks. Some Koreans spend between 30 and 50 thousand dollars to come to the U.S. illegally. It costs many Chinese about $70 thousand to come illegally and $100 thousand to come legally. Do not get involved. Remember, we are not natives here and Americans do not accept that we just trusted our friends and that our friends were not supposed to cheat us when something like this happens. This is a land of law, not of instant gratification. There is a process that we all have to go through to get somewhere. Nothing is easy in life. If it were so easy, we would not be here. Remember, we are the trailblazers. Just marrying an American may not solve the problem.

14. Eat healthy.

Most of us do not have health insurance, which means that we cannot afford to be sick. Doctors and hospitals are very expensive. It will take your life savings to get any surgery done. Even the rich are often unable to afford it. Will yourself to not get sick. Rest and sleep, and don't get anxious or depressed because of your visa issues. In my practice, I'm increasingly seeing depressed and anxiety-ridden people who are worried sick about their status. They get so angry. Negative energy is transferable and transparent. We have made a choice of coming to America to give ourselves and our kids a good life. We do not have the luxury of getting sick.

Protect your bodies physically, mentally, and spiritually. Even when we're very stressed, we need to try to eat and sleep properly. Pray, and stay healthy. When you do become sick, go see your friends who may know some doctors who are from our countries so that they might be able to help us. Rest and focus your energy somewhere else.

If you do have to go to the hospital, you can negotiate a payment plan and pay them monthly. Also, if you are to go see a doctor, do not walk into the emergency room, unless you have to - make an appointment first. It will be much, much cheaper that way.

15. Good will be rewarded with good.

I received so much help from my college after coming to the U.S. that now I am trying to give back by sitting on the Boards of organizations that do good for foreign borns. I am trying to give back to my law school, the State University of New York Law School at Buffalo, and Cleveland State University in my home town, by sitting on their advisory boards. I also give scholarships to help Notre Dame College in Cleveland.

What goes around comes around. I work closely with my church, because without everything it has taught me, the values they imparted to me, and its scholarships, I would not be where I am today.

Remember: the good that America has done for us and all the kindness to others will be paid back one day. Only in this country can we reinvent ourselves in less than one lifetime and see the changes and joy that the freedom can give us. It is not fleeting. We can go get a cup of coffee and enjoy it in the sun outside or at night in our own homes without the fear that it would be taken away from us or that we would be jailed for no reason. Even most of our jails here are nicer than the jails in our birth countries.

Most people in the United States do not discriminate as much as we think they do. When they do treat us a little oddly, usually it is because we are doing things a little differently from what they expect (not holding doors open to others behind us, crossing the street when we're not supposed to, etc.). Sometimes they are just jealous that we work so hard and make them look bad for not putting in as much effort. But we do so mostly because we don't have much choice – unlike them, we don't have as many friends and family to fall back on in times of economic hardship. Once we educate them about the reasons why we are here, they will understand us better. If they don't, that is their problem and not ours. We can only do so much within our power to change the world. Let's try to take one step at a time.

16. Do not do stupid things which you know are stupid.

One example is renting a warehouse to help a friend store their phony Gucci or Louis Vuitton bags so that they can sell them. It is a serious crime, even though you thought you were only renting the warehouse and not committing the crime of selling counterfeit goods. American courts view it as you conspiring with the person committing the crime, and you can be fined or jailed for it. The fact that you knew about the fake goods makes it a criminal act even if you were not at the scene when the fake goods were sold and you didn't make any money from it. This will make your clean record with the courts not so clean anymore. Our firm handled a case with this exact fact pattern.

Selling drug paraphernalia is a crime even if you are not selling the drug. Ecstasy is a drug. It is not just for a party or for having private fun with a friend. Giving your friend an ecstasy pill in her mouth, even if it is not swallowed or chewed, makes you both guilty of committing a criminal act.

We may not think this is fair, but these are the laws of this country. I have seen so many cases like this. I know you did not mean to do any harm and did not even know that this was against the law. But be careful! You are new in this country. You are the ones that the government is watching even more closely than others. Do well. Do not hurt your families and make them lose faith, lose love, and lose face because you were stupid.

17. Develop your core skills. Strengthen your weaknesses.

Life is more than just making money and sending it home to pay for a new house for our families back in our birth countries. They want us to do better, also, and be the best that we can be. It takes at least two to three years to be good at anything: being a carpenter, a professor, a grounds maintenance person, cook, lawyer, etc. The sun shines everyday, and we go to work every day. We're often willing to work six, or even seven days a week. If you want to succeed, if you want to be at the front of the pack instead of the back, you just have to work harder than others.

18. Keep up with current events.

Try to read at least two English newspapers a day – local and national news. I personally read the Cleveland Plain Dealer, the New York Times, and the Wall Street Journal.

You can learn from reading the newspaper both the current news and the culture within the United States, as well as international news and topics reminding us of where we came from and pointing us in the direction of where we want to go.

The New York Times has a liberal bent. The Wall Street Journal is very pro business. Your local paper will help you learn what and who is important in your city and state. This way, you will know whom to call if you need help (whether it would be with the government, non-profit agencies, or businesses).

An alternative is to force yourself to watch the morning, evening or nightly news. While you generally will get less information from these sources, it is cheaper, and will also help with your listening and pronunciation skills.

19. Keep a daily journal.

It will help you keep track of the many ups and downs, successes and hardships you have gone through. This will also help keep you focused on your long-term goals.

Remember to look back once in a while. What has happened in the past week, month, year, decade? See how much you have accomplished in this time. If you have not moved forward toward your goals, perhaps in the next week, month or decade you can try something else. I like the line from this old black and white movie, Swing Time. When you fall, "Pick yourself up. Dust yourself off. Start all over again."

20. Keep your faith.

Never lose your calling and belief. We are people who wanted to come to the U.S. and came. Remember how you heard and read stories when you were very young at home about neighbors and friends who became a "somebody" in the U.S., and you knew you could do as well? You nagged and nagged mom to let you leave and to help raise some money for you. You had an epiphany that somehow you would get here. But, after getting here, now what? You may be working three jobs, living in a dingy apartment, taking the bus, and watching the rich people go shopping.

Don't ever lose that feeling and remembrance that somehow we will make it. It does take about five years. There will be so many times when we have regrets, kick and scream, and miss home, but I know we can do it. We are here in the United States. Trust me, after three to five years, you could survive and thrive working one job, and be happy.

21. Motto - A family, education, and hard work – If you think in this order, good things will come.

22. Moral Compass – Don't forget it!

INTRODUCTION

I had no idea that I would become a successful immigration lawyer and a good businesswoman. My sister Cecilia and I came to the United States, each with two suitcases and $100. We arrived at Tacoma Airport in Seattle, not knowing if our host family had gotten our letters with the flight information in time to pick us up. That was in August 1969, at the height of the Vietnam era, with no computers or internet. The airlines were not deregulated, and a one way fare from Hong Kong to the United States was about $3,000 (8 Hong Kong Dollars was the exchange rate, so about 24,000 Hong Kong Dollars). My father was a publisher/writer and despite his big title, was making about 1,500 Hong Kong Dollars a month.

Now, fast forward to 2009 when I was approaching the age of 59. I realized that before time ran out on me, I needed to write all this down to inspire and to encourage the foreign-borns and immigrants, in that we all do have a common bond. No matter what country we come from, or how or at what port of entry we arrived, we share a common thread and need to strive, survive, and succeed to prove to ourselves that we can do it, to prepare a better life for the ones that we have left at home, and to promulgate our legacies.

Although times have changed and the world has progressed, we all face the same issues: how to stay and work in the United States once we get here, how to obtain a green card, and then, U.S. Citizenship, how to find and get a job that we can be passionate about and in which we can help our boss(es), how to contribute to society, and how to bring our loved ones to share in our lives here. Along the way, we must try to understand the Western and uniquely American way of life, learn the U.S. taxing structure, discover how to get and keep our jobs, and let our bosses know that we are good workers and good people. We must try not to violate any laws, fight or threaten others, or run when law enforcement officials ask questions. We must learn to look people in the eye and not give soft handshakes, to smile and not look defensive, to get a clean haircut – the list goes on and on.

To do well in this country, education is very important. You cannot succeed if you cannot speak, read and write English. When you work in the U.S., exceptional work does shine and speak for itself, you will succeed, and money will come. You will never make it by being a person without status in the U.S., working $8/hour jobs, which after tax leaves you with $6/hour, all while you have to support your family overseas as well as yourself. Keep in mind that we do look and act a little differently, so we need to make this into a positive aspect and not let first impressions hurt us. At first, I could not find or keep any jobs because in the 1970's there were no Asian women lawyers or waitresses in this city. We will survive and do well in this country if we understand and study, work hard and do not get into fights or drink while driving.

I understand that it's difficult. You feel that you can't leave the U.S. because you would be banned from coming back for more than 10 years. Who's going to support your family both here and there, straddling two coasts? What's more, if you go back, you face the shame of having accepted defeat. However, if you stay, you can't even get basic things like a Driver's License, Social Security Number or work papers.

I do not purport to have all the answers, but along the journey I've traveled I've accumulated knowledge which I can share with you about how we can all realize our goals.
It was a long and difficult climb from being fired from waitress jobs, to completing my education and building a career. After enduring the poverty and hunger of the early years, escaping an abusive relationship, finding a loving husband, and facing the prejudice and injustice of racism and sexism, I have seen first-hand the myriad problems immigrants must overcome to make their homes in America. Like the first European colonists hoping to find the legendary fountain of youth or gold for the taking, immigrants almost invariably find that America's wealth does not come effortlessly, but, rather, through hard work and persistence.

It is both a boon and a detriment to the state of U.S. immigration that many of the same experiences that I went through years ago remain unchanged. Reflected in the stories of my clients, I have seen the same hopes that I and so many other immigrants before me fostered while taking our first steps into American society; I have also seen many of the same fears. Old problems have been resurrected through conflict or economic difficulties, while new obstacles constantly arise to challenge immigrants, lawyers, and the system itself.

Because I have personally encountered or helped others deal with so many issues that an immigrant may face, I try not to use the word "you," and instead use "us" for solidarity purposes. I also try to avoid using the word "alien" because it sounds so weird and reminds me of the movie "ET" directed by Steven Spielberg. The words "illegal" and "unauthorized" also bother me a lot because they have become so politically charged. Accordingly, in this book I use the terms "person(s) without status" and "person(s) with status" (legal alien)).

Practice in the immigration law arena has evolved dramatically throughout the last 30 years. I still remember giving a speech at John Carroll University in Cleveland in the early 1980s, and an activist student asked me point blank why I didn't testify more often on the hill and push actively for legislative change given all that I knew and my high level of involvement in the field. This question has stayed with me throughout the years. Most older-generation lawyers such as myself study and work to <u>represent one client at a time</u>. Just like Tip O'Neill's quote, "all politics is local." We find loopholes, walk through the fields, and bring new cases with novel theories to the immigration judges. If we win, we get green cards for our clients. If we lose, we appeal to the Board of Immigration Appeals, and if we lose again, we bring the case to the circuit courts. This is where we can effect changes. In the past ten years, circuit court decisions have been varied because of the sheer volume of cases brought before them. Some have been conservative, others liberal. However, I'm angry. Maybe it's just me, but how the Department of Homeland Security (DHS) treats us is wrong. It does not pass the smell test. I had a conversation with the former Secretary of Homeland Security, Mr. Chertoff, who is a decent fellow and a great lawyer who knows what he is doing and the comment he made was along the lines of "aren't these people you are talking about illegal?" He is right, but what he didn't get, and what many U.S.-born people don't understand, is that the system makes it so easy to lose your legal status in the U.S. The system is setting us up to fail. It might be because you forgot to file a visa extension, you took a wrong turn on a bridge and ended up at the Canadian border, got sick and couldn't attend school full time, or even got below a C average while on an F-1 student visa.

The American media should change the way they represent immigrant issues. It's very easy to fall from legal status for anybody in the U.S. who is not a citizen. Thus, the best advice which we can give to any green card holder is that she apply for United States citizenship. This way, she can travel overseas without worrying about how to get back (green card holders need to return to the U.S. at least once every 6 months), encountering problems with a wrong fingerprinting, or being denied entry at the border if her name is not spelled right.

Yet, through the most trying times of crisis and sacrifice, the American dream has weathered adversity and the United States remains a country of freedom and opportunity; a true beacon of hope for those from places where hope has long been forgotten. The principles most central to the American ideal espoused by the founding fathers in the Declaration of Independence, those of freedom and opportunity, are promised to every person living in the United States. As immigrants and Americans, we can and must make full use of what faculties and resources are given us to strive, survive, and succeed.

Toward this end, it may be beneficial for today's foreign borns to have a set of guidelines by which they may direct their efforts while adjusting to American life. I do not purport to have solutions to every challenge that an immigrant may face, nor would I presume to tell others how to live. However, along the journey I have traveled through both hardship and happiness, I have discovered several general rules which have aided me immensely in my life. I share them here in the hope that they may help other immigrants who are working to realize their dreams.

I also talk of my personal journey to and within the United States. My history and character were shaped by my maternal grandmother, the disgraced first wife of a powerful publisher/writer, and her tenacious first born daughter, my mother, whose love and courage sent her first two daughters to the new world at the height of Asian anti-American sentiment during the Vietnam War. Her faith in us was so strong that she then sent her younger two children to join us. My start as a Catholic girl of nineteen accompanied by her eighteen year old sister, making the voyage from Hong Kong with two hundred dollars and four suitcases, to her happy settlement in Cleveland and the addition of nine nieces and nephews to her family, my diverse experiences can be reflected in the stories of the millions of immigrants who have come to America over the years, yet like every individual who braves the arduous and uncertain voyage in hopes of a brighter future, remain powerfully unique. I always tell my husband that the best days of my life were the day I got my citizenship, the day we got married, the days my kids were born, and the day I passed my first bar exam. I took two bars; in New York in 1976 and then in Ohio in 1977 when I moved after a failed and abusive relationship. Well, that's another story.

My sister and I came to the U.S. on scholarships and had to work in the school cafeteria as part of the package. Under the strict guidance and mentoring of Ottumwa Heights College Catholic nuns, we got up every morning at 5:30 to work in the cafeteria. We were late a lot, but somehow, breakfast for the nuns, college kids, and staff was always ready at 7 a.m. Even now, 40 years later, I still remember the early morning freezing weather, getting up and putting on clothes, getting ready for school and the day's testing, and that breakfast for 500 people.

In the summer months, my sister and I would travel to stay with my New York family, Mr. and Mrs. Chan. They always picked us up from the airport or bus station and drove us safely to the Catskills where many wealthy families vacationed.

I worked for seven summers, being promoted every summer, first from a chambermaid and bus-girl to waitress, and finally to head waitress. I was the first in the 50 year history of the hotel to rise so far when I started at the very bottom of the ladder.

So you see, hard work does pay off. From the mentoring and yelling of the Catholic nuns, from my New York host family, and from my boss at the Catskills, I learned and became who I am today, developing the ability to help immigrants on our path to fulfillment and success. As with any professional service provider/practitioner, I try not to be boastful about accomplishments because the purpose of this book is to help *you* – both in your immigration case and understanding your immigration situation. It's not about me. However, I want you to know that there *are* millions of us who have firmly and successfully resettled here and have kids and grandkids here. We can do this.

THE AMERICAN DREAM

> "*Leaving behind my writing brush and removing my sword, I came to America . . .*
> *[to attain] my ambition and become successful...*"
>
> -anonymous author, carved into the walls of one of Angel Island's detention centers

Printed on all of the American coins are the words, "E Pluribus Unum," the unofficial motto of the United States means in Latin: "From Many, One." In the book the Wizard of Oz, America is only referred to as "The Land of E Pluribus Unum." Some may think: the American Dream is only a dream for Caucasian Protestant Males, or it is not for the average American or the new immigrant. Many individuals prove the theory to be incorrect including Barack Obama, the first African American to become president. There still exists inequality between the genders, but progress has been made towards closing the wage gap and breaking through the glass ceiling. The election of women to higher office has never been more prevalent, and the possibility of seeing a female nominee for the office of President of the United States has never seemed so real.

It is for this vision of the American dream that most immigrants leave their homes to embark on this journey. First, they must work hard to save in order to afford the trip to the United States. Next, they must apply for a visa which is often denied the first time. The excitement of landing here soon turns into the anxiety of learning English, finding a place to stay, and changing home currency into U.S. dollars.

It's not easy being a first generation immigrant. For many, the reality they face upon arrival falls short of expectations, and there doesn't seem a way to remedy this. Problems such as racism, sexism, religious intolerance and other forms of bigotry have not yet been eliminated. A significant number of native-born Americans believe that immigration harms the country or them personally, so they are biased against immigrants. While this manifests itself in anti-immigration law on Capitol Hill, mainstream America may experience it through slurs like "Chink," "Gook," "Jap," "Dago," "Kike," "Spic," etc., which are derogatory and thought to be the equivalent in severity to the use of the word "nigger" to describe African Americans.

While trying to rise above living hand to mouth, immigrants are faced with more serious issues, not least of which is the language barrier. For most immigrants, English is not their mother tongue and, even after learning English, it may be impossible to shake the foreign accents which differentiate them from the native born. Many will never stop thinking in their mother tongues and must translate their thinking from the language of their country of origin to English every time they speak. Due to this language barrier, most immigrants spend their first years in America working in the jobs that most native born Americans rarely apply for. They work in restaurants as waitresses and waiters, in hotels as bellhops, and in American homes as housecleaners and nannies.

Many immigrants come with little money and no furniture. It is very common for newly arrived immigrants to have to hunt for discarded furniture. Some would initially spend their free time picking up used cans to deposit for 5 cents each.

Yard sales are places for immigrants to buy essential household items instead of just places to browse and pick up pretty but useless junk. To save money, many immigrants initially share apartments or houses with others. There is a saying in English, "it takes money to make money." When better-paying jobs are reserved for those already fluent in English and an immigrant may want to start a business of her own, it is very hard for her to get a loan from a bank (due to not having a credit history) or save enough money to buy property and equipment when being underpaid.

Viewed as a land of opportunity and freedom by those of us seeking a new life and a better future, America is a popular destination for new immigrants from around the world. In this nation, with its 200 year history, the vast majority of Americans are not far descended from immigrants producing the phenomenon of hyphenated Americans. With the exception of the Native Americans who may have come following buffalo herds across the Bering Strait and most African Americans who were taken forcefully from their homes in West Africa, most immigrants journeyed to the United States only after much deliberation by conscious choice. New immigrant groups traditionally face discrimination and poverty. The American dream is far from being a reality for most first-generation immigrants. Now the United States is under global scrutiny for its foreign policy and has caused many, even within the West and America itself, to feel that the U.S. has fallen from its position on the moral high ground. Despite this, people have continued to choose to leave their ancestral homes behind and come to this foreign land in which we have few or no acquaintances, family or friends. Though our American dream is under fire, we remain one of the most liberal and pluralistic nations in the world.

A recent study by the group Public Agenda found that 71% of the immigrants they surveyed would still come to the U.S. if given the opportunity again, while only 19% would instead stay on in their birth country.[1] The United States admits over 1 million immigrants a year, and the Census Bureau reports that 12 percent of the population is foreign-born (34.2 million people). There are also an estimated 12 million undocumented immigrants in the country.[2]

"Life, Liberty, and the Pursuit of Happiness," are unalienable rights recognized by our founding fathers in the Declaration of Independence. Most other countries deny these basic tenants to their people. It is perhaps this, more than any other incentive, which encourages people to cross oceans and rivers to gain entry into this country. Many leave behind all but what they can fit in a suitcase or two; others come with nothing, having sold all of their belongings off at losses just to pay for their passage. Some even go into substantial debt and must work two to three jobs to pay off their creditors, effectively becoming the indentured servants of today.

The American dream is to be able to start with nothing, but through hard work, become self-sufficient, ultimately own our own home, and not have to worry about having enough to eat. Many factors contribute to allow individuals to start with so little and gain so much in the course of our lifetimes. There are no international borders or language barriers within the continental United States, roughly the size of continental Europe. Along with social mobility, there is great freedom to travel and relocate anywhere within the fifty states. No residency permits are required to live in certain areas like cities, such as is necessary in communist countries. The unrestricted travel also allows businesses and workers to move about freely within the United States without fear of encountering tariffs or quotas. We can own our own business without fear of the government requisitioning it arbitrarily or shutting it down without legal cause. In America, the unemployment rate is typically lower than in most other countries, so as long as one is willing and able to work, in most economic conditions, s/he will eventually find a job.

What's more, no matter where an individual lives within the United States, s/he has the right to believe or not believe in any religion, to assemble in large groups and rallies, to speak his/her mind (with only a few exceptions), to monitor, report on, and protest corruption within the government, and to sue government officials as well as private citizens without fear of reprisal. Every person living in the United States has a right to due process, a trial by jury, and to be free of cruel and unusual punishment. Though discrimination is far from being eradicated, there are laws which protect individuals from being treated unfairly due to differences in race, gender, religion or sexual orientation.

These individual freedoms have been made possible by the fundamental nature of democracy and the establishment of this country under the rule of law. The government itself has been divided in a system of checks and balances to protect against abuses of power by any one person or branch, and all government officials are subject to the laws of the nation, which cannot be arbitrarily or easily changed by any individual. Citizens themselves, along with the general media, serve as the watchdogs to ensure that the government remains within legal boundaries and remains accountable to the electorate. The greatest enemy to individual freedoms in America today may be the lack of educated voters. That is why it is important for everyone to keep informed of current events in one's locality, nationally, and internationally. It is much easier nowadays to find information and news, whether it is by reading the newspaper during morning commute, listening to the radio, watching television, or checking the internet news feeds. The right to vote and to affect the choices made by future leaders of America is a power taken for granted by most Americans, but it is something that most immigrants did not possess before. Many in countries around the world have died in efforts to gain these rights and freedoms, just as the founding fathers and their contemporaries fought to secure these rights for future generations of Americans.

In days past, the dream was perpetuated mostly by letters and correspondence between the first to go to America and the families they left behind in their home countries. The discovery of gold in California in the mid-1800s saw the rise of phrases like "Golden Gate," "Golden Door," and "streets paved with gold." People all over the world can see the glorified and stereotyped American way of life, as depicted by Hollywood films and heard in pop music. In these films, everyone owns a house, and the biggest problems seem to be drugs and alcohol, relationship troubles, or choosing one lucrative job over another. Few people in movies are worried about how to get food for their kids, get a job, or stay in their homes.

New immigrants hear only of success stories but rarely of those who have failed to achieve the American Dream. Maybe a former neighbor sent back money to his/her parents to build a new house. Maybe a relative came back from the U.S. wearing designer clothing and bringing chocolates and pistachios. Some hear about a friend of a friend who is buying a second car for the family when only the extremely rich in his/her country of birth can afford one car. Pictures are sent back of gorgeous homes which have two floors, a basement and an attic; 4 bed-rooms, 2 bathrooms and a backyard that is not used for farming, but rather flowers.

It is rare for first-generation immigrants to have many friends or family members in high places who can refer us to jobs with good pay. Immigrants seeking employment must often take the longer route: by writing a job application or sending in a resume and cover letter. For the most part, few immigrants know people working in nicer workplaces, which are usually run by Caucasians and not others of their ethnicity, whom they may more easily communicate or connect with. To make matters worse, some immigrants are exploited by employers who may take advantage of their workers' lack of legal status to pay them less than the minimum wage, mandate longer hours without overtime pay, and thereby force them to live in crowded and unsanitary conditions.

These problems are nothing new. Many of the problems of racism, low wages, religious discrimination, and unfriendly political movements faced by immigrant groups in the past were just as bad as the ones new immigrants face today. In those times discrimination was more prevalent, socially acceptable, and severe. One example is the experience of the Irish immigrants in the middle of the 19th century. Initially, when the Irish came to the United States, the English and the Irish were enemies since the English had sought to dominate Ireland. When the Irish came to the United States, however, they found that they had only jumped out of the frying pan and into the fire. The men took jobs of hard labor building bridges and railroads while the women took on jobs cleaning houses and acting as nannies. These were mostly jobs that Protestant native-born Americans scorned at having because they viewed these jobs as only worthy of servants. There was talk that the new abundance in cheap labor was depressing wages, which caused much animosity because the Irish immigrants were willing to work for longer hours and less pay than the native-born Americans. There were at times even newspaper employment ads in the New England area that had the words "No Irish Need Apply," an occurrence so commonplace that a song about the discrimination was written.

"I'm a dacint boy, just landed from the town of Ballyfad;
I want a situation: yis, I want it really bad.
I saw a place advertised. It's the thing for me, says I;
But the dirty spalpeen ended with: No Irish need apply."

-excerpted from song "No Irish Need Apply"
Written by John F. Poole and sung by Tony Paston

It is a tribute to American society that Irish Americans are now completely assimilated and are only viewed as Caucasian and not differentiated based on country of origin. Though it may be difficult for first generation immigrants to accustom themselves to the United States, history has proven that with time each group of newcomers soon become integrated in the great melting pot of the United States. The American dream may initially seem to be unattainable for many but most find that after a decade of hard work one will be able to accumulate wealth and enjoy conveniences which may have been impossible to achieve without immigrating to America.

MONEY TALKS

"No matter what other nations may say about the United States, immigration is still the sincerest form of flattery."

Clayton Cramer

Many anti-immigrant Americans argue that foreign borns have a net negative effect on the U.S. economy due to the belief that immigrants create excessive competition in the labor market, take more out of the system in social benefits than they contribute in taxes, and send too much money out of the country as remittances, decreasing the amount of liquid capital within the U.S. This stereotype has been perpetuated by the mainstream media's bias towards reporting on poorer illegal immigrants who may be more dependent on social benefits and work in low-wage occupations.

One of the biggest complaints opponents of immigration have is that the influx of new immigrants depresses wages for the native-born unskilled American workers and creates too much competition. This argument has been one of the longest standing anti-immigrant rationalizations throughout U.S. history, only preceded by moral and religious lines of reasoning. Economic concerns due to immigration were first raised on a large scale when the Irish came to the United States fleeing the potato famine and the Chinese came during the California gold rush; the Irish took up unskilled work on the East Coast, while the Chinese did the same in the West. After the Irish had more firmly established their position within American society, they in turn clashed with the wave of Italian immigrants who came afterwards and began to compete for the same urban low-skilled jobs. Mexican contract workers were encouraged to come to America during several economic booms, only to be deported during subsequent recessions. There is also a tendency for people to overestimate the impact that immigrants may have on the economy because immigrants may concentrate in certain areas, creating the perception in those localities that immigrants are flooding into the country. The Japanese, who came to California to work in the agricultural sector and eventually bought farms of their own, only comprised a relatively small percentage of the overall population. Yet they attracted much animosity from the native-born whites. Nowadays, the newest era of globalization has facilitated travel to the United States and economic interaction between nations like never before, leading to an increased volume of immigrants and resurrecting old concerns.

It is true that an influx of labor will lead to a decline in wages in the short term, but in the long run, many of these immigrants will create businesses of their own, which in turn creates new jobs. In fact, immigrants may create more businesses than native-born Americans, for many immigrants prefer to take their fortune into their own hands rather than work for others. As an example, due to the urban flight and depreciating land values in Boston during the 1990s, the mayor of Boston intervened to facilitate the creation of new businesses by immigrants, helping them obtain loans in the absence of long credit histories. This attracted immigrants to the city, bringing Boston's population back to up its peak levels in the 1970s and the city's tax revenue likewise increased. In Philadelphia, due to the initiative of the Pennsylvania Welcome Center for Immigrants, 200 local immigrant-run businesses created 900 new jobs over a short period of time. Every dollar put into the Philadelphia program created approximately $1.60 in tax revenue for the city. Furthermore, increased competition within any market puts downward pressure on the prices of consumer goods and leads to increased efficiency within businesses and industries.

An analyst writing for *Wonkroom* says research suggests that had the Comprehensive Immigration Reform Act of 2006 passed "it would have generated a much needed $66 billion in new revenue during 2007-2016 from income and payroll taxes, as well as various administrative fees."[3] She adds:

> [A legalization opponent's] proposed solution of "attrition through enforcement," a harsh strategy used to "wear down the will" of undocumented immigrants through deportations, detentions, and anti-immigrant ordinances, would cost taxpayers at least $206 billion over five years, or $41.2 billion annually. [While a] 2006 Zogby poll . . . showed that the majority of Americans prefer harsh enforcement policies . . . 2009 polling indicates that 68% of voters believe that undocumented immigrants should be required to register, meet conditions, and eventually be allowed to apply for citizenship.[4]

Though some studies show that as much as 43% of the decline in wages of low-skilled workers can be explained by immigration into these areas of high immigration, on the whole there is very little evidence that more immigrants in the area would lead to lesser wages for the entire native population.[5] Studies have been done of the Mariel boatlift in which 120,000 refugees from Cuba immigrated to the Miami metropolitan area between May and September 1980, resulting in a 7% increase in the local labor market indicating that surprisingly, for the five years following the Mariel boatlift there was no effect on either unemployment or wages of whites, blacks, or Hispanics in the region. According to Bodvarsson, Lewer, and Van den Berg (2008) this is mainly due to the fact that the wage depression by the increased labor supply was partially offset by increased spending, which led to an increased demand for labor in the service industry. Immigrants' spending often creates demand for the items that they help to produce.

The libertarian CATO institute recently published an analysis measuring the economic benefits of immigration reform.[6] Using a methodology called the U.S. Applied General Equilibrium model (USAGE) developed for U.S. government agencies, their study finds that "increased enforcement and reduced low-skilled immigration have a significant negative impact on the income of U.S. households."[7] This study predicts that the minor savings in public expenses for these immigrants would be offset by economic output losses and job opportunities to the tune of $80 billion if the low-skilled immigrant population is reduced by 28.6% from otherwise projected levels. By contrast, the study argues that "legalization of low-skilled immigrant workers would yield significant income gains for American workers and households," by eliminating smuggler fees and other costs for illegal immigrants, allowing them to be more productive and to create more opportunities for U.S. citizens in higher-skilled professions.[8]

Another recent study, by Rob Paral and Associates for the Immigration Policy Center, argues that immigrants complement the native labor force rather than displacing US workers.[9] Paral et al. argue that "the substantially different characteristics of immigrant and native workers mean that the two populations are not simple substitutes for one another."[10] As they put it, "[a]sking unemployed auto-workers to move to California to pick tomatoes may be a short-term solution for some desperate workers, but it is not a strategy for economic recovery."[11]

As for the idea that immigrants who come to the United States are beggars and/or supplicants rather than contributors to society, the question inevitably arises: do immigrants pay their way or are they a burden on the welfare state? The results for studies of this issue are inconclusive; some say that immigrants contribute more taxes in their lifetimes than they use in social services (when only taking into account education, wages and social security); others declare the opposite is true (when other factors are included and given more weight). There are those who argue that immigrants comprise a greater percentage of the population within the United States living below the poverty level, and so will accrue more benefits from welfare programs than native-born Americans. However, illegal immigrants are not eligible for such programs, and most legal immigrants are unable to receive benefits for some number of years after entry, depending on the program. Additionally, most immigrants come to the United States at a young age, and so contribute much more to Social Security and Medicare than they receive. 2% of immigrants are over 65 years of age upon arrival to the United States, compared to 12% of the native population. As immigrants stay longer within the U.S., their income also rises, and they contribute more to federal programs. In 2005, new immigrants had a median household income of $32,000, but those who had been in the country for twenty-five years had median household incomes of more than $50,000.[12]

Another issue that fuels the anti-immigrant sentiment is the issue of remittances. There is concern amongst some Americans that too much money earned by immigrants in the United States gets sent back to their home countries and is spent there. When this money is sent back to immigrants' home countries, the benefit of money in banks increasing the amount of potential investment and the benefit of the money when it is spent on goods and services are enjoyed by countries other than the United States.

Finally, immigrants tend to save more than native-born Americans by living more frugally. Most immigrants feel that they need to save and remain fiscally responsible because they lack extensive social networks to fall back on when a member of the family becomes unemployed or in the event of a medical emergency. This additional saving translates to greater overall funding for investment by U.S. businesses.

On the whole, there are some valid economic arguments against immigration but there is equally as much proof that new citizens of the United States improve the national welfare by creating new jobs and increasing competition. Perhaps the issue should be less about whether or not immigration is beneficial and more about how to take advantage of willing new workers to increase American standards of living. After all, as a land comprised of immigrants, the United States has become the leader in national income, healthcare and technological innovation. As immigration in the past has brought the brightest and most hard working people from countries around the world, the new wave of immigration may help America remain one of the world powers in the next century.

DO MORE FOREIGN BORNS COMPROMISE SAFETY IN THE US?

One major exception to the beneficial aspects of immigration manifested in the terrorist attack by foreign nationals on September 11, 2001, which took the lives of thousands on American soil. When the first plane rammed one of the twin towers, it was initially unclear what had precipitated the crisis. At first, some thought it was a terrible accident; after all, plane crashes were rare, but made the American news regularly enough. Once successive plane strikes had hit the second tower and the Pentagon, however, and a fourth plane had crashed in Pennsylvania, the American public began to realize that the country had been attacked. As in previous times of uncertainty and conflict, the nation banded together to help those who had been hurt and tremendous acts of civil service and mutual assistance were performed. However, as recovery progressed and the official death toll rose, Americans began increasingly to ask for and seek out those responsible, and as in previous times, many innocent immigrants within the U.S. would suffer for it.

It is important to understand the American psyche pre-9/11 and post-9/11. Before 9/11, the United States had enjoyed well over half a century of relative peace at home. No foreign agent had committed a large scale attack on United States soil since Pearl Harbor in 1941, and such an attack by a foreign entity within the continental U.S. had not occurred since the War of 1812. Petty crime, riots, gang violence, serial killings – these Americans could understand and deal with; these were all committed domestically. However, long protected by two great oceans, far-away wars, coups, terrorism, and even genocide could be observed and then discussed with detachment (or as with the case of too many Americans, forgotten or ignored altogether). Since the general public had been largely unaffected by crises overseas, and as such, many Americans grew complacent and stopped paying close attention to world affairs.

Such problems have existed for the length of human history, and such occurrences are still commonplace around the world. America had made numerous enemies abroad through its actions during the Cold War. After the dissolution of the Soviet Union, even those who specialized in studying issues related to national security had a hard time understanding where the next threat would come from. Some had studied terrorism in the decades preceding 9/11/2001; there had certainly been enough examples of terrorism throughout human history and within the 20th century to warrant it. However, the majority of political and military theorists had been trained during the Cold War era to think in a dualistic fashion; the Soviets vs. America, superpower against superpower. Even the majority of large and well-publicized terrorist organizations were of an old breed. Primarily politically motivated, terrorists of the mid-late 20th century tended to be older, more educated, and worked within the confines of having to avoid drawing political and social condemnation. Knowing that they could be exposed if public opinion turned against them, many of those branded terrorists fought like guerrillas, but only targeted military and political personnel or events related to their cause instead of civilians. Due to the long lack of foreign attacks on U.S. territory and general complacency of the American public, there was a belief that America was effectively invulnerable.

This sense of security was demolished along with the twin towers. Since the attack had been perpetrated by sub-state actors who could slip into the country relatively easily through America's porous borders, security officials and citizens could not quickly identify the enemy. As such, there was much paranoia and speculation about how extensive terrorist networks were within the United States. People feared that similar attacks would follow to disrupt the already shaken economy and the government began placing restrictions on certain personal freedoms which Americans had previously taken for granted. The surge of patriotic feeling that overtook the country in response to the attack allowed the government to institute sweeping changes in the name of national security. Americans adopted an "us vs. them" mentality as the "War on Terror" progressed, and as before, the nationals hailing from the same ethnic region as the enemy became scapegoats. While not all Americans misplaced blame and anger upon those of Middle Eastern descent, an unfortunate degree of suspicion fell upon those who had lived within the United States peaceably for years. For the first time in a long time, the attention of the entire country was riveted upon the news, as viewers devoured information and misinformation brought to them by the media frenzy in the months following the attacks. Extensive coverage of al Qaeda and its method of using independent sleeper cells exacerbated this heightened state of alarm and suspicion. Also, political pundits discussed to seemingly no end the nature of fundamentalist Islam and its radical supporters, throwing around words such as "Jihad," and instilling the fear of suicide bombings into an already fearful public. The divide between America, a predominantly Christian country, and Islamic terrorists based in the Middle East and Central Asia was likened to the Crusades a millennium earlier. The public outcry prompted the government to choose to err on the side of caution in its national security initiatives.

After the September 11th attacks, immigration law and enforcement became more stringent and port and border security was tightened. There are now more hoops to jump through before USCIS will award any sort of visa. For a time, F-1 student visas were so hard to come by that colleges and universities in the U.S. suffered somewhat financially. This was done for good reason, as many of the terrorists involved in the 9/11 tragedy had arrived on student or tourist visas. However, as so often happens when the country is under attack, Congressional action went far beyond what was warranted and immigration was limited severely while funding for security-related programs and the military increased. The Bush administration also began to reform national security-related institutions, bringing many formerly independent agencies or agencies from other departments under the newly created Department of Homeland Security.

Among other functions, immigration, formerly under the domain of the Department of Justice and INS was brought under the umbrella of the Department of Homeland Security. By assigning immigration to the Department of Homeland Security, America was in essence placing emphasis on immigration as a national security concern, marking a major shift in immigration policy. This policy change was brought on by a major shift in public sentiment against immigrants. Because the 9/11 attack was an immediate cause of the first recession of the 2000s after a decade of phenomenal growth, the rise of anti-immigrant sentiment due to the attack correlated the almost inevitable antagonism toward immigrants in times of financial difficulty. For the first time since WW-II, immigrants are viewed as not only threats economically but also threats to national security.

BEING FOREIGN-BORN IN AMERICA

There are certain things that immigrants or non-immigrants should not do until they become a U.S. citizen.

1) As mentioned before, do not buy or carry a gun. There are different permit requirements for gun ownership, and you need to fill out forms stating your nationality and/or citizenship before purchasing a firearm. Some clerks may fill these forms out for you to save time and ask you to sign your name. If either you or the clerk states (inadvertently or not) that you are a U.S. citizen, it is a criminal act and may subject you to deportation/removal.
2) Do not drink if you will be driving later. That includes beer. The U.S. has very strict laws on drunk driving. This is very different from most countries, where people are allowed to drink at a young age. Another thing to remember is not to leave empty liquor, wine, and beer bottles or cans in cars. If police stop you and see this, they can and will charge you. There are a lot of profiling-based police pick-ups. If you look different, they may stop you because it's their job to protect their communities from criminal problems. Too often, different means suspicious. We just have to keep educating these people that we are not so different from natural-born Americans – we want the same things that they want, and picking us up, putting us in jail, and notifying Immigration to begin the 72 hour processing is not going to lower the crime rate. It is only a waste of taxpayer dollars, profiting the owners of private jails.
3) Do not steal butter, cheese, pencils, and the like from any store, including grocery stores. I've seen many of these petty theft cases in my 30-odd years of practice, and I always wonder what the person is thinking. I still remember the first few years of my life in the U.S. while attending college in Iowa and Illinois, still awed by our huge, clean grocery stores with all the candies and food out in the open. I was so hungry that I felt like putting them in my pockets, going home, and savoring them. I couldn't afford to pay for them, and nobody was ever looking for shoplifters. It was very different from where I came, where men stood everywhere watching the movement of shoppers. I suppose it was ultimately my Chinese Catholic guilt which allowed me to resist the temptation. You know you are becoming truly American when you go to a mall or grocery store and no longer feel wonderment and awe at seeing the wide, clean walkways and having the ability to walk in and pick up what you need while complaining about the long line at the checkout. My mother always commented that only in America do you have to stand in a long line to give someone money. Most everywhere else, no matter what business they are in, the first thing a shopkeeper does is to make sure there are enough

clerks to do business, take your money, and wrap up your merchandise.

4) When driving, do not drive like a maniac. If anything, go under the speed limit instead of over. We already look different; if you have no status, a final order of deportation has been issued (with or without your knowledge), and a police officer stops you for a minor infraction, they will notice that you are driving without a license and put you in detention. Fines are becoming ever more expensive, and the humiliation of going to jail and time wasted is really not worth a few minutes saved here and there. Recently, in Ohio, some cities have issued fines of $500 or more for driving without a license. It's ridiculous, but we must stop any conduct that gives officials an excuse to fine us.

We need to learn U.S. ways to live here. It's the same as Americans going to our old countries where people look at them and call the tourists names because they appear so uncultured, silly, and naïve. I still remember that when I was in Hong Kong in my teenage years, there were many American soldiers stationed in Hong Kong because of the wars in the Far East and the Vietnam War. I was awed by their white skin and at how they became red after just a few hours in the sun. Most were tall and fat with sweaty Navy shirts, broad shoulders, their stomachs round and huge, sticking out of their loose pants, always hugging a Chinese bar girl. No educated girls in their right frame of mind would go near these men because they always smelled of liquor. Now, 40 years later, I have dramatically changed my opinions.

I also remember how I and other girls in Hong Kong wanted to be like an American doll. I'd never really seen an American girl until I came to the U.S. in 1969 except on TV or in American comics. I was envious of them - their big breasts, clean, sexy and beautiful skin, white teeth, straight blonde hair and blue eyes. I imagined they never needed to do homework, did not have nuns or parents yell at them, and had no pimples. Even now, I can vividly recall my old image of the ideal American girl, and I sometimes still wish to be like them, until I come back to my senses. Because of this, I did not allow my children to play with Barbie dolls or any dolls that look like this; why try to be someone nobody can ever be? It is unhealthy to put someone or something, as idealized as these dolls are, on a pedestal.

When you have a green card or are still in no-status land and facing criminal charges, it is wise to talk to an immigration practitioner because the last thing you want is to be subjected to deportation after the criminal plea or trial. In earlier days, state court judges were allowed to issue a state order for "Judicial Recommendation against Deportation," which solved the deportation issue. This law ended about 15 years ago, and the state courts no longer have any judicial authority over federal deportation issues.

Although state judges have no say over recommendations against deportation, state police are becoming more vigilant in jailing persons without status or even green card holders when they are not sure if they should. Every day, we get calls from clients who are in jail, or whose grandparents and parents are in jail, because a final order of deportation was issued years ago which they do not even know about.

If a friend gets into trouble like this, you need to find out the "A number" of the person (the file number that each person's immigrant visa and work permit has). If she does not know it, or does not think she still has one, get her date of birth and country of birth, and be specific. Taiwan is not the People's Republic of China; it is the Republic of China. The Soviet Union is no more, so be sure to name specific countries. The U.S. Immigration Office files cases under an A file if it is an ICE case or a green card case. If it is a matter regarding a non-immigrant visa or if it is a change of status case, the case is listed under an LIN, WAC, EAC, or SRC number. Without this number, you cannot identify, or even talk to, the officers. The other piece of information you'll need is whether the person has been issued a final order of deportation. The number to call to find out if you have a final order of deportation is 1-800-898-7180 (follow the instructions). If you do have a final order of deportation, unless there are serious inequities, the chances of ICE detaining them for at least 90 days are high. The 90 day detention applies even if the person has no "A number." After 90 days, there will be a review, and if not, the person will be subject to review in another 90 days. Even if she wants to get deported, it will take weeks or months because of the difficulty of getting passports and/or one-way travel documents (as I mentioned earlier). Immigration officers in the field (not the people at desks, writing and studying immigration policy) have their jobs cut out for them. They are just like us immigration lawyers, getting pulled from all angles, their bosses changing policies on them every few years, working with ever-shifting anti-immigration and pro-worker forces, being viewed inside the agency as "soft" or "hard-nosed," etc.

I personally do not know how criminal lawyers practice their craft, but as immigration lawyers, the hardest part of our practice is to work on detention cases. In the 1980s and early 1990s, we may have gotten one or two of these calls per month, and those cases were simpler; usually we went to or called the nearest immigration office to negotiate, paid a bond, the client got out (assuming there was no criminal record) and then we went through the hearings.

In the past three or four years, however, detention of person(s) without status and green card holders has really gone up, along with the anti-immigration sentiments amongst the general American population and the political clout of the privately owned prison industry. The federal government pays about $100 each night for each person to be housed. Person(s) without status do not have a voice in government and cannot form voting blocs. Thus, it is important for green card holders to gain citizenship, begin to vote, and get involved in the American political system. Unless we speak out and push for a lot of issues, changes are not going to happen.

Some common misconceptions are that immigrants want to come illegally and work, live on free government healthcare, and send the money home without paying taxes. This is untrue for the majority of immigrants. Most immigrants come legally but it is so easy to fall out of status. If their country is at war or if bad economic times hits, students may lose their tuition for a semester of school. Instead of giving them a reprieve or a humanitarian work authorization so that they can pay their tuition and remain at school, these students are rendered immediately out of status and SEVIS will notify the schools.

In a situation like this, a student needs to file an I-539, related documents, and a completed form I-20 to show that she has been out of status for less than five months. Here, it is important to count months correctly. A student need not go to school in the summer, so if she missed the third (spring) quarter of school and also missed the summer months, she may still be less than five months out of status.

If a student has indeed been out of status for more than five months, we need to prove that there were exceptional circumstances and that the request to reinstate was filed as soon as possible. She needs to show that she had not engaged in unauthorized employment and that she does not have a record of being a repeat violator. The exceptional circumstances need to have arisen from forces out of her control, e.g. illness and serious injury, closure of the school, a natural disaster, or inadvertences. Note that this reinstatement only applies to her stay in the U.S. and that she must stay here to wait for approval. If she leaves without an approval, she will have to explain her situation overseas to the Consulate in order to apply for her visa to come back to the U.S.

Falling out of status in the U.S. on an F-1 visa has no "bar" consequences associated with it because the I-94 is marked "D/S" (Duration of Stay) to start with. This means that if the person leaves the country and an American Consulate/Embassy gives her a new visa to enter, she will be able to come back and go to school. She has to attend the same school that issues the I-20. If she attends another school, she's out of status again. A student may begin work on campus immediately after school starts as an F-1, but can only begin to apply for off-campus employment work permits after at least one academic year (nine months) of school. The sponsor needs to submit a letter to the school stating that there are unforeseen and uncontrollable economic circumstances causing severe economic hardship and an inability to pay the tuition. With this, the student may be approved for an economic hardship work permit, be able to help her parents pay tuition, and complete her education before going home.

Another type of work visa that a student can get is the curriculum practical training "CPT" visa. This has to be approved by both a foreign student advisor and USCIS officials, and it allows the student to intern/co-op, which may fulfill a requirement under her degree program. A pharmacist student, for example, needs this training period to work in a pharmacy before she can take the license test. On the other hand, a future lawyer in a JD or LLM program does not need to apply for this visa because internships are not a requirement to apply to take the state Bar Exam and practice in that state.

One of the most important work permits in the life of a foreign student is the optional practical training (OPT) permit. In the 1960s and early 1970s, and when I applied for my own OPT in the mid 1970s, it was 18 months. Through the years it has been reduced to 12 months. To compensate for the reduced length, a student can now apply for a 12 month period after each progressive degree. After graduating with a bachelor's degree, if a student wants to take a year off before she goes back home, or wants some training in a field related to her studies, she may ask for the 12 month period of OPT. For post-graduation OPT, the work permit application can be filed 90 days before graduation, but no later than 60 days after graduation. Otherwise, the student must leave the U.S. within 60 days of graduation or else be rendered out of status.

If at any time the student becomes ill or suffers an injury such as breaking her leg, she needs advance permission from the foreign student advisor to not finish off the semester and/or drop courses to maintain a grade point average equivalent to a "C". Foreign students can't get federal aid and need permission to doing anything. They cannot even get a driver's license and a social security number without a letter from their university.

Public high schools can only accept a foreign student on an F-1 visa for one academic year, and the student has to pay tuition for the year to be accepted. For example, an F-1 student needs to pay at least $16,000 to the Shaker Heights, Ohio public high school (one of the best and most integrated high school systems in the country) for nine months of study. After the nine months, the F-1 student will not be allowed in again. U.S. lower and middle schools are not allowed to accept foreign students at all, even if they are willing to pay. If a foreign-born child is adopted by a U.S. family, the U.S. parents will need to advise their school district that the child has no status and thus is not an F-1, and then wait for the two year legal physical possession requirements of the adoption law for a green card to come through. Even then, it's at the discretion of the school whether to allow the child to attend classes. This means that the law is configured in such a way that adopted children from abroad are in a better position if they are illegal than if they have F-1 status.

Students who attend vocational schools do not get an F-1 visa, but will get an M-1 instead. The admitting officers at airports or drive through check points have the authority to put an end date to students' I-94s, thus subjecting the students to a 3/10 year bar. They have 30 days to leave the U.S. after the end of their two or three year study period as stated in the SEVIS I-20.

After the 9/11/01 terrorist attack, pilot schools have been much more careful about accepting M-1 students, and the American Embassies and Consulates denied entries. Just the thought that one out of the tens of thousands of applicants could have caused death to our people on our own soil paralyzed most of the U.S. Consulates in Middle Eastern countries and many other parts of the world.

From 2001 to about 2006, our foreign student enrollment went down, and many well-educated students from wealthy and/or upper middle class families went to Europe and other countries for higher education, not to the U.S. After serious complaints to the Department of State, which issues visas for education, colleges and universities, the State Department reversed the trend and began to increase its approval rate for F-1 visas.

I can see why the State Department officials overseas grow tired of the games foreign-borns play when they apply for visas. There is a lot of fraud involved; travel agencies which charge quite a bit of money, phony documents and bank notes, people stating on visa forms that they are married instead of single, and all for the sole purpose of their burning desire to enter the U.S. There is a cultural divide between the views of U.S. immigration law, in which "a lie is a lie," and some foreign countries where "a lie is not a lie unless there is a victim." Each culture takes a different approach when dealing with issues. Let's say a woman's application for a tourist visa had been denied by the American Consulate in Guangzhou, China six months before the American Consulate in Beijing, China approved a tourist visa in her passport. However, the DS-156 asks the question "was a visa ever denied to you?" At the direction of a travel agency, the answer she put down was "no." The American authorities will say she lied and will probably not issue a green card after the foreign-born successfully entered the U.S. Her position from a Chinese cultural standpoint might be "I do not understand English and paid good money to a travel agency in order to navigate the application process, doing exactly what the agency required me to do and signing all the forms." However, American law determines that although the representative had misadvised her, she is still responsible because she signed the forms. She's stuck.

There are hundreds of examples like this. The best way to prevent such occurrences in the future is to keep disseminating information between the U.S. and other countries, and between the officials and foreign-borns. The more we educate and communicate with foreign nationals, the more public opinion of us and our country will improve. Times have changed. We did not have the internet during most of the Cold War era. Now, most information is accessible and it's easy to get knowledge. The question is how to get knowledge into someone's head and have them apply it, understanding that the American Consulate does not accept "lies" or "misrepresentations."

Denials of visa applications from the American Consulate can not be appealed in the U.S. This means that even though we may disagree with such a decision, we cannot appeal it or file motions with our U.S. judicial system/administrative decision/executive branch to reconsider. A foreign-born can always start a new application, albeit with a new filing fee and new documents. She can apply as many times as she wants. We have a client who applied for a tourist visa nine times in Russia and finally got it. It took me three times to finally get my F-1 student visa. The will to survive and succeed is strong in people like us. The visa application process is not for the weak of heart. Foreign-borns stand in lines for hours, and for the most part, the waiting rooms do not have enough chairs for all the people.

The U.S. government cannot, and will not deport a non-U.S. citizen from the U.S. just because "they can" or they "want to." There is a procedure. If a foreign-born loses her case in court and all appeals have been exhausted, she will be deported. The law in the past 40 years has always been that if a final order of deportation was entered by an immigration judge, a "bag and baggage" letter was sent by the legacy INS or ICE, and the foreign-born does not report to them in accordance with the instructions, the foreign-born becomes an "absentee" and "absconder or fugitive." It becomes difficult to help these people stay in the U.S. afterwards. If you fall into this category, which is separate from people who fell out of status or have not been detected by immigration services with a written notification, you need to ask yourself the following questions.

1. Did you know, or were you advised by a judge or lawyer that you have been issued a final order of deportation or voluntary departure? If so, why did you not leave? Aside from your burning desire to stay here and to raise and help your family, were you sick, was your wife pregnant, did someone have an accident, and did you even know that the consequences are so dire? These are situations in which you can file a motion with the court or ask for government attorneys to join with you to reopen the case so that you can stay. However, you need to think, work together with your legal counsel to review the case law, and study how the immigration judge, BIA and circuit courts have ruled on these real scenarios in the past. It's not sufficient to say "Oh, let's go to the newspapers to get a sympathetic story written." Years ago, immigration officers were not bombarded with the ever changing laws, the "darned if you do and darned if you don't" reporting of

statistics to OBM (Office of Budget and Management), and the forever watchful eyes of headquarters. As I said earlier, you will succeed and fulfill your life's ambitions as long as you prepare and don't forget the big picture of what life is about.

2. Did you attend every master calendar hearing and individual hearing scheduled by the court? If so, did you understand the translation? If not, why didn't you tell your legal representation? Did you understand what she was telling you? If not, did you let her know? If not, why not? If you did not show up to court, why didn't you? I've had cases where the translator spoke Spanish but not Portuguese or Cantonese and not Mandarin. These are grounds for an appeal or a motion to reopen, and will be successful. Did you get notices for the court hearings? Did you let them know any change of address you had? If you never changed your address and were not notified of the hearings, did you check the notices later when you found out about your order to see if the address on the notices was mistyped, e.g. 3010 rather than 3001? We have a lot of cases like these. You need to be meticulous about remembering dates, places where you lived, and the year that you came to the U.S., and keep all paperwork, including dental/medical bills and receipts to prove that you were in the U.S. The longer you stay here, the more equity you build. Equity here does not just mean the accumulation of material things. Of course, that helps as well. However, equity in the eyes of immigration means merit in the U.S. Do you have a family here? Have you been a responsible resident here? Do you contribute to any charities or donate blood? Have you regularly filed tax returns and reported your true income? Do you have any criminal records, any record of domestic violence, a DUI, or any other brushes with the law? For American citizens, an indictment or criminal charge brings wrath from the police and the jail system. Shame and silence may not be an issue. In our culture, if someone has violated our bodies or cheated us, aside from the shame within our communities, we also worry about what law enforcement will or will not tell the immigration officers. What do we tell our parents and siblings, here or back home? There is nothing they can do anyway, except to worry, nag you, and feel guilty because they probably do need your help and support. It's a matter of survival. It's difficult.

My advice is that you do report these criminal activities, and it's not because I'm becoming "Americanized" or "an American." I am one and proud of it, but as I matured and saw so much through my work with other foreign-borns, I've realized that our blessings of stoicism and silence can also be our downfall. We may feel that we are strong, and with the need to survive being so huge, we may think that it will be okay and "it" will go away. But "it" does not go away. One day, it will come back to haunt us if it's not dealt with, and by then, it will be too late to do much but have regrets. I've heard so many stories from clients and friends, and I strongly believe that we need to be powerful and voice ourselves. Keep a record, write things down. After 200 years (America only has 200 years of history as a nation, after all), foreign borns are still making history, and maybe one of our offspring will be the President of the United States. Miracles happen; people like us do survive and thrive. We shouldn't underestimate ourselves, with or without lawyers (although this doesn't mean that you should become arrogant, either).

In the 1980s, generally the deportation law was that if a foreign-born did not show up in court, the judge could administratively close the case or terminate it, and the foreign-born would not have the deportation order entered. The law changed in the 1990s, and makes it mandatory for judges to enter an "in absentia final order" to foreign-borns who did not show up for scheduled hearings.

With each change of the laws, I find that our firm's staffing has needed changing. With the advent of the employer's need for I-9 checking in 1986, most large law firms and labor lawyers began hiring immigration lawyers and/or merging with them to bring in the corporate cases. Employer sanctions and requirements for I-9s do not apply for employees hired before 11/7/1986 (they are grandfathered), and unless one get a new job with a separate employer, a current employee is not to be fired by the entity hiring her. I-9 forms are required for all employees hired after 11/6/1986 and still employed on 6/1/1987. 1986 in U.S. immigration history became the watershed year in which employers were fined for hiring foreign-borns unauthorized to work.

The 1980s and 1990s saw a whole area of new laws on I-9 fines and penalties, knowledge (constructive vs. actual) and good faith defenses. The thing is that as the years went on, the government did not really make that much on fines, and law firms began to dismantle their I-9 departments because great cases did not materialize. Immigrants kept becoming out of status, either by design, or through being set up for failure by our broken system.

Immigration laws are enacted by congressman and senators, elected by the people in their states, who are then sent to Washington, D.C. These politicians need the citizens' votes and the state's media for continued support and reelection. The media has become increasingly outspoken on causes both liberal and conservative. That is the power of the written word. Most people who are writers and reporters were born in this country or are second or third generation descendants of immigrants, so the main body of journalists hasn't experienced the U.S. visa application process and the subsequent ebb and flow of keeping one's visa status afloat. I teach my young lawyers that each immigration matter is an entity on its own. Each has its individual characteristics like a child. It has a spirit, a soul, a heart, a frame, and just like a medical procedure each case can go horribly wrong for no reason. Sometimes they just fall through the cracks. Atul Gawande, the New Yorker writer and famous cancer surgeon, gave a presentation that I was present at recently and I had an epiphany when he talked about how each surgery case is individual, even though human beings all have a heart, a head, hands, and legs. Things do go wrong, and we need to anticipate them and be proactive to prevent them.

We need to change the perception of foreign-borns. Madeleine Albright, Henry Kissinger, Dr. Wulf Utian, Tony Pena, and Sandy Alomar are all foreign-borns. They have done it and made it. So can we. I understand that you may think this type of outlook is too simple and that I'm naïve when I say these things. I don't think so, sir.

In the last few years, I have also noticed that because employers are so much tougher now in their hiring practices, non-citizen workers are filling in the third square on the I-9 (stating that they are a U.S. citizen or national of the U.S.) to get a job. Please don't do this. There may be a criminal penalty in doing this, and there may be problems for you when applying for a green card because you misrepresented information to obtain employment and possibly for making a false claim of U.S. citizenship. Now, the law on this is that the benefit obtained under the material misrepresentation has to be a benefit under the Immigration Act to be an offense. One argument is that getting a job is done to enhance one's ability to pay bills and to advance one's career, so this type of misrepresentation would not be a "lie" under immigration laws. The other side of the argument is that it is a lie, because it was done for the purpose of evading the employer sanctions statute. If the government's argument prevails, then that one mistake renders the foreign-born inadmissible and deportable.

My experience has been that if you are an employer who comes under the immigration office's scrutiny, and you produced your payroll records and the I-9, you shouldn't feel bad. It's difficult to run a business. It doesn't matter how well you checked your I-9s or how big or small your business is; my experience is that the employer will be fined. Minor things like an I-9 not being completed within three days of hire, a missing date, a check mark being left out, and the employee and employer reversing signature positions all led to fines.

Employers can invoke safe harbor provisions when they receive a "no match" letter from the Social Security Office. In the past few years, the Social Security Office has routinely sent letters to employers after receipt of the employer's 1099/W-2 information when social security numbers listed in the employer's documents have not matched those in the records of the Social Security Office. After legacy INS got transferred to DHS, and according to final regulations dated 8/15/2007, no match letters received by the employer triggers a "constructive knowledge" of the possible unauthorized status of the employee. This provides a lot of enforcement issues and turf wars between the Department of Justice and the new Department of Homeland Security, and employers and employees are both unhappy with this provision. However, this rule has not been enforced, which really is the right thing to do. The Obama administration recently came out with a memo reversing the situation.

Employers need "only" exert good faith efforts to check the documents given by the employee to prove their status. Employers also need to know the difference between "actual knowledge" and "constructive knowledge" when negotiating with DHS on the civil penalty. It's not sufficient to apply the "wink" principle. Bosses cannot wink and think DHS won't find out. DHS can fine an employer who has either actual or constructive knowledge of illegality/misrepresentation. However, fines cannot be issued if the employer has no knowledge of a phony social security number. In the past year, rather than fining employers, the U.S. Attorney's office and Department of Justice have indicted and criminalized large scale employers after raids, putting both employees and employers in jail.

DHS can begin the I-9 inspection process with the issuance of a 72 hour Notice of Inspection (NOI). This notice can be delivered personally by an officer or by Certified Return receipt mail. After the inspection, a Notice of Intent to Fine (NOF) will be issued, with the stated amount and the reason. I always advise clients not to allow DHS on the employer's premises to do the search. It's just not right to have federal enforcement people come in to a work place and interrupt the daily routine of a successful business. DHS can inspect the papers in their own place of work and on their own schedule. However, I do recommend that at times like this, when failure to complete an I-9 could result in referrals by ICE to the U.S. Attorney's office, to consult with a good I-9 and immigration attorney who can maneuver through the internal workings of a vast bureaucracy.

The immigration officer in DHS looks mythical and sounds intimidating. Headquarters pick up phones readily, but not District offices and ICE. Everything we do with them exhausts us. You have to keep pushing the phone system. One, two, three, and nobody picks up. Voicemails take two or three days to be responded to, if at all. The Service Centers with which we file most of our green card applications, naturalization applications, and change of status forms do not have easily navigable systems that a common person without the survival instinct, high energy, tenacity, passion and "never give up" attitude can use for information. It's mind-boggling. I look at my 59 year old face and ask, how did I make it through the past 32 years of practice in this arena?

Burn-out rates for DHS workers and Immigration Judges are high. It's a difficult place to work for even the best intentioned and most hardworking people. The field adjudicators are pushed everyday to do dozens of interviews at scheduled time slots. They don't even have time to go to the bathroom, let alone to read up on new laws and spend a lot of time analyzing them, or drafting appeals and denials. Laws, policies, headquarter memos, regulations, field memos and directories change by the day. They are also not paid a lot.

Every Friday at four p.m., my assistant prints all updates from Westlaw, AILA, and Immigration Briefs, has his list for me, and I religiously read it every Saturday morning with my cup of coffee. To be effective and to operate in this marketplace, we, as professionals, really need to know of changes and apply loop holes to our clients, both employers and employees, and nonprofits. Can you imagine any city without a diverse and different-looking population? All big cities – New York, Chicago, Houston, Dallas, San Francisco, Los Angeles, Miami etc. – are filled with vibrant foreign-born working communities. The mortgage scandals and debt scandals hardly touched the immigrant population, because by nature, people like us do not like debit or credit cards. We buy what we can afford and save up. I can go on and on.

I was at the New York USCIS (8th Floor of 26 Federal Plaza on Broadway) for 2 days in a row recently, on 8/24/09 and 8/25/09, for 2 cases. I was more nervous than my clients, and, of course, I could not show them that I was. They would think "why do I need you as my lawyer?" Fortunately we got the results we wanted. I watched the waiting rooms and the adjudications, the front desk clerks, the lawyers and the clients, and marveled at the complexity of our work and our intertwining lives. Every foreign born went through this kind of nervousness and fear of arrest when we stepped onto the floor. I went to the bathroom 3 times prior to the interview and I did not even drink any liquid except my usual early cup of coffee.

After the issuance of the NTA (that the foreign-born may get in the mail or have personally delivered to her), the first thing that she should do is to check the correctness of the form. Check the date, names, date of entry, and the country that you are from. Was it typed right? Any mistakes like this, even though they seem innocuous, could help in the case. The mode of entry, or how you arrived in the U.S., has been extremely important after the 1997 law. If you entered with a visa and married a U.S. citizen three years later, you can adjust your status in the U.S. to that of a permanent resident. If you entered without a visa and walked from Mexico or Canada, you cannot. If you entered with a phony passport or a real one that wasn't yours, you can apply for Adjustment of Status in the U.S., but you will need to file a 601 waiver, an apology to the U.S. government, and an extreme hardship waiver. As service providers, I always advise those in our office that because of the shame and a client's distrust of attorneys, we really need to pay attention and listen to them closely. Did they take a boat (a big one or a small one?) and come to shore on another boat? If they did, then we must check the NTA or OSC. If a foreign-born has been picked up by a law enforcement officer, he may not be treated as an arriving alien because he's already on U.S. soil. If he had entered and was picked up by law enforcement people (border patrol, state police, city police or immigration officials), even if he married a U.S. citizen or has parents who are green card holders and/or naturalized as U.S. citizens, he cannot adjust status in the U.S. to that of a green card holder. Most foreign-borns do not know of or understand the differences or thousands of other nuances. We can keep listening and helping them, and on the way, maybe bring more cases through the courts and set precedents to help generations of foreign-borns to come.

We had a gay client who came from Georgia (the former Soviet Union). He applied for asylum but because he could not speak English and needed his friends to translate for him he never told his former lawyer he was gay because he was afraid of consequences in his home country. I started representing him after he was detained and he lost all appeals. A man called me panicking and said his friend needs help and that he will be deported soon. It just happened (I lucked out) to ask is he gay, and he said yes. Then we filed a motion to reopen the deportation order with this new fact. It turns out our client never knew that being gay is a ground for his asylum claim. The lesson from the case is to make sure you tell your lawyer everything. A good lawyer will help you think outside the box and will keep asking you questions until she comes up with a vision and roadmap for your case.

Now, after reviewing the story of entry and checking all the facts, we need to focus on what we want to do. We must weigh the opportunity cost of staying here in the U.S. versus going back home or going to a third country. If you want to go back home and need time to pack, you can request voluntary departure from the government. The maximum amount of time allowed under this is 120 days. After requesting this, you have to leave or you are barred and cannot apply for a green card for 10 years (if proceedings start after 4/97, or five years if they started before). ICE is authorized to extend the time allowed for voluntary departure for another 60 days. That's it. So you really need to think it through. We have a lot of clients who thought they wanted to go back when they were facing a stern judge but changed their minds later. You cannot do this.

If you decide to stay, the court will schedule master calendar hearings and you need to show up each time. As long as you show up, the judge will not give you an in absentia removal order. In the event you can't show up because of illness, incarceration by the criminal system, or a funeral, you need to file a motion with the court to ask for permission to not show up. Unlike regular courts, where the bailiff or court scheduler is human, the immigration court system does not provide for a human to talk to so they'll at least listen. If your motion is not responded to, you need to show up and if you don't, you will get an in absentia. "Not knowing" is not an excuse.

We need to also think about relief. Just "wanting" to stay here is not enough of a reason for the court to allow you to stay. Think. Do you have a green card pending because your church sponsored you? Is your birth brother or sister a green card holder or U.S. citizen, and can they sponsor you (or did they)? If you go home, would you be subject to interrogation by the police? Will you or your children be harmed if you go back? Do you have a fear, and if so, what? Did you go through the sterilization process or forcefully have your child aborted because of the "one child policy"? Why did you want to come to the U.S. in the first place? To escape abuse from uncles, parents, or an ex-husband? Why couldn't you get a job back home? Is the political situation stable? Are you from the former Soviet Union bloc that broke up? Did you come from Honduras or El Salvador in the 1980s or 1990s? What religion are you? Would you be persecuted and put to shame if you go home? Why? Did you file anything, such as a visa petition (prior to 4/01 if you entered the U.S. before 12/02)? Did you or anybody else file a visa petition for you before 1/98, regardless of your entry date to the U.S.? Are your parents in the U.S.? If so, you may be eligible to be grandfathered into their petition and be 245(i) protected.

If you are a green card holder and you are issued the NTA or OSC because of a criminal issue, a different set of questions needs to be answered. How did you get your green card? Prior to your admission as a green card holder, were you ever in this country, and if so, with what kind of visa? Were you ever out of status? What is the nature of your criminal act? Did you plead guilty or go through a trial? If you went through a trial, was it a trial by jury or a bench trial? When was that? If it was a first time offense, how old were you? Were you a juvenile? If not, was it a misdemeanor or felony? If a weapons charge was added, what kind of weapon was it? Was it a credit card to open the door to an empty house where you stole all the TVs and DVD players, a 9mm gun, or a knife? If it was a knife, what kind of knife? If it was domestic violence, who was the victim? Are you still living with them? If you are not living with them, you might be charged with assault or battery instead, because domestic violence means that you hurt or attempted to hurt someone in the same household. Was it an aggravated felony under the immigration law definition (which is different from the criminal law definition)? If so, you may need to argue against mandatory detention. If it was an aggravated felony, what options for relief do we have? Did the crime involve drugs? If so, what kind?

When is the last time you came back to the U.S. with your green card? Under law prior to 4/97, the admission date was the date on which foreign-borns got a green card. Under the new law, each time coming back to the U.S. is considered a new entry, something that is important to remember for your defense. Are your parents U.S. citizens, green card holders, or still in a foreign country? If they are U.S. citizens and/or green card holders, when did they get their citizenship/green card, and how old were you at that time? What are the statuses of your spouse and children? How old were they? Check your NTA. Are they citing one incident or different incidents? It's not the number of charges that is important; it's the number of separate incidents.

Again, think macro. One thing you might say is, why should we let people who are criminals stay in the U.S.? They should all be deported. My answer to that is that they are still entitled to due process, the best legal representation, and a fair ruling under U.S. law. If all else fails, aliens with criminal records often come to me after losing the legal battle in the Immigration arena. America is about second chances.

When a foreign-born is charged with a criminal offense, aside from seeking the help of a criminal lawyer, she should also seek the advice of an immigration attorney. The two roles are different. A criminal lawyer's job is very much to avoid a jail term and fines, whereas an immigration attorney's job is to keep a client's green card, fight deportation, and allow her to stay in the U.S. It's parallel track thinking. Think. How does the trial or the plea hurt my green card or U.S.C request?

Immigration court proceedings are non-jury. The same judges run the same courtrooms with their assistants. They all have their quirks. Some judges always need their lunch breaks and do not appear in front of the court when they are hungry. They may be crabby. The deputies and District Counsels that represent ICE are the same people. Most of them are tough and sort of mean, but it's ok. If they weren't, they wouldn't survive doing their jobs. Our relative positions are very clear (we want our clients to stay, the District Counsels want them to leave), even though a District Counsel's job is to uphold the law of the land. The Judge sits there and gets aggravated because s/he has forty master hearings in the next three hours and we get stuck arguing some minute point of the law. After a while, foreign-borns all look alike to a judge when the pressure is on. The Judges, unlike Federal Judges, do not have the research and scheduling help that they may need. For the sake of expediency, they dictate their own decisions a lot of times or type their decisions and send them out just so it's done. The newer court rooms are pretty, but many courtrooms smell, and people linger all over the halls and rooms. It's like a zoo.

This is the reason why our stories need to be told. All of us players in the system are doing the best we can with the circumstances, findings, limited finances and limited resources that are given to us. We all have a role.

I watch a lot of our younger colleagues staying or leaving their practices. I'm impressed with their eagerness to learn, but I also remind them to sit in the courtroom, watch, learn, and have fun. Think – why did so and so do this? As the years go on, and as us old timers get tired, aged, or burnt out, they will have to take this over. Out of maybe 100 young ones, one or two stars will emerge. We'll see how they shine. We all do have our time.

Young lawyers nowadays are also different from when I started out. I would watch and sit for hours mesmerized watching the judges (like Judge Manos from Ohio Northern District Court) and experienced seemingly arrogant lawyers (like the Messermans, Duvins, Zashin, McCarthy, Patrick McLaughlin) practice their craft. They were arrogant because they could afford to, confident in their craft. I followed them like I follow a great writer today. Any chance I get I would sit next to them and absorb it all. A few years ago I got to sit next to David Bois who represented the rehabilitated Mr. Charlie Keating from Phoenix. I was just so star-struck. Now that I thought it is "my turn" to be admired by the young ones, times change. Oh well, they'll find out. Ha.

We need to read the Immigration Courtroom Practice Manuals and the local rules, and we need to know the temperaments of the Chief counsels, ICE officers, and the local U.S. Attorney's office regarding immigration indictments. Are they doing their jobs as a stepping stone to higher jobs? Will they do the right things?

Will they be flexible and give clients the benefit of doubt? Are they angry people by nature? Many lawyers are. Are they angry because they are passionate, or do they have family issues? Are they having affairs with federal employees? We need to get to know our players. Knowledge is king, and this puts us all on a level playing field. We do not have the resources of the federal government available to us, but we can be powerful in our own right.

After a few Master Calendar hearings, the Individual Hearing will be set. Remember, we already took pleadings and informed the Judge of our relief in the first Master. Now, it's a trial. We must make sure to prep our clients the week before, and the day before, going through what will happen, and advising clients to tell the truth and not get nervous. We may have done these hearings hundreds or thousands of times, but it's the first and only time for our client (hopefully there will not be a next time). Make sure the clients remember things that you think they should know. I've had many clients that got so nervous that they forgot their own or their spouse's birthday. The client must be able to name all their children, both those born here and overseas. If they have lived in a third country aside from the U. S. and their home country, make sure that fact is brought up in direct testimony before District Counsel thinks that we are trying to pull a fast one. Do not ask for a separation of witnesses unless District Counsel asks for it, so that our witnesses can hear what the main parties have testified. Go through the case and the legal theories months prior to the trial, and especially the day before. The Patriot Act and Real I.D. Act changed a lot of the evidentiary and Burden of Proof requirements, and Judges can now deny cases based on things that they couldn't before.

Put everything on record. The Judge has a tape in front of her. When she gets angry or she asks for something, she may turn the machine off. You want everything on record and the machine to be on, because in the event you file an appeal, the BIA and the Circuit Court can hear the Judge, and the transcripts will show what the Judge and/or the District Counsel said. This is a Court of Law, not just three legal people arguing about some nonsense with a befuddled and bewildered client.

I appeared in front of Judge Shapiro in Boston with my partner Scott Bratton, representing President Obama's aunt. Both Scott and I have argued in front of Judge Shapiro before and he is also an old-timer. I asked the judge to go off record so that we could schedule some dates for our next hearings. He is smart, smiled, looked at me right in the eye and said I do not go off the record for anybody. See, they are listening and learning also, and this time he turned the table back on me.

We need to work a case with the skills and craft of a true and great lawyer. Read up on all new laws and changes and think, why can't this hairdresser, who came from the Philippines when the politics in her home country were so bad and who has been here for more than 10 years, stay? Do the necessary research. Read about the non-precedent setting laws. Develop your core skills; immigration is not rocket science if we read and practice it every day. Stick with it. Read the Acts again and again. This is why we went to law school. It's a wide open area for you to appeal in and for the Circuit Courts to form new opinions and new rulings. The Child Status Protection Act (CSPA) is a ripe area for litigation. Deportation rules are another one. Push our congressmen and senators to give us more numbers for H-1B and H-2. Enforcement for ICE has nothing to do with benefits in USCIS. Well, it does, but it is parallel track philosophy again. It's like Medicaid, Medicare and welfare. Just because some people commit welfare fraud doesn't mean that deserving people should not be on it or be able to get those benefits.

The individual hearings last for 2-6 hours, or sometimes longer. If we lose, we have 30 days to file an appeal to the BIA. If we win, we will get the relief. There are no hearing notices issued by the BIA, the appeals proceedings and work are all on paper. It is all advocacy writing. The turnaround time is about 9 months to 2 years. The relief may be to remand the case back to the IJ, or it may be to dismiss the appeal, meaning that the appealing party lost. The Attorney General of the U.S. can also certify the case to herself and issue a ruling which will become the law of the land. If we lose at the BIA level, we have 30 days to appeal to the Circuit Courts. There are 11 Circuit Courts in the U.S. and the Court of Appeals for the District of Columbia Circuit. DC is not as relevant for deportation appeals; it is relevant for habeas petitions however. New York is in the 2nd Circuit, Ohio and Michigan are in the 6th Circuit, New Jersey is in the 3rd Circuit, Georgia is in the 11th Circuit, California is in the 9th Circuit, etc.

Chart S: Circuit Courts Map

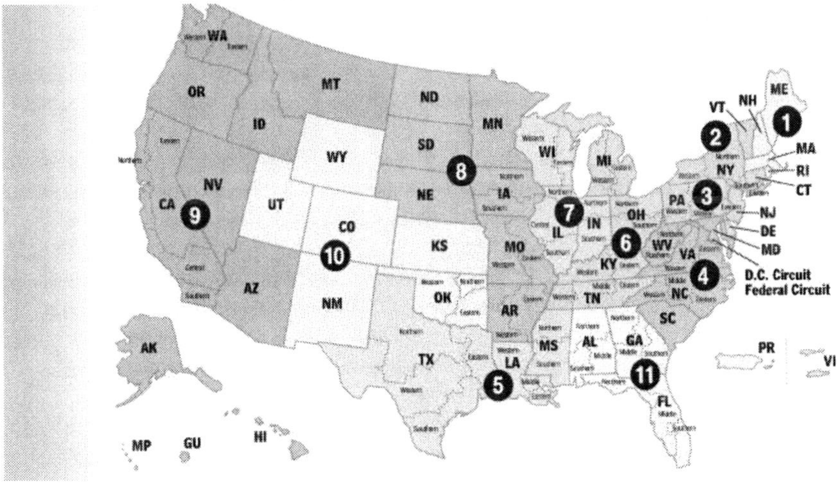

Source: http://www.uscourts.gov/courtlinks/

Unfortunately, we cannot go circuit court shopping for the best deal. It would be great if we could, because different circuits have different rulings and precedent setting cases based on the same situations. Different Circuits also have different rules and processing times. For someone for whom deportation is imminent, it's important to know Circuit rules regarding the stay of removal, as well as the local ICE rules. ICE in Detroit manages the Cleveland, Columbus, and Cincinnati offices. This information is important when we get an urgent call from a person without status who is detained. We need to know who to call.

What you can do is check local circuit laws prior to the IJ hearing. If the circuit rules are in your favor, you can move to that state. Since the appeals process needs to be heard where the IJ ruling was, your case will be pushed up to that circuit. Our Firm has done at least 10-20 published precedent setting cases in circuit courts and we have filed hundreds of lawsuits in federal court.

For clients, if you stay where you live, you may create some precedent-setting laws in your circuit, so be wary. If your circuit decides your case differently than the other circuits, it is a "circuit split." This means that your lawyer may be able to file for certiorari (cert) with the U.S. Supreme Court to see if they will hear the case.

Our firm has filed quite a few cert petitions in the U.S. Supreme Court. So far, none of our cases have been granted. It's my and my partners' dream to have one of our cases (before I retire into the sunset) granted cert so that I can tell my children/grandchildren that we have appeared in front of the U.S. Supreme Court. I have prepared for that day for 30 years, since I was certified to appear in front of it. However, it's very difficult to get cases heard. For example, in the term starting in October 2007 the U.S. Supreme Court only issued 70 decisions.[13] I have talked to all sorts of U.S. Supreme Court experts, and most have told me that they keep filing, and in spite of their views on the importance of their cases, the Supreme Court has also denied them. Still, just the fact that we have cases that we can bring up is an honor. I feel that I am an immigrant success story.

Some local ICE officers will jail the foreign-born even if there is a case pending with the circuit courts, because the rule is that a pending case is only a stay granted. This means that the foreign-born will not be deported, but it doesn't mean that he cannot be detained.

If the final order is an "in-abstentia" one, the filing of a motion means that a stay is also being filed. If the final order is appealed to the circuit courts, we need to also file a motion to stay. ICE's position in the past year has been that unless the motion to stay is granted, even though the circuit case is still pending they could still deport the foreign-born back to their home country if they possess a valid passport or a travel document. This morning (October 23, 2009) on my last stretch of editing this book I got a call from an officer from Cleveland ICE letting me know that a case that we have filed with the 6th Circuit will be given an OS (order of supervision) even though we have not filed a motion for stay.

You need to be strategic and not file a motion of stay for every case. If you have filed one and it is denied quickly, then ICE will detain them in jail or deport your clients very quickly because the BIA and the Circuit Courts usually will not grant a stay if they feel that your arguments on your case are not solid or winnable one. It also tips your hand to ICE that you may not have a solid winnable case.

After the filing of a mandamus action or an APA action, getting clients out of detention centers falls under the jurisdiction of the District Courts. This mandamus also needs to name, as defendants, the name of the jail that's detaining the foreign-born. This makes our job difficult because there is no computerized database or system to track where people are. They just disappear into a black hole. Worse, there are now a lot of privately run jails. Due to the excessive building in the 1990s and 2000s with the easily obtained tax credits, these private jails are jailing immigrants with DHS paying them more than $100 a night, per person. The jailers do not have guard training and are not really federal, state or local government workers. They are not paid very well and really don't know the difference between immigration and criminal detainees. People like us tend to be stoic; we sometimes do not know that we could and should voice our physical illnesses and discomforts. Immigrants are often just so scared to start with and probably think that complaining will only make matters worse.

The question we need to ask on a macro scale, and as a nation, is whether it is right to waste taxpayer money to jail and detain foreign-borns for up to 180 days when they are violators of immigration law, and not criminal law. Worse, many of these people, some of whom don't even have final orders of deportation, never knew about the serious consequences of violating immigration law.

I (who am not *that* old) remember in the 70s, 80s, and 90s when we waved them off and said "save your legal fees," just tell the IJ that you want to go home, and they granted voluntary departure. The government never really enforced it. The foreign-borns still had their social security numbers and drivers licenses and kept working. When their children became 21, they could sponsor their parents.

In those days, the mode of entry did not matter. Persons could still get green cards either by going back to their American consulates or local district immigration offices (for example, Cleveland was the district office for Ohio, branches or sub-offices include Columbus, Toledo, Cincinnati) in the U.S. since there was no 3 year/10 year bar.

This changed when our economy went downhill. For the first time in my 30 plus years doing this kind of work, I am getting calls every day from families of jailed foreign-borns seeking help for getting their relatives released. At the time of this writing (Sept. 2009) I had a client that was detained while she was reporting to her appointment at Cleveland ICE on her order of supervision. She was picked up by ICE and by the time she got to us it was already 3 pm. It is important to know the hours when your district office will accept bonds to allow your clients to get out of jail. In OH our district office only accepts bonds until 1 pm. I immediately called the big boss Mr. Vincent Clausen in Detroit (ICE supervisor). At that time, I found out he had just retired. I was heartbroken. I then found out who his replacement was, not only for this case, but for future clients as will both in MI and OH. As an immigration lawyer I have no shame in kissing up or kissing down. The female guards outside and inside the offices love the way I dress. I try and remember what each person likes and try and dress knowing what days they come to work. Whatever helps. Even though the law is federal and is supposed to be the same everywhere, it is important to have that human touch and to educate people who we work with everyday that we are not just another illegal overstay getting picked up. Years ago we could buy candies or donuts for immigration officials on a bad day when we were discussing a lot of cases. Nowadays it is considered bribery and unethical so we stopped doing that.

I still remember years ago when most immigration officials did have a heart and when one of us retired or got married or gave birth to a child we all celebrated and had a drink. The current boss in CIS-Cleveland Kim Adams is the child of Pat Adams, who also worked at Cleveland Immigration for years. We used to go to the same nail salon and hair salon and I would chase after them if I didn't get answers to some of my cases and wait for them in the salons. Now of course we have to stop. Pat was the Assistant to the District Director and was very intimidating. Somehow Kim grew up and started to work there and I still see her as family because Pat was such a good friend. Now friendships with them are discouraged.

Another time I chased the then-District Counsel Russell Ezolt to his lunch restaurant and at another time to the men's bathroom because he simply refused to give me the answer to a case we were working on together. Judge Cassidy from Atlanta (at that time Assistant Chief District Counsel representing Immigration in Cleveland) and I recently reminded each other that he was so upset at me that he left me alone after a late trial in an empty federal building late one evening with my client who was a foreign-born criminal person. The judge actually winked at me and strolled out of the courtroom with the deportation hearing judge. Luckily nothing happened to me and my client was such a chicken I had to walk him to his car before I walked out to mine. It was a late Friday night and our judges at that time had to "circuit-ride" since Cleveland did not have our own immigration court. Judge Cassidy firmly believed that since I represented my client I must have had total faith and trust in my client that he would not hurt me. Ha. It's fun to be at this stage of my life where we have a lot of war stories to tell.

District Court and Court of Appeals immigration cases have increased more than 50% in the past few years. This is a ripe area now for immigration practitioners and federal litigators. These cases are not for the faint of heart. We are going against the best and brightest Ivy League US Attorneys who work with the government. I interned and applied for jobs with the Department of Justice in the 1970's and never got hired.

I recently met with the inner circle of a very famous artist whose work has been auctioned for millions of U.S. dollars. The artist and his spouse got their green cards through the EB11 category (distinguished and extraordinary). However, because it took him so long and the procedure was so torturous, his protégés are worried that he will be too discouraged to apply for citizenship.

He continues to work as an adjunct art professor at a well-known university, but he wants to stop teaching and focus solely on his artwork. Is this legal under immigration laws? Should he, or does he have to apply for U.S. citizenship? Could he quit his professor job after nine years of working there? If the immigration officers find out, will they revoke his green card since he got it through work as a distinguished professor and artist?

I checked his green card paperwork, and noted that he had obtained his green card through self-petitioning under EB11. The job description stated that he is a professor and a renowned artist in his own right. The new AC-21 law states that you only need to have worked in the field that you got the green card in for the past 6 months. As long as you intended to do it in the future when you got the green card, you are fine. This particular artist had done the same job as a professor for nine years, and he had practiced his artwork for five years. Also, because he is going to focus on his artwork, he could leave his university job and would not need to worry about losing his green card.

He could also apply for citizenship now because he has been living in the U.S. for more than 30 months out of the most recent 60 months. He has no criminal record. He speaks rudimentary English, but will improve his English speaking skills by listening to tapes and practicing every day. The process of getting U.S. citizenship is generally not difficult once you are eligible. We need to fill out the N-400 form. Always check USCIS.gov on the internet to get the latest updated forms and information. There are quite a few pages on this form, but the instructions are all clearly stated on the web. Even the U.S. government is getting on board by being really professional and exacting on their USCIS.gov website regarding updates and instructions. In my early days of practice, we had no such help. Information did not travel that fast. The agency for immigration was a tiny agency that nobody paid attention to and which had no budget to work with. It took months and days to be notified that a government address had changed and there was a new location to do filings.

If you have lived in the U.S. for 2.5 years after getting your green card, then transferred to Europe to work, returning to the U.S. twice each year, can you apply for citizenship after five years of initially receiving the green card? The answer is yes, if you file tax returns as a U.S. resident, thus foregoing the $85,000 tax exemption for foreign income allowed for U.S. citizens, keeping a U.S. residence.

Another example: you got GC in March 2002, were immediately transferred to Europe and have been coming back twice a year for two years up to June 2004. If after leaving the US in June 2004 you cannot return to the U.S. until July 2005 because your job was so busy, when and under what conditions can you apply for U.S. citizenship? Answer: Since you left the country and did not return for less than one year, you are eligible to apply for N-400 in July 2008 provided you stay in the U.S. for a total of at least 30 months from July 2004 to July 2008 (i.e. 2.5 years within 4 years and 1 day). You need to file all U.S. tax returns as a U.S. resident and keep U.S. residency.

U.S. immigration law is not following up with global trends. If I were a U.S. policy maker, I would want these legal, foreign-born green card holders without criminal records to pay U.S. taxes and to become U.S. citizens. They can spread our U.S. culture or our U.S. thinking and U.S. goodwill around the world.

Now that countries in Europe are joining the EU, countries in Asia are forming their alliances, South and Central Americans are forming partnerships, American cannot afford to be too lonely and alone.

The secret is not just to fill out the forms, but to understand why and how the forms are so configured. Remember to answer "yes" regarding criminal charges, even if your charge has been dismissed. In the middle of the form, remember to put down all of the information regarding your driving tickets, speeding tickets, parking tickets, all incidents, and all other minor misdemeanors and infractions.

Another thing you should be sure to do is to put in all the associations, churches, temples, mosques, and any groups or organization that you contributed to and became a member of/belonged to. The last thing we need is for you to have contributed to an organization which was an international aid group many years ago and is now designated by our government as a terrorist organization.

Regarding bonds to release foreign-borns in jail; if I had not been an advocate for immigrants, I would think that this is a national conspiracy because the public really doesn't understand this. We are paying the debts for private jails that should not have been overbuilt as they have been when we jail illegal immigrants which cost the federal government $100 a night, per person. By the way, the food is terrible, and it's only getting worse. The food there is worse than any local jail, county jail, or federal jail. The owners aren't accountable to anybody, and the immigrants are so voiceless.

Notes for Friends of Foreign Borns

1. Talk to the foreign-born national - reach out. Don't be afraid.

2. Listen to her – take things one case at a time. Don't think too big.

3. Treat the immigration matter as a legal issue, not a political one. The one person in front of you needs help, and you have already taken the first step to help her.

4. Know that for your efforts, your reward will be 10 fold. The best thing to do is not to expect it – then, it will come.

5. Each ethnicity expresses gratitude differently – they may bring you a lot of food, or a live chicken, or just look at you with sad puppy eyes, or shake your hands softly. But they are grateful.

6. Ask and see what the most serious needs are, and see if you can help them to find solutions aside from wanting a green card, work permit, or a driver's

license. For example, get them out of their abusive relationships, help them find a ride to go to the library, help them with their inability to get library cards because they lack proper ID, etc.

7. Don't pander or show pity; most illegals are proud people. The fact that we are already in the U.S. means that they are brave and strong.

8. Learn something yourself – explore their culture and language. The biggest joy of my job is that every day I get to meet so many people, the nice and not so nice, and even the arrogant ones who think that after becoming American citizens they can look down on their old countrymen. Have fun and go along for the ride.

9. Join an association or a group that offers a lot of help to immigrants. Try not to do it alone because you will end up scratching your hair out. Learn from their experience and practice.

10. Remember that in whatever you do, you are showing them that Americans are not as mean as some people think we are. They will always remember you. I still remember all three schools that I went to from undergraduate school to law school and all the scholarships they gave me. Now I contribute to their causes. My boss in the Catskills, who had taken me under his wing, advised me to take off my Catholic cross around my neck so I would get more tips because Jews don't mingle well with Catholics. I never had a Jewish friend in Hong Kong because we perceived them as white and privileged. This cross is now still in my drawer, and whenever I look at it every morning I remember my boss, Mr. Verbie Konvisar. Both their daughters are still in New York and we remain friends. I would not be here if they had not helped me. Now, I repay them in part by helping others. Nobody can survive alone in this world.

11. Anyone can help. You don't have to be somebody who knows it all. It could be as simple as a little smile on a bus, talking to someone who has a foreign accent and is asking for directions, volunteering to teach English in a public library to help a future citizen pass a citizenship test, or helping your neighbor carry her groceries upstairs.

SECTION I

HISTORY OF IMMIGRATION AND IMMIGRATION LAW

1. TIMELINE OF SOME KEY DATES AND LANDMARKS IN AMERICAN IMMIGRATION HISTORY[14]

1492
Christopher Columbus arrives in the Americas.

1619
First shipload of indentured African slaves arrives in Jamestown, Virginia.

1654
First Jewish immigrants to New World (originating from Brazil) settle in New Amsterdam.

1717
English Parliamentary Act legalizes transportation of criminals to work in American colonies as punishment.

1718
Large-scale Scottish and Irish immigration begins. Most settle in New England, Maryland and Pennsylvania.

1789
Constitution takes effect, succeeding the Articles of Confederation.

1790
Naturalization Act of 1790 establishes uniform rule of naturalization and two-year residency requirement for aliens who are "free white persons" of "good moral character".

1795
Naturalization Act of 1795 restricts citizenship to "free white persons" who have lived in the US for five years and renounced allegiance to their former countries.

1798
Naturalization Act of 1798 permits President Adams to deport foreigners deemed to be dangerous and increases the residency requirements to 14 years to prevent immigrants from becoming citizens.

1802
Jefferson Administration revises the Naturalization Act of 1798 by reducing the residency requirement from 14 to five years.

1808
Importation of slaves into the United States officially banned, but continues illegally long after the ban.

1819
Secretary of State required to report annually to Congress the number of immigrants admitted.

1821 - 1830
143,439 immigrants arrive.

1831 - 1840
599,125 immigrants arrive.

1840
Crop failures in Germany, social turbulence triggered by rapid industrialization in Europe, political unrest in Europe, and Irish Potato Famine (1845-1851) lead to a new period of mass immigration to the United States.

1841-1850
1,713,251 immigrants arrive.

1848
Treaty of Guadalupe Hidalgo ends Mexican-American War and extends citizenship to the approximately 80,000 Mexicans living in Texas, California, and the American Southwest.

1848
Gold is discovered in the American River, near Sacramento, California.

1849
California gold rush spurs immigration from China and extensive internal migration.

1850
United States Census surveys "nativity" of citizens (born inside or outside the US).

1851-1860
2,598,214 immigrants arrive.

1854
"Know-Nothings," nativist political party seeking to increase restrictions on immigration, win significant victories in Congress. Protestant Americans feared the growing Catholic immigration.

1861-1870
2,314,825 immigrants arrive.

1861
Outbreak of American Civil War.
1862

Homestead Act provides free plots of up to 160 acres of western land to settlers who agree to develop and live on it for at least five years, spurring influx of immigrants from Europe seeking land of their own.

1862
"Anti-Coolie" Act discourages Chinese immigration to California and institutes special taxes on employers who hire Chinese workers.

1863
Central Pacific hires Chinese laborers and the Union Pacific hires Irish laborers to construct the first transcontinental railroad, which would stretch from San Francisco to Omaha, allowing continuous travel by rail from coast to coast.

1870
Naturalization Act of 1870 expands citizenship to both whites and African-Americans, though Asians are still excluded.

1870
Fifteenth Amendment is ratified, granting voting rights to citizens, regardless of "race, color, or previous condition of servitude."

1871-1880
2,812,191 immigrants arrive.

1881-1890
5,246,613 immigrants arrive.

1881-1885
1 million Germans arrive in the peak of German immigration.

1881-1920
2 million Eastern European Jews immigrate to the United States.

1882
Chinese Exclusion Act restricts all Chinese immigration to the United States for a period of ten years.

1882
Immigration Act of 1882 levies 50 cent tax on all immigrants landing at US ports and makes several categories of immigrants ineligible for citizenship, including "lunatics" and people likely to become public charges.

1885
Alien Contract Labor Law prohibits any company or individual from bringing foreigners into the United States under contract to perform labor. Exceptions made only for immigrants brought to perform domestic service and skilled workmen needed to help establish a new trade or industry in the US.

1886
Statue of Liberty dedicated in New York Harbor.

1890
Demographic trends in immigration to the United States shift as immigration from Southern and Eastern Europe substantially increases, while the relative proportion of immigration from Northern and Western Europe begins to decrease.

1891-1900
3,687,564 immigrants arrive.

1891
Congress makes "persons suffering from a loathsome or a dangerous contagious disease," those convicted of a "misdemeanor involving moral turpitude," and polygamists ineligible for immigration.

1892
Geary Act extends Chinese Exclusion Act for ten more years, and adds requirement that all Chinese residents must carry permits, as well as excluding them from serving as witnesses in court and from bail in habeas corpus proceedings.

1892
Ellis Island, the location at which more than 16 million immigrants would be processed, opens in New York City.

1901-1910
8,795,386 immigrants arrive.

1901
After President McKinley is shot by a Polish anarchist and dies a week later, Congress enacts Anarchist Exclusion Act, which prohibits entry into the US of people judged to be anarchists and political extremists.

1902
Chinese Exclusion Act is again renewed, with no ending date.

1906
Naturalization Act of 1906 standardizes naturalization procedures, makes some knowledge of the English language a requirement for citizenship, and establishes Bureau of Immigration and Naturalization in the Commerce Department to oversee national immigration policy.

1907
Expatriation Act declares that an American woman who marries a foreign national loses her citizenship.

Under an informal "Gentlemen's Agreement," the United States agrees not to restrict Japanese immigration in exchange for Japan's promise to voluntarily restrict

Japanese emigration to the United States by not issuing passports to Japanese laborers. In return, the US promises to crack down on discrimination against Japanese-Americans, most of whom live in California.

Dillingham Commission established by Congress to investigate effects of immigration on the United States.

1910-1920
2 million Italians arrive at the peak of Italian immigration.

1911-1920
5,735,811 immigrants arrive.

1911
Dillingham Commission, established in 1907, publishes a 42-volume report warning that the "new" immigration from Southern and Eastern Europe threatens to subvert American society. Commission's recommendations laid the foundation for the Quota Acts of the 1920s.

1913
California's Alien Land Law prohibits "aliens ineligible for citizenship" (Chinese and Japanese) from owning property in the state, providing a model for similar anti-Asian laws in other states.

1917
The US enters the First World War.

Congress enacts literacy requirement for immigrants, overriding President Wilson's veto. The law requires immigrants to be able to read 40 words in some language and bans immigration from Asia, except for Japan and the Philippines.

Immigration Act of 1917 restricts immigration from Asia by creating an "Asiatic Barred Zone."

Jones-Shafroth Act grants US citizenship to Puerto Ricans, provided they can be recruited by the US military.

1919
First Red Scare leads to outbreak of fear and violence against people deemed to be political radicals and foreigners considered to be susceptible to communist propaganda and more likely to be involved in the Bolshevik Revolution.

1921-1930
4,107,209 immigrants arrive.

1921
Emergency Quota Act restricts immigration from a given country to 3% of the number of people from that country living in the US in 1910.

1922
Cable Act partially repeals the Expatriation Act, but declares that an American woman who marries an Asian still loses her citizenship.

1923
In United States v. Bhaghat Singh Thind, the Supreme Court rules that Indians from the Asian subcontinent cannot become US citizens.

1924
Immigration Act of 1924 limits annual European immigration to 2% of the number of people from that country living in the United States in 1890. The Act greatly reduces immigration from Southern and Eastern European nationalities that had only small populations in the US in 1890.

Oriental Exclusion Act prohibits most immigration from Asia, including foreign-born wives and the children of American citizens of Chinese ancestry.

Border Patrol is created to combat smuggling and illegal immigration.

1929
National Origins Formula institutes a quota that caps national immigration at 150,000 per year and completely bars Asian immigration, though immigration from the Western Hemisphere is still permitted.

1931-1940
532,431 immigrants arrive.

1933
To escape persecution by the Nazis, Albert Einstein, the greatest theoretical physicist of the century, immigrates to the United States from Germany.

1934
Tydings-McDuffe Act grants the Philippines independence from the United States on July 4, 1946, but strips Filipinos of US citizenship and severely restricts Filipino immigration to the United States.

1940
Alien Registration Act requires registration and fingerprinting of all aliens in the United States over the age of 14.

1941
Japan's surprise attack on Pearl Harbor, Hawaii galvanizes America's war effort. More than 1,000 Japanese-American community leaders are incarcerated.

President Roosevelt signs Executive Order 8802, forbidding discrimination in federal hiring, job-training programs, and defense industries.

1942
President Franklin Roosevelt signs Executive Order 9066, authorizing the building of "relocation camps" for Japanese Americans living along the Pacific Coast.

Congress allows the importation of agricultural workers from within North, Central, and South America. The Bracero Program allows Mexican laborers to work in the U.S.

1943
Magnuson Act of 1943 repeals Chinese Exclusion Act of 1882, establishes quotas for Chinese immigrants, and makes them eligible for U.S. citizenship.

1945
War Bride Act and G.I. Fiancées Act allow immigration of foreign-born wives, fiancé(e)s, husbands, and children of U.S. armed forces personnel.

1948
The Supreme Court rules that California's Alien Land Laws prohibiting the ownership of agricultural property violates the Constitution's 14th Amendment.

The United States admits persons fleeing persecution in their native lands; allowing 205,000 refugees to enter within two years.

1952
Immigration and Nationality Act allows individuals of all races to be eligible for naturalization. The act also reaffirms national origins quota system, limits immigration from the Eastern Hemisphere while leaving the Western Hemisphere unrestricted, establishes preferences for skilled workers and relatives of U.S. citizens and permanent resident aliens; and tightens security and screening standards and procedures.

1953
Congress amends 1948 refugee policy to allow for admission of 200,000 more refugees.

1955-1964
Europe accounts for 50% of all U.S. immigration. By 1988, Europe accounts for only 10%. Asian immigration was 8% from 1955-1964, jumped to 41% in 1988.

1957
First Origins of Fraud Waiver. Congress creates provision that excuses deportation of an alien who is excludable at the time of entry on the basis of fraud or misrepresentation and who is a spouse, parent, or child of a US citizen, or a lawful permanent resident.

1959
Fidel Castro's Cuban revolution prompts mass exodus of more than 200,000 people within three years.

1961
Cuban Refugee Program handles influx of immigrants to Miami with 300,000 immigrants relocated across the U.S. during the next two decades.

1964
The Civil Rights Acts ensures voting rights and prohibits housing discrimination.

1965
The Immigration Act of 1965 abolished the existing quota system in favor of quota systems with 20,000 immigrants per country limits (the same limit for each country). Preference is given to immediate families of immigrants and skilled workers. Congress removed race for categories governing immigration and national exclusion. This was the first federal statute regulating immigration that did not have words like Negro, White, Oriental.

"Freedom flight" airlifts begin for Cuban refugees assisting more than 260,000 people over the next eight years.

The Bracero Program ends after temporarily employing almost 4.5 million Mexican nationals.

1966
The Cuban Refugee Act permits more than 400,000 people to enter the United States.

1980
The Refugee Act redefines criteria and procedures for admitting refugees.

1986
The Immigration Reform and Control Act (IRCA) legalizes illegal aliens residing in the U.S. unlawfully since 1982.

Immigration Marriage Fraud Amendments (IMFA) restrict immigrants who apply for green cards after marrying a U.S. citizen to a two-year green card. A permanent green card can be applied for only after one year and nine months of marriage.

1990
Immigration Act (IMMACT 90) increases legal immigration ceilings by 40 percent; triples employment-based immigration, which emphasizes skills and extraordinary ability; creates a diversity admissions category; and establishes temporary protected status for those jeopardized by armed conflict or natural disasters in their native countries.

1996
Personal Responsibility and Work Opportunity Reconciliation Act ("welfare reform") ends many forms of cash and medical assistance for most legal immigrants and other low-income individuals. Illegal Immigration Reform and Immigrant Responsibility Act (IIRIRA) expands INS enforcement operations, eliminates basic rights of due

process for immigrants and cuts down on avenues for immigrants to legalize their status. Anti-Terrorism and Effective Death Penalty Act groups provisions regarding immigrants with those designed to curb terrorism, including a new court to hear cases of alien deportation based on secret evidence submitted in the form of classified information.

2001
The Patriot Act creates significant new restrictions on immigration procedure in an effort to combat terrorism.

2005
Real ID Act directly imposes federal driver's license standards on the states.

2. PRE-REPUBLIC

a. Ancient Discovery

It is difficult to imagine the crossing made 30,000 years ago by the first immigrants to North America, the very first people to set foot on soil that would later become known as the United States of America. We do not know why these pioneers to the New World braved the arduous journey over a 1,000 mile-long path spanning what is now known as the Bering Strait. Whether they came in search of more hospitable climes, pursued migrating herds upon which they depended for their daily meals and resources, or were driven away from their ancestral homes by rival peoples, what they found was a New World in more than just name. From the seed of these first few hardy nomads sprouted ancient tribes, nations, and civilizations extending throughout the Western Hemisphere. The great Maya civilization dominated Mesoamerica for centuries before its collapse; the Pueblos made their homes amongst the cliffs and canyons of the American Southwest, and other cultures such as the Incas and Aztecs flourished and made advancements in agriculture, astronomy, and architecture. In North America, diversity flourished, and Native American factions spoke over 300 languages by the 15th century despite the dominating presence of extensive alliances and networks such as the Iroquois League and the Mississippian culture groups. Soon, however, European steel, gunpowder, and disease would bring an end to the Native American dominion over the Americas.[15]

b. European Discovery 1492

In 1492, a young Genoese navigator, Christopher Columbus, signed a contract with King Ferdinand and Queen Isabella of Spain to fund an expedition to the East Indies, center of the lucrative silk, spice, and opium trades. While such journeys had been made before, Columbus proposed to establish a new route to the Far East, one leading not overland through Arabia, but west, across the largely uncharted Atlantic Ocean. Ferdinand and Isabella were eager to gain a competitive advantage in the spice trade, especially over its neighbor and rival, Portugal. The Spanish monarchs were ready to gamble Columbus's life on the voyage, widely believed to be impossible.[16]

Although Erik the Red had led Norsemen to Greenland in 984 and his son, Leif Erickson, had sailed on to Newfoundland circa 1000, knowledge of the journey had not been passed onto other Europeans and would remain undiscovered for another half millennium after Columbus's voyage. Scholars in 1492, assuming that the waters of the Atlantic pervaded all space between Europe and Asia to the west, estimated that sailors from Europe would die of starvation and thirst long before reaching Asian shores. Columbus, on the other hand, severely underestimated the distance due to a series of incorrect calculations and assumptions, believing that the almost 19,600 km crossing from Europe westwards to Asia was actually 5,500 km. On August 3, 1492, the *Niña*, *Pinta*, and *Santa María* thus sailed from the port of Palos de la Frontera, first to the Castile-owned Canary Islands, and then westwards across the Atlantic. Land was sighted on October 12, just five weeks after the fleet's departure.[17]

The indigenous people Columbus met were friendly to the explorers, but Columbus had far more in mind than simply trade, noting in his writings that the natives were a people who would be easily subjugated. After exploring part of Cuba and leaving a small contingent of men to establish a settlement in present-day Haiti, Columbus sailed back to Spain, bringing with him gold, tobacco, and kidnapped natives, only seven or eight of whom survived the journey.

In Europe, word of Columbus's success spread like wildfire. Copies of his letter describing the lands and peoples encountered on the expedition were circulated widely and the promise of gold lurking beyond the western horizon, tempted European monarchs and adventurers alike to try their fortunes in the New World. Columbus's next voyage would be far larger than his first, comprised of a seventeen-ship fleet, 1,200 men, and with the express purpose not of discovery, but of colonization.[18]

c. Spanish

The Spanish crown was first to exploit the opportunity. For a time, Spain's operations in the Americas went relatively uncontested. Giovanni Caboto (known in English as John Cabot), a Venetian explorer, arrived in 1497; Portuguese explorer Pedro Alvarez Cabral landed at Brazil three years later. However, the lack of gold in Newfoundland dampened King Henry VII of England's brief enthusiasm for discovery in North America. Furthermore, the marriage between Henry VII and Catherine of Aragon had also stabilized relations between England and Spain and given English merchants limited trade rights in Spain's American colonies. England was in no position to challenge Spanish naval supremacy, and in any event, would gain little in jeopardizing its trade rights by attempting to colonize the New World. The French king who ascended the throne in 1515, Francis I, was all too willing to ignore Spanish claims while at war with Spain and the Holy Roman Empire, but his capture in 1525 curbed French incursions into New World territories.

Portugal, the only remaining competitor to Spain's quest for colonization, had turned its eye to the great African continent. As a compromise between indulging Spanish and Portuguese colonial interests, Pope Alexander VI of Spain had divided the world along a line of demarcation extending between the North and South Poles a hundred leagues west of the Cape Verde Islands at 38°W longitude, giving all non-Christian lands east of the line to Portugal, and those west of the line to Spain. This line was later extended another 700 miles west to 46°W by the Treaty of Tordesillas, placing Brazil (undiscovered at the time) within Portuguese-controlled boundaries, and a last line of demarcation at 150°E was drawn in 1529 at Saragossa, truly dividing the world in two and placing the lion's share of the Americas under Spanish control. From amongst all the European powers, it was thus the Spanish adventurers and administrators who first established permanent settlements in Central and North America and who would open the door for the second major phase of immigration in the continents' history.[19]

In the Old World, the Spanish monarchy was concerned with repopulating its European holdings after years of conflict, yet the Americas contained vast resources and the wealth of ancient civilizations to be discovered and taken. The effect of this duality of interest was the establishment of the *repartimiento* system of slavery, later adjusted to the quasi-feudalistic *encomienda* system, in the hope of subjugating, organizing, and assimilating native labor under Spanish administration to prevent mass emigration across the ocean.

Under the *encomienda* system, Conquistadors, soldiers, and officials were given authority over communities of Native Americans with the task of teaching them Spanish, converting them to Catholicism, exacting tribute and taxes, and putting them to work for the Spanish crown throughout the New World's mines and fields. While the lands remained technically under native control and the Spanish were required to pay wages to their native laborers, the conquistadors maintained control over the vast native populations through fear and coercion, and enforcement of the finer points of *encomienda* serfdom was not forthcoming from far-away Spain. Working and living conditions for Native Americans were so horrendous that native women even aborted or killed their children to prevent them from suffering under Spanish rule.[20]

Greater and greater numbers of indigenous people fell under the yoke and lash as the empires of Central and South America were toppled in turn by Spanish steel. Hernán Cortés famously led some 600 soldiers to defeat the Aztec Empire, aided by the Tlaxcalan people, who had been long subjugated by the Aztecs, and the blight of European diseases borne by the Spanish to which the hapless Native Americans had no immunity. Smallpox, measles, and influenza decimated the native populations, the population of Central Mexico falling from 25 million at the time of European contact to 1.3 million by 1600. After the fall of Tenochtitlan to Cortés's troops in 1519, Cortés was rewarded with control over 23,000 native workers. To the south, conquistador Francisco Pizarro destroyed the Incan Empire and claimed its wealth for Spain.[21]

Such promise brought 250,000 Spanish to the Americas throughout the 16th century, and another 200,000 for the following half century. Although Spanish settlement remained focused primarily to the south, where labor and precious metals were found in abundance, conquistadors made several forays into the Northern continent looking for similar treasures. Ponce de León discovered Florida whilst searching for the fountain of youth, and the Spanish established St. Augustine in 1565. Francisco Coronado went as far north as Kansas after crossing through Pueblo territory and capturing the Zuñi city; the Pueblos eventually submitted to Spanish rule in 1598. Hernando de Soto fought the Mississippians in a quest for gold and slaves that took his party from Florida through modern North Carolina, Tennessee, Alabama, and Arkansas.[22]

The Spanish subjugation of Native Americans continued well into the following century, the *encomienda* system being applied to the Pueblos as with other conquered civilizations. With the exception of a brief 13-year period following Popé's Rebellion in 1680 (in which 17,000 Pueblos revolted after suffering decades of drought, starvation, disease, raids from neighboring Apaches, and the prohibition of traditional religious ceremonies), Spanish dominion in the American Southwest continued until Mexico emerged from New Spain in 1810. Other uprisings inspired by the Pueblos' success, collectively known as the Great Northern Revolt, were suppressed. However, the sparsely populated continent and lack of established empires to conquer or precious metals to seize left Spanish exploration of North America moving at a slower pace than in the south. In fact, French settlers' early attempts to colonize North America predated the first Spanish settlement at St. Augustine.[23]

d. Huguenots (French Protestants)

French explorers had sailed to Newfoundland in 1506 and 1508, as other Europeans had, and had brought back word of the abundant fisheries there. Royal interest, however, remained focused on Asia and its lucrative spice trade. Because Spain dominated the Americas to the south, King Francis I had taken a strong interest in discovering a northern path to the Pacific Ocean, but conflict on the European continent had delayed his plans. In 1524, Francis I had sent Italian explorer Giovanni da Verrazano to search for a northwestern route to the East Indies. Verrazano had sailed from Cape Fear, North Carolina, to New York Bay and onwards to Newfoundland without discovering such a passageway, although he did claim all lands from South Carolina to Maine for France (the French arguing that the earlier Papal decision had granted only lands known at the time of demarcation to Spain).

It was then, in 1525, that Francis I was captured. The French king was only able to secure his release in 1526 after conceding significant amounts of land to his enemies, and returned to his realm with plans for reprisal already in mind. A protracted and ultimately futile effort to recoup his losses followed, and the crown did not pursue further exploration of the New World until 1534. The explorer sent in that year, this time Frenchman Jacques Cartier, had as much success as his predecessor. Although excitement followed the initial discovery of the St. Lawrence River, Cartier discovered on subsequent voyages in 1535 and 1541 that the waterway was indeed a river and not a strait, causing Francis I to ultimately lose interest in the endeavor.[24]

Although the French crown would not commission further attempts to explore North America, religious events on the European continent precipitated American immigration. While Francis I sent expeditions across the Atlantic, Martin Luther's Protestant Reformation had overtaken large portions of Germany and the Netherlands, Scandinavia, and most of England, but had converted less in the Catholic bastions of Spain and France. Admiral Gaspard de Coligny, the most prominent of the French Protestants (known as Huguenots), petitioned the boy-King Charles IX of France to allow Huguenots to establish a colony in the Americas. Charles IX's mother and the de-facto ruler, Catherine de Médicis, agreed. She wanted to rid France of the Huguenots, and had no qualms about ruffling feathers by infringing on Spanish territory in the New World. Thus, in 1562, 2 ships of Huguenots led by Jean Ribaut landed in northern Florida and marched into South Carolina, establishing a settlement dubbed Charlesfort. The settlement was intended both as a Huguenot refuge and as a base for French forces and privateers preying on Spanish ships. However, after Ribaut departed for France to procure additional supplies, internal strife overtook the settlers and all but one of those he left behind attempted to sail back to Europe on newly constructed ships. Those who survived the ill-fated trip did so only by resorting to cannibalism until rescued by another vessel; the settlement they left behind was burned by the Spanish in 1564.

By the time of the Huguenots' return, civil war between Protestants and Catholics had broken out. Another group of Huguenots fleeing the conflict thus made a second attempt at colonizing the Americas. This group of 300 arrived in northern Florida and established Fort Caroline there, being bolstered by another shipment of colonists in 1565.

Aware of the French presence in Florida, Philip II of Spain, successor to Charles I, moved to extirpate the rival incursion. To the Catholic Spaniards, the fact that the French had violated Spanish rights was infuriating; the fact that the settlers were Protestant was simply intolerable. Pedro Menendez de Avila, newly appointed governor of Florida, founded St. Augustine in 1565 and led ships northwards to confront the Huguenots. While Menendez maneuvered to threaten Ribaut's ships and keep them at sea, a separate Spanish force went overland and took Fort Caroline, sparing women and children but killing all of the Frenchmen for their Lutheran beliefs and presumptuous intrusion onto Spanish lands. Ribaut's fleet was later caught by inclement weather and captured by the Spanish.

The first religious refugees from Europe to America thus met an unfortunate end, and Spanish control over the region continued for decades more. However, by the end of the 16th century, the Spanish Empire was in decline; its constant wars against Protestantism and its vast global empire had stretched Spain's resources to the limit. Its weakness was seized upon and exploited by the once-more burgeoning English, coming to the forefront for the next phase of North American colonization under the rule of Queen Elizabeth I.[25]

e. English and Scottish

Enid Armstrong, Scottish Immigrant, 1941[26]

- Sent to live with her uncle in the US during the blitz because everyone thought the Germans about to invade
- Had culture clash issues concerning clothes – her Scottish clothes not the thing, wore orphan stockings
- By the end of war and in her final year of high school she went back home.
- Not much food
- Couldn't go to Scottish college because of US education
- Came back to US
- Got citizenship when married

Once it began, English immigration to the New World was more accessible, less regulated, and ultimately, far messier than the Spanish experience. Whereas Spanish immigration had been heavily regulated for military and administrative personnel and discouraged for the common man, the English monarchs paid little attention to the number of its citizens seeking opportunities in the colonies. Mercantilism was the order of the day, an imperialistic/colonial model designed to bring resources and wealth back to homelands in Europe, but while the Spanish set about exploiting local peoples in the Americas with militaristic efficiency to achieve that end, the English settled in North America in droves. Entire families made the perilous journey, seeking refuge from religious persecution or relief from economic hardship. Instead of the rigidly structured *encomienda* system granting governance of natives to a select few, the English headright system granted land to settlers who were able to pay for the additional passage of a laborer or indentured servant. Thus, not only could soldiers and officials go to the colonies, as with the Spanish, but private citizens could gain passage whether wealthy or poor. The success of the

English in colonizing North America where the French had previously been thwarted, however, was dependent upon events in the Old World.

No English monarch was so cunning in his/her simultaneous expansion of empire into North America and manipulation of European and British politics than Elizabeth I. Having ascended the throne in 1558, Elizabeth faced opposition from many enemies, both under her writ and on the Continent. As a Protestant, she was constantly at odds with Catholic elements within England and Scotland who believed that Elizabeth's cousin, Mary, was the rightful ruler. Spain also looked disfavorably upon the increasingly Protestant Church of England, formed after the Protestant Reformation had cleft Western European Christianity in two.

In the first few decades of her rule, Elizabeth did not formally condone the actions of English sailors profiting from trade and piracy within the Spanish West Indies, often coming into direct conflict with Spanish ships and settlements. It was during this time that Francis Drake famously took his revenge on numerous Spanish ships on an expedition of pillaging and piracy along the South American Pacific coast. Although immensely pleased by his actions and the valuables he brought back to England, the Queen was yet unwilling to openly challenge Spain.[27]

In 1584, 19 years after the founding of St. Augustine by the Spanish, Queen Elizabeth I granted a charter to Sir Walter Raleigh in the hope of creating a settlement in Virginia from which England could begin to reap the benefits of the New World. Her secondary objective was to stick another thorn in the side of the Spanish, although her orders to Raleigh were to colonize only non-Christian lands. Raleigh's half-brother, Humphrey Gilbert, had persuaded the Queen to allow him to establish a settlement in Newfoundland the year before, but the expedition had failed due to the inhospitable terrain. Sir Walter Raleigh's colony was aimed farther south (closer to the Spanish), and was to be used as a base from which English privateers could intercept and capture Spanish trade galleons bearing gold and raw materials from South and Central America.

The first expedition of around 100 men, mostly soldiers, thus founded the colony of Roanoke on the outer banks of what is now North Carolina. The venture was unsuccessful; its leader, Sir Richard Grenville, ordered the destruction of an entire Native American village in retaliation for the suspected theft of a silver cup, making instant enemies of the neighboring tribes. Grenville returned to England in 1585 for additional supplies and settlers, but his efforts there were ultimately futile. When Sir Francis Drake visited Roanoke in 1586 on his way back from the Caribbean, the settlers, having depleted their resources and grown tired of their misadventure, went with him back to England.

In 1587 a second expedition of settlers (including 17 women) under the command of John White was sent to the colony, and White sailed back to England to procure more supplies. However, the imminent threat to England from the Spanish Armada and the nation's need of the merchant marine prevented the governor from returning to Roanoke until 1590. Upon his return, the settlement was found completely abandoned, with the word "Croatan" carved on the side of its fort remaining the only clue as to the fate of the settlers.[28]

It was the fate of the Spanish Armada, however, that upset the long-standing naval dominance of Spain over England and emboldened the island nation to further its interests overseas. The execution of Mary of Scotland in 1587 had provoked the devout Catholic Philip II of Spain into sending direct military aid to

Catholics in England in the hopes that such action would finally instigate an uprising against Elizabethan rule. However, beaten by the more maneuverable English fleet and finished off by a bout of inclement weather, the campaign proved disastrous for the Spanish fleet, and the last significant threat to Queen Elizabeth's authority had been defeated.

Undeterred by the loss of its first colony, the English once again set out to gain a foothold in the New World after the Treaty of London brought an end to open conflict with Spain. In 1606, King James I established by royal charter the London Company and the Plymouth Company, both authorized to establish a settlement within their respective land grants. Although the Plymouth Company's settlement in Maine, the Popham Colony, was abandoned after only a year (and the company was subsequently dissolved), the London Company's settlement at Jamestown in 1607 would survive to become the first permanent English colony in the present-day United States.

Representation amongst the 105 initial settlers of Jamestown, all men, was vastly different from patterns followed by Spanish expeditions. 35 of the men were listed as gentlemen, but craftsmen and laborers also accompanied the party. Throughout the first few years, the residents of Jamestown clashed several times with the indigenous Algonquins and suffered terribly from hunger, disease, and instability in management.[29]

In fact, a series of cultural and social missteps led to almost immediate conflict between the settlers and Algonquins under the rule of Powhatan. 4 Powhatan tribes attacked Jamestown only 13 days after its founding, and peace was not achieved until Powhatan himself intervened to establish trade 3 weeks later. After the leadership of Jamestown changed hands 3 times in the following 18 months and the colony appeared poised for disaster, the arrival of John Smith and his timely negotiation with the Algonquins gave new life to the struggling colony. Agreeing for the settlers to become Powhatan's vassals in exchange for sustenance through the winter, Smith succeeded not only in maintaining peace between the men of Jamestown and the Native Americans for a time, but was able to enforce the planting of maize through martial law so that the settlement might sustain itself over winters to come. Although enormously unpopular, Smith's measures ensured that when conflict resumed in the summer of 1609 and Powhatan ordered the end of trade relations and Smith's execution, Jamestown yet managed to survive.

A gunpowder accident eventually necessitated Smith's return to England, and the colony again fell into a lack of discipline and leadership, once more narrowly escaping complete dissolution. A poor harvest and a lack of trade options resulted in what came to be known as the starving time in Jamestown, and the desperate settlers had boarded vessels and just started their voyage back to England when they encountered ships bearing fresh arrivals and supplies. Martial law was again imposed. Raids between the colonists and Powhatans escalated until 1614, when a marriage between John Rolfe and Chief Powhatan's daughter Pocahontas, who had been held hostage in Jamestown during the first Powhatan War, helped foster a revival of trade and diplomacy.[30]

The newest settlers who arrived at Jamestown had been enticed by promises of an utopist and fulfilling life at Jamestown via pamphlets widely circulated by the London Company, and they were driven by the possibility of land and the chance to escape relatively poor socioeconomic conditions in England. The wealthiest settlers, who paid for the passage of the less fortunate indentured servants, were granted land for each person accommodated. Indentured servants, in return for their labor, could be promised clothes, money, or even land after completing their terms of service. Still, whether one would live to see freedom was questionable, at best. It is estimated that 70% to 85% of English colonists to Virginia and Maryland during the 17th century were indentured servants, coinciding with an abnormally high mortality rate. The life expectancy for a Chesapeake male was 43 years, over a decade less than in England. A quarter of children did not survive infancy, and another 25% died before they turned 20.[31]

Still, indentured servitude was a system which was to prove enormously successful at generating revenue; immigration to the New World on a large scale had become a business in itself, and because of it, the English language and culture would be dominant over those of the other European powers by 1700. When John Rolfe discovered a new strain of tobacco, and farmers in Jamestown began to produce the crop in mass quantities in 1616, the colony became financially viable. 3 years later, the London Company sent unmarried women to Jamestown to expand the settlement. The success of the Chesapeake Bay's tobacco plantations induced rapid immigration, the area's population expanding from 350 in 1616 to 13,000 in 1650 and 41,000 in 1670. The amount of tobacco produced grew from 200,000 to 3 million pounds between 1624 and 1638 alone. Maryland, originally intended to be a Catholic refuge by royal favorite and former Secretary of State Sir George Calvert, also eventually became a tobacco colony.[32]

Despite the heady profits to be made in the Chesapeake for those with sufficient capital with which to invest in land and labor, some English immigrants in the New World aspired to more than just riches gained in tobacco. 17th century England, dominated by the Church of England and the monarchy, was still a society of relatively low social mobility. Non-Anglican subjects of the crown, such as Roman Catholics, were unable to hold political office or easily advance themselves within trade guilds. For the Puritans, however, the Church of England remained uncomfortably close to Catholicism, as King Charles I even allowed his Catholic wife, Henrietta Maria of France, to attend private masses. As such, a group of British Puritans journeyed to Holland in 1609, and upon finding that their situation there was yet unsatisfactory, contracted with the London Company in 1620 to gain passage to Jamestown as indentured servants. Instead of arriving at Jamestown as planned, however, the Puritans landed at what is now Massachusetts, an area outside of the London Company's ownership and jurisdiction. Before departing the ship, the pilgrims therefore drafted an article swearing allegiance to the king of England, but also establishing self-governance through majority rule, the first such article to be created throughout the British colonies. The 41 pilgrims who signed the Mayflower Compact and established Plymouth thus became the first immigrants to America to formally embrace the democratic principles which would later shape the nation.[33]

Although the London Company's brief success turning a profit in tobacco had maintained the momentum behind English immigration in Virginia, the Company fell back into fiscal trouble and lost its charter in 1624, Virginia becoming a royal colony of approximately 1,800 people. Soon after the Company's disbandment, however, political and economic events in England stimulated mass immigration to the colonies to an extent far greater than the London Company ever had. When Charles I dissolved Parliament in 1629 and raised taxes, citizens were angered; a faltering textile industry and a series of poor harvests compounded the problem as the crown continued to squeeze revenue out of its subjects. The Bishop of London, William Laud, had meanwhile been increasing the pressure on English Puritans to join the Church of England. Unwilling to conform to an organization they considered still tainted by Catholicism, persecuted by the monarchy and the Church of England, and facing increasing taxes and falling incomes, thousands of Puritans left for America in search of religious freedom and economic opportunity.

In 1630, a fleet of 11 ships bearing 700 Puritans, craftsmen, farmers, and servants set sail for Massachusetts under the Massachusetts Bay Company and Puritan leader John Winthrop. First establishing a settlement named Charlestown, the Company soon moved to Boston, where the colony began to expand under local governance of the Massachusetts General Court. Despite grievous losses during their first winter, the colony had grown to accommodate 2,000 people by the next year, and would continue to attract settlers by the thousands during the rest of the 1930s. The much higher survival rate in New England over the Chesapeake made Massachusetts an even more appealing destination for those seeking succor from royal and Anglican oppression. Those who survived infancy could expect to live to 70, and as many as 20% of first generation New England males lived to the age of 80, with female figures only slightly lower.[34]

For the local Pequots, the English had been a harbinger of death. An epidemic of smallpox in 1616 had killed 90% of the natives, who had developed no immunity to the terrible disease; another epidemic in 1630, combined with fierce conflict, resulted in the dissolution of the Pequot nation in 1638.[35]

The following decade saw approximately 21,000 people immigrate to New England under Puritan leadership while another 49,000 settled amongst other colonies, the flood of settlers only slowing after Oliver Cromwell, a Puritan himself, deposed Charles I and gave relief to those suffering from religious persecution. Still, the population of New England grew from fewer than 20,000 to almost 120,000 by end of the 17th century. New Englanders were comprised primarily of independent farmers/yeomen who bartered for the tools they could not produce. Puritanical strictness was tempered by an emphasis on valuing religious, familial, and community ties over materialism and worldly pleasures.[36]

The Massachusetts Bay colony itself gave rise to four more colonies: New Hampshire in 1677, which experienced slow settlement and remained economically dependent on Massachusetts; Connecticut in 1662, although the Connecticut River valley was settled as early as 1636; New Haven, which was absorbed into Connecticut; and Rhode Island, settled primarily by non-Puritan "exiles and troublemakers" beginning in 1636, and chartered in 1663. Newport, Rhode Island, became a haven for privateers and slave traders by 1700. Many captured Native Americans passed through Newport on the journey to life in bondage in the Chesapeake or Caribbean. However, with the exception of Rhode Island, the Puritan New Englanders harbored no patience for nonconformists, a quality ironic in those who had themselves fled persecution. In 1644, Massachusetts banished Baptists, and in 1656, the Quakers. The most well-known example of Puritan intolerance yet remains the infamous witch hunts which swept New England like fire in a brush. The first New England hanging of a woman identified as a witch occurred in 1647 in Hartford, Connecticut, the palpable fear of witchcraft intensifying and feeding upon itself with each successive conviction. The mania culminated in the 1692 Salem witch trials, in which 13 women and 6 men were hanged, and an 80-old man was crushed to death for staunchly maintaining his innocence.[37]

Not all men and women amongst the first phase of European immigration to North America did so voluntarily, and those who did not were perhaps more likely to commit evil deeds than the multitude of convicted witches. Along with devoted Puritans, craftsmen, and landowners seeking to become aristocracy in the New World, the dregs of English society were sent to supplement the labor force in Virginia, satisfying the demand in the New World which would later be met by the slave trade. Parliament had authorized courts to ship all "rogues, vagrants, and sturdy beggars" to the colonies in 1663, and in 1717 established deportation to colonies as an alternative to the death sentence. Although several of the condemned actually chose the death penalty over a life of hard labor, over 50,000 felons were ultimately transported to the American colonies after the 1717 law. The colonial governments were quick to object to such undesirables coming to live amongst them. Although they had no seat in Parliament from which they could voice their dissent or change imperial policy, the colonies established their own regulations concerning the unloading of criminals at colonial ports. Maryland simply refused entry to convicts as early as 1676, Pennsylvania and Massachusetts placed tariffs on the importation of criminals, and at least one colonial legislature required ship masters to post bond as insurance for the good behavior of such passengers.[38]

After the turn of the century, thousands of Scots from Scotland and Scots-Irish from northern Ireland were also driven to leave for America. Scots in northern Ireland suffered political exclusion, economic discrimination in the wool market, and ballooning rents. Scots-Irish likewise sought to escape intense poverty and a lack of adequate farmland. Around 60,000 Scots-Irish arrived between 1730 and 1770, while around 35,000 Scots from Scotland came to America between 1730 and 1775.[39]

f. French

After failed attempts to find a Northwest Passage, French exploration of the New World recommenced in search of gold and natural wealth. However, unlike the Spanish, who subjugated the indigenous labor and taxed the wealth of ancient civilizations, or the English, who transplanted considerable numbers of their own population to build settlements and cultivate the land, the French preferred to extract resources through building a lucrative fur trade with Native Americans. Most of the earliest French settlements, concentrated in Acadia (Nova Scotia) and the Gulf of St. Lawrence, did not survive the harsh winters and scurvy amongst the population. The settlement at Sable Island lasted from 1598 to 1603, and that at St. Croix River lasted only from 1604 to 1605 due to a dearth of food and water. Acadia's capital, Port Royal, was established in 1605 to replace the settlement at Ile St. Croix, but only fared marginally better in its early years. It was abandoned in 1607, re-established in 1610, and pillaged and burned by an English pirate in 1613.[40]

Although Samuel de Champlain founded Quebec and established a fur trading outpost, initiating friendly relations with the surrounding Algonquins and Hurons, rapid French settlement in the region was not forthcoming. Because of their reliance on trading rather than direct resource extraction and production, the French population in the New World did not proliferate nearly to the extent of the English, and was overtaken in many regions. The Huguenots, likely the only French who might have looked eagerly upon settlement in America, were excluded from New France and moved instead to the English colonies. Subsequently, the population in Quebec experienced limited growth, exacerbated by limited support from the French crown. The census of 1663 counted only 3,035 French residents in Quebec and only 15,000 in 1700. The French in Acadia were thus ill-prepared to withstand English encroachment without Native American support. Moreover, Champlain had made the Iroquois eternal enemies of the French when he and his men assisted their Algonquin allies in a brief skirmish in 1609. From trade with the Dutch, the Iroquois became the first Native Americans to adopt the use of firearms and fought the French nearly to extinction. The enmity tipped the balance of power in the Northeast in favor of the English.[41]

Farther west around the Great Lakes, however, the French were able to establish a presence uncontested by England. French exploration of Lake Huron and Lake Michigan had begun as early as 1634 under the direction of Jean Nicolet, a follower of Champlain. He was succeeded by Jesuit missionary Claude Jean Allouez, who traveled around the Great Lakes in his efforts to convert Native Americans and established a mission in 1666 between Lakes Superior and Michigan. As more French Jesuits entered the region and established missions, the governor of New France, Louis de Baude, Count Frontenac, decided that French military expansion was necessary. Besides founding Fort Frontenac in 1673, the governor enlisted the aid of fur trapper Louis Joliet in investigating the possibility of a waterway leading past the Great Lakes to the Pacific. Along with missionary Jacques Marquette, Joliet traveled to the Mississippi River, then 700 miles downstream to a point where it became abundantly clear that the Mississippi emptied into the Gulf of Mexico. Although the two turned back for fear of coming too close to Spanish territory, explorer Rene Robert Cavelier, Sieur de la Salle later retraced their route and claimed all land watered by the Mississippi and its tributaries for France. The territory encompassing all land from the Appalachians to the Rocky Mountains was named Louisiana (*Louisiane*), in honor of King Louis XIV.

Meanwhile, clashes continued between the French "Acadians" and English "Nova Scotians," as English outposts created by the Hudson's Bay Company were overrun by the Acadians in 1686. The beginning of the Nine Years' War, also known as the War of the Grand Alliance, the War of the League of Augsburg, or King William's War (as it was known in the colonies), in 1689 marked the advent of well over a century of extended conflict between the two powers, the outcome of which would determine the fate of New France and New England. While French and English forces did battle on the fields of Europe, their respective colonies fought a war much more brutal and visceral in nature. The Iroquois struck at New France with the support of New York governor Thomas Dongan, slaughtering 200 French settlers at Lachine and taking 90 prisoners. In response, the reinstated governor Frontenac organized a French-allied Native American invasion of New York in January of 1690. However, while on the path to Albany, a winter storm halted the snow-shoed war party's progress; instead, the warriors attacked the Dutch town of Schenectady, whose inhabitants had left the palisade gate open with only two snowmen on guard in jest at the possibility of a Native American attack in winter. The lapse in judgment proved fatal; the townspeople were exterminated in the night, and the war party retreated north. Similarly ruthless raids pervaded the duration of

King William's War, with the only result that the European powers agreed to restore colonial holdings to the pre-war status quo (Nova Scotia passed back to the French as Acadia after its conquest by Massachusetts forces), and the French and English colonists had grown to hate each other immensely.

The events of the War of the Spanish Succession (known as Queen Anne's War in the colonies) played out very much like those of the previous conflict. In the Northern reaches of colonial America, the unlucky residents of Deerfield, Massachusetts met a similar end to those of Schenectady in the previous war, and once more, Massachusetts moved against Acadia in response. After the Acadian capital of Port Royal rebuffed the English colonists' first attack, five Iroquois warriors brought to London by former governor of Virginia and Maryland so swayed public opinion that English troops were sent to the colonists' aid. Port Royal was besieged and taken in 1710 and renamed Annapolis Royal, never again to return to French control. With the Treaty of Utrecht and the end of the war in 1713, all of Acadia was occupied permanently by the English and renamed Nova Scotia.

As France grew stronger with the consolidation of the Louisiana territory through the establishment of settlements such as Mobile in 1710 and New Orleans in 1718, it also attempted to toe its way back into Canadian dominance with the creation of Louisbourg at Cape Breton Island. The balance of power, such as it was, remained tenuous after the less-than-decisive outcome of King George's War, and French influence in the region was only struck a mortal blow during the 1754-1763 French and Indian War. The eventual French defeat also became the death knell for the French resistance to British occupation in Nova Scotia.

Unwilling to tolerate the increasingly rebellious Acadians any longer, the governor of Nova Scotia, Colonel Charles Lawrence, demanded that they swear allegiance to Great Britain or be forcibly removed from the territory. The majority of Acadians refused to defect, and some 6,000 to 8,000 dissenters were deported to prevent further insurrection. Scattered around the colonies for a time, some Acadians chose to return to Nova Scotia and swear allegiance to the British crown; others eventually found their way to Louisiana and evolved into what we know today as the Cajun population. Louisbourg fell to British forces in 1758 and was utterly destroyed, followed by the French surrender of Quebec in 1759 and Montreal in 1760. In 1763, the Treaty of Paris ended the Seven Years' War in Europe and the French and Indian War in North America, France ceding all of New France (Canada) and the territory of Louisiana east of the Mississippi to Great Britain. Britain also gained Florida from the Spanish in exchange for the return of Cuba and the Philippines. French rule within the continental mainland thus finally ended after the long struggle, leaving the eastern half of North America firmly under British mandate until the American War of Independence.[42]

g. Pennsylvania Dutch and Quakers

Aside from the English Puritan and French Huguenot migrations, religious conflict in the Old World encouraged emigration to the New World from Germany, as well. The Thirty Years War between Catholics and Protestants taxed the German people's lives, as well as their pockets. German princes raised income taxes as high as 60%, while 1/5th of the German population was lost to the war, disease, and starvation. Toward the end of the seventeenth century, William Penn, a Quaker convert, arrived in Germany to spread knowledge of Quakerism. He soon realized that the people, fatigued by years of religious conflict, would make good candidates for emigration to his inherited estate in America, which he had named Sylvania. Preaching religious tolerance, he successfully recruited large numbers of Germans seeking to leave their war-torn homes. In 1683, a contingent of 4,000 German immigrants led by Francis Pastorius established Germantown, outside of Philadelphia. Because the Germans were not well received by colonies in other parts of New England, these settlers settled elsewhere to escape the pressures of Anglicization which affected many other ethnic colonies, thus maintaining a distinctly German culture.

Quakerism, too, became a source of tension with the religiously insular Puritans; while tolerated somewhat in the Chesapeake, where greater pluralism and the business of tobacco farming made religious conformism secondary to profit, Quakers often proved too meddlesome and outspoken for Puritan communities to bear. While some Germans found their homes in other areas such as the Carolinas and New York, Pennsylvania remained the predominant center of German immigration, settlers to that region becoming known as the Pennsylvania Dutch. From 1710 to 1770, 85,000 Germans emigrated from their homes and arrived in America.[43]

h. Dutch

Meanwhile, the last great seafaring power in Europe, the Netherlands, had not been idle. The Dutch East India Company had commissioned navigator Henry Hudson to find a western trade route to the East Indies, and he had explored the river which now bears his name in 1609. Dutch traders began interacting with the local Native Americans, but often became entangled in Native American power politics. The involvement of Dutch traders in conflicts between the Mohawks, Mohicans, and Munsees grew to such an extent that the Netherlands feared war with the Iroquois Confederacy would result. Accordingly, in 1621, the Dutch West India Company was granted an official charter to conduct business in North America and manage Dutch settlements and trade more equitably and efficiently. The Dutch West India Company sponsored two settlements: Fort Orange, replacing Fort Nassau (washed away by a spring flood in 1619), and New Amsterdam on Manhattan Island, which remained free of ice year-round and featured a good harbor. The island was famously purchased from the Manhattan tribe for 60 guilders' worth of finery, most often calculated as being the equivalent of $24.[44]

While Manhattan grew as a Dutch naval base and hub for trade with the Old World, the Dutch government attempted to encourage immigration in its North American holdings through its own system of patroonships. The patroon system was similar to the British headright system in that wealthy men could gain land in exchange for bringing settlers to the Americas. However, the patroon system was far more demanding on the patron, as it required the translocation of 50 Dutch families rather than individuals (as under the headright model). There was also relatively little incentive for Dutch families to leave Europe and settle in New Netherlands. The patroonship operation was largely a failure in comparison to other colonial initiatives, although some number of French Huguenots, English settlers, Swedes, and Finns came to the region or were incorporated into Dutch settlements. The first group of Jewish settlers to come to North America also fled to New Amsterdam after the Portuguese occupation of Recife in Brazil.

In 1664, the British occupied New Netherlands and renamed the region New York, relegating Dutch involvement in North America to trade with other nations' colonies. However, the Dutch also continued to facilitate and exploit immigration to America, conveying thousands of settlers and slaves to the New World. Throughout the 18th century, Dutch companies were responsible for bringing almost half of the German immigrants to American shores as "redemptioners," indentured servants who negotiated the terms of their passage only after it was given and when they had little choice but to accept what terms were offered. Dutch agents known as "newlanders" posed as immigrants visiting the old country after having made their fortunes in the colonies, enticing the poorest Germans to emigrate. After luring their targets aboard ships bound for the Americas, ship captains often starved their passengers to pad profit margins, causing many redemptioners to eat rats for sustenance. On one such trip, only 48 of the 156 passengers reached American shores alive. Upon arrival, prospects for the unfortunate survivors often grew worse. Some were forced to serve additional terms for family members who had died during the ocean voyage, families were often split apart at auction, and many were heavily abused while indentured. However, this was not the worst to come; slavery soon overtook indentured servitude as the colonies' primary source of imported labor, and it would come to leave its indelible mark upon the pages of American history.[45]

i. Slaves

The shift from the American farmers' reliance on indentured servitude to slavery occurred slowly. The first Africans to travel to the United States did so as indentured servants, and those who survived were freed after serving their obligation. In one known case, a slave was freed, became prosperous, and later owned slaves himself. However, slavery became institutionalized as labor-intensive tobacco, cotton, rice, indigo, and sugar plantations grew, and as the slave trade grew to fill the demand. Normal immigration had proved to be insufficient for the task, as conflict with Native American tribes, disease, and poor harvests kept populations low; the demand for labor far outstripped what indentured servants lured by the headright system or free labor could provide. Jamestown was nearly wiped out in 1622 by a Native American attack, and diseases killed over 500 more settlers in the following year. In fact, the attrition rate in the early stages of Virginian colonization was such that the colony recorded an English population of only 1,200 in 1624 despite 7,600 English having journeyed there over the 17 years since the founding of Jamestown.[46]

After the civil war in England ended and the monarchy was reestablished, the economy stabilized, and fewer English were willing to indenture themselves or emigrate. King Charles II chartered the Company of Royal Adventures of England Trading into Africa in 1660 to barter for slaves and goods in Africa. The Spanish, Portuguese and Dutch all had prior involvement in slave trading, and had soon found that it was usually more profitable to trade with the most powerful West African states for slaves than attempt to capture slaves themselves. Many of the slaves bound for the Americas had been taken by rival African states through battle, raiding, or tribute, and were sold to Europeans only after changing hands between several African slavers.

The Portuguese had held a virtual monopoly on the African slave trade for approximately two hundred years. However, during the period of increasing demand for slave labor in North America in the 18th century, the English became the dominant slave trading nation and transported 2.6 million slaves from West Africa to the New World. Although the majority of these were taken to South America and the Caribbean to replenish the slave populations there, in America, lower mortality for the slave population and a higher proportion of enslaved women allowed for a higher birth rate, reducing the demand for African slaves.

Tragically, passage to New World colonies proved too treacherous and abusive for many of the enslaved, who were brutalized and subjected to inhuman conditions for the length of the ordeal. The brutal marches in Africa to slave traders' coastal forts, the infamous Middle Passage, and the ruthless measures taken to break the slaves' spirits upon disembarking caused many of them to perish. The mortality rate during the Atlantic crossing alone was as high as 30% in the early 18th century for those who had survived the African leg of the journey, although the death toll on a 6-week trip to Brazil was significantly lower than that on trips to the Caribbean and the English colonies. It may have dropped to as low as 5% by the 1820s, when slave smugglers were unable to transport their human cargo en masse. However, given the extent of maltreatment and conditions in which Africans were confined and transported, it is remarkable that attrition aboard slaver-rigged brigs and barks during the era of legalized slave trading was not greater. Large ships carried, on average, 700 slaves distributed amongst the lower decks. Decks were often spaced just 4 feet apart, and slaves were often chained together in groups of six or more, sometimes with one person's head between the legs of another to maximize the usage of space.[47]

On one slave ship, the *Brooks*, a space of only seven square feet was allotted to each slave. In such claustrophobic conditions, slaves would have to endure lying in each others' excrement, fighting typhoid, smallpox, measles, and yellow fever in the stifling holds while receiving the minimum amount of nourishment slavers deemed their human cargo needed to survive. Those slaves who could muster the strength to resist did not take this abuse passively, and it is estimated that rebellions took place on as many as 10% of the mid-Atlantic voyages. At times, entire ships, including their crews, would succumb to the deadly conditions, and other ships even created epidemics in their ports of call.[48]

The terrible mortality did little to deter the growth of the slave trade in light of the heavy demand for slave labor. Newly imported men could sell for £28 to £32, and women about £3 cheaper by the early 1750s. An African-born boy sold for between £10 and £25, and a girl between £10 and £21. The price varied greatly depending on a slave's skills, age, tractability, and place of birth. African slaves were not only less malleable than slave owners might wish, but had to learn the English language and be acculturated in other ways. A "seasoned," or American-born, slave was significantly more expensive than an African-born slave, one such woman fetching a price of £57. Slave children born in the New World were thus considered extremely valuable to slave owners. Although the status of slaves' children was called into question in the early years of the trade, a Virginian law was passed in 1662 relegating the status of a child to the status of the mother in order to avoid legal complications (mostly concerning children fathered by slave owners). Another Virginian law in 1705 declared all non-Christian people brought to the United States to be slaves. Due to both importation and domestic growth, the slave population expanded at a quick pace. In 1649, the 300 slaves in Virginia comprised less than 2% of the Virginian population; by 1710, the 23,100 Africans and descendants of Africans constituted 42% of Virginia's total inhabitants. In 1790, over 15% of the U.S. population of 3.9 million was in bondage.[49]

At least half a million slaves were imported to British colonies (and later, America) from the start of the transatlantic slave trade to its (legal) end in 1808, although slave smuggling continued after that year. About 10 slave ships per week docked at New Orleans' port between 1808 and 1863 carrying 15 slaves each, other slave ships operating regularly out of ports all the way to New York. Despite laws, which threatened fines and imprisonment for slave traders, the deployment of a naval squadron to the West African coast in 1819, and the death penalty being placed on slave trading in 1820. These laws were virtually never enforced. Some officials even cooperated with slavers for profit. It is telling that the first conviction and execution for slave trading did not occur until after the outbreak of the Civil War. The majority of slaves were born to parents already living in the United States, and several slave states actually exported more slaves than they imported.[50]

The agricultural nature of the Southern economy continued to be a force driving slavery. The Province of Georgia, initially conceived and established as a free (non-slave) territory, was granted to a group of philanthropists to act as a refuge for debtors in 1732. Besides relieving the pressure within overcrowded prisons in England, Parliament and the King wanted to establish a buffer between South Carolina and the Catholic Spanish and French territories to the south and southwest. The land was to be distributed by the philanthropic board of trustees in 50-acre parcels in order to encourage the growth of self-sufficient small and mid-size farms. However, the land failed to attract settlers or debtors, despite advertising in Britain. While Georgia's neighbor, South Carolina, was enjoying significant agricultural growth and success, most felt that such had been made possible only by the importation of slaves to perform the daily tasks on southern plantations. Politically active pro-slavery factions cropped up in Georgia between 1735 and 1740, petitioning the trustees to adopt a more lenient attitude towards the practice, and failing in that endeavor, opting to bypass the trustees entirely by petitioning Parliament and the King. The opponents of slavery, including the trustees, resisted the introduction of unfree labor not for the indulgence of abolitionist ideals, but rather for more harshly pragmatic reasons. Life with slaves, they argued, would make freemen idle and susceptible to temptation. Furthermore, slave labor would encourage the growth of large plantations and a widely dispersed population (as opposed to a more densely populated collection of subsistence farmers), making the colony unsuitable as a military buffer, and provide slaves greater opportunity for escape to Spanish Florida, where they perhaps would even be armed and turned against Georgia once freed.

Despite these arguments, economic viability won out over ultimately unachievable military interests. Without slaves, the colony could not attract enough white settlers to be an effective buffer to Spanish territories, and even with slaves, the colony's military usefulness would be similarly compromised. The project was abandoned; Georgia was turned over to the King and became a royal province in 1752 after the government declined to renew the subsidies which had formerly sustained the province. It was a blow to the mission of members of Parliament who concerned themselves with the increasing problem of debtors in Britain. However, in broader terms, the failure to attract small farmers and the subsequent fiscal insolvency of Georgia as a free territory served as a clear indication that slavery would continue to take hold of the South.[76]

Initially, the tobacco farming industry was primarily responsible for the colonies' insatiable demand for slaves. While slaves worked on sugar plantations in Louisiana and harvested wheat, rice, and other foodstuffs elsewhere, the particular nature of the tobacco crop contributed greatly to the spread of slavery. Tobacco farming was extremely labor intensive, and because the plant depleted nutrients in the soil quickly (after 3 or so years), farmers expanded their operations to include more land. Furthermore, farmers attempted to offset a decline in tobacco prices by expanding their operations and producing even more tobacco, which required more labor. When sugar crops failed in the Caribbean, large numbers of slaves were transported to America to work in tobacco fields.[51]

Tobacco was not the most infamous crop to be associated with slavery, however. The invention of the cotton gin in 1793 spurred the production of cotton in the South, and with the rising population in America, became the dominant slave-dependent industry in the nation. Even more labor dependent and nutrient-dependent than tobacco, cotton production had previously been constrained by the inability of cotton growers to quickly clean the fibers harvested from a particular species of cotton of its seeds and thus make the majority of their harvests usable in (and sellable to) textile factories. Once the gin was invented, cotton production of the species *gossypium hirsutum* increased by a factor of more than 40 in just 2 years.[52]

Although the price of cotton subsequently started to fall, the demand from textile factories in the North and in England encouraged cotton producers to increase their holdings. As financial crises caused smaller, non-slave-owning farmers to go bankrupt, large plantations absorbed the smaller farms and bought additional slaves. Moreover, the high speed at which topsoil was depleted by cotton caused farmers to move west as treaties with Native Americans opened up more land for American cultivation in Georgia and the U.S. gained the Mississippi Territory. Demand for the fiber was such that cotton grew from 7% of U.S. exports in 1800 to 57% of U.S. exports in 1860; overall cotton production grew from 36.5 million to almost 2 billion pounds in the same time, and the Southern slave population grew from 851,532 to 3,950,511.[53]

Indentured servants were often treated as badly as slaves. Because indentured servants could not be viewed as permanent property by their masters, their long term well-being was neglected. Achieving maximum output within the years of servitude was paramount to the owner, and whether the servant survived to see freedom was an unnecessary concern. Like slaves, indentured servants were sold and traded (some even gambled away in games of cards), sexually exploited, and most often overworked, but slaves enjoyed a modicum of health benefits typically denied to the indentured servant. Although health care varied greatly according to individual owners' practices, historians surmise that in general, that provided to slaves may have been better than that available to the free population at large. Associations of plantation owners placed an emphasis on preventative medicine, maintaining hygiene (due to the prevailing belief was that slaves would pay little attention to their hygiene on their own), and ensuring that slaves had a balanced and adequate diet.

That is not to say that the life of a slave was anything but harsh. Field hands worked from daylight to dark at least 6 days a week, families could be separated at any moment through sale to distant plantations, and attempts to become literate were seen as a severe offense – sometimes, a capital one. Although slave owners wanted to protect their human assets and typically were against using the lash as anything but a last resort, favoring such punishments as extra work, confinement, or a loss of "privileges," overseers did not have a vested interest in the health of slaves. These intermediaries between slave and owner were instructed to see to the production of a large crop while not harming the slaves to excess. The latter condition was disregarded in the interest of the former more often than not, and slave owners were typically willing to overlook the transgressions if their slaves survived and the plantation turned a profit. Slaves quickly learned to hate their overseers no less than the life under the lash that such figures came to represent.

Those slaves who were not ensnared by the burgeoning agricultural industry of the South were employed in a wide variety of occupations by 1860. Besides domestic service, slaves worked in mines, docks and shipyards, sawmills, gristmills, textile mills, rock quarries, and fisheries, while others served aboard ships as deckhands and firemen. From logging to the production of barrels and staves, slaves also increasingly began to make the transition to becoming artisans and craftsmen. Some worked as blacksmiths, carpenters, wheelwrights, barbers, shoemakers, or bakers. To the conservative slave owner, the elevation of slaves to a higher status was seen as a dangerous proposition, and one that was to be discouraged. [54]

As with previous groups, animosity and conflict arose between these unwilling immigrants and their oppressors. A palpable fear of slave uprisings permeated communities in which the slave population was high, and owners were exceedingly harsh with their measures to punish those who would not accept their lot in life. Slave rebellions were put down in brutal fashion; escapees were punished by degrees ranging from whipping to castration, dismemberment, and death. In perhaps the most famous of these, the Stono Rebellion near Charleston in 1739, 20 slaves seized firearms and burned plantations, killing 25 whites and recruiting another sixty or so slaves before being confronted by militia and captured. These incidents were hardly limited to the South. In New York City in 1741, where the slave population was considerable and a slave revolt had been suppressed 29 years earlier, arson was blamed on at least 12 white and 160 black inhabitants of the city; 4 whites and 31 blacks were summarily executed by hanging or burning at the stake. Indeed, slavery was an affliction shared by all of the British colonies at the time of the American Revolution. Conflict between slaves and slave traders continued well afterwards, the injustice provoking uprisings and mutinies such as the successful slave capture of the *Amistad* in 1839. Although the slaves who had taken control of the *Amistad* were deemed free men by a federal court in 1840 due to the illegality of the slave trade, the abolitionist movement would not gain sufficient momentum in the North until after the Revolutionary War. All slaves would not gain their independence until the end of the Civil War in 1865.[55]

3. INDEPENDENCE, 1776

The years following the American Revolutionary War were also times of fluctuating immigration and emigration within the fledgling nation. The war itself had deterred or prevented many from coming to the United States, especially since the majority of immigrants prior to the Declaration of Independence had been from the British Isles. In fact, after the Treaty of Paris in 1783 ended the war, loyalists within the colonies began emigrating from New England to Canada. 7,000 loyalists left New York in what remains the largest single emigration from the United States. Some number of English, Scottish, Scotch-Irish, Swedish, and French immigrants did arrive in the United States during the next few decades, although not in the amounts seen before the war. Swedish families continued to flee the simultaneous famine and population boom in their homeland; an estimated 10,000 to 20,000 French colonists came to the United States after the 1791 St. Domingue slave revolt (in present-day Haiti); Irish workers and rebels escaped to the U.S. in 1798 after a failed rebellion against English rule.

By and large, events in Europe discouraged, rather than encouraged, immigration to the United States. The already-poor and still deteriorating relations with King George III of Great Britain led in part to a ban on the emigration of skilled workers from Ireland in 1788, and in 1803, the British Passenger Act placed restrictions on the number of passengers allowed to board ships bound for America. The French Revolution in 1789 and the Napoleonic Wars which followed prompted members of the French aristocracy to leave their homes for the U.S., while the socioeconomic changes sweeping across revolutionary France and the wide disparity in wealth and mobility between the classes forced the peasantry to stay and fight for better lives under the new regime. The successful revolution in France was viewed with fear and trepidation by other European monarchs; many united to fight Napoleonic France and put an end to the social experiment. The end of peace between England and France in 1803 proved problematic for American traders and once again slowed American immigration. Both nations forbade American ships from trading at its rival's ports. American vessels were consequently unable to safely sail to either, and those attempting to make the journey were often seized. This, combined with a continued hostile British presence in the western reaches of the American frontier, led Congress to declare war upon Britain in the War of 1812. Immigration to America would not recommence until the war's end in 1815.

That is not to say, however, that the United States population had stagnated. A census taken in 1790 counted approximately 3.2 million non-slave residents of the U.S., with ethnicities from the British Isles comprising approximately 75% of that number. It is estimated that the American slave population at the time was approximately 700,000. 30 years later, the non-slave and slave populations in the U.S. had more than doubled to 8.1 million and 1.53 million, respectively. Because of the increasingly large U.S. population, Congress recognized a need for federal legislation concerning immigration and naturalization, which had previously been left to the jurisprudence of individual colonies/states. The Naturalization Act, passed in 1790, set a 2-year residency requirement for naturalization, but citizenship was still exclusive to free whites. The requirement was raised to 5 years in 1795, and immigrants seeking naturalization were required to declare their intent to seek citizenship 3 or more years prior to gaining it. Furthermore, the Naturalization Act of 1795 required citizens to relinquish all foreign allegiances and titles. Finally, the Naturalization Act of 1798 raised the residency requirement to 14 years, mandated the recording of immigrants naturalized, and required the registration of all non-citizens living in or arriving at the United States. The residency requirement was lowered again to 5 years by another Naturalization Act in 1802, but the act added requirements for good moral character and allegiance to the constitution.

The first federal law concerning immigration itself was the Aliens Act of 1798, passed only a week after the Naturalization Act of that year. Within the act, the president was given authority to arrest and deport non-citizens deemed threats to the country, and captains were required to provide lists of all immigrants aboard their ships at U.S. ports. The Alien Enemies Act, passed on July 6, 1798, gave the president authority to detain and remove non-citizen males 14 years of age and older during times of war if they were of the enemy's nationality. Finally, the Steerage Act of 1819 required that the passenger lists of arriving ships be copied and sent to the Secretary of State and Congress for records, limited the number of passengers beyond crewmembers to 2 per every 5 tons of a vessel's weight, and established fines for the deprivation of passengers on a voyage. While rudimentary in nature, these laws established principles regarding transportation, naturalization, security, and immigrant safety within American immigration law which became the foundation for future legislation as the next wave of immigrants reached the shores of the United States.

4. BUILDING THE NEW AMERICAN FRONTIER (CA. 1821-1880)

a. Irish

As the 19th century progressed, immigration to the United States gained steam alongside the American economy. However, the most populous group to immigrate to the fledgling nation would do so under desperate circumstances. The Irish population had almost doubled every 50 years for 2 centuries, ballooning from 1.1 million in 1672 to 8.2 million in 1841. Systems of land tenure limited the transference and redistribution of land amongst the booming population, and social mobility was virtually nonexistent. Thus, when disaster struck in Ireland and its potato crops were lost first in 1846 (when 90% of the crops were destroyed) and again in 1847, the flow of Irish immigrants to America became a tide of hundreds of thousands. British Canada attracted some of the Irish emigrants through cheap passage, as British subsidies made fares to Canada as low as £2 (approximately $11) available, compared to fares of 3£10s (approximately $17.50) to the U.S. in 1846. The Passenger Act of 1847 passed by Congress increased regulation (and subsequently fares) for transatlantic shipping, prompting more Irish immigrants to board Canadian-bound ships. Tragically, an estimated 32%, or 30,000 of the 97,000 Irish who left for Canada in 1847, died on what came to be called "coffin ships" or died shortly after disembarking, compared with 9% of the Irish immigrants bound for the United States in that year. Those who survived the crossing often left Canada for the United States shortly after arrival. The amount of Irish Catholic immigrants was so large that the American Catholic population, which had only numbered 663,000 in 1840, was at 3,103,000 by 1860. From 1840 to 1860, nearly 1.7 million immigrants, representing over one third of the total number of immigrants (4.3 million), came from Ireland.[56]

The sudden rise in immigrant populations after long periods of stability, combined with financial troubles from 1837 to 1844, caused state and local governments to introduce legislation restricting the movement of poor foreigners into their municipalities. Factions appeared supporting heavier regulation and restrictions on immigration. Some citizens feared that the arrival of immigrants would lead to increased crime. The stereotype was not entirely fabricated; as of the late 1840s in Boston, 75% of those in the county jail, 58% of paupers, and 90% of truants and vagabonds were reportedly of Irish descent. However, on the whole, discrimination against the Irish arose from the fear that the influx of foreign labor would create excess competition, thus severely depressing wages and working standards. A secret anti-Irish organization named the Order of the Star-Spangled Banner, founded in 1850, came to be called the Know-Nothings in 1853. From the Know-Nothing party, mayors in 4 major cities (Boston, Philadelphia, San Franscico and Chicago) and over 100 U.S. Congressmen were elected. The Massachusetts state elections of 1854 were particularly dominated by the Know-Nothing party. However, their members' philosophies quickly bled into other forms of anti-pluralism.[57]

Violent anti-Catholicism within the majority-Protestant population became prevalent. In Philadelphia, the anti-Catholic riots of 1844 against the local Irish grew bloody, as protesters burned Catholic churches and left 30 dead. Periodicals and publications also railed against the loyalty of the Irish to Catholicism. Statements made by a conservative Pope against liberalism led some to claim that the Irish were against democracy. Contrary to such opinions, the Irish worked to counteract discrimination and improve their standing by banding together to improve their situation through collective economic and political action. Mostly working on public works projects in labor gangs and construction crews (where there existed more equality amongst the workforce) or finding employment from the government (such as on police force), Irish immigrants worked to form both labor unions and voting blocs. Emphasis was placed on strength and improvement through solidarity and organization, as opposed to individual advancement.[58]

Smaller ethnic groups, while somewhat overshadowed by the large Irish migration, were also brought to the U.S. in the mid part of the century. With the end of the Mexican-American War in 1848, the Treaty of Hidalgo gave U.S. citizenship to approximately 80,000 Mexican residents in New Mexico and 4,000 in California. In 1849, the California gold rush attracted those looking to make a quick fortune, with immigrants coming from Europe, Mexico, China, and Australia. Despite the high number of immigrants, Congress had done relatively little to implement new immigration and naturalization laws. The May Act of 1824 amended the temporal requirement for a prospective citizen's declaration of intention to 2 years instead of 3, the Passenger Act of 1847 increased regulations for passenger safety and space on merchant ships (functionally raising transatlantic fares and discouraging immigration to the U.S.), and the Passenger Act of 1855 added a requirement for ship captains to distinguish between temporary and permanent immigrants in their reports. However, the volume of Chinese immigration, like that of the Irish, began to spark protests which finally compelled Congress to act.

b. Chinese

Chinese Immigrant Quote:

> Chinese immigrants in the early days became laundrymen and couldn't bring wives over.[59]

The Chinese were driven both by tales of high wages in mining camps and by the Taiping Rebellion, during which 20 million died and economic operations were ground to a halt amidst a famine lasting from 1851 to 1864. From 1840 to 1880, around 370,000 Chinese came to America, mostly from the Guangdong province. Some of these Chinese came not as free persons, but as coolies, contract laborers who were treated little better than slaves for the duration of their contracts. The Chinese who signed such contracts often did so because they had little choice, as the Opium Wars from 1839 to 1842 severely damaged economy of Southern China.[60]

Arriving on Californian shores, the Chinese immigrants were greeted with the same hostility as the Irish on the East cost. The large cultural divide between the Chinese and the traditionally Western European descendants in America further increased antagonism toward the newcomers. A slew of anti-immigrant legislation was passed by the state of California. Laws in 1852 and 1855 taxed the importation of foreign labor. During the early 1850s, laws were passed requiring immigrant miners ineligible for citizenship to pay a monthly license fee. From 1858 to 1862, Chinese people were prohibited from landing on Californian soil except in cases of weather emergency. The Chinese Police Tax placed a $2.50 monthly tax on many Asian inhabitants of the state in 1862. Legislation revoking Chinese immigrants' civil rights and access to social services was also passed, including laws prohibiting Chinese from testifying in court, going to public schools, working on public projects, and owning real estate.[61]

Although many of the laws were later repealed, and much of the unskilled European labor that had come to California during the 1849 gold rush soon left the state, anti-Chinese sentiment persisted in the region. In 1869, 60 white men, organized as the Anti-Chinese league of Unionville, Nevada, expelled 35 Chinese, although they later returned. In 1871, 15 Chinese immigrants were hung, 4 were shot and killed, and 2 were wounded during a riot in Los Angeles as part of an ongoing campaign of violence against immigrants. The riot was due to the accidental death of a white policeman caught in the crossfire between Chinese immigrants.[62]

State legislation often reflected the xenophobic public sentiment. Nevada laws stipulated that nonwhites (often specifically defined as Indians, blacks and Chinese) were not allowed to vote, hold office, serve in juries or the militia, enter public schools, marry a white person, or testify against a white person. There was either an anti-Chinese movement present or anti-Chinese legislation passed in the states of Utah, Arizona, Idaho, Texas, Oregon, and Montana, as well.[63]

In the later part of the decade, the anti-Chinese Workingman's Party was created under populist Irish American Dennis Kearney, whose rallies were openly racist in the same manner as the openly anti-Catholic and anti-Irish protests in the East. Adopting the slogan "the Chinese must go," the party rallied against the Central Pacific Railroad, which employed a workforce that was 90% Chinese. It is somewhat ironic that the great transcontinental railroad, designed to unite the country and satisfy California's need for new residents, was completed by the two most persecuted immigrant peoples of that century. The Chinese, employed by the Central Pacific Railroad, and the Irish, employed by the Union Pacific, labored under dangerous and abusive conditions to complete one of the greatest American projects of the era, facilitating American expansion and growth into the western frontier.[64]

In Washington D.C., the influx of immigrants and shifting needs for labor during and after the American Civil War prompted Congress to become more deeply involved with immigration regulation. The Burlingame Treaty of 1868 established formal diplomatic relations on amiable terms between the U.S. and China and guaranteed freedom from religious persecution for Chinese subjects in America and U.S. citizens in China. In 1862 and 1869, laws prohibiting the importation of involuntary Asian "coolie" labor were passed by Congress. The Page Act of 1875 prohibited the importation of convicts and prostitutes. Officials abused its enforcement against Chinese women. The immigration rate of Chinese women decreased 68% from 1876-1882 after an excessively rigorous interview process was installed for Chinese women seeking to enter the United States.

However, as a representative body of the American people, Capitol Hill itself was hardly free from protectionism and some degree of bigotry. The Immigration Act of 1882, which blacklisted paupers and the insane, also placed a 50 cent tariff on immigrants. Furthermore, while Congress recognized an early need for Chinese immigrant laborers to complete the transcontinental railroad, it was not willing to extend citizenship to them, and eventually barred the Chinese from entering the country for any permanent purpose. Although the Naturalization Act of 1870 provided for the naturalization of African immigrants and descendants of such immigrants, it denied such citizenship to Asians. Finally, in 1882, the Chinese Exclusion Act prohibited the importation of Chinese labor to the United States for 10 years, codified the deportation of Chinese illegal immigrants, and confirmed that naturalization would be denied to Chinese immigrants. The successive acts of 1884 and 1888 were even harsher. To hinder Chinese immigration into the United States, Angel Island in the San Francisco Bay was set up as the western equivalent of Ellis Island. Many early Chinese immigrants were detained there while awaiting validation of their paperwork from relatives in the United States.[65]

c. Germans

Friedrich von Dietze, Germany, 1947[66]

- invited 1947 when US inviting German specialists w/ unusual knowledge to US, called Operation Paperclip
- in the war in Germany research/development for German navy, key in torpedo direction, so invited
- whole family killed in the war, had no work, wound up fixing radios or digging ditches
- got job offer from military police in 1947, winter
- left May 1947, went to work for the Dept of the Navy in DC
- went back to Germany to marry again in late 1947, and brought wife back

Although Chinese immigration had become so volatile an issue, the number of Chinese coming to the U.S. comprised a relatively small percentage of the aggregate amount, and was far surpassed by other ethnic groups. More socially palatable groups of immigrants such as the Germans and Scandinavians escaped the wholesale discrimination experienced by the Chinese and Irish.

Both Chinese and German immigration reached their highest annual rate in 1882; the Chinese at 40,000 and the Germans at 250,630. Although English and French immigrants continued to come to America during the period, the volume of German immigration was second only to the Irish. Over 5.6 million Germans came to America from 1825 to 1924, with almost 3 million of those arriving from 1840 to 1880 and another 2 million in the 1880s and 1890s. The influx of Germans was so large that 25% of those living in America could claim German descent by 1900, compared to only 9% in 1790.[67]

German immigration had risen in the 1830s as peasants fled a series of poor harvests and political instability which reached a flashpoint in the revolution of 1848. Many had just recently gained the freedom and mobility to emigrate due to the emancipation of serfs in Germany and Austria-Hungary. A large number of middle-class intellectuals also moved as well. Word spread quickly of the "land of unlimited possibilities," as America had come to be called, and chain migration brought successive waves of German immigrants to try their luck in the New World. The prospect of free farmland, which eventually attracted large numbers of Scandinavians as well, and general dissatisfaction with Otto von Bismarck's anti-Catholic *Kulturkampf* (cultural struggle) and anti-Socialist policies led to increases in German immigration in the 1860s and 1880s. Germans settled heavily in the Mid-Atlantic or East North-Central states in the early stages of their movement, with over 75% of German-born persons in the U.S. living in those areas in 1850. New York,

Chicago, and Philadelphia held the greatest percentages of the German population in America. Later, after the passage of the Homestead Act in 1862, many chose to live in rural areas of the U.S. and develop farmland. In 1870, 25% of German-born population in the U.S. worked in the agricultural sector, and Germans comprised more than a third of foreign-born farmers in the U.S.

That is not to say that Germans settled exclusively in rural areas; from 1860 to 1890, about 40% of Germans in America lived in cities of 25,000 people or more, although Germans tended to settle in different cities than did the Irish. Of the top 9 cities chosen by the those ethnicities, only New York was shared in common; whereas the Irish chose to settle primarily in New England, most Germans chose to live in Midwestern cities such as Milwaukee, Cincinnati, St. Louis, Chicago, Cleveland, Toledo, Dayton, and Detroit. The "German triangle" encompassed the majority of German-born immigrants in the United States by the late 19th century, the points of the triangle being Milwaukee, Cincinnati, and St. Louis.

Germans also occupied different sectors of the economy than the Irish. In 1870, 37% of German immigrant workers held skilled jobs, their Old World expertise exhibiting itself in the beer industry. Over 2,000 beer gardens and saloons could be found in Cincinnati in 1860, more than one for every hundred residents of that city. The free use of alcohol in German communities thus became ingrained in American lore, although Germans often worked as bakers, tailors, cigar makers, machinists, or butchers. Many German women did not work outside of the home, but those who did found employment in a wide range of occupations, from hotel keeper to nurse. Others worked as saloon keepers, bakers, and tailors in family-owned businesses. Finally, German fine art flourished in America to an extent arguably greater than that of any other ethnic group, from the prolific German American theaters to singing societies, singing contests, and professional orchestras. In Minnesota Germans staged over 1,600 theatrical performances from 1857 to 1890; in 1900, 174 German singing associations existed in Brooklyn. Although the German theater was to irreversibly diminish in the decades ahead, the symphonic orchestras survived and became a lasting German contribution to American culture.

On the whole, the majority Lutheran Germans were well suited to living with the Protestant-influenced Anglicans who had dominated the American religious landscape for so long. Still, rarely did an immigrant ethnicity avoid conflict altogether. The one third of Germans who were Catholic and the 250,000 who were Jewish found a less cordial reception awaiting them than had been given to their Lutheran countrymen and women. German Catholics became embroiled in a struggle over the direction of the American Catholic Church with the Irish, whose clergy were relatively more conservative on social issues and who eventually prevailed. The German Jews, being the first large group of Jews to immigrate to America, encountered different problems. While most worked as peddlers and struggled to work their way up the mercantile ladder, the refusal of virtually all American banks to hire Jews resulted in the creation of a handful of Jewish banking houses. Discrimination meant that Jewish success was heavily contingent on economic interaction within the Jewish community, both in retail and in finance.

Additionally, the idiosyncrasies of the German people and the ideas they imported from Europe did not sit well with some. The Know-Nothings disliked not only Catholic Germans, but others who harbored more rationalist, or even atheist beliefs about life. Those of a Puritanical bent also bemoaned the stereotypical

German's penchant for alcoholic drink. Several German American picnics and festivals took an ugly turn when anti-German agitators incited riots in Columbus, Cincinnati, and Louisville. A number of German anarchists were also hanged for suspected involvement in the 1886 Haymarket bombings in Chicago, and the publicized event made the German radical a dangerous element in the American consciousness.[161]

Heavy use of the German language became a contentious issue, as well. In areas with heavy German concentrations, the German culture persisted strongly, sometimes even into the fourth or fifth generation in America. German parochial schools often did not teach English to students, and states such as Pennsylvania and Ohio passed laws allowing for German instruction in public schools when a given percentage of parents requested it. English-speaking residents in several Missouri school districts had to fight to prevent German from becoming the language of instruction in public schools in 1888. By 1890, a reactionary movement against liberal use of the German language in public schools had come into full swing, and states such as Massachusetts and Texas mandated the use of English in public schools. Due to the large German presence in America, however, German remained the most popular foreign language studied by high school students until World War I.[68]

d. Scandinavians

The number of Scandinavian immigrants to America also increased dramatically starting in the 1830s. A high rate of population growth in Norway, Sweden, Denmark, and Finland throughout the 19th century served as a constant stimulus for the movement throughout most of the Norse countries; only in Iceland did the population less than double during the period, as droughts and famine took their toll. Considering that only 14,000 Icelanders emigrated from 1851 to 1930 despite the encouragement of emigration by the Icelandic government, the population boom in the other Norse countries may be identified as the primary factor which induced millions of Scandinavians to leave their home countries. The events of 1860s America, while divisive and deleterious to native-born Americans, were favorable for immigrants vying for land and employment in a depleted postbellum United States. The availability of steamships as a mode of transportation became a boon to those crossing the ocean, passengers gaining the luxury of concerning themselves primarily with seasickness and maltreatment rather than starvation and mortality. However, each nation's peoples were subjected to unique pressures which incentivized or necessitated emigration, as well.

e. Norwegians

The first of the Norse countries to experience a significant rise in emigration was Norway. In a land where only 3% of the area was tillable, a population increase boded ill for the rural community. The remainder of Norwegian society relied upon the timber and fish industries until the advent of industrialization and a shift to the railroad, mining, hydroelectric, and shipping/shipbuilding industries. Ironically, Norway's strides in public health and nutrition and a period of relative prosperity in the 1850s were the downfall of farmers' fortunes. Farmers were dependent upon annual loans under the best of circumstances. They anticipated extended growth in the years ahead and invested heavily in modernizing their operations to conform to a model of commercialized agribusiness. Thus, when the end of the Crimean War brought increased trade and competition from Russian grain in the 1860s, many farmers had made the shift from traditional small and subsistence farming to commercialized grain production but were yet unprepared to compete on an international scale. Unable to sustain themselves, deeply in debt, and unable to pay back their loans as Russian grain encroached upon the Norwegian market, some farmers switched to cattle raising. Those who did not have enough land to support cattle or were displaced entirely looked increasingly across the Atlantic for the salvation of their futures.

Approximately 80,000 Norwegians immigrated to America between 1825 and 1865, the movement primarily rural and familial in character; nearly 10 times that amount emigrated from Norway over the following half century, the trend tilting increasingly toward individual migration. Like many other individual immigrants, it was predominantly Norway's young adults who left seeking a better life in America. In fact, so severe was the effect on Norwegian society that of all nations which sent settlers to America, only Ireland lost a greater percentage of its youth in that movement. Not all were landless farmers. Fearing a decline in prospects as Norway failed to industrialize in stride with other parts of Western Europe, craftsmen and shipbuilders began to emigrate in larger numbers in the latter half of the century.[155]

Those who left Norway for America in the years directly prior to 1865 usually did so by taking ships to Canada, then crossing the border. The end of the British Navigation Acts in 1849 had proved fortuitous for Norwegian shipping lines, allowing them to carry emigrants to Quebec and lumber to Britain on the journey back. 90% of Norwegian emigrants in the years 1854-1865 accordingly boarded ships bound for Canada, not the United States. The advent of steamships and access to cheaper fares on British steamship lines in the 1860s, the passage of the Homestead Act in 1862, and the end of the American Civil War in 1865 decidedly reversed that trend. The first group of Norwegian immigrants who preceded the great exodus also aided in the migratory effort, with 40% of Norwegians' tickets bought and paid for from America in some years. The majority of Norwegian immigrants settled in the rural regions of the new American frontier according to their agricultural heritage and skill, with well over half of the Norwegian-born population living in Wisconsin, Minnesota, or North Dakota by 1910. The Homestead Act, which offered 160 acres of free land to immigrants who intended to become citizens and were willing to work and live on the land for 5 years, became a major force for enticing newly landless Scandinavian farmers. Swedes who were more likely to remain in cities included craftsmen, professionals, artisans, and seamen, the last of whom contributed significantly to building America's merchant marine.[69]

f. Swedes

The Life Stories of Undistinguished Americans As Told By Themselves was originally published in 1906. It collected interviews with a number of ordinary Americans such as former slaves, immigrants, sweatshop workers, housewives, and farmers' wives.

These articles were first published in Holt's 's reformist newspaper *The New York Independent* during the early 1900s.

Quote: In America they gave you good land for nothing, and in two years you could be a rich man; and no one had to go in the army unless he wanted to. That was what my uncle told us.

- The teller was a boy in Sweden.
- His brother Gustaf immigrated to Minnesota as he needed money - he wrote back that it was a good place to live, like Sweden in that you could grow the same things, good opportunities – he sent money back each month.
- Gustaf bought a farm and his brother went over to help and brought over family members.
- People wanted them to come back to Sweden, but they did not want to.
- Quote: Another thing that makes me like this country is that I can share in the government In Sweden my father never had a vote, and my brothers never could have voted because there is a property qualification that keeps out the poor people, and they had no chance to make money. Here any man of good character can have a vote after he has been a short time in the country, and people can elect him to any office. There are no aristocrats to push him down, and say that he is not worthy because his father was poor.
- He would go home to Sweden for Christmas, then come back to US, sometimes with family members.
- He wants to bring the whole family to the US.

Sweden's early efforts at colonization in America had been fairly short-lived, as New Sweden had existed for only 27 years from its inception in 1638 to conquest by the Dutch in 1665. Perhaps the greatest legacy left by New Sweden was the popularization of the log cabin along the American frontier, the cabin being a staple of the Scandinavian north and equally well suited to sheltering settlers against harsh American winters.

The Swedish government banned general emigration for a time. The law was finally repealed in 1840. It was therefore not until the 19th century that large numbers of Swedes finally immigrated to America. Like Norway, Sweden was heavily rural, with 90% of its population living in the countryside and 78% of its workforce in agriculture as of 1850. A growth in population from 2.3 million in 1800 to 5.5 million by 1910 lead to land distribution problems in a similar fashion to Norway, although 3 consecutive crop failures in Sweden from 1866-1868 aggravated the situation.

Accordingly, many of the same stimuli driving Norwegian emigration applied also to the Swedes, as 1.2 million left Sweden from 1851 to 1930. Likewise, many of the same factors which attracted Norwegians to the United States (the speed and fare of steamship crossings, available farmland, and job creation after the conclusion of the Civil War) were not lost on Swedes seeking opportunity.

Many Swedes took advantage of the Homestead Act and 45% settled in the North-Central states, becoming particularly concentrated in Minnesota. The period from 1862 to approximately 1890 during which Homestead land was available coincided with the peak years of Swedish migration; 40% of Swedish immigrants of the time came in the 1880s alone. Swedish immigrants also bought land from railroad companies which had been granted every other plot of land adjacent to railroad lines for the purpose of financing construction, and a few chose to purchase more expensive land in the East. Some of these represented the traditional farming aristocracy, who felt it was beneath them to earn an industrial wage and sought land in America. Those who worked as farm hands to raise enough capital to support their homesteads enjoyed wages 2 to 3 times higher than those in Sweden. Unsurprisingly, Swedish-Americans displayed a high propensity to settle in rural areas in comparison to the Irish, as 40% of Swedish Americans in 1900 worked in farming and only 32% worked in the iron, construction, or lumber industries. However, despite the availability of land in the United States, industrialization and urbanization ensured that fewer would choose the life of a farmhand or landowner as had done so in the old country.

The trend within Swedish immigration shifted towards that of individual migration by the turn of the century. Married couples and children comprised two thirds of Swedish immigrants to America in the 1840s and 1850s, but only one third by 1900. This was in part due to the presence of a high demand for maids in America, reflected in Swedish women outnumbering Swedish men in American urban centers. Another contributing factor was certainly a shift within Sweden itself away from farming and towards urbanization, as landless peasants were forced to seek employment in cities where industrial jobs were not always forthcoming. The proportion of Swedes living in the countryside and working in agribusiness had dropped to 75% and 54%, respectively, by 1900. The slow pace of industrialization in Sweden prompted a portion of the new urbanites to emigrate, fearing stagnation or crisis and electing to preempt disaster by relocating to the more modernized United States. Other young men fled the country illegally to escape compulsory enlistment in the Swedish army (an experience decried as humiliating and degrading by those who served at that time).

One last item of particular note within the Swedish movement was the presence of a religious component amongst certain Swedes. The Conventicle Act of 1726 had prohibited religious assembly other than that administered by the state church, thereby restricting the religious freedom of Baptists, Mormons, and Methodists, amongst other groups. Many adherents to these organizations subsequently chose to leave for America, where Protestantism of any form was generally well accepted and Swedish immigrants could create and maintain churches freely. As early as the 1840s, a small group of Janssonists (named after their vehemently anti-Lutheran prophet, Eric Jansson) moved to America and established a settlement at Bishop's Hill in Illinois. Jansson proved to be even more tyrannical than the establishment the Janssonists had fled. The colony ultimately failed following a cholera epidemic, the murder of Jansson, and the town's bankruptcy. Nevertheless, the colony set a course for later religious refugees to follow.[70]

g. Danes

Religious motivation for emigration was also evident in sections of the Danish population. Mormon missionaries baptized more than 20,000 Danes from the 1850s to 1900, telling converts of a gathering in the "Zion" of Utah. The majority of these Mormons chose to leave for Utah, taking advantage of an exceptionally efficient Mormon organization which aided converts in planning their pilgrimage and provided the poor with funds. Although the Book of Mormon had been translated into Danish by the time missionary efforts began and the government gave Mormons free reign to spread their beliefs, persecution and violence from the citizenry was not uncommon and lent weight to the idea of a refuge in America.

The majority of Danes, however, chose to emigrate for non-religious reasons. Besides economic motivations, the annexation of the Danish provinces of Holstein and Schleswig by Prussia and Austria in 1864 encouraged Danes to leave Europe, and the agents of shipping lines, railroad companies, land companies, and even U.S. state governments far outnumbered the handful of Mormon missionaries working to recruit immigrants. Indeed, a striking facet of the Danish populace was its secular nature; as many as one third of all Danish immigrants did not attend a church, and Danes did not put forth a widespread effort to create ethnic churches or other religious institutions in America as had the Lutheran Swedes and Norwegians. This may have also been due in part to the dispersed distribution of Danish immigrants in America and their exceedingly quick pace of assimilation into the American amalgamation of cultures. Although many Danes gravitated to the same regions as other Scandinavians, such as Iowa, Wisconsin, and Minnesota, only 57% of American-born children with at least one Danish parent were of "pure" Danish descent in 1910; the Danes intermarried with Germans and Swedes almost as often as not.

In Denmark, as in Sweden and Norway, a rise in population led to the fall of prospects for farmers and the body of immigrants exhibited a shift from family to individual migration. However, from its position on the Continent, Denmark was swept into the age of industry earlier than its northern counterparts of the Scandinavian world. From 1868 to 1900, only 43.2% of Danish immigrants were farmhands, and the majority of the others unskilled laborers and craftsmen from the cities of Denmark. During that time, unmarried Danish immigrants outnumbered the married by almost three to one. Even landless peasants often immigrated to the United States only after trying their luck at finding employment in cities, the rate of emigration directly from cities being double that of the country. All told, approximately 400,000 Danes emigrated from 1851-1930, less than the Swedish and Norwegian emigrations, but similar in volume to the Finns.[71]

h. Finns

In light of the commonalities exhibited within mass Scandinavian emigration, perhaps it was immigrants from Finland who were most distinctive. A dearth of land and a population increase (the sharpest in any of the Norse countries), exacerbated by slash and burn techniques in Finland, resulted in a rise of rural family emigration. However, Finns did not move to cities before leaving the country, as in Denmark, nor did the women of Finland seek domestic work in America. Only one tenth of Finnish immigrants were from cities, and two thirds were men.

Mass emigration from Finland began in the 1890s, significantly later than the exodus from Norway, Sweden, and Denmark. Finnish men found Homestead Act land difficult to come by. Although many settled in the rural areas of Minnesota, Wisconsin, and Michigan, Finns commonly became wage earners in copper mines, in forests as lumbermen, or as farm hands. Subsequently, the Finns were also set apart by engaging with socialist and labor movements. Because the Finns were considerably more active in labor radicalism and their homeland lay farther East than those of the other Scandinavians, Finns eventually developed a reputation as dissidents and became considered part of a wave of morally and intellectually inferior "new immigrants" from Eastern Europe.[72]

5. THE IMMIGRANT NATION (CA. 1881-1913)

Although the Chinese Exclusion Act of 1882 had curbed Chinese immigration, toward the end of the 19th century and in the beginning of the 20th there were increasing numbers of immigrants from other parts of Asia and Eastern and Southern Europe. The end of the age of sail and the advent of steamships had made crossing oceans easier than ever before, and work offered by the Industrial Revolution's new jobs provided added incentive for the poorest immigrants. These newcomers frequently did not agree with Western European sensibilities and were treated accordingly. The urban manufacturing sectors where many of them settled and worked were dirty, crowded, and unsafe, leading more affluent Americans to view immigrants as the very embodiment of urban vice and depravity.

a. Italians

Quote (in 1902): Now and then I had heard things about America that it was a far off country where everybody was rich and that Italians went there and made plenty of money, so that they could return to Italy and live in pleasure ever after. One day I met a young man who pulled out a handful of gold and told me he had made that in America in a few days.

- Went to US with 'brother' – kind of scammed though by 'rich man' from America
- Did not have enough money upon landing so were going to be sent back – a man he didn't know swore he was Rocco and Francisco ('brother')'s uncle and would take care of them, so were let in
- Lived with 'uncle' picking rags
- This 'uncle' Bartolo ran boarding house and had boarders work digging sewers – Bartolo would be paid, and give them only a quarter of their rightful wages and would charge them rent ('padrone') – told them if they did not work for Bartolo would be put in prison
- After a year heard that Bartolo was playing them so left and got new work – Bartolo went after them but their new boss told Bartolo to get lost
- New boss Irish
- Taught each other English, reading, writing, etc.
- Learned bootblacking and started own bootblack business w/ Francisco
- Culture clash regarding churches – many Italian immigrants viewed paying money to church as like buying religion; sense of two tiers, immigrants who can read and write like author who understand why you pay for US churches, and those that can't and don't (just off the boat sort of mentality)
- Quote: We had said that when we saved $1,000 each we would go back to Italy and buy a farm, but now that the time is coming we are so busy and making so much money that we think we will stay.
- Voting quote: They wanted us to vote last fall, but we did not. A man came and said that he would get us made Americans for fifty cents and then we could get two dollars for our votes....went to a Republican meeting and the man said that the Republicans want a Republic and the Democrats are

against it. He said that Democrats are for a king whose name is Bryan and who is an Irishman. There are some good Irishmen, but many of them insult Italians. They call us Dagoes. So I will be a Republican.[73]

In the period prior to the onset of World War I and immediately thereafter, no immigrant group was more maligned through its association with criminal activity than the Italians. Prior to the late 1800s, Italians preferred to head to the South American countries of Brazil, Argentina and Paraguay. However, an onset of yellow fever in Brazil and bad economic conditions in Argentina and Paraguay eventually led more Italians to head to North America.

Italians hailing from Northern Italy were fairly distinct from those originating from regions further south. Northern Italians typically arrived prior to 1880 and were composed largely of merchants and businessmen. Southern Italians, on the other hand, were primarily poor farmers from rural areas who had lost land to a combination of high taxes and rents, depreciating home goods values, and agricultural competition from globalization and increased importation. After the unification of Italy in 1880, the Italian government was dominated by Northern Italians who had little interest in developing the agrarian southern portion of the country. The unification also brought tariffs and increased corruption to Southern Italy, and tax revenue collected from southerners was typically not reinvested into the land. However, a host of other problems presented themselves to the Southern Italian farmer. Italian agriculture suffered from rain arriving in abnormal seasons, destroying crops and vineyards. Furthermore, famine, drought, earthquakes, heat waves, floods, and volcanic eruptions continually threatened to ruin farmers' livelihoods, and landless or destitute Italians often had no choice but to become wage earners. Because Italian workers could earn 3 times as much in the United States as they could in Italy, many Italians sold what few possessions remained to them for steamship tickets, hoping to recoup their losses after sojourning overseas. Subsequently, by 1900, 484,207 Italians were counted living in America.[74] Letters from America bore news of jobs and steady wages to Southern Italian villages, and chain migration brought another 3 million Italians to the United States between 1900 and 1914.[75]

The body of post-1880 Italian immigrants mostly lacked trade or professional skills, almost half ultimately performing manual labor in American cities. While some fortunate farmers found work in barbershops or bars, even Italians with extensive education were relegated to performing menial tasks due to their lack of proficiency in English. Children, too, often worked (not uncommonly, at the time) in factories and mines or were virtually enslaved under the *padrone* system of gang labor alongside adults. Italian-born employment agents used a form of loan sharking and indentured servitude which was so exploitative that it was outlawed by Congress in the Foran Act of 1885, although the practice continued underground.

Put mildly, therefore, urban life and toil was a large change from the life of a farmer, but despite the expressed longing of many for the fields of their hometowns, manufacturing and construction work was seen as a more expedient means than farming of earning money. Many Italians planned on eventually returning to their native country after earning enough to make a new beginning there, and had one of the highest return rates of any immigrant nationality.[76]

Indeed, almost half of the 4.5 million Italians who came to the United States between 1876 and 1924 returned to Italy. Because of this, many Italian immigrant families lived extremely frugally, saving all they could for use in Italy. More often, families remained in Italy while young men known as "birds of passage" worked in the U.S. They typically lived in conditions that were crowded and unsanitary, and many women worked in their windowless and cramped tenements to accompany their children and maintain close family ties. Diseases such as cholera, typhus, and tuberculosis spread quickly. However, Italians tended to be drawn to areas with high numbers of other Italian immigrants and formed the Italian communities within cities known as Little Italy today. Within these communities, non-English speaking Italians could find a microcosm of their home culture, and many new immigrants could find others from their towns and villages already living there. Hundreds of closely-knit mutual aid societies formed within the larger Italian community, and larger organizations rallied to expose and eliminate the exploitation and maltreatment of Italian immigrants by their landlords. Italian immigrants therefore typically enjoyed stronger social networks and community ties immediately upon arrival to the United States than other immigrant groups at the time.

Even living in their densely concentrated communities, however, Italians could not escape conflict with anti-immigrant and anti-Catholic groups. Although Italian Americans only constituted about 1.5% of the U.S. population at its peak, over 3 million Italians immigrated to the United States between 1890 and the start of World War I. The influx of unskilled workers and their heavy concentration in certain areas raised concerns in the minds of some U.S. citizens that the uneducated Italian population would eventually overtake and corrupt American society.

Italians also encountered difficulties with their fellow Catholics, the Irish. In religion, the two ethnicities disagreed significantly about the role of the parish. The Italians, for example, objected to the amount of fundraising activity inherent within the Irish-dominated American Catholic Church. Furthermore, as the Irish had long occupied the positions that Italian immigrants began competing for, a considerable rivalry developed which has since been immortalized into American lore as the Irish cop vs. Italian mobster. After World War I, infamous leaders within organized crime syndicates such as Al Capone contributed to the negative perception of Italian Americans, but in fact, prejudice existed much earlier. The Mafiosi immigrated in the 1880s and ran protection rackets and smuggling and prostitution rings.

Of course, most Italian immigrants were not involved with organized crime, and most, at one time or another, were discriminated against or otherwise wronged by a prejudicial public. In one egregious incident, the killing of a police superintendent in New Orleans in 1891 resulted in the arrest of hundreds of Italians, 19 of whom were put on trial. When the court found the defendants not guilty for lack of evidence, an angry mob broke into the jail holding them and attacked 11 of the Italians in the largest mass lynching in American history. In another incident in Buffalo, New York, the killing of one Italian by another led to the detention of 325 Italians for fear that concealed weapons were omnipresent amongst the Italian population. On the 325 arrested, only 2 weapons were found.[77]

b. Greeks

As another Southern European nation, Greece was stigmatized for its Mediterranean culture and suffered from late industrialization and development. A greater challenge to the well-being of Greeks presented itself in Turkey, where a 1908 decree had declared that Turkish Greeks were obligated to serve in the Turkish army. Not wishing to comply, many Greeks in Anatolia left and established permanent residence in the United States.

However, with the exception of Greeks in Turkey, Greek men, like Italian men, left for America with the expectation that they would someday return to their home towns and live a life of relative prosperity and comfort. A collapse in the European raisin market in the 1890s undermined Greece's chief export and prompted over 15,000 to leave the country. Correspondence bearing news of high wages along with prepaid tickets to America brought successive waves of Greek immigrants to the U.S. From 1900 to 1930, 402,804 immigrants came to America from Greece alone. A number of Greeks from Turkey, the Balkans, Egypt, and Cyprus immigrated to America during the time, as well.

Some left for the procurement of funds to pay for daughters and sisters' dowries, a task which traditionally connoted honor to Greek men but was becoming increasingly difficult to achieve in the face of declining agricultural prices. Ironically, these best of intentions became the ruin of Greek women's prospects for marriage. Because Greek women stayed in Greece to await the return of their men, the ratio of women to men in the home country became inordinately high as the years passed. From 1900-1910, less than 5% of Greek immigrants to the United States were women, a figure which only rose to 20% in the following decade. In roughly the same period, nearly a quarter of all Greek males aged 15-45 went to America. Consequently, Greek women left behind found suitors few and far between while dowries became ever higher. A generation of Greek women was thus forced to accept matches with far older or otherwise undesirable men.

For their part, Greek men who declined to return to Europe faced an uphill battle as they fought to find their niche in American culture. Wherever they traveled and worked, Greeks were greeted with a degree of hostility by other immigrant populations. Those in the Western United States who worked on railroads or in mines were harassed by both the Mormons and the Ku Klux Klan to the extent that some Greeks suspected the groups were one and the same. In textile shops and shoe factories of the Northeast, Greeks clashed with the Irish and French Canadian competition; Greeks who worked in New York or Chicago performing menial labor or as entrepreneurs confronted their share of antagonism, as well.[78]

c. Hungarians

1.7 million people from Hungary immigrated between 1880 and 1914, peaking in 1907, when 185,000 (or 1% of Hungary's population) came to America. Most were young men from peasant families who wished to earn enough money in America to return to Hungary and purchase land of their own. Indeed, two thirds of Hungarian immigrants were males, most were under the age of 30, and nearly half of the men returned to Hungary to marry and/or bring portions of their families back with them to America. Large families were often separated for years, as siblings did not immigrate together.

Only 54.5% of immigrants listed as Hungarian were ethnic Hungarian and spoke Magyar, the remainder being a mix of Rumanians, Slovaks, Germans, Rusyns, Croats, and Serbians. In the early stages of immigration from Hungary, ethnic minorities outnumbered Magyars as the Hungarian economy declined in the 1880s, and only a quarter of "Hungarian" immigrants spoke Magyar as late as 1899. It was not until the late 1890s that the more affluent Magyars decided to leave as the economic situation worsened, and by 1903, Magyars comprised the majority of immigrants from Hungary.[79]

Magyar immigrants represented the most educated portions of the Hungarian population, as 88% of the 450,000 that arrived between 1890 and 1914 were literate, while only 58% of the total population of Hungary could read and write. Still, the immigrants found that they lacked modern industrial skills, and were forced to accept dangerous low-wage jobs in coal mining and heavy industry in the Northeast and Midwest United States (particularly concentrated in Cleveland).[80]

d. Ukrainians

The numbers of Ukrainians who have immigrated to the United States is uncertain. Due to a number of factors confounding the identity of many of those whom we would now identify as Ukrainian, the official U.S. figures for that population are accepted to be low. Initially identifying themselves as Rusyn, Rusniak, (Anglicized as Ruthenian) or at times Greek Catholic, these immigrants primarily hailed from regions dominated by the Austro-Hungarian Empire, although much of modern Ukraine was under Russian control. A number of immigrants from the Austrian-owned regions of Galicia and Bukovina, the primarily Hungarian-influenced Carpatho-Ukraine region, Poland, and Russia were of Ruthenian ethnicity. An estimated 34,000 Ruthenians immigrated to the United States from 1877 to 1887, and another 75,000 between 1888 and 1898. Official U.S. records indicate that 254,376 Ruthenian immigrants arrived from 1899 to 1914, most of whom settled in Pennsylvania, New York, and New Jersey.

A clearer picture can be seen of the Ruthenian migrants' motivations for leaving Europe. Due to a general lack of industrialization, the 1890 Austrian census found that 77% of Galicians worked in agriculture, where wages were exceptionally low and fathers would divide land amongst their sons. An 80% population increase in the region between 1880 and 1900 decreased the amount of land available to each peasant, and high taxes compounded the problems extant in rural areas. Since industrial jobs were not readily available and relatively affluent Poles tended to occupy higher-wage jobs in cities, Ruthenian peasants chose to escape to the United States. The anticipation of a better life across the Atlantic was so gripping that Austro-Hungarian authorities sometimes withheld letters originating from the United States for fear that entire villages would emigrate.

The body of Ruthenian immigrants was indicative of the peasantry's destitution in central Europe. Of the 14,473 Ruthenians recorded by the U.S. Bureau of Immigration in 1905, only seven possessed what could loosely be called higher education; of these, there were 4 priests, a musician, a teacher, and a lawyer. 209 of the immigrants were skilled laborers such as blacksmiths and bakers, and a staggering 12,854 were unskilled laborers. The remainder had no listed occupation or were under the age of 14. The flight of unskilled laborers from Austria-Hungary and nearby regions explains the poor literacy rates observed in Ruthenian migrants. In the 1890s, 65% of males and 72% of females over the age of 6 in Galicia were illiterate, and 49% of Ruthenian immigrants to the U.S. in 1910 could not read or write. Consequently, most Ruthenians immigrants started their American journeys working either in coal mines as helpers earning roughly one third of what an experienced miner might earn, or in cities as workers in factories, mills, and refineries.[81]

e. Poles

Tanya Shimiewsky, Poland, 1950[82]

- Was in Nazi occupied Poland.
- Husband taken to concentration camp.
- Then she, mother, young daughter taken – mother and daughter killed.
- After war walked back to Poland, but none of her family was left.
- Committee of Jews helping the people coming back gave money, she lived in a kibbutz.
- Cared for orphans.
- The kibbutz illegally sent people to Israel (Poland didn't want to let them out).
- Wanted to go to Israel too.
- Found out her husband was working in Germany, so she pretended she was a displaced person going back to Italy lived with husband, got food from Americans and money from Hebrew Immigrant Aid Society (HIAS.)
- Made money in a kosher food store.
- All set to go to Israel, but because of the devaluation of the mark, lost all their savings.
- Had relatives in US that wrote and said they should go there, so they did in 1950.

Wojtek Pobog, Poland, 1949[83]

Polish, not Jewish, but in concentration camp for being Polish

- After the war, heard no good going back to Poland
- Canada – lumber work – but wouldn't take families
- Belgium – coal mines – horrible conditions, people ran, they would be arrested for breaking contract
- Put a picture in a Polish newspaper looking for a US sponsor, and the embassy said a man in Minnesota was sponsoring them
- Arrived June 19, 1949 – got ten dollars each and a ticket to Minnesota
- Turned out St Cloud, Minnesota was nowhere
- This old guy only had work for the parents to clean sties and dig on a farm, paid 50 cents a day
- He and brother got work nearby, then a doctor they'd worked with in a camp in Germany got them jobs in a hospital in NY, and parents got jobs in nursing home
- Went into army during Korean War
- Afterwards when working he had difficulty with Italian unions, and situations where the foreman was English/Irish/Scots, Italians were lead

men, and Polish people only swept the floor – so went to college at night, got a chemistry degree

Poles were frequently listed under different classification systems which ensured the mystification of their growing population within the United States. In the years 1885 to 1898, 1899 to 1919, and 1920 to 1932, immigrants were listed by country of birth, by the country to which they belonged, and by both country of birth and by race/people, respectively. Similar to the Ruthenians, such systems of categorization presented problems for the Polish, who until 1920 could be listed amongst Austrian, Prussian, or Russian immigrants. The remnants of the last Polish state had been eliminated in 1795 and such a state did not reappear until 1919 with the end of the First World War. It is thus reasonable to scrutinize the official INS figures which report only 96,700 Polish immigrants between 1819 and 1900, but 1,324,460 from 1899 to 1932.

Some believe it is likely that over 400,000 Poles came from Germany alone after 1850, the vast majority before the turn of the century. In these estimates, the German Poles were followed by approximately 800,000 from Austrian Galicia who arrived in America between 1890 and 1914 and were succeeded in turn by another 800,000 Poles from Russia, most of whom immigrated after 1900. However, due consideration must be given to the finding of the 1910 census that over 900,000 of foreign-borns in the United States spoke Polish as their native tongue. Because Poles both lacked an established nation-state and the region from which they hailed contained various minorities within itself, primacy of the Polish language may be the best characteristic by which that population which identified itself as Polish can be distinguished. Religion, too, would prove a useful tool for identifying ethnic Poles, for the Catholic majority lived alongside the highest concentration of Jews in the world. Discrepancies thus may be explained to a large degree by misclassification (whether by place of origin, or ethnicity) and emigration.[84]

Reports of emigration during the early 1900s and into the Great Depression vary significantly, as well. INS reports document 295,426 emigrants from 1908 to 1932, while historians' estimates place the number at approximately 600,000. Regardless of the precise amount, records are indicative of a high volume of Polish immigrants who traveled back and forth between Poland and America.

Beyond statistical incongruities, a characteristic of the first mass of Polish immigrants shared with that of the Ruthenians was their general impoverishment and a high occurrence of illiteracy. Three quarters of Polish immigrants recorded in 1909 were farm hands or servants, and only 3% of the Polish immigrants in that year entered American borders with $50 or more. The literacy rate in Russian-occupied Poland was only 41% in 1897. Many Poles settled in cities and industrial centers such as Chicago, New York, Pittsburgh, and Buffalo, taking up low-wage jobs and engaging in competition with other Eastern and Southern European immigrants under the skillful manipulation of their employers. Unlike the Ruthenians, however, later Polish immigrants were more likely to read and write than their forbears, in large part due to educational reforms in the interbellum period. In 1909, the literacy rate had risen to 66%, and by 1929 was an astonishing 96%. In later years, the vocational skill of the Polish immigrant had improved somewhat, but migration took place under more desperate economic and political conditions.

Official figures in this regard reflect the rising incidence of Jewish immigrants within the flow from Eastern Europe. Prior to their displacement and mass migration, 3.4 million of the 35.5 million Polish residents in 1939 were Jewish. Notably, only 10% considered themselves members of the Polish nation and spoke Polish for day-to-day purposes, but those who immigrated to America were classified as such (through country of birth) per INS procedures. 3.2 million of the 12 million displaced people later rescued from Nazi concentration camps after World War II were Polish, and most of these were also Jewish. However, both voluntary and compulsory emigration of Jews in Eastern Europe had started much earlier.[85]

f. Jews of Eastern Europe and Russia

Elise Radell, 1939[86]

- As a child when Brown Shirts came, became aware Jewish, a kid threw a rock at her, her parents pulled her out of school had her tutored.
- Kristallnacht – stuff ruined, all Jewish men arrested – father was out of town, came back, found out all men arrested so went and turned self in.
- Father eventually came back, much changed.
- Couldn't get visa to US unless had relatives there.
- Had aunt in US so got visas and came over August 1939.
- Grandparents didn't want to come – were killed.
- Had appendicitis in US –treatment free because couldn't pay – culture shock in hospital as couldn't speak English.
- At first school v difficult, when learned English skipped ahead.
- Father stockboy in fabric store – in Germany had owned textile firm – mother was seamstress.
- Went to college – would've gone to grad school but father sick, no money.

Ruchel Dwajra Zylska/Rachel Deborah Shilsky[87]

- Arrived in the U.S. on August 23, 1923, on a steamer called the *Austergeist.*
- Kept on her person for over twenty years the paper attesting to her arrival in the U.S., so nobody ("government, my father, anybody") would throw her out.
- Her mother "used to talk about the Czar or the Kaiser and how the Russian soldiers would come into the village and line up the Jews and shoot them in cold blood."
- Her mother said, "I had to run for my life . . . I held you and your brother in my arms as I ran."
- Her mother was "terrified of Europe and happy to be in America."

Never particularly well-treated, the Jews of Eastern Europe faced growing hostility as their population expanded throughout the 19th century from 1.5 million to almost 7 million. Although not significantly wealthier than their neighbors, Jews were perceived as enjoying a higher standard of living and became subjects of resentment, the prejudicial fervor encouraged by government and church leaders alike. The ascendance of Alexander III of Russia in 1881 had heralded an effective reign of terror in Russia and Poland. Under Alexander's rule, Jews suffered the revocation of occupational, educational, and residential rights, deadly assaults, and commonly, outright expulsion. The May Laws of 1882 forbade Jews from settling in villages, displacing half a million. Those in several cities suffered a similar fate, 20,000 Jews being exiled in chains from Moscow alone. Many fled to other cities such as Vienna, Warsaw, Bialystok, and Lodz.

Beyond oppression, it was in the interest of the Eastern European Jews, like so many others, to simply seek better economic opportunities in America. Jews within the Russian Empire were prohibited from owning land or pursuing certain vocations, forcing many to become merchants and artisans who catered to rural towns' needs. However, the glimmerings of industrialization in the late 19th century displaced many of these workers, and a continuing population boom in which the Jewish population more than quadrupled over the course of the century led to the growth of a Jewish proletariat receptive to socialist ideology. This radical turn amongst Jewish youth in turn fueled the Russian government's efforts to cast Jews in an unfavorable light as dissidents and subversive elements to the Christian majority. A multitude of pogroms ultimately resulting in the killing, lynching, robbing, rape, or mutilation of thousands of victims continued throughout most of Alexander III's reign and into that of Nicholas II.

Accordingly, between 1880 and 1920, over two million Jews from Poland, Russia, Austria-Hungary, Romania, Galicia, Silesia, Bohemia, and Slovakia immigrated to the United States. These sojourners, approximately 80% of whom were from Russia and Russian-occupied Poland, found passage to the United States difficult due to legal complications and the possibility of a lengthy journey to reach German ports. Although the proximity of Black Sea ports might have attracted other Eastern European immigrants, Jews, especially those of an age to serve in the military, were unable to gain Russian passports and wished to avoid the ill-reputed Romanian border sentinels on the path to Odessa. 90% of all Romanian emigrants from 1881 to 1920 were Jewish, along with 60% of those from Galicia and 50% of the Russians. Aware of the patronage Jewish travelers could bring to the German shipping industry, German officials also encouraged the use of their shipping lines by developing a certain laxity for border enforcement. In this, Jewish organizations within Germany played a large role by lobbying European governments and arranging for special rates with railroad and steamship companies in a collective effort to both alleviate the plight of their religious brethren and to prevent Western Europe from being burdened itself with so many refugees.

It was at this time that the head of the Hamburg-American shipping line, a German Jew, outfitted empty cargo holds with bunks and thus invented the concept of carrying passengers in "steerage." Conditions in steerage were sometimes not much improved over those on transatlantic voyages during the age of sail decades earlier, although the shorter transit time of as little as 6 days prevented mortality rates from climbing. Still, crowded and unsanitary surroundings for malnourished passengers led to the spread of disease, and many immigrants were quarantined at Ellis Island for days or weeks. As many as one out of every 40 immigrants were promptly deported due to health or poverty-related concerns.

Those who passed inspections at Ellis Island inflated a Jewish population which had previously been only 250,000, approximately 80% of whom had been of German origin or descent. The United States, home to only 3% of the world's 7.7 million Jews in 1880, contained 23% of its 15.6 million Jews in 1920. Additionally, these immigrants were marked by the lowest rate of remigration of any group of that time, at an estimated 5%; besides the Jews, only the Irish had a 90% or greater likelihood of staying in America. This can be explained by the fact that the Jewish and Irish had the highest proportion of females within their numbers of immigrant groups of the period, at 45% and 55%, respectively. Nearly a quarter of the Jewish immigrants were children, indicating that like the Irish, male Jews tended to make the journey accompanied by their entire families. Over 70% of these stayed in New York City after passing through the halls at Ellis Island, the city growing to contain almost half of all American Jews by 1920. The remainder dispersed amongst other large cities in the Northeast and Midwest such as Boston, Baltimore, Cleveland, Chicago, Newark, and Philadelphia.[88]

Relations between poor Jews and their more affluent counterparts were at once symbiotic and strained. Although well-established Jews provided some financial assistance and employment for nigh-penniless newcomers, accommodations and living standards could still be pitiably low, comparable to those simultaneously endured by the Italians. A 1908 survey found that in the apartment buildings of New York's Lower East Side which housed over 500,000 Jews, half of apartment rooms were shared by 3 or 4 people, and a quarter were inhabited by five or more. Most Jews who lived in such quarters paid unduly high rents to a Jewish landlord, and the great majority of the 300,000 or more who worked in New York City's garment industry worked in factories owned by fellow Eastern European Jews. Furthermore, Americanized Jews often disagreed violently with the Eastern Europeans on political and religious issues, the newcomers often socialist or Zionist, the old guard decidedly not.

Despite these inconsistencies, both groups of Jews found unity in the movement to combat the anti-Semitism which threatened to rise with the tide of Jewish immigration. Their concerted efforts to help less fortunate Jews abroad is also reflected in the amount of aid sent to Jews in blood-soaked Europe after World War I, over $60 million.[89]

Initially, German-descended Jews feared that the influx of Jewish immigrants would contribute greatly to a growing anti-Semitic element within America. Yet, many of the grievances held against Jews were caused, albeit innocently, by the old blood. Belief in an international Jewish conspiracy was nurtured by the decline of American farmers' prospects and a financial panic in 1893-1894. Several of the Jewish immigrants of the mid-19th century had come to occupy prominent positions in the financial sector, and controversy arose concerning the maintenance of the gold standard and the deflationary pressures associated with it. Jews and financial manipulation came to be inextricably linked in the mind of the undiscerning American. Faced with these pressures, and despite their differences, old and new Jewish immigrants were able to reconcile their beliefs and eventually achieve a greater degree of solidarity. Many of the heavily acculturated Jews, in danger of being completely assimilated by a sometimes hostile majority, instead experienced a partial revitalization of their traditional observances with the arrival of the Eastern Europeans.[90]

g. Japanese and Filipinos

Taro Murata, Japan, 1907[91]

- when he came over to America, Japan was poor, he had no money, and he had heard that the U.S. was a good place to make money.

- first job was working on Rail Road in Washington state, 9 hours a day – there were around 2,000 Japanese boys working there, he would interpret between them and the foreman.
- many immigrants worked on the Rail Road, and sometimes different groups fought.
- individuals stuck with their own groups as they understood people from their own countries better.
- after three years he went back to Japan and had an arranged marriage.
- worked for Oriental Trading Company (import-export) in Seattle as stock boy then office worker – after 3 or 4 years started dry cleaning business – his children went to university.
- arranged deal with Teamsters Union so Japanese businesspeople could drive own trucks instead of hiring Teamsters, so the government got to know his name.
- daughter worked as a nurse at a hospital, son got aeronautical engineering degree but couldn't get a job because he was Japanese and employers feared subversion (right before WW-II) – Japanese consul invited son and other boys to go back to Japan and get a job, government paid fare – son went back, worked at airplane factory, father didn't hear from him at all throughout the war.
- as leader of the Japanese community, was picked up by the government on Dec 7, interned.
- wife couldn't sell the business, finally had to give it up back to the real estate owners due to owing back rent.
- tried to bring his son back to live in the US after the war, but couldn't because the boy had fought for Japan.

Willie Barientos – Filipino Farmworker[92]

- born in April 1908 in Philippines, in 1924 he went to Hawaii to work on pineapple plantations.
- in 1924, when he came to Hawaii, there were 1600 Filipino workers striking on 23 of 45 plantations – lasted 8 months – Honolulu national guard came in – 16 strikers, 4 policemen killed.
- in 1928, anti-Filipino riots in Yakima, Washington – spread in 1929, 1930 throughout California.
- in Hawaii, Barientos had a salary of a dollar a day.
- cutting sugarcane was very hard work so he told the plantation bosses that he would not do it, so they gave him a hoe and told him to cut grass.
- he complained, got a better job recording how many boxcars of sugarcane they filled.
- stayed in Hawaii until 1929, and came to the U.S. on Dec 20, 1929, got a job in Stockton, California picking asparagus – was too hard, he went to San Francisco.
- wanted to be educated so did housework in exchange for education, then became a janitor and learned English at night.
- earned 30 dollars/month as a janitor.
- in 1946 went to Delano and learned how to harvest grapes.
- he started a union in 1965.

- joined with Mexican and other farmworkers so the strike could be successful.
- never married because in 1924 when he came to the U.S. Filipinos could not marry white people, and there were no Filipina women – also, Filipinos couldn't buy land unless they fought in the war.
- is proud of what he has accomplished, but has never married, and bitterly remembers the way Filipinos were treated, he is proud that he did something about it in the strike.

Japan and the "Gentleman's Agreement"

For hundreds of years the nation of Japan had banned emigration and, indeed, almost all contact with the Western world in order to maintain Japanese isolation. However, in 1854 the American Commodore Matthew Perry officially 'opened' Japan to the West by sailing his steamships into Japanese harbors and signing a treaty that would allow the United States trading rights with Japan. Not long after this the Japanese decided to forgo their previous attempts at isolation and threw themselves into the project of modernizing in an effort to catch up with the Western world. For this reason the emperor of Japan had, in the late 1800s, lifted the ban on emigration from Japan. This lift, combined with overpopulation on a small island nation, led many Japanese to leave their country in search of somewhere with more space and better wages. Many Japanese immigrants intended to return to Japan after they had saved up money.

In 1904 American legislators had extended the Chinese Exclusion act indefinitely, creating a demand for cheap agricultural labor that had previously been provided by Chinese immigrants. This demand proved tempting, and Japanese immigrants, pre-selected by the Japanese government to be hard-working, frugal, and literate, came to work in the West Coast. Most Japanese immigrants came to the United States in order to work in the agricultural fields. The wages were lower than those given to white workers, and if Japanese laborers started demanding higher wages, their employers would refuse and bring in new immigrants from different countries who would work for less. Some Japanese immigrants progressed from being mere laborers to owning their own land or starting businesses, such as department stores, thus removing the problem of low wages. In 1913 the Alien Land Law barred "aliens ineligible for citizenship", or Japanese immigrants, from purchasing land, and retroactively revoked ownership of all land that Japanese aliens had already bought. However, Japanese immigrants got around this law by registering the land in the name of their children, who were American citizens. By 1920, people of Japanese descent owned 450,000 acres of land in California and controlled 10% of the annual crop revenue.

Japanese immigration had begun in Hawaii even before the Chinese Exclusion Act. The primary industry of Hawaii, which was not annexed until 1898, was the production of sugar cane. The growing of sugar cane was labor intensive, and the European sugar plantation owners had started importing Chinese labor to offset the native Hawaiian work force in the hopes that competition would be profitable. The plantation owners were also afraid that the hard work and living conditions would cause their laborers to strike, and hoped to offset that possibility by diluting the labor pool with culturally distinct workers and fostering animosity between them. When Chinese laborers became too much of a majority, the plantation owners brought in some Portuguese laborers and a wave of Japanese workers. Some of the Japanese laborers found the working conditions so atrocious that they broke their three or five year contracts and fled, while others attempted to strike in 1900, 1906, and 1909. However, a strike that only included part of the work force could not be successful, and plantation owners would often bring in other ethnic groups to replace the strikers, more specifically immigrants from Korea. The Korean government banned immigration to Hawaii in 1905, but the plantation owners simply switched to the Philippines for their source of cheap labor.

Although there was never a very large amount of Japanese immigration compared to that of other nationalities, the heavy concentration of Japanese immigrants in certain areas of the West Coast led people living in those areas to have a mistaken understanding of their numbers. Many American citizens were upset by what they perceived as an invasion, and an anti-Japanese sentiment, much like the anti-Chinese sentiment that had preceded the Chinese Exclusion Act, spread throughout the West Coast. This attitude was felt most significantly in California, where the labor unions believed that Japanese "coolie labor" was a threat to American workers. This fear led to the creation of the San Francisco Asiatic Exclusion League in 1905. In an extension of the anti-Japanese feeling, in 1906 the San Francisco school board decreed that Japanese students were to attend a segregated Chinese school. This news was reported in the newspapers of Tokyo, causing angry diplomats from Japan to demand explanations from President Roosevelt.

While China might not have been in a strong enough position to stop the Chinese Exclusion Act, Japan was a more powerful nation at the time. Japan's goal to catch up with the Western world had been achieved with shocking efficiency, and Japan made its debut on the international arena with a victory over Russia in the Russo-Japanese War from 1904-1905. This victory over a modern nation secured Japan's place as a major world power, and one which President Roosevelt did not want to offend lightly. Due to Roosevelt and the federal government's intervention, the San Francisco segregation of Japanese students was never carried out. However, the feeling that had propagated the initial decree still remained, and the Japanese immigration situation still needed to be dealt with.

Because of Japan's place in the international community, obvious exclusion legislation was not a desirable solution to the conflict surrounding Japanese immigrants. Instead, a compromise was reached. Under the "Gentleman's Agreement" of 1907-1908, the United States promised not to make any legislation specifically restricting Japanese immigrants, while Japan promised to stop allowing Japanese laborers to immigrate to the continental United States. In this way the flow of Japanese immigrants was stemmed while Japan was able to avoid embarrassing anti-Japanese legislature.

However, there were loopholes; the agreement did not extend to the immigration of wives of laborers, and a number of women, called 'picture brides', immigrated to the United States to join men that they had only met once, or had never met but married by proxy back in Japan. Because of these 'picture brides' and the children they had, who were United States citizens, the number of individuals of Japanese ancestry in the West Coast did not decline as much as some would have liked. For this reason many viewed the "Gentleman's Agreement" as an ineffective policy to restrict immigration.

While immigrants flooded into America from Eastern Europe, Japan was just emerging from long isolation on the other side of the world The end of the Tokugawa Shogunate in 1867 brought the end of a general ban on Japanese emigration in 1885, and for the next 9 years, the Japanese government allowed contract laborers to travel to Hawaii under a strictly regulated program of emigration. The Chinese Exclusion Act and its indefinite extension in 1904 had caused a shortage of cheap agricultural laborers, and the Japanese were quick to fill the gap. By 1890, there were 12,000 Japanese in Hawaii, and by 1898 (when Hawaii was annexed to the United States), the number had grown to 60,000.

Working conditions in Hawaii were often harsh, and the high supply of immigrant labor meant that workers could not even begin to negotiate for better pay without being promptly replaced. Indeed, some Japanese moved to sugar cane plantations in Hawaii which had previously been operated by Chinese and Portuguese workers. The plantation owners, who had imported Chinese labor earlier simply to increase competition with native labor, fostered animosity amongst their workforces and made sure to diversify the ethnic groups they hired in order to prevent collective protests. Japanese strikes often failed due to the lack of cooperation and organization amongst the different ethnic workers and the ability of employers to bring in additional laborers from Korea and the Philippines. A 1904 Japanese-led strike at a sugar plantation in O'ahu, for example, was effectively broken by the hire of 250 Koreans.

Korea banned emigration to Hawaii in 1905, but Filipino workers continued to seek work in Hawaii. During the years between 1909 and 1934, the Hawaiian Sugar Planter's Association brought 120,000 Filipinos to Hawaii. After the Commissioner General of Immigration exempted Filipino immigrants from the head tax on persons entering the United States, many Filipinos moved to Alaska and the contiguous United States, as well.[93]

Eventually, the new Asian workers began to travel beyond Hawaii to the contiguous United States. Some Japanese immigrants went to California, where they created businesses. Although the Alien Land Law of 1913 prevented immigrants ineligible for citizenship (such as Japanese) from purchasing land and took land from those who had already bought it, the Japanese often registered land under the names of their children, who had been born in the United States and were American citizens. By 1920, Japanese descendants owned approximately 450,000 acres in California and controlled 10% of its agricultural revenue. Such numbers were not lost on the other American citizens of the West Coast, who watched the growth of the Japanese population with alarm.

As Japanese immigrants graduated from being laborers to landowners, the anti-Japanese furor grew exponentially. Forming in 1908, the Oriental Exclusion League (OEL) claimed a membership of 110,000 and was the most dominant anti-Asian group in California prior to 1924.

The Philippines

Once Japanese laborers in Hawaii became too organized the plantation owners decided to bring in Filipino laborers to avoid costly labor strikes. During the beginning of the century the Filipino population was concentrated almost entirely in the Hawaiian islands. In 1910, out of 2,767 Filipinos in the United States, only 406 of them lived outside of Hawaii. However, because the Philippines had become a United States territory in the Spanish American War of 1898, Filipino workers were in a position of being able to enter the continental United States relatively easily as well. In 1903 a group of Filipino carpenters attempted to enter the United States in order to build an exhibit for the St. Louis Exposition. However, every person entering the United States at that time was required to pay a head tax, and the carpenters could not afford it. Because the carpenters could not pay the head tax, immigration officials decided that they would no doubt become a public charge, and thus denied the Filipino carpenters entry. However, the Commissioner General of Immigration overruled that decision and decreed that Filipino immigrants did not need to pay the head tax. Perhaps in part because of the exemption from the head tax, although more likely due to the exclusion of Chinese and Japanese laborers, by 1920 there were 5,603 Filipinos in the continental United States and Alaska.

h. Mexicans

Emilia Castañeda[94]

- she will never forget the morning in 1935 when she left her native Los Angeles at age 9 with her father and brother for Mexico, where she had never been.
- such departures were routine, part of a widely-accepted "repatriation" program designed to alleviate unemployment and poverty in the Los Angeles area.
- initially even the Mexican consul in L.A. supported the effort, but by 1935, Mexicans in L.A. were not given much choice.
- one study claims that 1 million people of Mexican descent were driven from the U.S. during the 1930s due to raids, scare tactics, deportation, repatriation and public pressure, of whom approximately 60% of those leaving were legal U.S. citizens.[95]
- L.A. county's own figures showed that Mexicans were on average only 10% of the people on welfare, yet repatriation was promoted and seen as a way of effectively diminishing welfare rolls.
- conditions in Mexico were harsh, and the people there often did not welcome repatriates.
- Castañeda recalls children taunting her as a 'repatriada,' she found this very offensive, an insult like gringo or wetback.
- in some cases bedridden Mexicans in nursing homes or asylums in L.A. county were sent to Mexico on the back of a truck. [96]

Like the Japanese and Filipinos, Mexican workers came to the U.S. to fill the gap left by the Chinese after the Chinese Exclusion Act, a gap made wider by the encouragement of labor-intensive irrigation farming in California and Texas by Congressional action in 1902. The shift from small farms to large ranches in Mexico displaced many workers from southern Mexico, who first moved northwards to work on Mexican rail, and then into the United States after hearing of higher wages in America. Furthermore, the population in Mexico grew from 9.4 million to 15.2 million between 1877-1910, primarily due to improved healthcare and a reduction in the mortality rate. Later, the Mexican Revolution in 1910 and the resulting political instability drove more Mexicans to cross the border.

Many of the Mexicans were lured by exploitative opportunists commonly called *enganchadores* (from "*enganchado*," meaning "hooked"), who spread stories of high wages in America and loaned migrants money for transportation. Upon arrival in the United States, workers found that wages were much lower than promised and remained indebted for much longer than anticipated. Still, wages were almost invariably higher than those that could be found in Mexico. In 1905, a worker in the Mexican state of Jalisco could earn only 12.5 cents per day, plus maize, while a truck worker in the American Southwest could earn $1.25 daily in fewer hours; a Mexican family could earn $5 per day from picking cotton in Texas at the peak of the season. Constant migration between Mexico and America became common, as Mexicans were exempt from the head taxes implemented in 1903 and 1907, and laws against contract laborers were particularly weakly enforced. As many as 80% of Mexican migrant workers were undocumented in the 1920s, and due to the mobility of labor across the border, many Mexicans did not bother to learn English, find permanent housing, or adapt to American culture.

Despite initially amicable relations between the United States and Mexico, attitudes towards Mexican labor soured during the recession of 1907. That year, many Mexican railroad workers in California lost their jobs and were deported to Juarez, Mexico; the event served as an early precursor to modern trends in immigration law enforcement.[97] Societal pressure against Mexicans was such that well-established Mexican American families distanced themselves from the newest immigrants in the early 1900s. Those who had been brought into the United States with the annexation of Mexican territory, an estimated 100,000, had long since found their political and economic clout slipping away as European Americans migrated west in the search for gold and land. As early as 1850, Spanish-speakers comprised only 11% of California's population; twenty years later, that population had shrunk to 4%, and by 1900 was only 1-2%. Although the political sway of Mexican Americans in New Mexico did not wane as quickly due to that area having been more densely settled than California at the time of annexation, society became increasingly segregated, Mexican Americans were increasingly marginalized, and neither new nor old immigrants were able to stop public opinion from turning against them both.[98]

The increasing controversy over immigration and the economic recession led Congress to pass the Immigration Act of 1907, which established the United States Immigration Commission (also known as the Dillingham Commission, named after Senator William P. Dillingham). The Dillingham Commission was a 3-year study of immigration to the United States, with the result being that "old" immigrants from Western Europe were declared pioneers and entrepreneurs, and "new" immigrants from Southern and Eastern Europe were depicted as unskilled, illiterate, and unable or unwilling to adapt to American culture.

It is unsurprising that such stereotypes had proliferated and that anti-immigrant sentiment had permeated the highest circles of American government. The wave of immigrants who came during the Industrial Revolution and settled in urban areas were, after all, typically poorer and less educated than the more established families from Western Europe which had been in America for generations. However, as often happens with prejudice, stereotypes, reinforced by selective examples, ballooned into widely accepted fiction and provoked violent action. The Haymarket bomb incident in Chicago in 1886 at an anarchist protest for the dispersion and killing of immigrant strike workers was blamed on immigrants. Later, President McKinley's assassination in 1901 by Leon Czolgosz, the anarchist son of Polish immigrants, had seemed clear confirmation of all immigrants' inherently radical and criminal nature. Darwinism and eugenics combined to create pseudoscientific theories regarding the superiority of the Nordic race and the corruption of its purity by immigrant populations. This led the Dillingham Commission to suggest that the United States admit immigrants in amounts relative to their existing proportions within the U.S. in order to maintain a Western European majority.[99]

i. French Canadians

The other major immigrant group from the Western Hemisphere prior to World War I, the French Canadians, exhibited certain similarities to the Mexicans in their slow acculturation and constant remigration. An explosion of the French-speaking population of Quebec from 1763 (60,000) to 1871 (more than a million) led to the immigration of hundreds of thousands of Quebecois into New England in the late 19th and early 20th century. Despite the vast amount of land in Quebec, the quality of the soil and climate, similar to that in Scandinavia, left much to be desired for farmers. However, few actually decided to continue farming in New England; far greater numbers of French Canadians acquired jobs in textile mills and factories.

Because of the constant migratory flow back and forth across the U.S.-Canadian border, it is difficult to ascertain the exact number of Quebecois who immigrated and settled in America. Notably, the French Canadians became the first and only immigrant group to immigrate to America primarily by rail, and the ease with which they traveled only places immigration statistics in further doubt. However, some indication can be gleaned from the number of foreign-born and native-born French Canadians in the United States. In 1890, a total of 526,934 French Canadians were reported to be living in the United States, 57.4% of who were foreign-born. Although the aggregate number of French Canadians increased to 830,335 in 1900 and 932,238 in 1910 before shrinking again to 848,309 in 1920, the percentage of foreign-borns within that population shrank in each decade to 35.6% by 1920.

Despite the increasing number of native-born French Canadian Americans, such families somewhat isolated themselves from the rest of New England, as they lived in French-speaking communities, read French newspapers, and worked with other French Canadians. Furthermore, French Canadians did not involve themselves politically for a time, with one of the lowest naturalization rates of any ethnicity and a substantial rate of emigration back to Canada. Use of the French language also persisted strongly in French Canadian descendants. Even by 1970, half of the 2.6 million Americans who spoke French as a mother tongue were not only born in the United States, but had parents who were born in the United States, as well, and one tenth of New England's population was among the French speakers.

Although the Quebecois did not clash significantly with the English-speaking workers of New England (indeed, much of New England's population had moved westwards a century before), they were not particularly well-liked by

Protestant New Englanders. French Canadians even challenged the Irish dominance of the Catholic Church in America, as the Germans had before. Disparities in the language and form of worship in addition to opinions about the level of autonomy that should be allowed individual parishes led to conflict. Even worse for French Canadians was the pressure placed upon them to Americanize their parochial schools. Fierce resistance and appeals to Rome regarding the adoption of the English language in such schools met with failure, as the Vatican chose not to interfere and even the leaders of the opposition could not continue their efforts in the face of excommunication.

Nor did French Canadians ultimately remain socially isolated, although most preferred not to intermarry with the majority English-speaking ethnicities of America. In 1880, only 7.5% of French Canadian-descended children in America had one parent of another ethnicity; 26.5% had one second-generation French Canadian parent, while 66% of the children were of parents both born in Quebec. As late as 1926, only 11% of French Canadians in Woonsocket, Rhode Island had married outside of their ethnicity (mostly to Irish Catholics). However, in areas where less French Canadians were present, acculturation and assimilation were inevitable, and intermarriage between French Canadians and those of other ethnicities (and even other religions) occurred more frequently.[100] The surge of patriotism and nationalism during the First World War, especially, placed great pressure on nonconformist groups to Americanize.

6. WORLD WAR I, 1914

The Great War erupted across Europe with little warning or preface, plunging 1914 Europe into a destructive campaign of men and material that would lead scholars to label the conflict as the "war to end all wars." When the United States abandoned its long-standing doctrine of isolationism and entered the war in 1917, the German American population, having long escaped persecution, now found itself the subject of general suspicion and distrust.

Although many of them had been in America for generations, some in the German American community had celebrated the Prussian victories over France in the 1870-71 Franco-Prussian War, and German American newspapers had defended Germany's actions in Europe at the start of World War I. Some German banks had even sold German war bonds to support the Axis war effort, and a portion of the German American population chose to donate to the German Red Cross in lieu of the American Red Cross. Questions about the mixed loyalties of the Germans in America even led to the theory that they put glass in Red Cross bandages.[101]

Once U.S. involvement in the war moved beyond the sale of munitions to the Allies and entered the realm of armed conflict, fear of subversion and sabotage from within the German American population intensified. Theaters banned the performance of German operas, and the charter for the German American Alliance was revoked. German book burning became occasion for celebration or riotous behavior in several cities and towns. The hamburger was renamed the liberty sandwich; sauerkraut, liberty cabbage. Schools stopped teaching German as a language, and its use was effectively purged from the American experience. Despite 10% of the U.S. population reporting German as their first language in 1910 and nearly a quarter of high school students learning German in 1915, the number of students taking German had fallen to approximately 1% by 1922. The rapidity and breadth of the transformation within America lead the *Tulsa Daily World* to declare that the German language was "deader than Latin."[102]

Due to overwhelming cultural pressure, many German American families bought liberty bonds, adopted Anglicized names, and made public statements denouncing Germany. President Wilson's Proclamation of War in 1917 had invoked the Alien Enemies Act of 1798, declaring all male citizens of Germany 14 years of age and older "enemy aliens," rendered deportable, and their property subject to seizure. Ellis Island was transformed into a detention center, and approximately 6,300 Germans were interned there, along with radicals and other undesirables. It is therefore unsurprising that although the Alien Enemies Act was soon extended to German women and 2.5 million German-born people were counted in the 1910 census, only 482,000 actually registered as enemy aliens during the war.[103]

The pervasive fear fueled a general movement for "one hundred percent Americanism." Those who did not demonstrate an acceptable level of enthusiasm for the war effort and the nation were rounded upon and abused or coerced into conformism. A Croatian in Pittsburgh was jailed and fined for sitting during the playing of the national anthem, while a writer in Tulsa was shot by an operative of the City Council of Defense for making pro-German remarks. Others were fired from their jobs, lynched, painted, tied up, tarred and feathered, or forced to kiss the flag or buy bonds. William L. Harding, the governor of Iowa, stated that the use of any language other than English was a threat to national security, consequently banning the use of German in public. 15 states passed laws requiring all schools, public and private, to use English. Schools and night schools were established to teach English, such as Jane Addams' Hull House in Chicago, which not only offered language instruction, but also gave immigrants advice on making the cultural adjusting to living in America. Mexican Americans in the South were courted by the Americanism movement with community meetings and outreach programs, asked to buy liberty bonds, and encouraged to Americanize their children. Some stated that the period was the first time they actually felt like American citizens. Wartime laws promising expedited naturalization for any man who served in the military led some Asian immigrants to enlist, although they were ultimately still barred from citizenship due to their race.[104]

The inexorable momentum of one hundred percent Americanism also took its toll on the press. The Trading with the Enemy Act of 1917 placed new burdens on foreign-language newspapers, requiring that such publications file English translations of all material concerning government policies and the war or obtain permits exempting them from the provision. Newspapers which had traditionally printed in German began to print in English. Public sentiment and government censorship ensured that most newspapers which had initially expressed opposition to America's entry into the Great War were, to all outside observers, loyal to a fault by the summer of 1917. Some suspended publication, whether they did so voluntarily, in response to increasing public pressure, or by the express order of a state council of defense. Still others were put out of business by the revocation of their second-class mailing privileges, without which the papers could not afford to operate. By 1920, only 234 German language publications remained of the 554 in 1910, and their circulation had fallen to a quarter of its 1910 levels.[105]

Despite the wartime fear of German American subversion, the end of the war brought the American people's attention back to their old pre-war prejudices. The Bolshevik Revolution in 1917 had brought an end to Czarist Russia and increased already-heightened xenophobic feelings within America. Those within the U.S. who already suspected Eastern Europeans of radical socialism and anarchism saw the revolution as the realization of their fears, thereafter accusing Russian immigrants of seeking a violent, revolutionary overthrow of the American government. This belief had been reinforced by the public denouncement of the war and the organization of anti-conscription meetings by the Socialist Party of the United States, even though the statement had caused many patriotic socialists to split from the party. Socialist papers, too, often lost their second-class mailing privileges, and many socialists were imprisoned. The terms anarchist, socialist, and even labor unionist became synonymous with Bolshevik, and newspapers frequently used the terms interchangeably. Such beliefs would shape U.S. immigration law in the interwar period.[106]

U.S. immigration policy in the early 20th century continued along protectionist lines established in the latter part of the 19th. Although the country had emerged from isolationism to engage in greater cooperation with Europe and trade with Asia, Americans, by and large, were still wary of immigrants and the effects they might have on American living. Per the prevailing theory (reinforced by the Dillingham Commission's report) that immigrants in recent years were less intelligent and less educated than their 17th and 18th century counterparts, Congress repeatedly attempted to establish literacy requirements for incoming foreigners to stop unskilled workers from entering the U.S. Bills were passed in Congress in 1897, 1913, 1915, and 1917 and vetoed each time by Presidents Cleveland, Taft, and Wilson, but proponents of the bill finally garnered enough support to override the 1917 veto, making literacy in a known language a requirement of all male immigrants over the age of 16 and females over 16 who did not accompany a literate male immigrant. The direct impact of the law on immigrant numbers was small. The literacy rate in Europe had increased since the law's original conception, and as such, the law did not prove as exclusionary as once hoped.

Still, anti-immigration members of Congress had not paused in pursuing their agendas; the momentum of their initial victory enabled and emboldened them to pass a flurry of additional anti-immigration laws. Included among these was the Immigration Act of 1917, which created the "Asia Pacific Triangle," or "Asiatic barred zone," an area encompassing most of South and Southeast Asia from which immigration was denied. The law also extended the allowable time after entry in which an immigrant deemed radical could be deported from 3 years to 5 as a response to the Bolshevik Revolution. In 1918, the President authorized immigration officials ban the entry of immigrants deemed a threat to public safety. The following year, a strike by the Boston Police which initiated a spree of looting and violence was succeeded by immigrant worker strikes in the steel and coal industries, increasing suspicion of widespread immigrant and radical unrest, although the strikers' complaints most often lacked a political bent. The situation worsened as bombs were sent to several prominent individuals' homes, including that of Attorney General Alexander Mitchell Palmer.

Palmer's agents infiltrated sections of the Communist party within America and struck at each in turn, apprehending any and all who were unlucky enough to be in the vicinity of the communists' various headquarters. The agents confiscated all property on the premises and jailed over 6,000 suspects for days or weeks without warrants while they searched for evidence of a widespread communist conspiracy. The government's fears ultimately proved unfounded. In all, Palmer's agents found 3 guns and no explosives amongst the communists' possessions. However, thousands of immigrants were deemed radical and deportable by Palmer's agents and members of the Lusk Committee (a New York-based group commissioned to combat radicalism), including 200 members of the Union of Russian Workers in New York City. Many immigrants who belonged to unions were unaware that their organizations had been linked with communists and anarchists by authorities. Assistant Labor Secretary Louis F. Post found that in nearly every case, technical membership in some organization had been cited as sufficient cause for deportation.[107]

Some groups escaped the government's sweeping changes and expanding powers of deportation and denial. Filipinos were exempt from the restrictions of the 1917 Immigration Act, and Mexican workers, who were still in high demand, were permitted to enter the country under temporary contract. Things also became easier for immigrant contract workers when some restrictive immigration laws were repealed by the Commissioner General of Immigration in 1918 under pressure from industry lobbyists. Mexican workers competed with the Californian Japanese on sugar beet and citrus farms, comprised 43% of Arizona's copper miners by the mid-1920s, and grew from constituting 17.1% to 59.5% of workers on 9 western railroads from 1909 to 1929.[108]

However, the pressing need for cheap labor provided by immigrants was continually at odds with notions of racial purity and the preservation of Western European societal mores. During the war, the United States Army conducted a psychology test in which soldiers of Western and Northern European descent scored higher IQs than those who had come from Eastern and Southern Europe, reviving debate about Nordic superiority and the corruption of bloodlines. Such beliefs were often openly and shamelessly expressed; articles by novelist Kenneth Roberts were published in the *Saturday Evening Post*, suggesting that the mixing of races, even between the Nordic, Alpine, and Mediterranean populations in Europe, would produce "worthless" hybrid children. A plan drafted by Senator Dillingham setting a hard cap of 357,000 immigrants per annum and proposing a system for admitting immigrants in proportion to the national composition of the 1910 census was issued into law in 1921, a system in which over half of the slots for immigration were reserved for Western and Northern Europe. The law was replaced by the Johnson-Reed Act in 1924, changing the national proportions used to those of the 1890 census (in which Southern and Eastern European descendants comprised an even smaller percentage of the overall population). The quota was so low that nearly 10% percent of its annual allotment in 1924 was equal to the amount of immigrants who had been processed at Ellis Island in a single day in 1917. An amendment in 1927 lowered the quota to 150,000 immigrants per annum. The act also banned all immigration by peoples ineligible for citizenship (non-Caucasians, as ruled by the 1922 case *Ozawa v. U.S.*) and ended the "Gentlemen's Agreement" with Japan. Such decisions reflect the unfortunate racial tensions and prejudices of the day, as lawmakers fought to preserve the Western/Northern European majority within the United States. However, despite its discriminatory nature, the Johnson-Reed Act also marked several major events in American immigration law.[109]

First, the act created the visa system in the U.S., with Consuls denying visas to immigrants they deemed undesirable. Second, the act reserved 50% of each year's quota for the parents and husbands of U.S. citizens and gave preference to the families of legal U.S. residents, placing an emphasis on family reunification within immigration law. Whereas the previous law had only provided exemptions for those seeking asylum from religious persecution and the children of citizens, the Johnson-Reed Act exempted from the quota husbands of citizens, women who had lost their citizenship through marriage to foreign nationals (prior to the 1922 Cable Act, wives adopted their husband's citizenship and lost their own), immigrants previously admitted to the U.S., ministers, and professors. Finally, those born and residing in the Western Hemisphere were exempt from the quota, an allowance made primarily for businesses in the American West and Southwest which relied on Mexican workers to operate. Because the quotas had a dramatic effect on slowing immigration from Europe, there became an insufficient supply of labor in the Northern states, as well.

Not surprisingly, Mexican and Canadian immigration increased significantly. During the period, Mexican immigrants moved beyond their traditionally inhabited locales in the Southwest and traveled north to fill the need for workers in the steel, rubber, and automotive industries. They did so in no small numbers; by 1927, Chicago recorded a population of 75,400 Mexican workers, and one third of its 2.7 million residents in the 1920s were foreign-born. Canadian immigration rose to nearly a million persons during the 1920s, of which Catholic French Canadians constituted approximately a third.[110]

The Johnson-Reed Act also had an indirect impact on the Filipino population within the U.S. Many Filipinos who remained exempt from immigration quotas had been recruited prior to the passing of the act by businesses in California and Alaska who feared a cutoff of Mexican labor. However, the rise in immigration was brief. When the stock market crash in 1929 brought about the worst economic downturn in the country's history, immigrants to the U.S. once again found themselves resented by a discontent and desperate public.

7. THE GREAT DEPRESSION, 1929

News of the stock market crash, bank failures, drought, and other harbingers of the Great Depression spread quickly. The Gross National Product (GNP) fell from $104 billion in 1929 to $73 billion in 1933, a contraction of more than 25%. In the same time period, business investment fell from $24 billion to a measly $3 billion. More than 5,000 banks failed, wiping out $7 billion in depositors' money. In Pennsylvania alone, there were 1,150,000 people unemployed in 1932, and only two fifths of the working population had full time employment. In 1933, 25% of the country's total workforce was unemployed, which amounted to 13 million Americans.[111]

With its unprecedented levels of unemployment and falling living standards, many were deterred from immigrating to the United States, and emigration exceeded immigration in some years. Nearly one third of the Poles, Slovaks, and Croatians, and more than half of the Greeks, Russians, Romanians, and Bulgarians returned to Europe. However, this was also due in part to the government taking measures to further curb immigration and preserve jobs for its citizens. As those entering the U.S. would likely be unable to find employment, visas were denied to all but the wealthiest immigrants under the "LPC clause" (likely to become a public charge) established under law in 1882, as well as in the 1917 Immigration Act.[112]

The sudden broadening of individuals excluded under the clause had the greatest effect in the Southwest, where most Mexican immigrants, with or without temporary work contracts, were denied entry. The literacy law of 1917 was extended to Mexican immigrants as well, and Mexican immigration dropped from 40,000 in 1929 to 13,000 the following year. Unsatisfied with applying restrictions to new immigrants, citizens and the government then turned to recent immigrants already residing in the United States. In the 1930 census, Mexicans were classified for the first time as non-whites. Many Mexicans were fired from their jobs and denied welfare, with the government offering transportation back to Mexico and forcing it upon those who did not take it willingly, as it had done during the recession of 1907. During the Great Depression, approximately one million Mexicans were deported, with a number of Mexican American citizens even illegally deported as part of the program. During the period, Mexican American children were segregated from European American children and placed in schools of much worse quality; 82.2% of public school teachers in European American schools had teaching degrees, compared to 46.6% in Mexican American schools.[113]

Filipino immigration also fell as laid-off American citizens accepted lower paying jobs and several immigrants returned to the Philippines spreading word of hardship. To further discourage Filipinos daring enough to brave the tough economic times, the Tydings-McDuffie Act of 1934 was passed. The act provided for the independence of the Philippines in 1945, but a quota was finally applied to Filipinos. In 1935, the government offered to repatriate Filipinos on the condition that they promise never to return to the United States. Although the government did not force Filipino residents out of the U.S., as it had done with Mexicans, the added stipulations on Filipino immigration ended decades of unrestricted travel.

Just as the last major avenues of immigration seemed to be closing, rumblings in Europe heralded the coming of a new wave of immigrants, arriving under very different circumstances than those of the Industrial Revolution. The Nazi movement in Germany was growing increasingly violent, and many of the persecuted sought refuge in the United States. Never having had to deal with such a volume of refugees seeking asylum before, prospective immigrants were issued or denied visas largely at the discretion of individual consuls. Despite urging from President Roosevelt for consuls to be sympathetic to the plight of most refugees, some consuls remained extremely selective in their issuance of visas, and others were biased by anti-Semitism. The outcome was tragic. The 1921 and 1924 laws reduced Jewish immigration to 73,000 from 1924-1931. Only one half of the quota allotted to German immigrants was used from 1933 to 1940; the combined German-Austrian (Anschluss) quota was only filled in 1939, and many who might otherwise have escaped death in Europe were denied admittance.

The fault did not lie exclusively with the consuls, as a tough stance on immigration during the Great Depression had been adopted by the majority of government officials. The Wagner-Rogers bill in 1939 proposing that 20,000 German children be brought to the United States outside of the quota never even made it to a vote. Still, some successes were made in loosening immigration regulations to save lives. In 1938, Secretary of Labor Frances Perkins extended the 6-month visitor visas of political refugees, an act which enabled 15,000 refugees to stay in the U.S. In 1940, action by the State Department allowed consuls outside of Germany to grant visas to German refugees, and a system was created in 1941 to allow refugees on temporary visas to get Canadian quota numbers and return to the U.S. on permanent visas.[114]

By the time the U.S. entered World War II, it had admitted over 150,000 refugees, the most of any nation. Although the majority of these refugees were middle-class and had held white-collar or professional jobs in Europe, many of them found that the language barrier and general unemployment during the Great Depression made employment extremely hard to come by. Some areas prohibited the employment of immigrants in professional occupations such as law and medicine, and it was not uncommon for these well educated Jewish refugees to perform menial jobs to get by in a time when any work at all was a blessing. Still, compared with life under the Nazi jackboot, many of the refugees found life in America infinitely preferable, and used their freedom to contribute to the war effort.

8. WORLD WAR II, 1939

After the surrender of France to the Nazis in 1940, it seemed as if the Wehrmacht would soon sweep away the last vestiges of resistance in Western Europe and that Adolf Hitler might thereafter turn his gaze across the Atlantic. After all, the infamous Zimmerman Telegram during World War I had exposed German designs against the United States, and Western Europe was falling with frightening speed. The U.S. government moved quickly to protect itself from foreign espionage, passing the Alien Registration Act in 1940, also known as the Smith Act. Comprised of 3 parts, or titles, the first title of the Smith act made subversive action a criminal offense, the second title broadened the activity under which aliens could be rendered deportable, and the third title required all immigrants to register with Immigration and Naturalization Services (INS), have fingerprints taken, notify INS of changes of address, and be issued a registration card. The act also prohibited aliens who opposed the American government or laws from being naturalized.

On December 7, 1941, the Japanese launched a surprise attack on Pearl Harbor, bringing America into the war. 4 days later, Germany declared war on the United States, and President Roosevelt called for an aggressive expansion of the somewhat neglected armed forces. As the great military-industrial complex transformed the nation and patriotism once again overtook the hearts and minds of Americans, old fears for national security resurfaced and immigrant descendants of enemy nations came under suspicion as dissidents and spies. All non-citizens of Japanese, German, and Italian descent were declared "alien enemies" and their conduct was regulated. This was later extended to Hungarian, Bulgarian, and Romanian immigrants. Those who had been labeled alien enemies were required to re-register with INS and carry new identification cards at all times.

Public opinion of the Japanese in California, never having risen to a particularly high level, quickly deteriorated. Extant xenophobic organizations capitalized upon the strike at Pearl Harbor to rally the general populace against the Japanese. Some unashamedly cited economic motivations for interning the Japanese, such as the Grower-Shipper Vegetable Association in central California, while others such as the Western Growers Protective Association masked their business interests behind patriotic rhetoric. Other groups, such as the American Legion and the Native Sons of the Golden West, supported the anti-Japanese movement.[115]

The combination of the Californian farmers' desire to kick out their competition, the public's fear of sabotage, and the politicians' desire to gain support by turning against an unpopular group led to a series of public proclamations that mandated the relocation of nearly 120,000 ethnic Japanese (both United States citizens and Japanese nationals) to hastily constructed and sparsely equipped internment centers.[116] These ethnic Japanese were often forced to sell their land, homes, businesses and other equipment at substantial losses because the forced relocation was so abrupt. Prior to the establishment of these concentration camps, the civil liberties of these ethnic Japanese had been slowly corroded. At one point, those living within what was defined to be the military zone (essentially the entire West Coast, extending up to 100 miles inland) were required to report every change of residence or employment to the FBI. Later, there was also a curfew established for ethnic Japanese in this military zone from 8 p.m. to 6 a.m. every day. An excerpt written by Columnist Henry McLemore reflected growing public opinion at the time:

"I am for the immediate removal of every Japanese on the West Coast to a point deep in the interior. I don't mean a nice part of the interior either. Herd 'em up, pack 'em off and give 'em the inside room in the badlands. Personally, I hate the Japanese. And that goes for all of them."[117]

Although INS primarily detained Japanese immigrants, 10,905 Germans were arrested and detained on charges or suspicion of sedition, and officials went so far as to intern some German, Italian, and Japanese immigrants living in Latin American countries. Like the Germans prior to World War I, some Italians in America supported Mussolini's actions in the 1930s and became a source of concern for the government. 3,000 Italian Americans were arrested in California, some of whom were held for 2 years. Others were detained for up to 2 months for curfew violations or the possession of contraband. Eventually, Italian American citizen pressure led to the relief of Italian immigrants from such close scrutiny and labeling as alien enemies, but Japanese Americans suffered far stronger enmity from the American people and Japanese American citizens and immigrants were interned alike en masse. Action by Congress enabling Japanese Americans to renounce their U.S. citizenship in a "denaturalization declaration" and be deported to Japan after the war's close was eventually invalidated by the judicial system, but only after over 1,300 of the approximately 5,500 individuals who had accepted the offer had already been deported.[118]

Like in the First World War, however, groups of immigrants from neutral and friendly countries benefited from the diversion of American ire towards the Axis powers. The absolute nature of the war and the drafting of much of the male workforce forced many American women to take up jobs left behind by their husbands, brothers, and sons, and the government began to draft incentives for Mexican labor to return to U.S. employ. The *bracero* temporary contract program was instated in 1942 and attracted over 200,000 workers, including some West Indian, Bahamian, Canadian, and Newfoundlander workers along with the Mexican majority. Although the Mexican government negotiated for a minimum wage, living and working condition standards, and paid transportation to and from jobs in the U.S., the Mexican government stopped its citizens from working in Texas for the first five years of the program due to the substandard working and living conditions there. Nevertheless, many Mexican workers remained in America after their contracts had expired, resulting eventually in a campaign of deportation that lasted well into the 1950s.[119]

Cooperation with China during World War II also brought about the end of the long standing Chinese Exclusion Act. The Citizens' Committee to Repeal Chinese Exclusion and Place Immigration on a Quota Basis was formed in May, 1943 to lobby the U.S. government for change, a change won in December of that year. Although 25% of the quota assigned to Chinese immigration was applied to ethnic Chinese of all nationalities, a stipulation not applied to other immigrant groups, Chinese immigrants were finally allowed to undergo the process of naturalization. After the war's end, the War Brides Act was passed, allowing the spouses and children of those who had served in the armed forces to join their husbands in the United States. The act was soon expanded to include fiancés, fiancées, and Chinese wives of citizens who had not served in the military. Filipinos and Indians were similarly permitted to undergo naturalization and more standard quotas were applied to immigrants from the Philippines and India.

The end of World War II brought a brief celebratory respite for the Allied nations and the United States. Yet, even as the world breathed a sigh of relief and looked forward to more peaceful times, the reality was that post-war Europe had once again inherited a harsh legacy. The policies of Nazi Germany, the destruction of European infrastructure, and the expenditure of its resources had displaced millions, with little hope for recompense or rebuilding. Survivors of concentration camps were often placed in displaced persons camps where living conditions were regrettably low. Some of these survivors feared a return to their old homes, where neighbors had turned a blind eye to Nazi activities or openly supported them. A pogrom in Poland in 1946 resulted in the death of 40 Jews. Most survivors simply had no homes to return to, and many displaced Jews chose to travel to the newly established state of Israel. Because of this, most immigrants attempting to enter the United States in the years immediately following the war were Catholics and Protestants from increasingly unfriendly countries in Eastern Europe (primarily Soviet-influenced) or Jews who wished to join relatives in America.

To alleviate the sudden competition for scarce quota spots, President Truman issued a directive reserving half of European quota spots for people displaced by the war. However, because the vast majority of these came from Eastern and Southern Europe, areas with low quotas to begin with, only 41,000 such immigrants entered the U.S. in the next few years, instead of the 40,000 per year that the president had hoped for. A further initiative passed in 1948, the Displaced Persons Act, brought another 200,000 displaced individuals into the United States. Preference was given to close relatives of U.S. citizens and Allied war veterans, but standard immigration restrictions applied to all those applying for entry under the act, and individuals who had participated in anti-American movements were ineligible. While some displaced persons were denied entry upon the grounds that they were likely to become a public charge, federally funded voluntary agencies, or VOLAGs, were permitted to vouch for many who had no fiscally sound American relatives. 90% of those who were admitted took advantage of this opportunity. At first, the act also contained additional restrictions for Jews, but an amendment in 1950 removed the anti-Semitic elements of the act, and over 80,000 Jewish displaced persons were able to immigrate to the U.S. by 1952.

Besides the passage of laws disregarding or expanding the quota system, it became common practice for immigration officials to "borrow" quota slots from future years and let more than the set annual amount of immigrants into the country. Such occurrences happened so frequently that several countries had quotas mortgaged hundreds of years into the future. The tide of displaced persons and refugees did not abate as tension mounted between the U.S. and U.S.S.R., although refugee origin shifted from previously Nazi-occupied territories to Soviet ones. It soon became clear that the quota system was inadequate to address immigration of the day.

9. POST-WORLD WAR II (1945 onward)

The territorial expansion of the Soviet Union at the end of World War II raised alarm in the West, which had viewed revolutionary Leninism with almost the same level of apprehension as the fascist regimes in Germany and Italy. After the resolution of conflict against the Axis, many Western policymakers feared that Stalin would continue to aggressively expand the Soviet sphere of influence into central Europe and Asia, as he had already extended his reach over Eastern Europe and part of Germany. The growth of communist movements in more remote parts of the world which had recently won independence from Western European colonialism, the communist takeover of China, and continued Soviet propaganda and rhetoric about the inevitable fall of capitalist societies culminated in a widespread fear of communist subversion and worldwide revolution. Because the United States had escaped the devastation of Europe and emerged from World War II as the strongest Western nation, many believed that the responsibility fell upon America to contain communism wherever it appeared to be gaining momentum, even if oppressive totalitarian regimes had to be supported to achieve that end.

As such, anti-communist paranoia began to overtake American hearts and minds in even greater measure than even the anti-German sentiment during World Wars I and II. While the German threat had been absolute, it had also been clearly definable. Those of an enemy nationality or ethnicity could be identified, watched, and detained. Those harboring political sentiments of the enemy were far less conspicuous. The clandestine and slowly subversive nature of communism (as Americans believed it to be) led to a shift back to social isolationism. Once more, immigration legislation was passed to maintain ethnic proportions within the American population, and people considered to be "un-American" were excluded from entry, even including accomplished comedian and filmmaker Charlie Chaplin. However, even as Americans withdrew from cultural exchange and engagement to the relative security of political conservatism, the United States was expanding its operational arenas overseas in the fight against communism and faced a decision about accepting refugees from Stalinist oppression and proxy wars. After all, how could the United States claim to be taking an ideological stand against Soviet occupation and oppression if it turned those away seeking asylum?

Because of these conflicting interests, general regulations for immigration were increased and potentially problematic residents within the United States were investigated, while simultaneously, large numbers of refugees were exempted from quota restrictions. This duality within immigration policy also reflected diverging opinions within the government. Senator Joseph McCarthy's infamous hearings which slandered and accused many undeserving individuals (including McCarthy's political opponents) of communist affiliations or sympathies had begun in 1950. The same year, Senator McCarran's Internal Security Act was passed despite a veto from President Truman, enabling easier detainment and deportation of aliens deemed threats to national security.

The Truman administration had pushed for a far more liberal stance on immigration. The Commission on Immigration and Naturalization, established by an executive order from President Truman, produced a report labeled "*Whom Shall We Welcome?*", in which the commission made seven recommendations for guiding future immigration policy, most of which were designed to create more egalitarian immigration practices. These included the abolishment of the national origins system; the establishment of a general quota without regard for nationality, race, or religion; the use of recent census numbers instead of those already decades-old; the creation of a Commission on Immigration and Naturalization, a regulatory agency to perform functions then split between the Departments of Justice and State; the allocation of visas based on family reunion, asylum, U.S. needs, and special needs in the free world; the reservation of 100,000 quota spaces per annum for refugees and displaced persons; lastly, the report suggested the review/reallocation of visa proportions every three years by the established commission. Although nearly all of these recommendations would be eventually implemented in 1965, finally abolishing the notions of ethnic preservation set by the National Origins Quota Act, Congress in 1950 would hear none of it. Senator McCarran went so far as to claim that the commission's report had communist undertones through favoring more immigration from minority ethnic groups, and the report was thereafter ignored. Congress chose instead to pass the Immigration and Nationality Act of 1952, also known as the McCarran-Walter Act, which reaffirmed the basic tenets of the 1924 National Origins law.

Despite hypersensitivity about communism and Congressional conservatism, prevailing theories supporting the quota system had changed. Although racism was still very much a part of 1950s America, the openly eugenic and fanatically genocidal policies pursued by the Nazis made most members of Congress hesitant to make similar arguments when it came to immigration policy. Instead, the 1952 law was justified by the citation of sociological theories regarding the time required for the cultural assimilation of new immigrants, as the "sociological and cultural balance" of the United States had to be preserved. The act included many provisions and stipulations seen in earlier periods of immigration law; the national origins system was preserved using the 1920 census, the "Asian Barred Zone" was replaced by an "Asia-Pacific Triangle," and the Western Hemisphere was exempted from quota restrictions. However, communists or those with suspected communist affiliations were banned from immigrating, Asia was condensed under a single quota for the Asia-Pacific Triangle, and preference from all nations was given to those with higher education or exceptional abilities, then to relatives of U.S. citizens and residents. Also, despite many refugees from World War II being exempted from quota restrictions, non-European refugees were not covered under the 1948 Displaced Persons Act, and were largely denied admittance. Although the first of America's forays into anti-communist conflict in the 1950-1953 Korean War rescued South Korea from North Korean communist occupation, only 8,000 refugees, children, and war brides were allowed into the United States from 1952 to 1960.

a. Refugees

Changes of leadership in both the United States and Soviet Union in 1953 brought shifts in foreign policy and emboldened reform movements within Soviet satellite countries. In Eastern Europe, two major uprisings amid a slew of others during the mid-1950s revealed that cracks were beginning to form in the U.S.S.R.'s political infrastructure after the death of the totalitarian Stalin. The first of these occurred in East Berlin, where mismanagement and strict policies had caused the economy to deteriorate and pushed workers to the brink of revolt. Although the uprising was suppressed by force in Berlin, protests continued to occur in more than 500 towns and villages across East Germany. The second major uprising in Eastern Europe took place in 1956 in Hungary, where student activists hoped for change in their own state after reformist Wladyslaw Gomulka had become First Secretary of the Polish United Workers' Party and negotiated for more favorable trade and a reduced Soviet military presence in Poland. For a period during and immediately after the revolt, travel out of Hungary was unsupervised, tempting thousands of Eastern Europeans to leave through the sudden gap in the Iron Curtain. However, the window of opportunity was hastily closed by the Soviets. Seeing in the Hungarian Revolution the seeds of democratic change and rebellion against Soviet influence as the Hungarian government declared its withdrawal from the Warsaw Pact, Soviet troops struck Hungary in full force. The resistance was crushed under the assault by Soviet tanks, artillery, and airstrikes. Many Hungarians fled the country, approximately 35,000 of them eventually heading to the United States.[120]

Because of the uprisings in Eastern Europe and additional conflict in Asia, the U.S. found itself flooded by refugees seeking asylum. Although the quota system remained in place, most restrictions continued to be bypassed by further legislation creating exceptions for refugees, with the result that less than half of the 2,515,479 immigrants to the United States from 1951-1960 were actually admitted under a quota. The first piece of legislation created for the benefit of political refugees was drafted during the Eisenhower Administration. Aptly named the Refugee Relief Act, the 1953 law provided for the admittance of refugees fleeing extreme circumstances caused by international political events. It eventually helped bring 214,000 refugees from Europe to the United States, including Italians, Germans, Yugoslavs, Greeks, and Hungarians. The Refugee Escapee Act in 1957 for communist and Middle Eastern countries brought 29,000 Hungarians, Koreans, Yugoslavs, and Chinese to America, and the Fair Share Refugee Act of 1960 authorized roughly a quarter of those still living in refugee camps from World War II to resettle in the U.S. These acts not only established a clear distinction in U.S. immigration law between refugees and other immigrant groups, but also led to the realization that significant reform within the U.S. immigration system was needed to accommodate and regulate the large volume of foreign-born individuals seeking admittance to the United States.

b. The *Bracero* Program and Illegal Immigration

The United States had opened its borders to political refugees in a demonstrably idealistic and humanitarian effort to serve as a bastion against the oppressive forces of communism. It was not, however, so welcoming to those who came for the less pitiable notion of finding work, especially those who did so illegally. As always, the porous Mexican-U.S. border was a cause for concern, especially in the cloak and dagger nature of Cold War maneuvering. If the average Mexican laborer could go back and forth across the border clandestinely, so could Soviet spies and saboteurs. Although the *bracero* program remained in effect after World War II's end by being extended annually until a law that made the program permanent was passed in 1951, U.S. farmers had no compunctions about hiring Mexican labor outside of the system, where workers did not have even the marginal protection offered by the program. In the peak year of the program, 1957, more than

450,000 braceros were recruited. Many Mexicans also immigrated to the United States outside of the program—in 1950 alone there were 469,000 illegal immigrants apprehended at the border. [121]

The end result was Operation Wetback, an INS initiative involving the seizure and deportation of illegal immigrants. As many as 750 law enforcement agents started combing the American Southwest in July of 1954, primarily targeting Mexicans. Over a million Mexicans were deported, including several American citizens of Mexican origin or descent. As criticism and opposition mounted and funding was expended, the operation slowed and was terminated a few months after it began. However, those few months had once more exposed dangerous trends in immigration enforcement. [122]

Anti-communism and fear of subversion had certainly played a role in the conception and acceptance of the operation in Washington; however, the old economic arguments against immigration, legal or illegal, had resurfaced. Although the need for labor had led to the implementation of the *bracero* program and even the encouragement of illegal immigration earlier, some argued that such immigrants hurt the economy more than it helped, displacing American workers and harming retailers. The racial component of Operation Wetback, implicated by its very name and carried through to its execution in the deportation of Mexican American citizens, was also indicative of a disturbing prejudicial tendency within enforcers of immigration law. In any case, the program's successes, such as they were, proved to be fleeting. While INS claimed that somewhere around a million illegal immigrants had been deported or fled the country, it is likely that the quoted figure was inflated for bureaucratic reasons, and some of those deported were almost certainly deported multiple times as they continually reentered the country. Soon after the operation's end, illegal immigration returned to its pre-operation levels and the Border Patrol returned to targeting only those who had violated *bracero* contracts. Between the years of 1951 and 1965, approximately 4.5 million braceros and an equal number of undocumented workers came in from Mexico. The program ended in 1965 as the agricultural business found that illegal workers were more convenient and stopped lobbying for extensions while Unions continued to lobby against them.[123]

10. IMMIGRATION AND REFORM DURING THE COLD WAR 1945-1980

Despite INS and Congressional efforts to deter illegal and non-European immigrants from entering the country, the number of Cold War refugees arriving in the U.S. and the promise of a higher standard of living more than offset the effects of the Immigration and Nationality Act and Operation Wetback. Aggregate immigration from other parts of the world still amounted to more than that from Europe in all but 2 of the 13 years in which the Immigration and Nationality Act was in effect. In that time, approximately 1.5 million immigrants beyond the quota-allowed amount had entered the United States.

Asian immigration reached record numbers between 1950 and 1980. During those years, the Filipino population ballooned from 122,707 to 781,894, the Chinese population from 150,005 to 812,178, and the Japanese population from 326,379 to 716,331. The first group of Cuban political refugees also arrived at the end of the 1950s. According to a 1963 study, of the Cuban immigrants in America, 7.8% were lawyers or judges, 34% held professional, managerial or executive jobs, and 36% had attended high school or some college.[124]

Nevertheless, when divided by nationality, immigration from European countries remained relatively high. The largest group of immigrants came from Germany, followed by Canada, Mexico, the U.K., and Italy. Immigration from Eastern European states numbered in the tens of thousands as people fled harsh Soviet socioeconomic policies and political instability, and Western European governments, such as that of the Netherlands, negotiated for non-quota-restricted immigration in an attempt to ease the postwar financial burden on the state by sending citizens to America.

As the Cold War progressed and the world grew accustomed to the nuclear standoff between the United States and the U.S.S.R., conflict in the third world and within Soviet satellite states continued to drive a significant portion of immigration to the United States. Unrest and dissatisfaction with communist overseers remained in Eastern Europe and Central Asia; student protests in Czechoslovakia provoked Soviet military intervention, which in turn only served to further incite youth movements across Eastern Europe.

The strife over civil rights also indicated that a large minority population was no longer willing to quietly suffer unequal treatment. The United States could not tolerate racism against its minority members, since that led to civil strife and instability. Such instability in turn threatened the national security of the country in the dangerous era of the Cold War, and national security was paramount.

U.S. Policies: Immigration Reform Act of 1965 (Hart-Celler):

The shift in public attitudes toward race and national origins that accompanied the Civil Rights era was clearly echoed in Congress; both Republican and Democratic parties had taken pro-immigration stances in the 1960 election. However, nothing substantive could take place until the 1964 election of President Lyndon Johnson, since the House and Senate immigration committees at the time were controlled by restrictionist Democrats.

Under pressure from Johnson, the holdout Democrats gave way to the other members of their party and allowed immigration bills onto the House and Senate floors. The debate that followed was remarkably similar to previous debates that had taken place since the turn of the 20th century, although the previously open prejudice and intolerance of some Congressmen was out of fashion in the Civil Rights era. The National Origins Quota system that had long shaped U.S. immigration policy was to be abandoned; it was hopelessly out of date with the ethnic makeup of the United States.

The heavily Democratic 89th Congress eventually passed the Immigration and Nationality Act in 1965, which replaced the National Origins system with more open provisions. But while categories describing the ethnic character of immigrants who could enter were liberalized, regulatory control was also extended.

- Race was removed from categories governing immigration and naturalization exclusion; no longer could it be used as a factor to prohibit or restrict immigration
- Immigration was allowed from every country, and each country had the same numerical limit (allowing significant Asian and African migration for the first time)
- The overall amount of immigration allowed was not increased; previously unlimited immigration from the Western Hemisphere was removed; the general immigration ceiling was raised from 150,000 to 270,000, but overall was actually restricted since half went to the previously unlimited W. Hemisphere.
- The "Asia-Pacific" triangle concept was abandoned, but specific restrictions regarding the earlier "LPC" clause that kept out those unable to support themselves, requirements for physical and mental health, various ideological and moral tests, etc., were retained.

Signing the bill into law, President Lyndon Johnson remarked that "this bill that we sign today is not a revolutionary bill. It does not affect the lives of millions. It will not reshape the structure of our daily lives, or really add importantly to our wealth or our power." His words reflected the wisdom of the experts of the day; yet the Immigration and Nationality Act of 1965 became the new foundation for U.S. immigration law. It also facilitated the unforeseen boost in Asian and other immigration, which relied upon the "family chain migration" practice of bringing over family and relatives.

The 1965 Act was not solely responsible for rising immigration, since that had been the trend since long before its inception. However, it did help sustain the trend in ways which the earlier 1952 Act would not have. As a result, many new immigrants from Asia and Latin America would be able to come to the United States over the following decades.

a. Arabs

Before the inflammatory events of September 11, Arab immigrants to the United States traditionally remained low-profile, a population not well understood, but well tolerated due to their obscurity. Yet, a sizable population of Arabs, both

Christian and Muslim, has come to America over the years; out of a total of 2,223 passengers, well over 100 Syrians traveling in steerage class died on the night the Titanic sank in 1912. As early as 1924, 200,000 Arabs were living in the U.S., approximately 95,000 from Eastern Mediterranean countries, and the rest from Yemen, Iraq, Morocco, and Egypt. 90% of these were Christian (mostly Maronite), while the other 10% was Druze or Sunni. A decline in the price of silk and a shortage of land necessitated most of the early Arabs' emigration, as well as a 1908 decision by the Ottoman Empire to make Arabs eligible for conscription. Army service was a less than desirable fate for the average Arab youth, as the Ottomans favored putting Arabs in the front lines of their armies. Finally, the Allied forces' blockade of Syria and Lebanon, the Ottomans' seizure of food supplies, an earthquake, and yellow fever caused starvation and death during World War I, prompting those who could afford the trip to emigrate. Like the German Jews, many of these early Arabs in America peddled to save money and start businesses.

Arab immigration to the U.S. waned during the years of the Great Depression and did not recommence in strength until after World War II, when relatives began to join their families in America. During post-war period, movements for independence and political turmoil in the Middle East also drove almost 6,000 Palestinian refugees to immigrate to America, along with political elites from Egypt, Syria, and Iraq, refugees from the 1952 Egyptian and 1958 Iraqi revolutions. Some Coptic Christians and middle-class Muslims arrived in the early years of the Cold War.

As conflict continued in the Middle East, so did emigration from the region. A number of Arabs became disillusioned from their shockingly rapid loss during the Six-Day War of 1967 and left the region, 90,000 Lebanese and Palestinians immigrated to America from 1965-1992 due to ongoing civil war and strife, and the enactment of UN sanctions on Iraq in 1990 and the 1991 Gulf War caused more Arabs to immigrate to the United States. The growing prevalence of Islamic fundamentalism in the region not only pushed several Christian groups away, such as the Iraqi Chaldeans and Egyptian Copts, but also led many secular and moderate Muslims to emigrate.[125]

Besides security and stability, the primary incentive for Arabs to come to the United States was economic in nature. The educational opportunities afforded Americans remained far greater than those in the Middle East until approximately 1975, when Iraq, Egypt, and Lebanon had established respected institutions of higher learning. However, the job market did not keep pace with educational progress, and many well-educated Arabs chose to seek suitably skilled jobs or postgraduate education in the U.S. All told, 802,827 documented Arab immigrants arrived from 1948-2003, with the majority of Muslim background.

The years following the attacks of September 11 became an unprecedented time of trial for both America and its Arab population. Never before had such an attack taken place and been displayed so dramatically to the American people, and the tragic attacks ranked only behind the Battle of Antietam in the highest death toll for violent attack in a single day. Predictably, America's outrage was misplaced upon the unfortunate Arabs in America. Anti-Muslim hate crimes were 17 times higher in 2001 than in 2000, with 1,717 incidents of backlash discrimination reported to the Council on American Islamic Relations in the 6 months after the attacks. Arabs were commonly fired from jobs, threatened, or pulled off of commercial flights, with 80 reports of illegal airline discrimination found by the American-Arab Anti-Discrimination Committee. Despite calls for tolerance from Washington D.C. and the declaration that America was "at war with terror, not with Islam," the Bush administration's aggressive rhetoric and policy led the aggrieved and the poorly informed to ignore such fine distinctions. Arab Americans in essence became unofficially recognized as the new alien enemy, an unfortunate state of affairs which has not yet diminished fully.[126]

b. Asian Indians

Much like the Koreans and other immigrant groups, very few Asian Indians came to the U.S. prior to the passing of the Immigration and Nationality Act of 1965. Those who immigrated to America in the early years were mostly poor laborers who settled and worked in the American West, although several smaller, more affluent groups (Hindu missionaries, students and merchants) also arrived.[127]

After 1965, the number of Indians in America increased dramatically; such immigrants were, and continue to be attracted to the United States by its high wages and stable political and economic environment. According to U.S. census data, the Indian population grew by 987% in the 20 years between the 1970 census and the 1990 census (from 75,000 to 815,447). Unlike the immigration patterns of many other ethnicities, however, Indian immigration has been particularly balanced between the genders, as many have availed themselves of investment and employment-based routes to permanent residency and brought their families to live with them in the United States. Moreover, many who eventually gain permanent residence in America come initially on student visas; one study suggested that as many as a quarter of all Indian medical students come to the United States.[128] Others come as experienced and well-educated professionals, while a number have become entrepreneurs, opening enterprises such as restaurants, motels and newspaper kiosks.[129]

c. Central Americans

According to official census figures, 565,081 Salvadorans lived in the United States in 1990 and 708,741 in 2000, while Central American figures for those years weigh in at 1,323,380 (1,046,099 foreign-born) and 1,811,676, respectively. However, those numbers are generally accepted to be too low, because many Central Americans crossed the U.S.-Mexican border illegally, relying on smugglers when the crossing became too difficult. An estimate placed the number of U.S.-resident Salvadorans in 2000 at 1,117,959, with 2,863,063 Central Americans living in America. Of the Central Americans, Salvadorans comprised the largest proportion, with Guatemalans, Hondurans, and Nicaraguans following in turn. An estimated 25 percent of El Salvador's population is outside the country, due to a combination of factors including the 1980–1992 Salvadoran civil war, economic insecurity, natural disasters, and family members' desires to join their relatives living abroad. Approximately 90 percent of these emigrants live in the United States.[130]

Most Central Americans who immigrated prior to 1979 were likely to have been professionals seeking economic opportunity. 101,330 Central Americans immigrated legally in the 1960s, and 174,640 did so in the 1970s. Of these immigrants, women outnumbered men, and Panamanians were the largest group. Some who worked for U.S. corporations or families in Central America followed their employers back to America to continue working, and subsequent network and chain migration contributed significantly to the acceleration of Central American immigration during the period.

Those who immigrated after 1979 through the 1990s were mainly political refugees or fled economic trouble directly caused by political instability. The Sandinista revolution in Nicaragua in 1979 was followed by peasant movements in El Salvador and Guatemala, and the Reagan administration's backing of both the anti-Sandinista "contras" in Nicaragua and the Salvadoran government made Honduras a staging ground for U.S. and contra operations. Labor activists, student organizers, priests, and opposition leaders were frequently tortured by U.S.-backed factions, and an estimated 200,000 civilians were killed by the death squads and right-wing paramilitary groups in El Salvador and Guatemala.[131]

Many Nicaraguans fled to Costa Rica and the United States (primarily Miami) due to the violence; first, those connected to the old regime overthrown by the Sandinistas, followed by middle-class professionals, then by poor workers and young men avoiding conscription into the conflict. Miami also attracted a number of old Salvadoran elites and Hondurans. Consequently, 50% of Guatamalan and Honduran-descended individuals and 60% of Nicaraguan and Salvadoran-descended individuals in the United States can now trace their or their families' American origins to immigration in the 1980s. Although primarily political refugees, these immigrants were not recognized as such, nor were they granted refugee protection and benefits. In the early 1980s, only 2-3% of Salvadorans and Guatemalans and 10% of Nicaraguans who applied for asylum were approved. A portion of immigrants caught crossing the border illegally were also pressured by INS officials to waive their right to apply for asylum. Accordingly, many of the immigrants remained illegally in the United States, hoping to outlast the violence and eventually return home. Predictably, the longer they stayed in the U.S., the less likely they were to return, and few decided to go back to Central America after peace agreements took place in the 1990s.

However, most of the immigrants can hardly be blamed for their decision to stay. Sporadic fighting between the remnants of guerilla armies and death squads continued in Nicaragua, El Salvador, and Guatemala. Soldiers without a cause found the transition to a life of banditry and crime easily accomplished, and El Salvador gained the highest crime rate per capita in the western hemisphere. Central America continues to be characterized by poverty and unemployment, and hurricanes and earthquakes since the 1990s left thousands dead and millions homeless. Consequently, Central American immigration remained high throughout the 1990s.

Most Central Americans went to urban areas and found jobs in factories, cleaning services, construction, restaurants and hotels, or domestic work, although a number became agricultural workers. In 1990, one third of Central American-descended people in America lived in Los Angeles, with Miami, New York, and Washington D.C. exhibiting large populations, as well. Nicaraguans were the only group of which the majority did not settle in L.A.; they concentrated in Miami, instead, and interacted with the considerable Cuban population in that area. Tensions flared between Central Americans and African Americans, the latter being the ethnicity most prone to displacement from jobs and housing.

Central Americans in America also suffered from relatively high poverty levels due to a combination of little education, the language barrier, and the lack of legal status for many. Moreover, while intraethnic networks made a life in America sustainable for many, they did not provide many avenues for social mobility and a progression to high-wage jobs.

Still, some progress was made in granting relief to displaced Central Americans. The Immigration Reform and Control Act in 1986 gave relief to those who arrived prior to 1981, although the vast majority was not granted amnesty, and the promulgation of stricter regulations regarding the employment of undocumented workers in the act made the immigrants' hold on employment tenuous. Several more victories ensued for proponents of the Central American immigrant cause, including the establishment of temporary protected status for Salvadorans and Nicaraguans in 1990 and a decision in *American Baptist Churches v. Thornburgh* which required INS to reopen 150,000 Guatemalan and Salvadoran asylum cases. 1997 brought the passage of the Nicaraguan Adjustment and Central American Relief Act (NACARA), which negated the effects of the Illegal Immigration Reform and Immigrant Responsibility Act of 1996 (with regards to requirements for the issuance of a stay of deportation) for Salvadorans and Guatemalans who arrived prior to 1990, and furthermore granted an automatic cancellation of deportation for Nicaraguans and Cubans who arrived prior to 1995. Temporary protected status was later extended to many Central Americans after the natural disasters of the late 1990s and 2001.[132]

d. Communist China

Significant changes had also occurred farther north; the Cultural Revolution and the reformation of social institutions within China under Chairman Mao's Red Guard in the 1960s had eliminated the last vestiges of opposition to Mao and his party. However, the interests of China and the Soviets had become increasingly divergent, and American political theorists began to recognize that China's brand of communism was far more independent and nationalistic in character than that in Eastern Europe. After a territorial dispute between the communist giants in 1969, President Nixon and his administration saw an opportunity to reestablish relations with China and coax its leadership further away from any Soviet influence or alliance. Chinese immigration to the U.S. remained low after President Nixon met with Chinese Premier Zhou En Lai, but the historic trip set the foundation for further diplomacy, which would eventually enable the next wave of Chinese to come to the United States.

e. Cubans

A large number of Cubans arrived in the United States after Fulgencio Batista's sudden departure to a life of self-exile on New Year's Eve, 1958, left political power in Cuba in the hands of the popular rebel leader Fidel Castro. Castro moved quickly to consolidate power, first striking at Batista's allies and disbanding the army, jailing or executing those who resisted. He then moved against American corporations and wealthy landowners, the Catholic Church, and the free press in turn, resulting in the expatriation of old regime political adherents, followed by an exodus of middle class and professional workers. By 1980, some 692,219 Cubans immigrated to the U.S. as relations between Fidel Castro and the U.S. government deteriorated and the events of the Bay of Pigs invasion and Cuban missile crisis (along with several misguided assassination attempts) drove Castro to increasingly align himself with the Soviets. [133]

f. Dominicans

Immigration from the Dominican Republic, as with that from other Caribbean and Central and South American states, has been a fairly recent phenomenon. Emigration was restricted until General Rafael Leónidas Trujillo's assassination in 1961, whose death initiated a period of instability after over 30 years of dictatorial rule. The anti-Trujillo Jean Bosch was elected in 1962, but the presence of powerful military, corporate, and religious enemies resulted in the overthrow of his administration a mere 7 months after his inauguration. A series of provisional governments failed in succession amidst a liberal insurgency until 1965, when U.S. troops acted in support of the Dominican government to defeat the insurrectionist *constitucionalistas*. An election was held in which the last of Trujillo's puppet presidents, Joaquín Balaguer, defeated Bosch, whose party remained literally under attack throughout the pre-election campaigns.

Although Balaguer vowed to reinstate many of Trujillo's old policies, he chose not to renew Trujillo's ban on emigration, primarily for political reasons. Trujillo had believed that a low population would inevitably cause a labor shortage and slow economic development. He had therefore worked to discourage emigration while promoting childbirth and European immigration, his success in that regard inflating the Dominican population from 900,000 in 1920 to 3 million by 1961. Balaguer did quite the opposite, being more interested in maintaining political power in the face of revolutionary discontent. He cracked down on dissidents but allowed them to emigrate freely, hoping to drive the rebel element out of the country and solidify his hold on the presidency. In 1959, for example, 1,805 of the 19,631 who applied for passports received them; in 1969, each of the 63,595 people who applied was approved. The simultaneous passage of the U.S. Immigration Law of 1965, which made visas easier to obtain for third world travelers, produced an exodus of Dominicans to America.[134]

As time passed, Balaguer's economic policies triggered wage depression and rising unemployment, forcing additional Dominicans to emigrate. Balaguer encouraged industrialization, but did so in a manner in which capital displaced labor. By 1981, the industries of the Dominican Republic created less than 5,000 new jobs per annum at a time when the working population was growing at a rate of over 56,000 per annum despite the implementation of family planning programs and an aggregate reduction in fertility rates. Even the agricultural sector grew less dependent on Dominican labor, as ranchers used approximately 2 acres per animal for cattle-raising and sugarcane fields imported laborers from neighboring Haiti.

The dual fangs of political oppression and economic recession accordingly led to a steady increase in the number of Dominican immigrants to the U.S. The number of Dominican immigrants recorded rose from 3,045 in 1961 to 12,624, 18,220, and 41,405 in 1971, 1981, and 1991, respectively. As the Dominican Republic lost an estimated 16-23% of its base population in the 1970s, a quarter of Dominican immigrants to America were listed as blue collar workers, 6% had professional or technical skills, and less than half of the aggregate had held jobs at the time of migration.[171] As unemployment rose, the Dominican peso lost value, and the government attempted to compensate by cutting back on public services, slightly more skilled workers immigrated from the Dominican Republic (8% of men and 7% of women), but the majority of Dominicans remained unskilled. As many as two thirds of these traveled to New York and established residence there. Dominicans in New York remained impoverished. In 1992, the death of a Dominican youth suspected of drug dealing at the hands of a police officer led to three days of rioting, drawing national attention to the Dominicans' plight.[135]

g. Haitians

In Haiti, the state-sponsored killing of 30,000-60,000 Haitians led to some degree of emigration during François Duvalier's 14-year reign. However, it was under Jean-Claude "Baby Doc" Duvalier that the economy, and eventually the civil administration, completely collapsed. The amount of Haitians living in extreme poverty rose from 48% in 1976 to 81% in 1985, and the end of the Duvalier era in 1986 was succeeded by a series of military coups and the repression of grassroots movements.

From 1971 to 1980, 56,335 Haitians legally immigrated to the United States, fleeing the terrible economic conditions under Baby Doc. Far more arrived in the following decades as conflict flared on the island, with 138,379 legal Haitian immigrants between 1981-1990 and 179,644 between 1991-2000. Unable to gain immigrant visas, a substantial number of Haitians immigrated illegally as well. From 1985 to 1996, 874,095 Haitians acquired nonimmigrant visas, and as many as half of them chose to overstay in the United States rather than return. Still others attempted to immigrate entirely without visas, as groups of "Haitian boat people" sailed to Florida starting in 1972. These were turned away by the Coast Guard when discovered because they were deemed as economic, not political refugees, thus inadmissible as likely to become a public charge. Some Haitians opted to flee to French-speaking Quebec instead of America.

Haitians who made it to the United States suffered not only poverty and the denial of asylum, but were otherwise generally unwelcomed and discriminated against. Among protests and other open forms of social vituperation, they have been accused of being AIDS carriers, the Food and Drug Administration even prohibiting Haitians from giving blood in 1990. The plight of the Haitians still remains unresolved, with poverty levels remaining inordinately high in both Haiti and the United States. Despite extensive international aid and intervention and relatively free and fair elections being held in 2006, Haiti remains one of the most corrupt states in the world, and Haitians continue to flee the country.[136]

For whatever reason, the U.S. never really treated the Haitians well. They are not entitled to our NACARA, TPS, DED, and most were never granted asylum.

h. Jamaicans

Until 1952, immigrants from Jamaica, as a colony of Great Britain, were included under the large national origins quota allocated to Great Britain, and approximately 150,000 immigrants to the United States hailed from the Caribbean from 1900-1940. However, Congress changed Jamaica's quota to 100 in that year, and did not apply the same provisions for the rest of the western hemisphere to newly independent Caribbean states until 1965. In the interim years, most Jamaicans migrated to Britain, establishing a sizable population in London, and post-1965 Jamaican immigrants to the United States mainly established residence in New York and South Florida. From only 8,659 Jamaican immigrants in the 1950s, 71,011 were counted in the 1960s, and almost 515,000 immigrated from 1971-2000. Additionally, a large number of undocumented immigrants may as much as have doubled the number of Jamaicans coming to the United States. Due in part to its relatively large size and population, the country has consistently ranked at or near the top of West Indian immigration.[137]

An uneven distribution of farmland, stagflation, national debt (with the fourth highest debt per capita in the world), and high crime rates driven by drug trafficking and poverty continue to be motivating factors for Jamaicans immigrating to the United States. There were nearly 1,700 homicides in 2005, and over 1,600 in 2008. The island's organized crime was largely controlled by Colombian groups shipping cocaine to America and supplied with weapons from America. Several egregious social problems also persisted, with violence against women on the rise and the criminalization of homosexuality a contentious issue in Jamaican civil rights.[138]

With a predominantly black population, Jamaica continues to be the largest source of African-descended immigrants to America. The influx has also been one of fairly educated individuals. The number of Jamaican immigrants with a tertiary education stands at 42%, and has become problematic for the country, as an estimated 77% of its most educated citizens have left the country. 6-7% of Jamaican emigrants have been professional or technical workers, many of them nurses.[139]

In the past 20 years or so, I have seen the U.S. immigration services working together with the federal drug force, and the FBI, to investigate Jamaican drug cases. I have seen Jamaicans being treated differently than African Americans and even during a Jamaican funeral the drug forces would come and separate the local African Americans from the Jamaicans and interview only the Jamaicans. Whether warranted or not warranted, I always advise our Jamaican clients to watch who they give rides to, to never borrow luggage or purses from their countrymen to travel, even within the US. We have quite a few cases where dogs at US airports find drugs in luggage where the Jamaican person borrowed the piece of luggage from a fellow Jamaican and did not realize there were hidden compartments with drugs there on a flight from New York to Chicago. We also have cases where the passengers or driver in a car have hashish or marijuana on their bodies and the police charge all the people in the same car with criminal conduct. It is just not fair that a small group of Jamaicans are giving Jamaicans a bad reputation.

i. Koreans

Korean immigration picked up tremendously as a result of the Immigration and Nationality Act of 1965, which abolished the old national origins system and allowed for more racial equality within U.S. immigration. According to U.S. census data, the number of ethnic Koreans in America increased by a staggering amount – 69,150 in 1970 to 798,849 in 1990.

Four main groups of Korean immigrants arrived between the end of the Korean War and 1965, the largest of which consisted of Korean war brides (wives of servicemen), Peace Corps volunteers, and other U.S. citizens. Another group of several thousand was comprised of Korean orphans adopted by primarily non-Korean Americans. The third category was comprised of Korean F-1 students who managed to change their status after graduation from that of students to that of immigrants, and eventually became citizens. Finally, there were a few hundred who came under the national origins annual quota of 100.[140]

Of the Korean immigrants who have entered the U.S. after 1965, most have been well-educated. Some have started small businesses after coming to America, while the rest have largely been professionals. After becoming citizens, most of these bring their families from Korea. Generally, those who come through family-based avenues have been less educated than the relatives who preceded them.[141]

Notably, the newest group of Korean immigrants has been mainly Protestant, and there are today a large number of Korean churches in America.[142] Until very recently, Koreans were predominantly Buddhist; the conversion of the population resulted from the work of American (and to a lesser extent, Canadian) missionaries.

There is a large number of Korean churches in the U.S., and if you have time, do go visit. It is a lot of fun. The newer Koreans mostly came on E-2 and F-1 visas. It is only a few months ago that Korea was added as a visa waiver country. We will see after a few years whether this policy will last, or whether the U.S. will take Korea off the list if too many Koreans overstay.

j. Puerto Ricans

Puerto Rico holds a unique place relative to the United States. After the U.S. took Puerto Rico from Spain in the 1898 Spanish-American War, martial law ruled the island until the implementation of the 1900 Organic Act, also known as the Foraker Act. The Foraker Act erected civil political institutions within Puerto Rico, but the U.S. government retained heavy influence and applied mercantilist policies to the island. The Governor of Puerto Rico (who spoke little Spanish) was appointed by the American President, a minority of the 11 seats in the Executive Council was held by native Puerto Ricans, and decisions made by the elected House of Delegates could be vetoed by Congress or the governor. The Puerto Rican economy was dollarized, unable to trade with other nations or set its own tariffs, and all trade was required to make use of U.S. ships under the Coastwise Shipping Act. U.S. laws applied to Puerto Rico unless specified otherwise, while the Constitution did not due to Puerto Rico being an unincorporated territory. Puerto Rico was granted only an observer status in Washington D.C., and Puerto Ricans were initially not considered U.S. citizens.

These terms were received by many Puerto Ricans, who had only just won greater freedom of self-governance from the Spanish in the 1897 Charter of Autonomy. The situation did not much improve with the passage of the Jones Act in 1917, which gave Puerto Ricans U.S. citizenship and created a 19-member Senate and 39-member House of Representatives in Puerto Rico, but left many stipulations of the Foraker Act unchanged. In fact, things worsened considerably for male Puerto Ricans, as they became citizens just in time for the implementation of the draft during World War I. Still, few Puerto Ricans elected to immigrate to the United States in the years preceding World War II, despite the disastrous 1928 San Felipe hurricane and economic decline. Landowners became indebted to American banks and lost their holdings entirely; and the land was eventually converted to sugarcane plantations. On such plantations in 1929, workers usually earned less than $4 per week and spent 94% of that income on food. Because of the substitution of sugarcane production for other forms of agricultural product, Puerto Rico was forced to import 80% of its food by 1930. During the Great Depression, 15,000 Puerto Ricans died per year as poverty, starvation, and diseases such as hookworm and malaria took their toll. Still, it is unsurprising that average Puerto Rican net immigration was only 2,111 per year from 1900 to 1945; conditions in the United States were not much better for the poor. Most of those who did immigrate during the phase had higher education and moved to New York City.

After World War II, however, a booming U.S. economy enticed Puerto Ricans to immigrate in much greater force. From 1946 to 1964, 34,165 Puerto Ricans immigrated per year seeking economic relief, peaking in 1953 when 74,603 arrived. Notably, this was the first great immigrant wave to arrive in the United States by plane. Two-engine commercial planes could take an individual from San Juan to New York City in 8 hours for the price of $75. By 1973, 40% of all Puerto Ricans lived in the United States.

Some Puerto Ricans arrived in America as agricultural contract workers who spread themselves thinly throughout the U.S. From 1950 to 1977, 350,000 such workers were employed in 22 states. However, like the earlier immigrants, most post-war Puerto Rican immigrants traveled to New York. It is ironic that both the U.S. and Puerto Rican governments facilitated the Puerto Rican migration because Puerto Rico was considered overpopulated at 618 people per square mile, yet most Puerto Ricans gravitated to New York City, where the population density was 90,000 per square mile.

The group was the first natively Spanish-speaking ethnicity to settle in the Northeastern United States en masse. The Puerto Ricans' struggle with learning English in schools, graduating to low-paying and unskilled jobs (for those who obtained jobs), and poor housing conditions grew as a source of concern. Schools usually tracked young Puerto Ricans into vocational training at a time when such jobs were in decline. In New York City, a shift from manufacturing to the service sector particularly hurt Puerto Ricans, 60% of whom were employed in manufacturing and were too frequently unable to speak English fluently enough to make the transition to service jobs. Because the newest immigrants tended to be younger, less skilled, less educated, more likely to be from rural areas, and darker-skinned than the first wave of Puerto Ricans, they also met with more open hostility, racism, and discrimination.

These problems continued to plague the Puerto Rican population in America well after the tide of immigration began to ebb. Between 1964 and 1973, only 66,829 Puerto Ricans immigrated (net), as opposed to 302,293 in the previous decade. Although less of these Puerto Ricans settled in New York City, the ethnicity as a whole experiences dispiriting high school dropout rates, unemployment rates, and poverty. Still, after the economic progress of the 1980s a greater number of Puerto Ricans attained the highest levels of academic and professional achievement, a trend which promises to continue into the future.[143]

I think mainstream Americans do not quite know how to take Puerto Ricans. They are neither Mexicans nor South or Central Americans. They are US citizens at birth, and the newer generations were stuck with not having an identity and not remembering how hard their forebears fought to be a part of America and to be able to fit in.

k. South Americans

Immigrants from South America, like those from Africa, are often overlooked due to their relatively small proportions within their respective ethnicities. South Americans comprise only 5.2% of the Hispanic and Latino population in America, and are spread thinly enough across national ties, class, and geographic location to escape notice. Of the South Americans in the U.S. (both foreign-born and native-born), however, Columbians far surpass the rest in number at an estimated 653,029 in 2000, and rank sixth on the list of most populous Latino groups in America.

From 1960 onwards, many Colombians immigrated to the United States by flying into New York or Miami on tourist visas and simply never leaving. Many of them had left after the terrible events of "La Violencia" in Columbia, an anarchical and violent political period in which civil war between left-wing guerillas and the military caused millions to flee their homes. Later, the ruthless operations of narcotics traffickers and an increasing incidence of kidnappings for ransom maintained Colombia's position as one of the most dangerous countries in the world. The Colombian foreign-born population grew from 12,582 in 1960 to 143,508 in 1980, and finally 509,872 in 2000.[144]

Following Colombian-descended American-residents in volume are Ecuador and Peru with populations of 380,428 and 339,027, respectively, then Argentina and Venezuela with approximately 125,000 individuals each living in the United States in 2000. The rigors of economies in transition and political instability were the stimuli for emigration from those countries, as in Colombia. In Chile, a military coup ending the Pinochet regime led to the exile of thousands in the 1970s, while gross mismanagement by the Argentine government led to economic and civil disorder. More recently, a weakening economy and rising national debt has spurred recent immigration to the U.S. from Argentina, whereas fluctuating oil prices combined with the far left-wing policies of President Hugo Chávez of petroleum-dependent Venezuela to cause both an economic downturn and internal strife.

A high incidence of foreign-born individuals amongst South American-descended residents is indicative of their relatively recent migration to the United States, comparable to the migrations from Central America. Within America, over 70% of Colombians, Ecuadorians, and Peruvians were foreign-born as of 2000. The early immigrants of the 1960s and 1970s were educated upper and middle-class individuals, while recent immigrants have been somewhat less so due to the number of poorer, undocumented immigrants coming from South America. Illegal immigration from South America has increased steadily, facilitated by the establishment of networks extending from the relatively wealthy South American diaspora in America to less affluent friends and relatives left behind. In one such network, Ecuadorians in America arranged for the illegal entry of poorer, rural

Ecuadorians and paid for their passage, allowing the immigrants to pay back the debt at a later date.

Interestingly, despite the relatively high percentage of foreign-born South Americans in the United States who remain unauthorized – 28% of Colombians, 36% of Ecuadorians, 22% of Peruvians, and 32% of Venezuelans – South Americans as an aggregate in the U.S. are generally in better economic standing than Central Americans, Mexicans, or West Indians, with higher mean earnings ($13,911) and a lower poverty level (13.6%) than those from other parts of Latin America. South Americans' socioeconomic standing thus even exceeds the Cubans' (with the caveat that Argentineans and Chileans bring up the mean earnings statistic considerably, as fully one third of immigrants from those countries were employed in professional or managerial occupations in 1999, compared to 17% of Colombians and 14% of Ecuadorians). South American immigrants also exhibit the highest average years of education among those groups at 12.6, a statistic which only Cubans (11.9) and Nicaraguans (12.0) approach.

As previously noted, South Americans not only display a wide range of socioeconomic backgrounds, but did not heavily settle in specific regions of the United States. Their largest concentrations, as of 2000, were in New York, Florida, California, New Jersey, and Texas, yet only in Florida did South Americans represent more than one fifth of the state's Latino population. Their dispersal has made South Americans more prone to rapid acculturation and assimilation, as indicated by a high rate of intermarriage with European-descended individuals, yet second generation South Americans have been shown to generally maintain strong cultural identification with their Latino heritage. Colombians, especially, have become active in campaigning for political candidates in Colombia and encouraging immigrants to vote at U.S. consulates.[145]

I. The American Civil Rights Movement

If some Americans ignored the worldwide turmoil and political upheaval in more distant parts of the world, it was perhaps because of the media's intense focus on the War in Vietnam, and perhaps because another force for social and political change had arisen within the United States itself. In the 1950s, the civil rights movement in the United States had begun, primarily amongst the disenfranchised African American population. Having faced prejudice, discrimination, and other forms of socioeconomic injustice and persecution for centuries, the largely peaceful movement involved the use of "civil disobedience" in the form of boycotts, sit-ins (in which people would occupy seats or spaces prohibited to them as a form of protest against segregation), marches, and demonstrations. Despite harsh or abusive punitive action against demonstrators and the existence of several more violent branches of the movement, including the militant Black Panthers, the movement remained mostly non-violent and began to win victories in court. The first such victory was *Brown v. Board of Education* in 1954, ending segregation by law. The Civil Rights Act of 1964 banned discrimination in public and places of employment, and the Voting Rights Act of 1965 established federal voter registration. This removed the ability of states to create literacy tests and polling taxes discriminatory to African Americans, finally giving such communities a voice in government and a democratic avenue for effecting political change. The Civil Rights Act of 1968 built upon the previous law to ban discrimination within the housing market and protecting civil rights workers, who courageously carried on under threats or acts of violence.

Amongst other feats in its championing of minority causes, the movement had a large impact on immigration law. Earlier calls from Presidents Truman and Eisenhower for immigration reform had fallen on deaf ears on Capitol Hill due to the political precedence of keeping one's constituency satisfied over making concessions for foreign policy considerations. However, the Civil Rights movement had raised awareness of the oppression of minority groups within the United States, and the public attitude towards intolerance and bigotry began to shift. Both major political parties were pro-immigration in the campaigns leading up to the 1960 elections. After Lyndon B. Johnson's election in 1964, several anti-immigration Democrats in Congress finally bowed to presidential pressure and allowed immigration bills to be introduced on the floors of the House and Senate, evoking spirited debates between those who still believed that the ethnic composition of the United States had to be preserved and those who aligned with the Civil Rights movement in promoting racial equality within America. Congress (still dominated by Democrats) finally passed the 1965 Immigration and Nationality Act, extending general regulatory measures but liberalizing or eliminating the provisions of the old national origins system which were based on ethnic and racial factors. Within the act, race and nationality were removed as factors used to restrict immigration, and every country was given an equal quota, including those in the Western Hemisphere. Upon signing the bill into law, President Johnson remarked that the bill was "not a revolutionary bill. It does not affect the lives of millions. It will not reshape the structure of our daily lives, or really add importantly to our wealth or our power." Revolutionary it may not have been, but the law set the foundation for U.S. immigration law as we know it today and allowed many immigrants from the Middle East, Latin America, and Asia to immigrate to the United States.

m. Vietnamese

In Indochina, the communist North Vietnamese led by Ho Chi Minh defeated and cast out French colonial forces. The United States then sent military forces to protect the non-communist South Vietnamese and to prevent the entire region from being swept up in a communist revolution, per the much-touted domino theory. The conflict, and America's eventual withdrawal from Vietnam, caused over 400,000 Indochinese to flee to the United States from 1975-1979, being admitted under 10 parole programs during the Ford and Carter administrations. The 1980 census counted 245,000 Vietnamese, 218,000 Laotians, and 160,000 Cambodians (Kampucheans). Many sought egress on makeshift boats out of desperation. Initially, they stayed in refugee camps while the federal government attempted to resettle them in other countries. Later, they were dispersed to all 50 states by the federal government after the passing of the Refugee Dispersion Policy. Most Vietnamese had to accept low-wage jobs, as the government urged them to find work as soon as possible and attain financial independence.[146]

The children of these Vietnamese Zero generation are now in their 20s to 40s. They are doing really well, writing books, owning restaurants, teaching at university, becoming architects, making their parents proud.

I was having Dim-Sum on September 6, 2009 in Boloong restaurant, a local Cleveland Chinese restaurant. I met up with my old Vietnamese friend and she introduced me to her whole family. She reminded me that I got her the green card in 1983 and since then she became a citizen and she brought her mother here and together they brought her siblings. All her three sons attended or currently attend St. Ignatius, one of the best Catholic high schools in NE Ohio. She is still working as a dishwasher. When I saw the three kids I just knew they would go places. Their journey spanned far greater than mine or us zero generation immigrants could every dream of.

One day they will write about their family's success and become inspirational.

n. African Immigrants

Immigration of Africans to the United States has been a recent trend. Most of the current African immigrants have come to the US within the last twenty or thirty years. During colonial times, the slave trade brought between ten and twenty million Africans to America.[147] Few Africans came to the US after slavery was abolished in the 1800s.[148] African emigration to the US only began increasing between 1900 and 1950, during the period of colonial rule in Africa.[149] During this time, over thirty-one thousand Africans immigrated to the US,[150] but African immigration has been on an incline since. According to the 1970 census figures, about 61,463 Africans were living in the US. By 1980, this number tripled to 193,723. The 1990 census showed more than 362,819 Africans, almost twice as many as in the previous decade. Most recently, the 2000 census counted a total of 881,300 Africans living in the US.[151] Notwithstanding this drastic increase, Africans make up only about three percent of the total foreign-born population in the US.[152]

The 1980 Refugee Act had a major impact upon the number of African immigrants entering the United States, particularly from Ethiopia and Somalia. The Act was largely enacted as a way to allow the United States to live up to the 1967 United Nations Protocol Relating to the Status of Refugees.

In the early 20th century, most African emigrants who left the continent headed for Europe as a consequence of the colonization process. This began to change after 1960 when most African nations became independent from European imperial powers and especially in the 1970's and 1980's when the United States began admitting larger numbers of refugees.

For purposes of classification, the US Census Bureau divides the point of origin for African immigrants into six categories: West Africa, North Africa, Middle Africa, South Africa, and Other (or Unclassified).[153] The countries which fall into each of these regions are as follows:

- North Africa: Morocco (with Western Sahara), Algeria, Tunisia, Libya, Egypt, and Sudan
- West Africa: Mauritania, Senegal, Gambia, Cape Verde, Guinea-Bissau, Sierra Leone, Liberia, Guinea, Burkina Faso, Cote D'Ivoire, Ghana, Mali, Niger, Benin, Togo, and Nigeria.

- Middle Africa: Chad, Cameroon, Central African Republic, Sao Tome and Principe, Equatorial Guinea, Gabon, the Republic of the Congo, the Democratic Republic of the Congo (DRC), and Angola.
- East Africa: Ethiopia, Eritrea, Somalia, Djibouti, Uganda, Rwanda, Burundi, Kenya, Tanzania, Zambia, Malawi, Zimbabwe, Mozambique, Seychelles, Comoros, Mauritius, and Madagascar.
- Southern Africa: Botswana, Namibia, South Africa, Swaziland, and Lesotho.

As of the 2000 Census, West Africans comprised 36% of the total foreign-born population in the United States (326,507 persons counted).[154] After that East Africa comprised 24%, North Africa 22%, Southern Africa 8%, and Middle Africa just 7% of all African immigrants.[155]

As of 2000 the three countries that had the most emigrants living in the United States were Nigeria (134,940), Egypt (113,396), and Ethiopia (69,531), but there is a good chance that all these groups have been undercounted.[156]

Since the 1980's the number of African immigrants being admitted into the United States has been increasing significantly. In 1989 the number of Africans granted permanent resident status was just 25,166. By 2001 this had risen to 53,948.[157] By 2009 this number had more than doubled; 127,050 African immigrants were granted permanent resident status this past year.[158] That many African immigrants were of recent arrival was confirmed by the 2000 Census; over half of African-born individuals had arrived in the 1990's.[159]

Though not as significant as in the past, African immigrants continue to be admitted into the United States under refugee or asylum status. The number of individuals who can enter the United States as refugees has a fixed ceiling every year; in 2009 that ceiling was 80,000 individuals (up from 70,000 in 2007). However, the actual number admitted was only 74,602.[160] The number of individuals admitted into the United States overall has declined significantly over the course of the late 20th century. Immediately after World War II, several hundreds of thousands of displaced persons had been allowed into the U.S. And as recently as the late 80's-early 90's, well over 100,000 people were entering under this status.[161] But shortly thereafter the numbers fell dramatically to a low in 2002 of just over 20,000 individuals. Since then they have risen again to the 74,000+ figure.

In 2009, the ceiling for the entire African continent was just 12,000 individuals. The ceiling has been cut almost in half in just a few years as resources are diverted towards the Middle East and South Asia instead. As a result only a small proportion of African immigrants are now entering the United States as refugees. The largest single groups admitted in 2009 were from Somalia (4,189), Eritrea (1,571), and the DRC (1,135).[162]

Relatively few immigrants are granted asylum in the United States: just over 22,000 in 2009, a full quarter of which came from China alone. The only African country to contribute a significant number to the pool of asylees is Ethiopia (1,113).[163]

West Africa

Western Africans make up the largest portion of African-born immigrants in the US.[164] The 2000 census indicated that the 326,507 Western Africans accounted for thirty-six percent of the African-born population in the US.[165]

Like immigrants from other parts of Africa, West Africans' journey to the US often follows a transnational migratory pattern, which involves traveling to and living in one or more other countries before obtaining the funds and visas for their ultimate destination in the US.[166] Two of the most cited motivations for coming to the US have been the pursuit of post-secondary education and to take advantage of economic opportunities.[167] Other reasons include reuniting with family members and escaping from political terror and instability.[168]

The majority of West African immigrants come from Nigeria (134,940), Ghana (65,572), and Sierra Leone (20,831).[169] As the most populous country in Africa, estimated at 148 million,[170] it is not surprising that Nigerians make up one of the largest groups of African immigrants in the US. There were very few Nigerian-born individuals in the US in the beginning of the twentieth century.[171] Their numbers began to increase noticeably after Nigeria's oil boom in the 1970s made it one of the wealthiest nations in Africa.[172] Many Nigerians, able to establish sufficient funds in order to obtain visas, began coming to the US to study during this period.[173] In fact, in the late 1970s and 1980s Nigeria was among the top six countries that sent students to study in the US.[174] While many initially returned to Nigeria after completing their studies, the political and economic instability in Nigeria that followed the civil war and numerous political coups spurred an influx of Nigerian immigrants during the mid to late 1980s. This internal instability caused a large exodus of professionals and middle-class Nigerians, which contributed to what critics call a "brain-drain" of Nigeria's intellectual resources. The number of Nigerian immigrants has continued to grow. The census counted 91, 499 Nigerian-born individuals living in the US in 1990; this number increased to134,940 by 2000.[175]

Ghana's population, an estimated twenty-three million, is a mere fifteen percent of the Nigerian population.[176] Nevertheless, Ghanaians make up the second largest group of West-African immigrants in the US (65,572).[177] The most significant wave of Ghanaians immigrating to the US occurred in the four decades after Ghana's independence in 1957.[178] After establishing its status of being the first African nation to win its independence, Ghana struggled to institute a successful form of government; it underwent four political coups between 1957 and 1981.[179] Ghana's political turmoil was incited by the fact that the various forms of government and leaders could not deliver on their promises to halt the decline in the country's economy.[180] After a new constitution came into force on January 7, 1993, Ghana's Fourth Republic was established. Since then, Ghana's has experiences relatively peaceful conditions, with 2000 ushering in the first democratic presidential change of power in the country's history.[181] Its political and economic changes have affected Ghanaians' emigration trends. Similarly to Nigerians, many Ghanaians came to the US as students.[182] During the 1980s and 1990s, however, many began coming to the US in search of business opportunities and specialized training and experience.[183]

With its recent peaceable conditions, Ghana has become the host of more than 31,000 refugees and asylum-seekers – the largest refugee population in West Africa.[184] Most of these refugees are from Liberia, another West African country.[185]

The Liberian refugee situation was caused by the country's civil war, which began in 1989 and continued through 1997.[186] The political instability caused Liberians to flee not only to neighboring countries, but to the US as well. Before the civil war, less than 1,000 Liberians came to the US each year.[187] This number began increasing after the war broke out. From 1990 to 1997, the INS reported 13.458 Liberian refugees in the US.[188] This number does not include the estimated 10,000 to 15,000 Liberians who received temporary protected status.[189] The 2000 census counted 39,030 Liberian born individuals living in the US. The end of the civil war meant repatriation to Liberia for some, while others have stayed in their new homes and naturalized. The census indicated that 10,785 Liberians were naturalized US citizens by 2000.

Sudan

Civil wars in Sudan have claimed at least 2 million lives and displaced more than 5 million since 1983.[190] From 1983 until 2005, 22,647 Sudanese immigrated to the United States, most as refugees. In the absence of large preexisting concentrations of Sudanese who could absorb so many immigrants, Sudanese refugees were widely distributed across the United States where church and community groups could provide the particularly high level of support needed for their acclimation to American life.

American television and newspapers have documented particularly well the heartbreaking stories of the young men brought to the United States in the spring of 2001. Airplanes landed in forty metropolitan areas throughout the U.S. delivering 3,800 refugees, almost all young men in the late teens and early twenties. Among the "Lost Boys of Sudan" were only eighty-nine young women. When villages were attacked, girls were raped, killed, taken as slaves to the north, or became servants or adopted children for other Sudanese families. As a result, relatively few girls made it to the refugee camps. The younger boys survived in large numbers because they were away tending herds or were able to escape into the nearby jungles.[191]

Somalia

The first Somali immigrants came to the United States in the 1920s and settled in the New York area, but their numbers were modest.

On July 1, 1960, former British and Italian Somalia merged to form the new, independent Somali Republic. From then until 1969, the democratic government gradually lost support, and, in that year, a popular military regime backed by the Soviet Union put an end to what was widely believed to be an inefficient and corrupt government. The U.S. withdrew its support, and after a territorial war with its neighbor Ethiopia, the Soviet Union, its protector and source of investment and aid, also withdrew support.

Somalia is almost universally considered a failed state, and it remains one of the most insecure places in the world, with an unprecedented humanitarian crisis. Despite the election of a moderate, former member of the Islamic Courts as President in January 2009, fighting between the Transitional Federal Government (TFG) and Islamist fundamentalist insurgents of Al Shabaab and Hizbul Islam continue unabated. In May, the fighting intensified in Mogadishu and displaced more than

270,000 people, causing the number of internally displaced persons (IDPs) to reach 1.5 million people.[192]

Not surprisingly, virtually all the Somalis to enter the United States during the past twenty years have come as refugees. In the mid-1980s, small numbers of Somalis were admitted to the United States as refugees. In 1990, as a result of the civil war, their numbers increased. From 1983 through 2005, they were the 8th largest group of refugees to come to this country. Approximately half their 46,000 number were settled in the five metropolitan areas of Twin Cities (14%), Washington DC (10%), Atlanta (9%), San Diego (9%) and Seattle (4%).[193]

Over a half-million Somali refugees still live in camps throughout Ethiopia (home to about 68,000) and Kenya (home to over 300,000 in a single refugee camp in Dadaab and hundreds of thousands of others in Nairobi and the northern part of the country).[194195]

One tribe of Somalis, the Somali Bantu, is eligible for automatic asylum in the United States if they can prove their origins. Tracing their roots to Mozambique, Tanzania, and Malawi, 25,000 to 50,000 of their ancestors were enslaved in the 18th and 19th centuries and brought to Somalia. Even after they were released from slavery beginning in 1895, they were forced to work for colonial plantations and remained at the lowest rungs of society. With their darker complexion, they look different from the more Arab looking Somali population. Their distinctive physical appearance has been the basis for continued discrimination and abuse in Somalia, where they are relegated to agriculture, manual labor, and mechanical work - all low-status jobs. Access to education is restricted, and the majority of adults have very little formal education. This means that many adults are pre-literate and most have had little exposure to urban settings and Western cultures. The U.S. government agreed to resettle the Somali Bantu only after efforts by the United Nations to move them to Mozambique failed.[196]

Southern Africa

Immigrants from Southern Africa make up a relatively smaller share of the total African foreign-born population in the United States. In 2009, 127,050 immigrants from Africa gained legal permanent resident status.[197] South African countries that have contributed to that total include: South Africa (3,171), Zimbabwe (983), Mauritius (110), Madagascar (71), Mozambique (66), Botswana (55), Namibia (53), Swaziland (42), and Lesotho (14).[198] These nine countries therefore only comprised about 3.5% of the total African population that gained permanent resident status in 2009. Of these, only South Africa and Zimbabwe have regularly contributed over 100 new permanent residents annually over the past decade.

The region also has produced relatively few refugees and asylum seekers over the past decade. Most of the countries in Southern Africa are relatively stable and not currently experiencing any civil wars, droughts, or unusual conditions of hardship. The one exception is Zimbabwe. Due to the political situation involving President Mugabe and the resulting food shortages, the number of asylum-seekers from Zimbabwe has risen sharply since 2000; ten years ago there were virtually none while since 2003 the country has averaged about 175 a year.[199]

South Africa

Before 1950 there were very, very few immigrants from South Africa coming to the United States. In fact, the country had been much more of an immigrant-receiving country for most of its history.[200] Strategically located on the cape of Africa on the trade routes between Europe and Asia, the Dutch first set up trading posts there in the 1600's. The British would seize these posts during the Napoleonic Wars and make South Africa a British colony in 1806. However, Dutch-speaking settlers known as Boers continued to make up a majority of the white population. That began to change with the discovery of huge despots of gold and diamonds in South Africa. The result was two wars between the Boers and the British, ending in British victory.

By the mid-20th century the industrialization of the country and mining industry had attracted thousands of immigrants from around the world, especially other British colonies. But in 1948 the white supremacist National Party gained power and enacted the system of apartheid that would last until 1990. Emigrants now began to flow in reverse; many would come to the United States. Since the end of apartheid the flow has not stopped. In fact, it has gotten stronger. Since 1994 more people have left South Africa than have immigrated there.[201] Just over half of all foreign-born South Africans living in the United States in 2000 had immigrated within the previous decade.

A large majority of South Africans who immigrated to the United States over the past 50 years are white descendents of the British and Dutch colonizers of the prior centuries; as of 2000 they make up around 82% of the total population.[202] Racial tensions after the fall of the apartheid system have led many whites to emigrate away from the country, primarily to other English-speaking countries. This immigrant group is one of the most highly-educated and economically successful groups in the United States today.[203]

Zimbabwe

Zimbabwe's past is tied to that of South Africa in many ways but the end of "whites-only" rule came more violently. With most of Africa gaining independence in the 1960's, the white minority in Zimbabwe seized the initiative from Great Britain and unilaterally declared independence in 1965. This was done to avoid Britain's plans for a multi-racial democracy; instead, it ushered in a civil war that would tear the country apart until 1979. Robert Mugabe, leader of the Zimbabwe African National Union, a militant resistance movement during the civil war, was elected President of the new country in 1980. He has held that position ever since, suppressing or crushing his political opposition, and creating an economic and food crisis within the country by the year 2000.

The result has been several 'waves' of emigrants leaving Zimbabwe. The first, which took place in the late 70's at the end of the civil war, seriously depopulated the white minority in the country. In 1978 Zimbabwe's white population stood at 280,000; by 1980 it had fallen to just 100,000.[204] The first group of Zimbabwe immigrants to reach the United States was therefore almost entirely white. Later waves, however, proved to be many asylum-seekers fleeing the government of Mugabe. Today about 41% of foreign-born immigrants from Zimbabwe in the United States are white and 49% are black.[205] Both groups tend to be well-educated and immigrants from South Africa and Zimbabwe, overall, tend to enter better-paying jobs in America than their counterparts from other African nations.

Botswana

Botswana's stability and prosperity have largely kept its population at home in modern times. Only very small numbers of native Botswanans immigrate to the United States. This was due to the discovery of huge diamond mines not long after gaining independence from the British in the 1960's. Unlike Zimbabwe and South Africa, Botswana was never dominated by a powerful white minority after independence and thus was spared many of the racial tensions that afflicted both of those countries. In fact the wide availability of jobs and its open borders made Botswana an attractive destination for refugees and others fleeing turmoil in its neighbors. Between 1971 and 2001 the foreign national population increased six-fold.[206] Before the discovery of its mineral wealth, Botswana was poor, sparse and sent many of its people abroad to work in mines. Today it is a favored destination for other peoples across the region.

Eastern Africa

East Africa, which has played host to human habitation which dates back several thousand years, encompasses the countries of Djibouti, Ethiopia, Eritrea, Somalia, Sudan, Kenya, Tanzania, Uganda and Mozambique.[207] East African immigration to the United States has been a recent phenomenon. During the first half of the 20th century, immigration from East Africa was particularly sparse; fewer than 1,000 East Africans arrived in the United States before 1960. The few individuals who made the journey to the United States were predominantly male students sent by their governments to study and then return to serve in high ranking positions. Among these early travelers was President Obama's father, a Kenyan economist who studied at the University of Hawaii in the late 1950s.[208]

Beginning in the early 1970s, an amalgamation of political and economic factors precipitated a dramatic increase in immigration from East Africa. Famine, drought and the violence of the regimes of Ido Amin and Milton Obote in Uganda and the Derg Military Junta in Ethiopia, to name particular examples, resulted in large scale migrations across the region. From 1970 to 1990, around 59,000 East African immigrants were admitted in to the United States. That number increased to 130,000 during the course of the last decade of the 20th century. These immigrants primarily settled in larger cities across the United States. Washington D.C., Portland, Oregon, Minneapolis–St. Paul, Columbus, Ohio and New York City are homes to large East African communities.[209]

Kenya

Kenyans have been among the most successful immigrant groups in the United States, ranking highly on statistical measures of social and economic success. On average, Kenyans exceed U.S. national averages for years of education, median household income, and poverty and employment levels.[210] This success may be explained in part by the familiarity of Kenya's people with western culture and the English language.

The British colonized Kenya in the late 19th and early 20th century, first through the establishment of the British East Africa Protectorate in 1885, followed thereafter by official colonization in 1920. British colonization dispossessed native Kenyans of their most fertile and arable lands, and denied them political representation.[211] The seeds of a post colonial Kenya were planted in the waning days of World War II. A number of Kenyans sought alongside the British, and after the conclusion of the war, these former soldiers brought their organizational and military skills to use in planning for a post-colonial Kenya. The bloody Mau Mau rebellion, which lasted from 1952-56 galvanized Kenyans to participate in politics. (Rudolph). Kenya finally gained its independence in 1963. Within two decades, Kenya became one of Africa's more viable and stable countries.

Mirroring general East African trends, Kenyan immigration to the United States grew exponentially in the 1980s and 1990s. Kenyan immigration in the 1990s nearly tripled from the prior decade; from around 9,000 people to almost 29,000. Unlike some immigrant groups from other parts of Africa, Kenyan immigrants were not motivated to emigrate because of sectarian strife and oppression, rather, an economic depression and a high unemployment rate motivated Kenyans, often well educated, to pursue economic opportunities in the United States. Additionally, immediate English fluency has significantly eased the transitions Kenyans face in adapting to life in the U.S.

Ethiopia

Ethiopia is the oldest independent country in Africa. The country can trace its origins back 3,000 remained independent from European rule for all but five years of its history.[212] The origins of modern Ethiopian immigration to the United States can be traced back to the ascension of Emperor Haile Selassie in 1930.[213] Emperor Selassie introduced Africa's first constitution, and after he was restored to power following Italy's withdrawal after World War II, the Emperor oversaw two decades of economic stability. Selassie's government encouraged Ethiopians to travel to the West to complete their higher educations. Between 1941 and 1974, over 20,000 accepted the Emperor's invitation. Many returned to Ethiopia, drawn back by the promise of lucrative jobs in Ethiopia's government.[214] Despite Selassie's success in maintaining a stable economy, the Emperor's regime stifled political expression and exploited ethnic, religious and class differences to maintain his rule. In September of 1974, a Marxist military junta, known as the "Derg", overthrew Selassie and imposed a Soviet style militant socialism.

The tumult which ensued from Selassie's overthrow forced thousands to seek refuge in neighboring countries. This instability was exacerbated by factionalism within the Derg. In 1977, Major Mengistu Haili Miriam became the new leader of the Derg. Mengistu imposed a particular brutal regime on Ethiopia, which became known as the "Red Terror". Famine and drought in the early 1980s made life unbearable in Ethiopia. Western governments, including the United States, began admitting Ethiopian refugees from the camps bordering Ethiopia.[215] Changes in U.S. law further benefitted Ethiopians fleeing the derg. Motivated in part by its desire to combat the spread of African Marxism, the United States passed the

Refugee Act of 1980, which had the effect of raising the numerical limits on refugee admissions and expanding the qualifications for persons pursuing refugee status.[216] The Mengistu regime was overthrown in 1991.[217] Conflict with Eritrea, which seceded from Ethiopia in 1993, continued to plague Ethiopia. In 1998, Ethiopia and Eritrea fought a two year war over disputed border regions. The war brought about mass displacement of the populations of both countries.

Ethiopian immigrants have primarily settled in Los Angeles, Washington D.C., Dallas and New York City; cities that already had established Ethiopian communities.[218] Many Ethiopians have found adjusting to life in the United States difficult. One study has found that Ethiopians could not adjust to the "fast pace and 'fend for yourself' mentality of a Western society.[219] However, those who migrated to areas with established Ethiopian communities have found the transition easier due to availability of a support network.

Uganda

Along with Kenya, Zanzibar and Pemba, Uganda became a British protectorate following the Treaty of Berlin in 1890. Although few Europeans settled in Uganda, large numbers of Asians from the British commonwealth moved to Uganda. There, they served as middlemen between the Colonialists and native Ugandans, and thus made up the backbone of the country's trade and industry.

Led by Milton Obote, a former schoolteacher, Uganda gained its independence from Britain in 1962. Thereafter, Obote suspended the country's constitution, and centralized power within his office. In 1971, Obote was ousted in a military coup led by commander Idi Amin who soon thereafter, declared himself president. Amin's regime was characterized by large-scale repression, murder and terror. Amin particularly distrusted Uganda's 80,000 strong Asian community. In 1972, Amin, claiming he was inspired by a dream, ordered 60,000 Asians to leave the country within 90 days. The majority of the Asian community were holders of British passports, and eventually settled in the United Kingdom.[220] In 1978, Amin entered into a disastrous war with Tanzania, which resulted in his ouster two years later. In 1980, Obote returned from exile. However, Obote's regime soon matched Amin's in its brutality.

Numerous native Ugandans fled Amin and his successors, though relatively few sought refuge in the United States. 2,549 Ugandans arrived in the United States between 1970 and 1979. That number increased to 3,143 between 1980 and 1989.[221] Of those who arrived, few were granted permanent residence. From 1946 to 1996, with several exceptions, generally fewer than 50 Ugandans annually received permanent resident status in the United States.[222] (Miller). Ugandan communities are prevalent in metropolitan areas such as Atlanta, Sacramento, Dallas and St. Petersburg. Ugandan immigrants face mixed acculturation problems. Because English is the official language of Uganda, newly arrived immigrants seldom face language barriers; however American culture and technology may seem daunting to some Ugandan immigrants.

SECTION II

IMMIGRATION PAPERWORK AND THE LEGAL PROCESS

1. IMMIGRATION LAW CHANGES 1980 TO PRESENT

The most recent decades of the U.S. immigration experience have been some of the most evolutionary and liberal in the history of immigration policy and law, the fears of the past have continually resurfaced to challenge our capacity to grow and unite. I'm very fortunate to have begun my practice in the 1970s and seen the evolution. So much has happened. The Cold War ended with the collapse of the Soviet Union and the fall of the Berlin Wall. Borders long closed were finally open again to trade and migration, the newest phase of globalization has connected economies like never before, and health and financial shocks have been translated throughout the intricate networks of human commerce and interaction to affect the entire world.

Reflecting equitable trends within immigration law, there was increased diversification of the foreign-born population within the latter half of the 20th century. In 1960, 75% of the foreign-born population was of European origin. That number shrank to 39% in 1980 and 15.3% in 2000, surpassed by immigration from Latin America and Asia, which grew (as a percentage of the foreign-born population) from 9.4% to 33.1% to 51%, and from 5.1% to 19.3% to 25.5% in those years. The Filipino population doubled from 1980 to 1990, growing from 774,652 to 1,419,711.[223]

Not all persons who apply for asylum status get approved. Each asylum officer and immigration judge works and thinks differently. Just because a client has a good, credible and non-frivolous asylum case, doesn't mean that we don't have to think outside the box to get them the green card faster.

Before you file for asylum, you need to be on U.S. soil. You can try to come illegally, but it is getting very difficult. It is always better to come as a tourist with an approved tourist visa. We have a client who came to us with a B-2 visa after a few denials. We filed for asylum and also a labor certification and I-140 for her prior to the adjudication of the asylum application. During the individual hearing the Immigration Judge approved her green card based on the labor certification and job offer.

On the legal side, the 1980 Refugee Act was the first major piece of legislation creating a systemic method for evaluating and admitting refugees for humanitarian reasons; setting an aggregate cap of 270,000 immigrants (70,000 refugees) with no more than 20,000 allowed from any individual country in a year. No sooner had the act passed than the Mariel crisis arose, as a dispute over the fate of some 3,500 Cuban asylees in the Peruvian Embassy at Havana resulted in an announcement by Fidel Castro that any Cuban wishing to emigrate would not be stopped. Despite harsh limitations on the belongings such emigrants could carry with them, 125,266 Cubans availed themselves of the sudden opportunity and boarded 2,011 boats captained largely by Cuban exiles living in Miami. All but 2,500 of the "Marielites" were able to gain permanent resident status in the United States, classified as "Cuban-Haitian Entrants" under a special provision. Haitians spotted attempting to make landfall on U.S. shores, on the other hand, were most often deemed economic refugees, denied entry, and towed back to their country by the Coast Guard.[224]

Despite the abolition of the old ethnic quota system and new measures taken to consider and alleviate the plight of refugees, illegal immigration continued to be a problem. To this end, the Immigration Reform and Control Act (IRCA) of 1986 both granted amnesty to the approximately 3 million illegal immigrants who had entered the U.S. prior to January 1, 1982, and imposed harsh sanctions upon employers who failed to provide valid I-9 forms for employees to the government. Although the IRCA was a compromise of sorts, controversy arose over its efficacy and justifiability. Opponents from both sides chimed in, arguing either that giving amnesty to illegal immigrants would further encourage illegal immigration, or that harsher penalties for employers caused unnecessary discrimination against legal foreign-appearing workers, of whom there were many. The Immigration Marriage Fraud Amendments Act put the burden of proving the legitimacy of marriages between USCs or permanent residents and foreign nationals on the couples, as such marriages would be henceforth presumed illegitimate until proven otherwise.

Throughout the 1990s, some 800,000 to 900,000 people immigrated to America each year. This was in part because of the Immigration Act of 1990 (IMMACT 90), a piece of legislation designed to replace the 1952 Immigration and Nationality Act. Prior to IMMACT 90, most, if not all, employment-based immigrants needed employer sponsors. The immigrants were required to work for the sponsoring employer for up to a year after receiving a green card. At present, under AC21, foreign nationals must work for at least 6 months after filing for their green card, and all of the 6 months following the green card's approval. Separate quotas for family-based and employment-based immigration were also established in IMMACT 90.

Within the law, allowed amounts for total immigration was increased to 700,000 per year from 1992-1994, with a flexible cap of 675,000 afterwards. Perhaps more importantly, the law redefined the ideological stance immigration officials should take regarding exclusion and deportation (for example, a bar was removed against communists), and diversity was actually promoted rather than discouraged as in the past. The "diversity lottery" system facilitated immigration from countries whose nationals were underrepresented in the U.S., and "family chain migration" increased from countries such as Mexico, India, and China. Irish immigration was also relatively high due to the efforts of proponents such as the late Senator Kennedy; between 1992 and 1994, 40% of the 100,000 lottery visas went to Ireland. In 1995, the diversity program was finalized, with 50,000 visas reserved for countries from which less than 50,000 people had come in the previous five years. IMMACT 90 also modified non-immigrant definitions and created new visa classifications such as the O (extraordinary ability), P (internationally recognized athletes and entertainers), Q (cultural exchange), and R (religious workers) categories.

The collapse of the Soviet Union prompted changes within immigration law, and several additional moves towards liberalization were made with the sudden disappearance of the rival superpower. Temporary measures to deal with issues of the time, such as the Chinese Student Protection Act after the June 4th Tiananmen Square incident, the Soviet Scientists Immigration Act of 1992, and the granting of Temporary Protected Status for refugees from Lebanon, El Salvador, and other countries reveal a certain degree of increased lenience towards foreigners and people without status whom lawmakers had previously sought to exclude. In 1994, the

North American Free Trade Agreement (NAFTA) Implementation Act was passed and allowed professional and certain business workers from Canada and Mexico to enter the U.S. for temporary work, much like the H-1B worker category, but without the levels of different tiers. Replacing the previous 1988 agreement with Canada only, NAFTA placed higher restrictions on Mexican workers, requiring Mexicans to carry more documentation, acquire nonimmigrant visas for children and spouses, and limiting the number of petition approvals per year to 5,500 while Canada had no admissions cap.

Illegal immigration to the United States did not abate; legal means to enter the country are unavailable to many, the borders of the country are simply too large to secure completely, and economic interaction with Canada and Mexico preclude controlling border crossings too tightly. As the federal government was slow to find effective means to control illegal immigration, political pressure within the sections of the country most affected once again provided the impetus for state-level action. Notably, California voters approved a proposition to deny illegal immigrants access to publicly funded healthcare, education, and welfare in 1995. Although ruled unconstitutional later, such moves prompted Congress to reform immigration law and related spheres with three laws in 1996. The first of the three, the Antiterrorism and Effective Death Act, provided measures for excluding and deporting foreign terrorists and criminals. The Personal Responsibility and Work Opportunity Reconciliation Act in August of the same year reduced the amount of federal social benefits such as food stamps and social security income available to even legal permanent residents in the U.S. in an effort to discourage all forms of immigration. Within the Illegal Immigration Reform and Immigrant Responsibility Act (IIRIRA), the 3/10 year bar was established, grounds for deportation were expanded, illegal immigrants' access to court hearings were hindered, border security was tightened, asylum was granted less often to refugees, and many avenues for illegal immigrants to gain legal status while within the United States were closed. IIRIRA also established minimum income requirements and the mandatory affidavit of support for family-sponsored immigrants. Despite the passage of IIRIRA, some number of refugees continued to enter the country. While the amount of African immigration amounted to a trickle relative to that from other areas of the world, perpetual conflict within African states provided for the relief of 25,929 Somalis, 14,551 Liberians, 13,200 Sudanese, 7,437 Ethiopians, and 5,675 refugees from Sierra Leone between 2000 and 2004.[225]

While some laws had limited immigrants' rights and the admittance of refugees, progress was made in the realms of family reunification and relief for victims of crime and abuse. The Child Citizenship Act, passed in October 2000, now grants citizenship to LPR children younger than 18 living with a USC parent in the United States. The Legal U.S. Immigration Family Equity (LIFE) Act was passed 2 months later and extended the deadline for benefits under 245(i) of the Immigration and Nationality Act to April 30, 2001. The LIFE Act also created 2 visa categories which facilitate family reunification. The K visa is given to fiancés (K-1, K-2) and spouses of USCs (K-3, K-4) and their children, while the V visa allows certain LPR spouses and children to stay in America while waiting for a green card.

The T visa category was created by the Trafficking Victims Protection Act of 2000, and allows people who have been trafficked into the U.S. to remain in the U.S. while the case against their trafficker is pursued. It is believed that as many as

50,000 people, mostly women and children, are trafficked into the US each year and are often forced to live in slavery-like conditions. The visa was created in the hope that victims offered a way to remain in the US lawfully would be more willing to contact authorities with information about traffickers.

In 2002, Congress passed the Victims of Trafficking and Violence Protection Act (VTVPA). The VTVPA created a special nonimmigrant classification, designated as the U visa, for victims of specific crimes. This visa status grants temporary immigration benefits to certain victims of crimes who assist government officials in investigating or prosecuting relevant criminal activity. A renewal of the Violence Against Women Act in 2005 later amended regulations for T and U visas to better protect trafficked women.

The 2002 Child Status Protection Act (CSPA) allowed many older children to obtain green cards via their parents. CSPA locks in the age of green card applicants' children on the date that the principal visa holder's priority date becomes current, less the number of days the petition is pending, as long as the beneficiary applies for permanent resident status within one year of the visa availability date. Also, CSPA locks in age of USC's child at time petition is filed.

Many things changed with the events of September 11, 2001. The day forever altered the way Americans who witnessed the destruction of the twin towers viewed the world and created lasting effects in many aspects of American life, not least of which was greatly increased security. Fearing that additional terrorist attacks would come and prove disastrous for the country, the government began to crack down on illegal immigrants and was granted greatly expanded powers for ferreting out those who meant to do the U.S. harm. The USA PATRIOT Act (signed into law on October 26, 2001) gave the government the ability to detain suspected terrorists indefinitely, some 1,200 residents of South Asian and Middle Eastern descent were rounded up and held without the right to due process. Broad changes were made to the very infrastructure of the government's security apparatus in the form of immigration operations being moved under the direction of the newly created Department of Homeland Security (DHS) as three departments: U.S. Citizenship and Immigration Services (USCIS), Immigration and Customs Enforcement (ICE), and Customs and Border Protection (CBP). By assigning immigration to the Department of Homeland Security, America was, in essence, placing emphasis on immigration as a national security concern, marking a major shift in immigration policy.

In 2002/2003, further measures were taken to provide Americans with at least the semblance of heightened security. No-fly lists prohibited those named from entering or reentering the country, and non-immigrant males 16 years of age and older from 24 Middle Eastern countries (all but one of which are notable for having large Muslim populations) were required to be registered and fingerprinted under "Special Registration" for a short time in 2002. 13,000 of these people were put in deportation proceedings in what became the largest such program targeting a specific ethnic group since World War II. Another event of 2003 was the passing of the National Defense Authorization Act, which expedited the USC application process for military personnel and allowed servicemen/women's parents, spouses, and children to become LPRs or USCs.

In 2005, the REAL ID Act made it harder for immigrants to get asylum, expanded grounds for deportation further, and limited the issuance of driver's licenses and state ID documents to certain classes of legal immigrants. A plethora of state legislation also began to appear, with 150 anti-immigrant bills introduced in thirty states. Although most of these proposals didn't make it into law, Arizona's Proposition 200 survived and required local and state government employees to report illegal immigrants attempting to procure public health and social services to immigration officials. Under the Georgia Security and Compliance Act, which easily cleared the state legislature in 2006, employers are required to check the legal status of immigrants seeking work in federal databases; proof of legal status was made necessary for dispensation of state social benefits; workers without taxpayer identification numbers are required to pay a 6% state withholding tax; immigrants jailed for DUIs or felonies are to have their status checked and reported to immigration officials if found to be in the country illegally; finally, local law enforcement officers are authorized to obtain federal training in enforcing immigration laws. One of the last major legal changes prior to the writing of this book was the initiation of PERM (Program Electronic Review Management), which started in March 2005 after more than 10 years of deliberation between the Labor Department and immigration officials. Prior to PERM, employers could pay as little as 95% of the prevailing wage to immigrant workers, which only had two wage levels. Under PERM, the employer must pay 100% of the prevailing wage under four wage levels. In July 2007, the Labor Dept. came up with new rules disallowing the substituting of employees in approved labor certificates to allow a different alien to apply for the green card. The rules also required an I140 to be filed within 6 months of the Labor certification approval. If this I-140 is not filed, the Labor Certificate is rendered useless.

Upon sailing into New York harbor, immigrants of the past were greeted by the majestic Statue of Liberty, not only a powerful symbol for freedom from slavery, oppression and tyranny, but also a constant reminder of the pact of friendship between the United States and France in which the nation was born. Her left hand holds a tablet representing knowledge, while the torch in her right embodies enlightenment, the advent of a new age of reason and the right of the individual. However, the nation was forged not only in amity and liberty, but the founding fathers codified the right of individuals to freedom under the rule of law. This seemingly paradoxical duality has become the strength of a society committed to a path of self-determination amidst the perils of tyranny on one side and anarchy on the other. Lady Liberty does not bear her burden alone; Lady Justice has an equal share in presiding over the land of the free.

Today, immigrants no longer pass through the gates at Castle Garden and Ellis Island, but the vision of America as a country of opportunity and freedom remains. Still, times have changed and the law has evolved in response to growing challenges to the existence of an American dream. An immigrant's journey toward a new life in the United States can become mired in an obtrusive, tedious and often nebulous legal process. The difficulties inherent in beginning anew may be many, but the bureaucracy and technicalities of the law should be the only first hurdle on one's path, not the last. Immigration law is still under constant scrutiny, and it is highly probable that a comprehensive review of the immigration system will occur in coming years. As xenophobia often becomes a problem in times of economic difficulty and national crisis, laws often reflect shifts in public opinion. Other international events may also change America's perception of foreign nationals – both those already in the United States and those who have not yet arrived.

Immigration, both legal and illegal, will continue to be an issue of vital importance for the American people well into the future, and may very well command the fate of the nation as the forces of globalization and integration continue to shape the world.

The immigration process is complicated, but ultimately conquerable. The remainder of the book is devoted to modern law and navigating the legal journey of the 21st century immigrant to America. The U.S. immigration system identifies four distinct categories of people in the United States: citizens, legal permanent residents (green card holders), visa holders, and illegal immigrants. Each immigrant's setbacks and triumphs while climbing the ladder of American society remain unique; each individual must follow a different path. However, from the very beginning of one's journey seeking legal entry to the U.S. to earning permanent residency, acquiring citizenship, and even fighting the loss of status, detention, and deportation, one truth remains constant: that having the belief and the will to overcome is the surest means to become an American.

Generally, because I am an immigration lawyer and my intent is really to write a book for immigrants and immigrant practitioners to help aliens, in the manner of the legal system, to stay legally and not be labeled an "illegal", this section may have repetitions since without the parallel tracks and repeated terms I can't explain concepts.

2. 66 POINTS TO REMEMBER

1. Most filings to immigration have associated fees – remember to add a personal check, money order or certified money order with the filing. Do not ever let your personal checks bounce. Asylum filings do not require a filing fee.
2. USCIS personnel's livelihood is supported by fees for filings, so our government wants your money. USCIS is solely supported by filing fees.
3. Certain visa petitions have premium processing. The fee is $1000 for premium processing, payable to USCIS. Check the web or check with your lawyer to see what visa petitions are eligible. If yours is, it may be worthwhile to pay – you will get an answer in less than 15 days. As of today's writing, old visas, H1, and extensions of H1 have premium processing. Certain I-140 petitions that are required for H-1B extensions also have it.
4. The filing fee for green card applications has been raised to $1010. This includes work permit requests and advance parole requests. Do not travel on your advance parole if you have any out of status issues (only exception is J-1 D/S and F-1 D/S status), because even though the advance paroles are granted by USCIS, you may not be able to come back. Even if you can come back, you may have other issues and may be precluded from adjusting status. A U.S. citizenship application N400 is $675. You are allowed to take a total of two tests (so you have another chance if you fail your first test on English, history, or writing).
5. You can access all forms at www.uscis.gov.
6. All priority dates and quotas are based on place of birth, not nationality. For example: If you were born in Russia, immigrated to Canada at a young

age and now carry a Canadian passport, and want to immigrate to the U.S., your quota is based on Russia, not Canada.

7. Remember your file number, it is referred to as A-number (Alien number) and is an 8 or 9 digit number which is preceded with a letter A. If you file only an NIV petition with USCIS, or a visa petition, there will not be an A-number. The file will be identified by the receipt notice number on the Filing Receipt, usually starting with LIN, EAC, WAC, etc.
8. You can call the number on your receipt for the status of cases. Be nice on the phone. Do not harass the phone people, who are probably subcontractors with answers in a book in front of them. The number is 800-375-5283.
9. All requests to USCIS, ICE and CBP always, always need to have the following information. Otherwise your letter goes to LaLaLand.
    - Alien number –OR-
    - Receipt notice number of the filing –OR-
    - Foreign-born's full name, underline last name, date of birth, and place of birth AND
    - Petitioner's full name, foreign-born's full name, date and place of birth AND
    - Petitioner's full name and A-number
10. If filing for asylum, remember the concept of "firm resettlement"; why can't the foreign-born and his family live in their adopted country that already granted them a passport or stay or a landed immigrant status?
11. If filing for asylum, remember to consider why you and your family can't move to another city in the country where you came from if the persecution is only in a region of the country. Our law is that unless you also cannot live in the other regions and cities of your home country you cannot be granted asylum. This may be a ground to deny asylum.
12. *Always* think strategy and ask what is it that you truly want to do. Remember the real reason why you came to the U.S. to start with – was it to realize your dream of being a doctor? To get a Ph.D.? To work and send money home to support your family? Do you want to retire in the U.S., or go back home? If you want to stay, you really do need a green card. If you want to really make money and send it home, then work with a legal work permit but save the money and don't spend it.
13. Make sure everything is correct and that the filing fee checks are addressed to the correct agency, with the correct name. If anything on the check is wrong, the whole filing takes a few weeks to bounce back and you miss your filing deadline. Make sure the forms are signed by the correct person. Children under 14 cannot sign their own forms, but do not leave this part blank. The parent can sign on their behalf. Make sure all the supporting evidence is included in order to avoid a Request for Evidence (RFE) or Notice of Intent to Deny (NOID).
14. Ensure you mail the application by a courier service or in a manner that you can track the package so you have evidence of delivery.
15. Keep all immigration documents and old passports. These are your proof of legal status and compliance with the laws.

16. Do not listen to rumors and chatter from friends, relatives, or the internet; do what you need to do to survive. Have faith in our country and that our government will do the right things. Don't be scared.
17. Always check USCIS, ICE, and State Department headquarter memos - they are binding rules for the USCIS/ICE/CBP adjudicators, though not for the courts. They are directives from the USCIS General Counsel's Office for field adjudicators on how to process cases. It's interesting reading them, and if we read them enough, we learn why they were hired by our President and understand the "wind" of our political climate in D.C. Read their agendas. Everybody has one.
18. Does whatever it is pass the "smell" test? Of course, it takes time to develop a "smell." Lately, ICE has sort of been going nuts on detentions and arrests. But it's ok, they'll change. We'll keep educating them. If we lose our focus, we will not get our greencard or citizenship. Look at the big picture.
19. Always check 245(i): if no visa petition or LC was filed prior to 4/30/01, and if the foreign-born became out of status, it's generally difficult to get green card. But think, don't give up.
20. Always check pre-245(i): if a visa petition was filed prior to 1/14/98, even if the foreign-born entered the U.S. after 12/00, they still qualify for a green card if otherwise eligible.
21. 245(i) also allows children, step-children (if marriage of the parent and stepparent took place prior to the children turning 18), previously acquired spouses, and even divorced spouses (as long as marriage happened prior to 4/30/01) to qualify for green cards, as they are grandfathered in 245(i).
22. The "grandfather" clause 245(i) also applies to an after acquired spouse (marriage after December 2000) as long as the benefits to be issued to the spouse are the same and at the same time as awarded to the principal foreign-born, her current spouse. Both can get work permits – what are known as (C) (9) cards – after 90 days. If the after acquired spouse divorces and marries another spouse, conceivably, the person can be grandfathered.
23. Widow cases do not need an I-864 – the spouse died already. If the foreign-born was widowed after less than 2 years of marriage, and the widow had already gotten a green card, we need to file an I-751 immediately. If the widow got a green card and her spouse died after more than two years of marriage, we need to file an I-360. If the widow never got or filed for a green card and her spouse died after less than 2 years of marriage, she's out of luck. This issue is being litigated in the federal courts now, it is called the widow penalty. If the widow filed for a green card and if the spouse died less than 2 years after marriage, but the green card was never approved, she should be able to get deferred action.
24. K2 & K4 children may be able to adjust status in U.S. even when the marriage of the stepparent and natural parent happened after the children are over 18. But if they did not adjust prior to age 21, there may be a problem. Our firm is currently litigating this issue.

25. Study AC21. Aside from the family visa petition, AC21 really helps a lot of foreign-borns, especially from China, Mexico, India, and the Philippines, stay legally in the U.S. while waiting through the long queue.
26. Hire the best lawyer you can find to protect your rights. A lot of these arcane rules are ripe for federal litigation. Federal courts in the U.S. are blessed with the best judges, law clerks, and lawyers to do research, who care about their jobs and love to practice.
27. Do not despair, we can and will become legal and be able to stay legally in the U.S. The goal of getting our green cards and citizenship will be achieved as long as we work and visualize success. We all went through the process. If you didn't, your parents, grandparents or great grandparents did – whoever came first, the pioneers of the country. America only has 200+ years of history. Where do you think our population of three hundred million came from?
28. Think macro, the big picture, and the future. If the work permit that you filed for takes longer to approve, do not get angry and start yelling, and then work without the work permit. We know how important it is. If we work without a work permit for more than 180 days, we fall outside of 245(k) and if you are not 245(k) you cannot get a green card without a waiver or 245(i) unless you are an immediate relative. Waivers are difficult, if not impossible to get.
29. In immigration, there are no "levels of deportability." If you are in a "deportable" state already, there is nothing worse immigration law can impose on you than being deported. It's not like criminal law, wherein if you sell more drugs, you go to jail and spend more days there. Deportation is (usually) not life or death.
30. If you really like the U.S. and want to live here permanently, you need to plan, and execute the plan. The U.S. is not like the U.S. of even 30 years ago, where you could come here, work a little bit, save some money, and then go home and get a green card. Our economic situation has declined and our people are not as generous to our guests, so think hard. You need to take risks, and be willing to go on this ride. Getting a legal visa and green card is not easy, especially for people who do not have four-year university degrees and are not the best of the best from their country. Although it's excruciating, it's also exciting, fun, and challenging.
31. Things have changed in the immigration field: the increased enforcement, the prolonged waiting time for green card approvals, the long waiting times for visa approvals, immigration numbers, 3/10 year bar, 5/10 year bar for removal, permanent bars for certain violations. Yet the core of immigration principles has not changed. The U.S. needs and wants children to be safe (hopefully the Dream Act will pass), so we have CSPA, the Child Citizenship Act, Adam Walsh Act, Special Immigrant Juvenile Status. The U.S. needs highly educated and world-renowned entertainers, scientists, artists and entrepreneurs with or without employers; these are the EB11, NIW categories. Since 1990, the U.S. has shifted its focus from family reunification to degreed and skilled worker immigration, and thus divided preferences into employment based/family based categories. To balance the amnesty program, which allowed a lot of people to get green cards (even

though it took years), we started employer sanctions and started finding employers who hired foreign borns without work permits. Thus, read the daily newspaper, and watch our global and universal trends. The U.S. does have a rhyme and reason and a plan for doing certain things.

32. You must process papers lawfully, and do not misrepresent or commit fraud. I totally understand that it's easy to just let things slip by when you think a mistake is so small. For example, we've had a case where the real birth date of a foreign-born was 11/12/75. The Chinese passport officer in China typed in 11/17/75. The foreign-born did not bother to go to the passport office (issued from the home country) to change the passport because it might have taken weeks or months to get a new one. The foreign-born got on a plane, and after the air hostess gave the passengers a copy of the I-94 to be filled in, she wrote down the wrong date of birth on the form so the customs officer by the gate would not deny entry. Now she had misstated the date of birth twice – on the passport, and on the I-94. After entry, a person in this situation will still need to apply for a social security number, tax ID number, driver's license, and credit cards. She would really need to keep using this wrong date of birth, and the time of reckoning would come if she were to go home or stay in the U.S. to begin applying for a Green Card. To apply for a Green Card, USCIS requires a birth certificate (and if the person does not have one, she needs to produce two affidavits from people older than her and government proof that there is no birth record). Her birth certificate would not show the same birth date and she would be in trouble. She would not be able to prove she is who she is. Worse yet, if she explained the chain of events to USCIS, she would be admitting that she had "lied" and will need to file for a waiver to get a green card. To file a 601 waiver, she would need a living parent with a green card or U.S. citizenship, or a spouse with U.S. citizenship or permanent residency. A U.S. citizen child would not be able to help her. If she were still single, and if she were a first generation immigrant, she would not be able to get the green card because her parents would not even be living in the U.S. Now she would be really stuck. This is one of the reasons why we have so many illegals in the U.S. It's not that we don't try, it's just we get stuck. Now this person wouldn't even be able to go home, because if she did, how could she come back? The 3/10 year bar would kick in, and even after 10 years, she would still need a waiver to come back.
33. Marrying a US citizen spouse is only one of the ways to get a green card. There are numerous other ways to do it if you do not want to marry. Don't feel pressured into marrying somebody you are unsure about.
34. It's a myth that we are guaranteed a green card if we marry a U.S. citizen. It's not always the case. If you entered illegally by walking over the border, and you are not covered under 245(i) (i.e. entered prior to 12/00 and had a visa petition filed for you or you are grandfathered into a parent's or spouse's visa petition), you would not be able to get the green card without leaving the country. Again, any or all "bar" issues will come in to play if you leave, and we'll need to file for a waiver if there is one available.
35. Labor certificates had really been going faster after PERM started in March 2005. In the last 9 months, it has considerably slowed down again. We

need to maintain status in the U.S. and have a visa for us to get a green card. If we are out of status and/or have no visa status in the U.S. at the time of application for the green card (485 pending), even if USCIS accepts the filing with documents and the fee of $1010, they can't grant the green card because since 4/01, illegals in the U.S. cannot get green cards anymore. Prior to 4/97, we could leave the country to apply in the U.S. Consulates, because there was no 3/10 year bar. Now, we cannot leave.

36. Do apply for the annual 55,000 Green Card lottery. Someone has to get it, and it could be you. If you don't ask, you don't get.
37. Do not underreport your income and earnings when you file your annual tax return. We can't get a good credit history and when we buy a house, how do we explain where the money came from?
38. Try not to get on government welfare, Medicare, or Medicaid, especially in big cities. Just because other people get it does not mean you should do it. This will perpetuate the media myth that we all come to U.S. and get health care benefits without paying into the system.
39. Just like other government agencies, USCIS, ICE, and CBP do have their problems. It doesn't mean we cannot educate and reform them. Impressions are formed in one minute, and first impressions are important. When you go to an interview, respect the officers, and pay attention to what they say. Do not twiddle your thumbs, roll your eyes, and sit when they ask you to stand. This is your "15 minutes." Dress nicely, smell good (I know, I know, us foreigners are all hard workers and may not care about our appearances, believing we are beautiful on the inside). Give a good strong handshake and look at them in the eye; we have nothing to hide. Don't go in there with slippers or cheap tennis shoes on (Again, I know we are cheaper people because of the U.S. exchange rates and we are nervous about spending too much). This is not the time to be silly or stupid. Also, it's important that the USCIS people feel good about their jobs. Can you imagine working there ten hours a day with smelly rooms, cheap government offices, crying babies, pressure and yelling from their bosses, and having to look at people who don't even look them in the eye? Why would they help us if they hate their jobs? We need to imply to them (they don't like to hear us talk a lot) that we are beautiful people, and it's their job to try to explain things and help process cases.
40. USCIS, ICE, and CBP are changing. Until not too long ago, it was not a diverse work force. Most officers were Anglo-Saxon, older, and had been there for years. Also, most came from the border patrol area, where they picked up foreign-borns, released them back to home countries, and then saw them again later somewhere. It was frustrating. Now, our government is serious about diversity in the work force. When I walk in with our own clients, the government employees do understand their languages, their cultures, and why certain things are done a certain way. They are smart and know what they are doing. I still remember when I was looking for a job and the U.S. Immigration Dept. wouldn't even interview me. Now that the world has changed, USCIS has tons of women and minority officers. Some are kind, some are not, but it's ok. Give them a chance; as we get older, we become kinder. Everything takes time.

41. Never be late to a scheduled appointment to see an immigration officer. Their motto is "you have to wait for us, we don't wait for you."
42. Smile at all immigration people. They may be tired and burned out. They are just trying to do their jobs.
43. Just do it. There are times when we despair with the arguments and decisions of the officer. Don't argue with them, because they are very busy. Each day, they do many interviews. Put your arguments in writing. Keep writing letters, and keep a record of your letters. One of the officers will eventually read one. This is why great immigration law firms always recruit the best writing people they can find. I routinely ask people who interview with us what the last 5 books they've read are and check writing samples.
44. Advocate, advocate, advocate. Ask yourself: who am I, and why am I special and different from the many others who come in front of the officer? Just because I have no criminal record and am not on government welfare does not make me different and special, although it should be commended. Learn a skill, and become the best you can be.
45. When filing for EB11/12 or asylum cases, don't assume that the immigration officers know your country's conditions, or know what an opera singer, scientist, or AIDS researcher does. We need to educate the officer, and also lay foundations to prove the authenticity of documents. USCIS is fraud detection-oriented. What this means is that if stories don't pass the smell test on the docks, our cases will not be approved. U.S. immigration officers have a crushing workload of cases to adjudicate and do not have time to ponder. Those few minutes in the interview can determine your whole life and future.
46. A child is still a child, even if she is over 21. As long as the parents file the asylum petition (I-589) prior to her becoming 21, even if the final granting took place after she turned 21, she can adjust to green card status and get a work permit in between. Make sure the child does not get married until the child's green card approved. This is the one instance where if she has an illegitimate child, this child cannot bring her own child in together with the newborn's grandmother's case.
47. Filings under an asylum grant case do not need to meet admissibility requirements for a green card. Even if she doesn't fall under 245(i) and her entry to the U.S. was with a phony passport, she entered without inspection, or she overstayed, she can still get a green card. If a waiver is necessary for fraud, no qualifying relatives are needed. The waiver provision is much broader for asylees than others.
48. All employers need to fill out I-9s for employees, principals, and owners. They do not need to do this form for consultants or independent contractors. If the employers pay with 1099s, they do not need to fill out I-9s. There are exceptions to this rule.
49. I-9 has two kinds of fines associated with it: paperwork violations and illegal hire. After ICE gives employers notice, employers have to allow ICE to check I-9 files and payrolls. Make sure all the i's are dotted, t's are crossed, and all space applicable is filled out.

50. Employers must keep employees' I-9s throughout the periods of employment. After employee termination, the I-9 must be retained for either 3 years of hire or one year after termination date, whichever is latest.
51. Employers, employees, foreign-borns, and U.S. citizens should give immigration officers only what they ask for. No more, no less. Don't think that you have nothing to hide or that you are not dishonest. Sometimes, they find things and start fining us. Just give federal officers what they require.
52. H-1B applications, labor cert filings, and PERM after March 2005 are totally different matters, although all are named as labor certifications filed with the Department of Labor. All need prevailing wage testing.
    - Prior to PERM, employers could pay up to 95% of the prevailing wage, which only had two wage levels. Under PERM, the employer has to pay 100% of the prevailing wage under four levels.
    - H-1B gives somebody visa status. Therefore, the employer has to pay the wages as stated in the Labor Condition Application (LCA) filing. If the wages are changed, either due to increase in responsibilities or economic woes, a new LCA needs to be filed with the labor department and the H-1B needs to be amended or a new one filed.
    - A PERM filing does not give visa status in the U.S. The only purpose of a PERM filing is to enable the employer who petitioned for the foreign-born national to apply for a green card for the worker under the EB-2 or EB-3 category. The employer is the only authorized party to sign the 9089.
    - The labor certification is a future prospective offer for employment, and the employer does not have to pay the stated salary in the PERM filing until the foreign-born national has a legal work permit, or until after the green card is approved.
53. All people in the U.S. can be divided into two types: either you are a U.S. citizen or an alien.

There are 2 types of aliens: Legal vs. Illegal

Legal aliens – People who hold a valid visa. A green card holder, a tourist in the U.S., a foreign student who is legally going to school and attending a full course of credit, and an H-1B holder who is working in accordance with the visa application forms and being paid the prevailing wage are legal aliens.

Illegal aliens – Examples: people whose I-94s have expired, i.e. the permitted duration of stay in the U.S. is over and they have overstayed; Non-visa holders, or have committed a crime and are rendered removable or deportable by the immigration office; tourist who is working here illegally and was determined by immigration to have been working illegally is also classified as an illegal alien. They include all people who entered illegally, stayed illegally, and worked illegally.

There are 2 types of citizens in the US:

There are basically two types of citizens in the U.S. You're either born here, or you derived, acquired, or naturalized. When I say you were born here, you could have been born in an American embassy when your parents were soldiers in Germany, and you're still an American, because the embassy is American soil. Through the years, the laws on derivative and acquired citizenship have also expanded.

1. Aliens

a. Legal

- Non immigrant with I-94
- Immigrant with green card

b. Illegal

- Overstay
- Illegal entry
- Illegal work
- Final removal order

2. U.S. Citizens

a. Born in U.S.

b. Not born in U.S.

- Naturalized
- Acquired
- Derivative

54. Documents needed to travel internationally for all people:

a. A passport or travel document issued by the person's home country. Make sure the correct name, date of birth, place of birth and picture are in them. The duration of the passport must be longer than your period of stay in the foreign country.

b. A visa to enter the country you're traveling to. Most countries' nationals are not as fortunate as us Americans, because they need to apply for a visa at their local American Consulate or Embassy before they come to the U.S. Canadian citizens can travel to the U.S. without a visa because of the visa waiver program, but Mexicans cannot. Canadian landed immigrants need a visa. All countries' nationals need to prove that they're otherwise admissible, and they're not trying to enter here to work without work permits, to marry a girlfriend or boyfriend, or to apply for a green card here. The visa is usually stamped in your passport. Americans on short trips abroad, for example, to France, Israel, etc., would not need visas. See full list of visa waiver countries in chart C. Different countries have different rules for different people.

c. After entry to a foreign country, you're given a piece of paper which should state the duration of stay in that country or the U.S. dates of entry and departure. In the U.S., this is called an I-94. It's white. Nationals from visa waiver countries get a green visa, and it's usually passed out on the airplane when you fly in.

55. Form names and types of benefits:

Visa petitions do not give us a benefit, status, or a stay period in the U.S. There are four kinds of visa petitions: the I-140, I-130, I-526, and I-360. Neither a Labor certificate nor a LCA is a visa petition.

Status and benefits in the U.S. – the following forms give you a visa status so that you can stay in the U.S. – I-129, I-485, I-539, I-589, N400, N600, I-826 (TPS status). These are different from visa petitions, which only allow you to file for a green card when the quota opens.

Other forms that give you a benefit, but not status in the U.S. (If the underlying status terminates, you became a Person without Status) – I-90, I-129F, I-765, I-20, G-325A, I-612, I-601, I-824, I-102, I-730.

- I-90 is a form that you fill out to replace a lost Green Card or if any information on the I-551 is wrong.
- I-129F is a fiancé request from USCIS, to be cabled to the foreign American Counsel after it is approved to allow the foreign born to enter the United States. We cannot do a change of status inside the U.S. from one type of visa to that of an I-129F (i.e. no such thing as I-539 to I-129F).
- I-765 gives you a work permit. This work permit expires if the underlying reason for giving you the work permit is terminated or expires.

- I-20 is issued by a school to accept a foreign student into its "full course of studies" and into its school program. It's controlled by SEVIS, a huge computer system that started after 9/11.
- I-589 is an application for asylum status. If it's granted, you can apply for a Green Card after one year of the final grant.
- G-325A is a form to be filed together with I-485. It lists all your past addresses and history so that the FBI and different security agencies can check up on you before they give you a GC.
- I-612 is a waiver for foreign residency requirement.
- I-601 is an "extreme hardship" waiver.
- I-824 is a form in which we ask USCIS to notify different agencies of an action, e.g. Green Card approval from parents in the U.S. when a child remains overseas to allow the child to follow and join the parent's green cards make the same quota.
- I-102 is a form for lost or misplaced I-94s. It's important because without this copy, you can't prove legal entry and won't be able to get a green card.
- I-730 has to be filed with CIS within 2 years of the asylum grant for the principal foreign-born to allow his spouse and children to be admitted to the U.S.
- U.S. State Department forms DS-156 and DS-157 are to apply for a tourist visa, student visa, or any nonimmigrant visa to come to the U.S from an American Consul or American Embassy to enter.

Other forms:

- I-751 "Petition to Remove Conditions on Residence" required to be filed jointly by both USC and Alien Spouse before 2nd anniversary of grant of permanent resident status if marriage is 2 years or less; This condition may be waived by USCIS and can be filed by one sponsor if marriage was entered into good faith and was terminated by divorce or annulment or the possible removal from the United States would cause extreme hardship on the non-USC ex-spouse.
- I-821 is to allow for TPS (temporary protected status). When TPS came out, only an I-765 needed to be applied to file for a work permit. I-821 was added later; without this, USCIS won't approve an application for a work permit. It was confusing when it was first introduced.
- AR-11 is to notify the government that you have changed your address. This form must be completed and sent to USCIS *each and every time* you move your place of residence. If you do not notify USCIS of your address, you will not receive important immigration documentation, such as the result of your visa or immigration application, RFEs, etc.
- I-290B is file an appeal or motion to reopen and/or reconsider. This form is used to argue that the denial of an application is incorrect.
- I-693 is the medical exam required for all adjustment of status applications; the form is completed by a physician registered with USCIS to conduct medical exams for immigration purposes.
- I-864 is the Affidavit of Support. This form is completed in family-based GC cases and some employment-based GC cases to show that the

immigrant will have financial support in the United States and will not become a financial burden on the US government.

- I-907 is the form to request premium processing for certain applications.

ICE also has their forms. For example, when a person leaves the country, she needs to bring a G-146 form (changed in October 2009 to 122) to the American Embassy overseas, which will send this form back to the local district office to confirm that the foreign-born has indeed traveled out of U.S. land. G-166 is a bag and baggage letter informing the U.S. of the date and place of travel and allowable tonnage of luggage to be carried with the body of the alien. The I-213 is used when the ICE officer questions the alien of their reasons for issuing the NTA.

56. Revocation of green card:
What they giveth they can taketh away. You can lose your green card in different ways. One such way is pleading guilty to a crime or being convicted of certain crimes after a trial. If you don't come back to the U.S. within 6 months, the burden is on CIS to prove that you intend to give up your green card. You may be stopped and questioned about whether you abandoned your residence. If you do not enter the U.S. at least once within a year, the burden is on you to prove that you do not intend to give up the green card. If you left the U.S. and did not return for more than one year, the presumption is that you have relinquished the GC. If you know that you will be leaving the country for more than one year and there is a chance that you would not be able to return, you need to apply for a reentry permit. This is a travel document which allows you to come back at least once in two years. If CIS finds out that the labor certification with which you obtained your GC is fraudulent, or that the marriage you entered into which allowed you to get the GC is fraudulent, they can start a removal or revocation procedure for your GC. Once the removal procedure has been started, you need to find some form of relief that allows you to keep the GC, and better yet, to apply for citizenship. Do not take any revocation procedure lightly, thinking that your whole family is here and that you've lived here for so long. Do not state that you are a US citizen in any forms, especially when applying for a job.

57. Comparison of civil, criminal and immigration law:

A simple way to understand immigration law is to compare it with the U.S. civil and U.S. criminal systems. America is a country only 200 years old. Our laws closely resemble those of Western Europe.
If you owe your landlord money, the landlord can sue you with a civil complaint. Money is the main object. Whoever loses has to pay the sum that the judge says she owes. The beginning of the proceeding is called a civil complaint. Service of the complaint to the defendant (the landlord is the plaintiff), and the notice of hearing is called due process.
Criminal law takes effect when you assault someone or steal something or otherwise commit a crime. It begins with the police or law enforcement officials issuing a charging document, indictment, or a ticket when you're

driving drunk. You need to appear in court and either go through a trial, pay a fine, or plead guilty/no contest. A prison term and fines may be involved. Immigration laws are neither civil nor criminal. When President Bush started DHS, Immigration moved over from DOJ to DHS and became one of its first agencies. Legacy Immigration also became three branches after the transfer; USCIS, which grants benefits, ICE, which does all of the deportation and fraud and criminal alien investigation, and CBP, which controls all of the port of entry and airport activities (i.e. entry). DHS's core mission is law enforcement. Although the purpose of the legacy Immigration and Naturalization Service is to adjudicate applications for benefits, because of the enforcement-oriented minds of DHS officials, immigration law became more fraud-orientated, rather than benefits oriented.

The different district offices work their cases differently. Different areas' immigration judges, depending on their philosophies and case loads, are different. Immigration judges are not Article 3 judges. Article 3 judges serve life appointments. Immigration judges are administrative judges serving at the pleasure of the President of the United States and the Secretary of Homeland Security.

58. Definition of aggravated felony (immigration system) INA Section 101(a)(43):

(A) murder, rape, or sexual abuse of a minor;
(B) illicit trafficking in a controlled substance, including a drug trafficking crime;
(C) illicit trafficking in firearms or destructive devices or in explosive materials;
(D) laundering of monetary instruments or engaging in monetary transactions in property derived from specific unlawful activity if the amount of the funds exceeded $10,000;
(E) explosive materials or firearms offenses;
(F) a crime of violence (but not including a purely political offense) for which the term of imprisonment is least 1 year;
(G) theft (including receipt of stolen property) or burglary for which the term of imprisonment is at least 1 year;
(H) demand for or receipt of ransom;
(I) child pornography;
(J) racketeer influenced corrupt organizations, or gambling for which a sentence of 1 year imprisonment or more may be imposed;
(K) owning, controlling, managing, or supervising of a prostitution business; transportation for the purpose of prostitution if committed for commercial advantage; peonage, slavery, involuntary servitude, and trafficking in persons;
(L) gathering or transmitting national defense information, disclosure of classified information, sabotage or treason; offenses relating to protecting the identity of undercover intelligence agents or undercover agents;

(M) fraud or deceit in which the loss to the victim(s) exceeds $10,000; or relating to tax evasion in which the revenue loss to the Government exceeds $10,000;
(N) alien smuggling except in the case of a first offense for which the alien committed the offense for the purpose of assisting, abetting, or aiding only the alien's spouse, child, or parent (and no other individual);
(O) an offense committed by an alien who was previously deported on the basis of a conviction in this section
(P) falsely making, forging, counterfeiting, mutilating, or altering a passport or other document fraud for which the term of imprisonment is at least 12 months, except in the case of a first offense for which the alien has affirmatively shown that the alien committed the offense for the purpose of assisting, abetting, or aiding only the alien's spouse, child, or parent (and no other individual)
(Q) failure to appear by a defendant for service of sentence if the underlying offense is punishable by imprisonment for a term of 5 years or more;
(R) commercial bribery, counterfeiting, forgery, or trafficking in vehicles the identification numbers of which have been altered for which the term of imprisonment is at least one year
(S) obstruction of justice, perjury or subornation of perjury, or bribery of a witness, for which the term of imprisonment is at least one year;
(T) failure to appear before a court pursuant to a court order to answer to or dispose of a charge of a felony for which a sentence of 2 years' imprisonment or more may be imposed; and
(U) an attempt or conspiracy to commit an offense described in this paragraph whether in violation of Federal or State law and applies to such offense in violation of the law of a foreign country for which the term of imprisonment was completed within the previous 15 years. Notwithstanding any other provision of law, the term applies regardless of whether the conviction was entered before, on, or after the date of enactment of this paragraph.

59. The definition of criminal felony (criminal system) differs between each state but is in general a serious crime for which the punishment is at least one year in jail although this varies among states. This is a higher level of criminal act than misdemeanors.

60. The three branches of the federal government and how they interact with 50 U.S. state governments

The federal government is comprised of the legislative, executive and judicial branches. The great thing about practicing immigration law is that we interact with all three. For the majority of U.S. persons living in America, immigration doesn't have a large impact on their lives. They don't know people like us. They think of us more as laborers than as people who work and contribute. When we apply for a GC, we apply for it through service centers and district offices, which are administrative offices. It's not adversarial, and it's all through writing. If status is denied and the foreign-born becomes without status, then she has to go in front of a judge after the issuance of OSC before April 1997, or NTA after April 1997. In the 80s and 90s, it was relatively simple because the laws were detailed and clear – either you were deportable, or you weren't. Now, with all the new laws, acts, regulations, headquarter memos, forms, regulations, and different circuit interpretations, it's really exciting. The state police are also getting involved now, albeit with no additional funding. They're informing Immigration about anybody who appears not to have valid immigration status.

61. Do not state you are a US citizen on any form especially when applying for a job (form I-9).

62. Deportation vs. Removal vs. Expedited Removal vs. Inadmissibility

Prior to 1997, deportation began with the issuance of an OSC (Order to Show Cause) by legacy INS. If the foreign-born was not notified of the issuance, or if the foreign-born did not get a copy of the OSC, the judge usually terminated or administratively closed the proceedings. The foreign-born would not have any final order of deportation. However, on some occasions the Immigration Judge would order deportation under these circumstances.

Removal begins with the issuance of an NTA (Notice to Appear) by legacy INS after April 1997, or after March of 2003, by ICE and DHS. It is now the foreign-born's responsibility to notify ICE and the judge of all changes of address. If the foreign-born does not show up at hearings, she will get a final order of removal. Rules regarding the review of this order became very complicated after 1997.

Expedited removal began in 1997. This applies to jailed and detained foreign-borns and foreign-borns at the border entering illegally. It applies if a foreign-born is not admitted or paroled and unable to prove his identity. He can be removed anywhere from a few hours to 14 days after the order is given.
After 1997, the idea of admissibility has become crucial. The terms "admission" and admitted mean with respect to an alien, the lawful entry of the alien into the United States after inspection and authorization by an immigration officer. 101(a)(13). You have to present yourself to an immigration official for you to obtain any benefits. You cannot obtain a GC if you can't prove that you've been admitted, even if married to a U.S.C.

Deportation

a Prior to 1997, began with issuance of OSC; if a foreign-born pled voluntary departure and did not leave the country within the days allowed, she would not be able to get a green card until after 5 years from the date of the plea. If not deported, and if she left the country with a final order and paid her own expenses, she couldn't come back into the U.S. for 5 years.

The foreign-born could apply for suspension of deportation as long as she would experience extreme hardship if forced to leave the U.S. – to qualify for this relief, she had to have stayed in the U.S. for more than 7 years. The mode of entry did not matter.

b After April 1997, began with issuance of NTA (Notice to Appear); The old concept of deportation changed to a removal concept – if a foreign-born pleads voluntary departure, she can't get a green card for up to 10 years – if she leaves the country with a final order, she cannot return to the U.S. for more than 10 years. The suspension of deportation changed to cancellation of removal; however, the foreign-born now needs to stay in the U.S. for more than 10 years for this relief. Exceptional and extremely unusual hardship also has to inure back to a green card/U.S.C spouse and/or parents and/or child, no more to herself. The core rule remains the same, that the immigration judge that hears the case remains in the locale where the foreign-born is living – if where the foreign-born lives is different from the place where she was picked up prior to the issuance of an OSC or NTA, she can request a change of venue to the immigration court in her place of residence. If a person is ordered removed, he or she has the right to appeal to the Board of Immigration Appeals. This is an appellate body that will review a judge's decision to determine whether to affirm, reverse, or remand the case.

Circuit court appellate review occurs by filing a petition for review with the appropriate circuit courts (in the jurisdiction where the IJ heard the case). For example, if an Ohio IJ heard the case, the appeal should be filed in the 6th Circuit after the Board of Immigration Appeals decision. If the case was heard in NY, the appeal has to be filed in the 2nd Circuit. Illinois is the 7th. This is important, because different circuits hold different precedent-setting rules. It's extremely important to know your circuit rules, because the Circuit has to follow its own rulings on similarly situated cases. Although there may be a circuit split decision, the U.S. Supreme Court may decline cert.

63. When helping your friend to pay bond to allow her to get out of detention, you can only pay by certified check or money order. If the foreign-born absconds, you cannot get your money back. If she keeps going to court and wins her case at the end, or leaves the U.S. if she loses and you have proof, you can get all the money back plus interest.

64. If you do not have immigration status, do not visit someone in jail or go to help someone out to do translation. You may be picked up. This is like feeding a sheep into the lion's den. You may laugh, but we do have a lot of cases like this.

65. When applying for asylum, think burden-shifting upon a showing of past persecution, future persecution, past persecution, inference of persecution, Real I.D. Act, 1 year rule, credibility. You must prove your case and submit corroborating evidence when it can reasonably be expected.

66. Asylum Filings:

The asylum application is filed with USCIS if you are not in deportation and removal proceedings. If you are in deportation or removal proceedings it is filed with the IJ.
You must file:
-An original I-589, Application for Asylum and Withholding of Removal.
-This must be completed in English and signed with the Preparer.
-All supporting evidence.
If filed with USCIS, it must contain 2 copies. The court requires one copy. There is no fee. It must be filed within a year of coming to the U.S.

3. NONIMMIGRANT VISAS

a. General

Many immigrants to America arrive with the intention of someday returning to their places of origin, but later choose to remain in this country. These people generally arrive on nonimmigrant visas (NIVs), of which there are many types.

Three documents are necessary when traveling to foreign countries: a passport, a visa, and a duration of stay document (form I-94 in the U.S.) after entering that country stating the time of entry and planned time of departure. Care should be taken to ensure that all information on documentation is correct and that one is informed of all relevant regulations. The lack of a valid passport (with correct information), the failure to undergo fingerprinting at the airport when required, and failure to comply with I-94 departure requirements may lead to the loss of legal status within the United States. Certain conditions may also render one inadmissible to the United States, such as health problems, criminal records, national security concerns, a high likelihood of an applicant becoming a public charge, or previous deportation. Illegal entrants (or those who cannot prove admission) to the United States cannot adjust their status within the U.S. to that of a legal permanent resident, even if married to a U.S. citizen. The only exception to this is those eligible for exemption under 245(i) (see section on 245(i)).

Denials of visa applications from the American Consulate cannot be appealed in the U.S. However, a foreign-born may apply multiple times, albeit with additional filing fees and documents. It is not uncommon for a visa to be granted after several failed attempts. U.S. nationals are fortunate in that they may travel to many countries for short periods of time without applying for visas. However, American students studying abroad must obtain visas to travel and to study there for an extended duration, as must those working in foreign countries.

I've had quite a few calls through the years from American university students a day prior to their flight to their European or Asian schools, indignant to discover they needed a visa.

Forms for Nonimmigrant Visa Applicants	
I-20	Form issued by a school to accept a foreign student into its school program
I-94	Arrival/Departure record
I-102	Form to replace a lost I-94
DS-156	Nonimmigrant Visa Application when

	applying for the visa overseas with the American consulate or embassy
DS-157	Supplemental Nonimmigrant Visa Application when applying for the visa overseas with the American consulate or embassy

Foreign nationals from visa waiver countries are allowed 90 days' stay in the U.S. However, nationals of these countries who overstay are deported without access to deportation hearings or any other recourse. Only those with serious illness are permitted an extended stay (10 days) for treatment. This 90-day visa cannot be otherwise extended in the U.S. and cannot be changed to any other type of nonimmigrant visa. Visa waiver holders who have not overstayed may opt to apply for permanent residency upon marriage to a U.S. citizen.

b. Visa Waiver Program

Countries that have agreements with the U.S. allowing their nationals to enter the U.S. without applying for a visa at U.S. embassies for up to a maximum of 90 days. These visa holders cannot request an extension of their stay nor ask for a change of status. They have to leave U.S. soil within 90 days.

Andorra	Iceland	Norway
Australia	Ireland	Portugal
Austria	Italy	San Marino
Belgium	Japan	Singapore
Brunei	Latvia	Slovakia
Czech Republic	Liechtenstein	Slovenia
Denmark	Lithuania	South Korea
Estonia	Luxembourg	Spain
Finland	Malta	Sweden
France	Monaco	Switzerland
Germany	The Netherlands	United Kingdom
Hungary	New Zealand	

Source: State Department Website

c. Other Non-Immigrant Visas

Special provisions have been made for citizens of Micronesia and the Marshall Islands allowing them to travel in the United States as nonimmigrants without a visa. Canadian citizens can travel to the United States without a nonimmigrant visa for business or tourism.

Those other than students or workers who wish to stay in the U.S. for more than 90 days should apply for a tourist visa at the U.S. Consulate or the U.S.

Embassy. This B-1/B-2 visa provides a person with a degree of flexibility regarding his/her duration of stay.

For those who live, work, or shop regularly near the U.S.-Mexican border, the Border Crossing Card or "laser visa" was created in 1998. A second generation of cards was issued beginning in 2008, containing a biometric data component utilizing face-matching and fingerprinting technology. The machine-readable card serves as both a B-1/B-2 visa and an expedient and convenient means to cross the border for short periods of time, valid for ten years of the date of issue or upon the holder's fifteenth birthday (if a reduced fee for children was paid). Currently, laser visa holders may enter the U.S. and travel to areas within twenty-five miles of the Mexican border for thirty days or less without the need to fill out I-94 form. Those who must travel elsewhere in the United States for longer periods of time may fill out an I-94 form and use their card as a B-1/B-2 visa.

Foreign students attending school in the U.S. may apply for an F-1 student visa. Some students also come to the United States under J-1 visas. This visa is for exchange visitors (and also applies to others like au pairs) and has a two-year residency in home country requirement after the program for which the J-1 visa is granted ends. This makes it especially difficult for J-1 students wishing to stay in the United States after their studies are complete. J-2 dependents are also subject to this two-year residency requirement and can apply for a work permit. The only recourse for J visa holders is to apply for a waiver of this two-year home country requirement.

There are only four grounds for a J visa waiver: exceptional hardship to a US citizen or permanent resident spouse or child, persecution of the exchange visitor if he or she returns to their home country, the exchange visitor's home country has no objection to him or her staying in the United States, or a US government agency recommends the waiver. J visa waivers can be difficult to obtain in certain circumstances, so it is wise to use an immigration attorney when applying for this type of waiver.

Waiver Form For J Visa Holders	
DS-3035 is to get DOS # then you use I-612 when applying for waiver to USCIS (I-612 is for hardship waiver)	Waiver for Foreign Residency Requirement

Foreign diplomats, ambassadors, officials, and representatives to international organizations are granted A or G visas. Because the U.S. only recognizes China (PRC), and not Taiwan, most diplomats from Taiwan come to the U.S. on an E visa. Traders and investors from countries such as Israel, Taiwan and Japan also may apply for an E visa. Only certain countries have signed agreements with the United States for the E-1 (Treaty Traders) and/or the E-2 (Treaty Investors) visas, individuals from countries that have not signed E-1 or E-2 agreements with the U.S. are not eligible for E visas.

The countries listed below are designated treaty countries with the United States. They are based on the signing of a treaty of friendship or commerce. If the foreign born holds a passport from one of these listed countries they may be able to invest in a business or projects in the U.S. and to apply for these visas to come work and stay. Their children will be able to attend school on an E-2 visa. Spouses can apply for yearly work permits, although the children cannot.

E-1 Countries

Argentina	Costa Rica	Iran	Macedonia	Slovenia[K]
Australia	Croatia 11	Ireland	Mexico	Spain[H]
Austria	Denmark[C]	Israel	Netherlands[F]	Suriname[I]
Belgium	Estonia	Italy	Norway[G]	Sweden
Bolivia	Ethiopia	Japan[E]	Oman	Switzerland
Bosnia and Herzegovina 11	Finland	Jordan	Pakistan	Thailand
Brunei	France[D]	Korea (South)	Paraguay	Togo
Canada	Germany	Latvia	Philippines	Turkey
Chile	Greece	Liberia	Poland	United Kingdom[J]
China (Taiwan) 1	Honduras	Luxembourg	Singapore	Yugoslavia[K]
Colombia				

E-2 Countries

Albania	Colombia	Honduras	Mexico	Slovak Republic [B]
Argentina	Congo (Brazzaville)	Iran	Moldova	Slovenia[K]
Armenia	Congo (Kinshasa)	Ireland	Mongolia	Spain 8
Australia	Costa Rica	Italy	Morocco	Sri Lanka
Austria	Croatia 11	Jamaica	Netherlands[F]	Suriname[I]
Azerbaijan	Czech Republic [B]	Japan[E]	Norway[G]	Sweden
Bahrain	Ecuador	Jordan	Oman	Switzerland
Bangladesh	Egypt	Kazakhstan	Pakistan	Thailand
Belgium	Estonia	Korea (South)	Panama	Togo
Bolivia	Ethiopia	Kyrgyzstan	Paraguay	Trinidad & Tobago
Bosnia and Herzegovina 11	Finland	Latvia	Philippines	Tunisia
Bulgaria	France[D]	Liberia	Poland	Turkey
Cameroon	Georgia	Lithuania	Romania	Ukraine
Canada	Germany	Luxembourg	Senegal	United Kingdom[J]
Chile	Grenada	Macedonia	Singapore	Yugoslavia[K]
China (Taiwan) [A]				

Country-Specific Footnotes

A. **China (Taiwan)** – Pursuant to Section 6 of the Taiwan Relations Act, (TRA) Public Law 96-8, 93 Stat, 14, and Executive Order 12143, 44 F.R. 37191, this agreement which was concluded with the Taiwan authorities prior to January 01, 1979, is administered on a nongovernmental basis by the American Institute in Taiwan, a nonprofit District of Columbia corporation, and constitutes neither recognition of the Taiwan authorities nor the continuation of any official relationship with Taiwan.

B. **Czech Republic and Slovak Republic** – The Treaty with the Czech and Slovak Federal Republic entered into force on December 19, 1992; entered into force for the Czech Republic and Slovak Republic as separate states on January 01, 1993.

C. **Denmark** – The Treaty which entered into force on July 30, 1961, does not apply to Greenland.

D. **France** – The Treaty which entered into force on December 21, 1960, applies to the departments of Martinique, Guadeloupe, French Guiana and Reunion.

E. **Japan** – The Treaty which entered into force on October 30, 1953, was made applicable to the Bonin Islands on June 26, 1968, and to the Ryukyu Islands on May 15, 1972.

F. **Netherlands** – The Treaty which entered into force on December 05, 1957, is applicable to Aruba and Netherlands Antilles.

G. **Norway** – The Treaty which entered into force on September 13, 1932, does not apply to Svalbard (Spitzbergen and certain lesser islands).

H. **Spain** – The Treaty which entered into force on April 14, 1903, is applicable to all territories.

I. **Suriname** – The Treaty with the Netherlands which entered into force December 05, 1957, was made applicable to Suriname on February 10, 1963.

J. **United Kingdom** – The Convention which entered into force on July 03, 1815, applies only to British territory in Europe (the British Isles (except the Republic of Ireland), the Channel Islands and Gibraltar) and to "inhabitants" of such territory. This term, as used in the Convention, means "one who resides actually and permanently in a given place, and has his domicile there." Also, in order to qualify for treaty trader or treaty investor status under this treaty, the alien must be a national of the United Kingdom. Individuals having the nationality of members of the Commonwealth other than the United Kingdom do not qualify for treaty trader or treaty investor status under this treaty.

K. **Yugoslavia** – The U.S. view is that the Socialist Federal Republic of Yugoslavia (SFRY) has dissolved and that the successors that formerly made up the SFRY – Bosnia and Herzegovina, Croatia, the Former Yugoslav Republic of Macedonia, Slovenia, and the Federal Republic of Yugoslavia continue to be bound by the treaty in force with the SFRY and the time of dissolution.

Source: State Department

There are many other types of nonimmigrant visas (NIV) for different categories of people who are permitted to stay temporarily in the United States. See complete list below.

VISA DESIGNATION	Who Can Use This Visa
A-1	Ambassador, public minister, career diplomatic or consular officer, member of the immediate family
A-2	Other foreign government official or employee, immediate family members
A-3	Attendant, servant, or personal employee of A-1or A-2 & members of immediate family
B-1(See also H1B / B-1 in Lieu of H-1B)	Temporary visitor for business
B-2	Temporary visitor for pleasure
B-1/B-2	Temporary visitor for business and pleasure
C-1/D	Combined Transit and Crewman Visa
E-1	Treaty Trader, spouse and children
E-2	Treaty Investor, spouse and children
E-3	Australian Treaty Trader, spouse and children
F-1	Student (academic or language training program)
F-2	Spouse and Children of F-1
G-1	Principal resident representative of recognized government to international organization (& immediate

	family)
G-2	Same as G-1 for other than principal representative
G-3	Same as G-1 or G-2 for non-recognized government
G-4	International organization officer or employee and members of immediate family
G-5	Attendant, servant, or personal employee of G1 through G-4 Classes
H-1B (See also H1B / B-1 in Lieu of H-1B)	Alien in specialty occupation (profession)
H-1C	Registered nurse
H-2A	Agricultural worker performing agricultural services unavailable in the United States
H-2B	Agricultural worker performing other services unavailable in the United States
H-3	Trainee
H-4	Spouse and child of H-1, 2 or 3
I	Representative of foreign informational media, spouse and children
J-1	Exchange visitor
J-2	Spouse or child of J-1
K-1	Fiancé of USC
K-2	Child of Fiancé of USC
K-3	Spouse of USC

K-4	Child of K-3
L-1	Intra-company transferee
L-2	Spouse or children of L-1
M-1	Student (vocational or other recognized non-academic)
M-2	Spouse or children of M-1
NATO-1	Principal permanent representative of member states to NATO & official staff, plus immediate families
NATO-2	Other representatives of members states to NATO, plus immediate families
NATO-3	Official clerical staff accompanying NATO-1 and 2 holders, plus immediate families
NATO-4	NATO officials and immediate families not eligible for NATO-1 visas, plus immediate families
NATO-5	Experts not eligible for NATO-4 status, plus dependents
NATO-6	Civilian component members accompanying NATO force or employed by allied headquarters, plus dependents
NATO-7	Attendant, servant, or personal employee of NATO-1 through 6 alien and immediate family members
O-1	Aliens of extraordinary ability in sciences, arts, education, business or athletics
O-2	Accompanying alien
O-3	Spouse or child of O-1 or O-2
P-1	Internationally recognized athletes or members of internationally recognized entertainment group

P-2	Artist or entertainer in reciprocal exchange program
P-3	Artist or entertainer in culturally unique program
P-4	Spouse or child of P-1, 2, or 3
Q-1	Participant in international cultural exchange program
Q-2	Participant in Irish Peace Process Cultural and Training Program
Q-3	Spouse or child of Q-1 or Q-2
R-1	Religious Worker
R-2	Spouse or child of R-1
S-5	Certain aliens supplying critical information relating to a criminal organization or enterprise
S-6	Certain aliens supplying critical information relating to terrorism
S-7	Qualified family member of S-5 or S-6
T-1	For individuals who are present in the U.S., American Samoa or the Commonwealth of the Northern Mariana Islands as the result of trafficking.
T-2	Spouse of T-1
T-3	Child of T-1
T-4	Parent of T-1
TN	Trade visas for Canadians and Mexicans
TD	Spouse or child of TN

U-1	Victims of certain crimes
U-2	Spouse of U-1
U-3	Child of U-1
U-4	Parent of U-1
V-1	Spouse of a green card holder whose I-130 petition was filed before December 21, 2000, the date of the enactment of LIFE Act, and has been pending for at least three years
V-2	Child of a green card holder whose I-130 petition was filed before December 21, 2000, the date of the enactment of LIFE Act, and has been pending for at least three years
V-1	Child of a V-1 or V-2

d. Student Visas

Those granted F-1 visas should take full advantage of their opportunity, as the denial rate is approximately 60 - 85%. Public high schools may only accept a foreign student on an F-1 visa for one academic year. U.S. public lower and middle schools are not permitted to accept foreign students on F-1 visas. The U.S. parents of an adopted foreign-born child must advise their school district that the child is not on an F-1 visa, and wait for the two year legal physical possession requirements of the adoption law to be fulfilled before acquiring a green card and sending the child to school. However, allowing a child to attend classes is ultimately at the discretion of the individual school. This means that the law is configured in such a way that adopted children from abroad are in a better position if they are illegal than if they have F-1 status.

I would also add here that since you are lucky to have an F-1 visa, do study hard and don't waste time in school. There are so many people, especially kids and college aged people, who want to come to the U.S., and the denial rate is approximately 60 - 85% on F-1 visas. You and I know that you are very fortunate to have this once in a lifetime experience of studying in the U.S. I did, and without my alma mater, I wouldn't be here writing, thinking, and practicing law.

F-1 recruitment is a big business now, both in the U.S. and overseas, because most of the foreign students are not granted scholarships like we were in the 1960s and 1970s. A word to the Foreign Student Advisors here: you were given the privilege and have the job of working with foreign-born students. Mentor them and teach them. Foreign Student Advisors are the first point of contact for any foreign student who travels from afar to this country. If they were not smart, did not come from a well-educated family, or didn't love your school, they would not be there paying tuition in U.S. dollars from their own or their parents' savings, so for goodness sake, be kind, passionate and embrace your job. Don't just think of a student as a foreigner who is stupid or nagging and always looks for ways out of attending class.

Students who attend vocational schools are admitted with M-1 visas. CBP officers at airports or border checkpoints have the authority to place a departure date on M-1 visa students' I-94s. M-1 students must leave the U.S. within 30 days of the end of their two or three-year study periods as stated in their SEVIS (Student and Exchange Visitor Information System) I-20s.

Exchange students could come to study in U.S. schools with a J-1 visa. This program could either be sponsored by a J-1 visa provider or the school itself if they are so authorizes. Depending on the foreign born's country skills list and the program number, and whether the students have accepted U.S. government funding and/or foreign government grant, they may need to apply for waiver of the 2 year foreign residency requirement to change their certain status in the U.S.

Following the 9/11 attacks, pilot schools became extremely cautious about accepting M-1 students, and American Embassies and Consulates frequently denied applications. From 2001 to about 2006, foreign student enrollment within the United States declined, and most students instead turned to Europe, Canada, and Australia for higher education. With the return of relative normalcy, F-1 recruitment has again risen and become a significant source of revenue, as most foreign students are not granted scholarships to study in U.S. colleges.

There are three kinds of work permits for students. Students may normally only work on campus. Some can work off campus with approval by DHS of a curriculum practical training (CPT) work permit. The revised I-20 must be approved by both a foreign student advisor and USCIS officials. It allows a student to intern to fulfill a requirement under his/her degree program. A pharmacist student, for example, is required to undergo this training period before she takes the license test. Students can work off campus if granted an "economic hardship" work permit. They can work off campus for up to 20 hours a week, and full time during breaks.

The third work permit available to foreign students is the optional practical training (OPT) permit. After graduating, a student wishing to acquire further training in a field related to his/her studies may ask for the 12 month period of OPT. The student must find a job within 3 months and provide his/her foreign student advisor with the employer's name and phone number. Students who do not find employment within 3 months must leave the country or be rendered out of status.

e. Work Permits

Before obtaining an employment-based green card, many immigrants need temporary work visas to maintain status in the United States and to work legally. There are essentially two categories of work permits. A non-LPR/non-citizen must possess one of these to legally work in the United States.

The first type, the Employment Authorization Document (EAD), is not employer-specific and thus allows an individual to change jobs, if desired. EADs do not confer a legal status upon the holder, and EAD workers must maintain the underlying basis for work authorization, e.g. C(9) work permit is one granted when the worker is I-485 pending, C(8) is asylum pending, C(10) is cancellation pending,

A(5) is after-asylum final grant. The second category is employer-specific and includes the H-1B, H-1C, and O visas. These work permits that allow workers to work legally within the U.S. also serve as nonimmigrant visas which provide legal status.

f. H-1B

An H-1B visa permits a foreign national to be employed legally in the United States for the petitioning employer for an initial period of 3 years, up to a maximum of 6 years if extended. Employees are only eligible for an H-1B visa if the position is professional in nature, i.e. the position requires specialized knowledge. If the employee has never previously obtained an H-1B, and the potential employer does not qualify for exemptions from the H-1B numerical cap, then the employer must petition for the employee through the annual random selection process. Congress currently places an annual cap of 65,000 on new H-1B workers with at least a Bachelor's degree and another 20,000 H-1B workers with a U.S.-earned Master's degree or higher.

On April 1, USCIS begins to accept petitions for the following fiscal year (employment beginning October 1). Petitions are randomly selected until the congressionally mandated 65,000 general category cap and 20,000 advanced degree exemption limit have been reached. USCIS first conducts the selection process for employees with "advanced degrees," i.e. a Masters degree or higher from a qualifying U.S. institution. "Advanced degree" petitions not selected become part of the random selection process for the general 65,000 limit. It is recommended that employers begin preparations early so that initial H-1B petitions are ready to file by April 1.

When petitioning on behalf of an employee for an H-1B visa, employers must comply with the Labor Condition Application requirements. The LCA, signed by the employer, is part of the H-1B petition, and obligates the employer to pay a minimum salary at the "prevailing wage" for that position during the employment period. The prevailing wage takes into account the geographic area of intended employment and the minimum educational, experience, and skill requirements for the position. Common methods of determining the prevailing wage include: (1) submitting an application to the State Employment Service Agency (SESA) of the state in which the employee will work, or (2) searching the Online Wage Library maintained by the U.S. Department of Labor. Both methods utilize the annual Occupational Employment Statistics (OES), but obtaining the prevailing wage through SESA provides the employer with "safe harbor" protection in the event of an audit by the Department of Labor. Evidence of the prevailing wage determination and the LCA should be maintained by the employer in its employee records in the form of Public Inspection Files. Finally, it is recommended that employers allocate at least two weeks for the prevailing wage determination to allow for SESA processing times.

Even if the employer does not have enough work for the employee, the employer is not allowed under the law to "bench" the employee by withholding salary or failing to pay the prevailing wage. The employer's only option is to terminate the employee. Once terminated, the employer should notify USCIS to withdraw the employee's H-1B. Because an H-1B allows a beneficiary employee to work for the petitioning employer only, a terminated employee must find another willing petitioner to continue working in H-1B status. There is no grace period to stay in the U.S. for the terminated H-1B visa holder. The visa expires and the alien is rendered out of status.

Only time spent in the United States in H-1B status is counted towards the 6-year H-1B eligibility period. Any time spent outside of the United States can be "recaptured" by filing an extension of stay with USCIS. Certain H-1B beneficiaries may be eligible for extensions beyond the 6-year maximum based on the American Competitiveness in the Twenty-First Century Act (AC21), such as those going through the green card application process.

Getting an H-1B can be complicated, depending on the job sought and the foreign born's qualifications. Our firm recently advised a Chinese woman in her twenties who was on 1 year Optional Practical Training (OPT) after her Associate of Arts degree in Surgical Technology. Her OPT was to expire in February 2010. She had been in the U.S. since 2005, and sought to work here long-term and gain permanent residency, ideally starting out on an H-1B. She wanted to know if she would be eligible next year. The answer is no, unless she has enough progressive professional experience to establish the equivalent of a Bachelor's degree. She also had to prove that the degree or equivalent is required for the position. She would be able to work as a Physician's Assistant on an H-1B if she got her B.A. degree.

There exists an H-1C visa specifically reserved for registered nurses within areas of the United States in which there are a shortage of medical personnel. The H-1C petition process is similar to that of the H-1B petition process in that the employer must petition on behalf of the registered nurse. H-1C visas, like H-1B visas, are employer-specific. An H-1C visa is valid for 3 years and cannot be extended. The cap for H-1C visas each year is set to 500, partitioned between states depending upon each state's population. If a state's population is in excess of 9 million, the state's annual cap is set at 50, while if it is less than 9 million, the cap is set at 25. [226] Due to the limited number of H-1C visas available each year and stringent requirements for the petitioning hospital, many foreign-born RNs elect to apply directly for the nursing green card, which is limited by the EB-3 quota (see section on employment-based green cards), or seek H-1B visas. However, because most nursing positions do not require a bachelor's degree or higher, it can be very difficult for a nurse to receive an H-1B, unless he or she can show that the position does require advanced knowledge, such as for a Nurse Anesthetist.

Another alternative to the H-1B visa is the O visa for persons of extraordinary ability. The requirements for the O visa are much more stringent than those for the H-1B visa, and similar to the requirements for an EB1-1 green card category. If one has reached the 6-year limit of her H-1B visa and does not qualify for further extension, qualifying for the O visa can keep her in legal status. O visas are also employer-specific. An O visa is valid for up to three years, and 1-year extensions may be granted indefinitely if the original project of employment remains incomplete.

g. E-3 Visas

The E-3 classification is available only to nationals of Australia who are coming to the United States solely to perform services in a specialty occupation. A specialty occupation is one that requires theoretical and practical application of a body of knowledge in professional fields and at least a bachelor's degree as a minimum for entry into the occupation in the United States. This status is very similar to the H-1B classification, but without the annual limit on visas issued per year and the limit on the amount of time one may renew an H-1B.

Applicants can apply either directly at a U.S. embassy or consulate abroad or through USCIS if they are already present in the United States in another status. Applicants must provide proof of a valid job offer in the U.S. and evidence of qualifications for the job. Employers are required to complete a Labor Condition Application (LCA) for the applicant, which must be submitted with the rest of the evidence for the E-3 application.

E-3 status is granted for an initial period of up to two years. The status can then be extended indefinitely, with only two years granted per extension. Therefore, one can stay in the U.S. for many years but will have to renew the status every two years.

Recipients of E-3 status can also obtain derivative E-3 status for their spouses and children. Spouses may work on E-3 status, but children cannot. Also, derivative family members do not have to be nationals of Australia.

h. TN Visas

In 1994, the North American Free Trade Agreement (NAFTA) was passed, which among other things, makes temporary employment in the U.S. easier for certain Canadian and Mexican workers. The TN visa is generally used by those engaged in the fields of accounting, engineering, law, pharmacy, science, and education. To be eligible for TN status, one must:

1) Be a citizen of Canada or Mexico;
2) Work in a qualifying profession;
3) Be offered a full-time or part-time position with a US employer that requires a NAFTA professional; and
4) Have the qualifications for the profession

There are different application requirements for Canadians and Mexicans. Canadian citizens are not required to apply for a visa with a U.S. consulate or file a petition with U.S. Citizenship and Immigration Services (USCIS). They can simply request admission as a TN nonimmigrant at a U.S. port of entry with proof of eligibility for TN status, such as proof of Canadian citizenship and a letter from the prospective employer detailing items such as the professional capacity in which the nonimmigrant will work in the United States, the purpose of the employment, the expected length of stay, and the nonimmigrant's educational qualifications. If the Canadian is found to be eligible following inspection by a U.S. Customs and Border Protection (CBP) Officer, then he or she will be admitted as a TN nonimmigrant with an I-94 card.

For Mexicans, the process is a bit lengthier. While Mexicans do not have to file a petition with USCIS, they do need a visa in order to enter the US as a TN nonimmigrant. Mexican citizens must apply for a TN visa directly at a U.S. embassy or consulate in Mexico with proof of eligibility for the TN visa, such as proof of Mexican citizenship and a letter from the prospective employer detailing items such as the professional capacity in which the nonimmigrant will work in the United States, the purpose of the employment, the expected length of stay, and the nonimmigrant's educational qualifications. Once the TN visa has been approved, the Mexican citizen may then apply for admission at a United States port-of-entry.

All TN nonimmigrants may receive an initial stay of up to three years. The status may then be extended indefinitely, either by applying through USCIS or at a US port of entry.The spouse and children on a TN nonimmigrant may be eligible for TD nonimmigrant status. These family members do not have to be citizens of Mexico or Canada. Spouses and children cannot work while in the United States, but they are permitted to study.

L-1 is another type of temporary work visa. L visas are for intra-company transferees, or employees who transfer from a foreign company to work at an affiliate, subsidiary, branch, or joint venture in the United States. Specifically, L-1A visas are for employees in managerial or executive positions, while L-1B visas are for those with specialized knowledge required for that U.S. position. The employee must have worked for the foreign, related entity for at least one continuous year in the three years preceding the L petition. L visas are specific to that petitioning employer, and cannot be "transferred" to another employer. L visas are valid for three years initially. L-1A visas can be extended twice, for two-years per extension, whereas L-1B visas can only be extended once for two years. L-1 visas, like H-1B visas, are very popular due to their dual intent. This means that one can apply for the nonimmigrant visa or have the intent to apply for permanent resident (green card) status and still be able to keep or extend the L visa with no negative effect. Another benefit of the L visa is that unlike with other non-immigrant temporary worker visas, the spouse of the L-1 visa holder may be allowed to work while in the United States on L-2 status. And the greatest advantage to the L category is there are no limits to the number of visas that be granted each year, like with H visas.

Work Permit Forms	
I-765	Application for Employment Authorization. If underlying basis for the work permit expires the work permit also expires
I-129	Petition for a Nonimmigrant Worker
I-539	Application to change or extend nonimmigrant status

i. NIV Quotas

Nonimmigrant Visa Quotas for FY 2010	
Specialty Occupation (H-1B)	65,000 (6,800 may be reserved for H-1B1 – Chile/Singapore) + 20,000 for Advanced Degree Holders from US universities
Intracompany Transfer (Executives) (L-1)	None
Investment (E-2)	None
Temporary/Seasonal Agricultural Workers (H-2A)	None
Temporary/Seasonal Workers (H-2B)	66,000 (33,000 Oct 1- Mar 31, 33,000 Apr 1 – Sep 30)
Job Training (H-3)	None
Student Visas (F-1, M-1)	None
Religious Worker Visas (R-1)	None

Source: USCIS

4. TEMPORARY PROTECTED STATUS (TPS) AND DEFERRED ENFORCED DEPARTURE (DED)

Individuals from designated countries are allowed to temporarily stay in the United States when it is unsafe for them to return to their countries of origin due to "ongoing armed conflict, an environmental disaster, or other extraordinary and temporary conditions." As long as a country is entitled to TPS or granted TPS through an executive order (DED), citizens of that country or persons without citizenship who last resided in that country are allowed upon application for TPS or DED to stay legally in the United States and are permitted to work legally through the application of an Employment Authorization Document (EAD).

TPS was created as part of IMMACT 90. Authority to designate countries and to extend or terminate TPS to these countries was transferred from the Attorney General to the Secretary of Homeland Security pursuant of the Homeland Security Act of 2002. At the same time, the responsibility to administer the TPS program was handed over to the USCIS by the legacy INS. TPS is granted in general for 6 to 18 months at a time and may be extended if deemed necessary when reviewed at the end of the designated time period. Those who are protected under TPS need to promptly reapply for extensions of TPS status. After the end of the TPS designation, those formerly protected by TPS revert back to their original visa status unless it had expired. If they never had legal status and did not gain legal status while under TPS, they will become illegal immigrants. TPS is a legal status unlike voluntary departure periods or grace period which do not render an alien in a legal status.

It is at the discretion of the President of the United States to grant DED, a form of TPS, to nationals of particular countries. DED has been granted to nationals of just 5 countries from its inception in 1990 to 2009.

We have had a number of TPS clients over the years. When the new DED law first started there was no separate form, we filed the 765 and our clients would get the work permit. Then immigration started using 821, but as long as both forms are filed together they will still approve the work permit. Sometimes they will approve the 765 before the 821 is approved. The third wave is here now where CIS will not approve the 765 unless the 821 is filed and approved. This is how foreign nationals fall through the cracks because these things change through the years and unless you are really up to date and with it your clients fail.

Worse, most foreign borns from DED or TPS countries are very economically poor. This means that most of their earnings go to their home to support their families, they do not have money in America to hire proficient and professional lawyers to help them. As a Catholic and a foreign born myself, I constantly struggle with how to charge, bill, be fair, ethical, not overcharge, but be able to run a successful law firm, keep our good people, pay for health care, vacations, 401k, life insurance and pension plans. Success begets success. If our clients do not succeed, neither do we. They are our constituents and they reflect who we are.

The opposite is also true. I like to remind our clients how great and successful and happy I, a normal Chinese immigrant, became. Since they have come in a newer and better era, they can do 100 times better than I could ever dream and be.

Forms for TPS applicants	
I-821	TPS Status
I-765	Application for Employment Authorization

5. GREEN CARDS

a. GENERAL

<u>Gaining proper visa status in the United States</u>

Always think along parallel tracks when you think about status in the U.S., just like in life: yin versus yang, black versus white, happy versus sad, personal goals versus career goals, and temporarily coming to the U.S. versus staying permanently in the U.S.

Once we come to the United States and like it here, how do we adjust our status from having a nonimmigrant visa to obtaining permanent resident status?

Parallel Tracks

Yin	Yang
Black	White
Sad	Happy
Depression	Euphoria

IBM	Apple
Bill Gates	Steve Jobs
Woman	Man
Personal Goals	Career Goals

Parallel Tracks

Non-Immigrant Visa Status	**Immigrant Visa Status**
How do I come to the United States, stay temporarily, and if necessary, get a work visa?	How do I stay permanently and get a green card?
People who come to the U.S. to travel on a tourist visa (or a visa waiver for visa waiver countries) and return to their home country after the trip - just like a U.S. citizen going to another country on vacation and then returning to the U.S.	2 types of people: -People who have documentation for coming to the U.S. and want to realize their dream while still in their home country -People who enter the U.S. with a NIV and want to stay.

In order to travel anywhere in the world and stay there legally, we need three things: a travel document (passport), a visa (a pass issued by the country we are traveling to), and a duration of stay document after entering that country, stating clearly when we entered and when we need to leave the country.

When an American national travels to Peru, we need a U.S. passport, approval from Peru for us to go there (on our own or with a tour group), and after we get off of the airplane, we need to go through the long lines at their immigration and customs office, to have the documents allowing us into that country for a specified duration.

U.S. nationals are lucky. We are sort of spoiled when we travel because most countries allow us to travel there with a pre-approved visa, saving us the trouble of having to apply for one overseas. If we travel to certain countries (e.g. China, Russia, etc.) we still do need a visa and need to apply way ahead of time.

Whether a foreign-born national comes to the U.S. to vacation, visit a sick relative, or to study, the same rules apply; we need a valid passport (travel document) from our country of nationality or birth, a visa to enter the U.S., and an I-94 after we get off the plane stating clearly the duration of stay allowed by the U.S. government to the particular person. Whenever we are missing any one of these documents, we become a person without status in the United States.

It's easy to lose legal status in the U.S. It happens if you do not have a valid passport with your picture in it, if you do not go to the right line at the airport to give them your fingerprints, if you do not check the small piece of paper that you filled out on the airplane and the stamp given to you by the immigration officer stating the date that you need to leave, if your date of birth on your passport was typed incorrectly and you were too busy, lazy, or careless to go get it corrected, if you filled out the I-94 incorrectly on the plane because you thought you were leaving the U.S. only a few weeks after the time stamp on the I-94 and the U.S. officials would not know, to name just a few of the ways.

All foreign nationals from visa waiver countries are allowed 90 days' stay in the U.S. If they stay longer, once they are caught they will be deported immediately to their home country. They are not allowed a deportation hearing or any other recourse. This 90 day visa cannot be extended in the U.S. (no exceptions) and it cannot be changed to a student visa or any other type of non-immigrant visa. Visa waiver holders can change status to that of a green card holder if they marry a U.S. citizen, but there are exceptions to this. For example, if you had a final order of deportation, USCIS will stop the green card processing and deport you.

We usually advise our clients that if they want to stay in the U.S. for more than 90 days for various reasons, it is wise to go to the U.S. Consulate and/or the U.S. Embassy to apply for a B-1/B-2 (tourist) visa, which gives a person more flexibility to stay in the U.S. longer and without all the restrictions.

It is not that difficult to apply for B-1/B-2 visas to come to the U.S., so you really do not have to come to the U.S. illegally. The first thing you need is a valid passport issued by your government. Years ago, before the fall of the Berlin Wall and when there were civil wars in different nations, it was difficult and expensive to get passports. Now, it's not that difficult. Different countries have different rules regarding the issuance of passports, and it's a sovereignty problem, i.e., if you cannot get a travel document that the U.S. government can stamp their passport in, then you can't come to the U.S. If your country conditions are so oppressive that valid grounds exist for you to apply for refugee status, then you would not need your country to issue a passport. We have known refugees who stayed in camps for years, were abused and suffered tremendously while waiting for an interview, but to no avail. You apply for refugee status when you are outside the country, apply for asylum status when inside the country.

I've talked a lot about the tourist visa, B-1/B-2, because most visitors to the U.S. Now let's move on to other reasons why people may want to come to the U.S. You need to also ask yourself why you want to come to the U.S. If you want to come to the U.S. to study, you can apply for an F-1 student visa. If you are working for your government within the United Nations in New York, you should come with an A or a G visa. Since the U.S. only recognizes China (PRC), and not Taiwan, most diplomats from Taiwan come to the U.S. on an E visa.

If you want to come to the U.S. to invest in a business, certain countries' nationals can apply for an E visa. Israel, Taiwan, Korea, and Japan have E visa agreements with the U.S., but countries like India and the People's Republic of China do not. Different visas are subject to specific rules and guidelines, but instead of complaining about them, we need to understand why American immigration officials enacted the rules in the first place. Since this is such a fast changing and fluid area, we all need to educate both our home countries' governments and the U.S. government to change and adapt to a fast changing world. The U.S. is a beautiful country; not only is this a land of immigrants, but it is also a land built by immigrants and children of immigrants. We need to continue applying our core values within the confines and the parameters of our laws and regulations so that this remains a civil and safe society.

Listed below are some of the most-used general visa categories, their respective purposes, maximum stay periods, and what not to do because it would void their status.

Common Visa Type	**Purpose**	**Maximum Length of Stay**	**Notes**
B-1/B-2	Business/Travel	6 months, possible to get one extension	Cannot work on B-2 visa, B-1 visa allows limited work permission
E-1/E-2	Treaty Trader/Investor	Can extend indefinitely in two-year increments	Must be citizen of a country qualifying for E-1/E-2 status
F-1	Seeking an education in academics or language	Length of time required to complete your degree, & I-20 duration	Has to be a full-time student and cannot work off campus without permission
F-2	Spouse/children of F-1 student	Length of time F-1 is valid and not divorced	Cannot work, study full-time
H-1B	Specialty Occupation Worker	6 years	Annual limit on the number of H-1B visas issued each year
H-4	Spouse/children of person in H status	Length of time principal H is valid and not divorced	Cannot work
J-1	Exchange visitor/student/scholar.	Length of time of program in old IAP-66 or new DS 2029	Some classes of J visa requires 2 years home resident in country of origin after end of program, prior to applying for GC or H or L status
J-2	Spouse/children of J-1	Length of time J-1 is valid	Can work after applying for work authorization Subject to 2-year home requirement if J-1 is subject
K-1	Fiancé of U.S.C	90 days to marry the spouse visa sponsor. If not, cannot adjust status	K-1 visa holders can not extend or change their visa status while in the United States

K-2	Under 21 year old child of Fiancé of U.S.C	90 days	Subject to same rules as K-1
L-1A	Intracompany Transfer Executive or Manager	Up to 7 years	If applicant is coming to US to set up new office, will only be granted an initial stay of 1 year instead of 3 years
L-1B	Intracompany Transfer Specialized Knowledge Employee	Up to 5 years	If applicant is coming to US to set up new office, will only be granted an initial stay of 1 year instead of 3 years
L-2	Spouse/children of L-1	Length of time L-1 is valid and not divorced	Can work
O-1	Extraordinary Ability	USCIS determines the length of time, but there is a 3 year initial admission, with extensions granted in 1 year increments	Must obtain consultation letter/advisory opinion
O-3	Spouse/children of person in O status	Length of time principal O is valid and not divorced	May not work, can study full- or part-time
TN	NAFTA Professional Worker	Initial period of stay is 3 years and can be extended indefinitely	Must be citizen of Canada or Mexico
TD	Spouse/children of TN	Length of time TN is valid and not divorced	May not work, can study; do not have to be citizens of Canada or Mexico

Now that you have come to America legally and have decided that you may want to stay in the U.S. for a longer duration than your I-94 permits, whether because you love your job or business here, because you've got nothing to go back to at home and this is your home now, because your children want an education in the U.S., or for some other reason, then how do you go about getting a green card so that you can stay?

Start early, plan, and strategize. Treat this like you treat your health. See professionals, and do not listen to ethnic chatter, rumors, and gossip on the street. Can you imagine your cholesterol level if you ate nothing but fat, meat, and eggs every day? Or having a mental health problem and not seeing a social worker or a good doctor? The green card application process is like life itself; it has a cycle of its own, ups and downs, madness and insanity. But if we work hard at it, do not give up, and push ourselves, meditate, pray, and do the right things, we can endure and get our green cards. It's difficult, neurotic, important, and glamorous, and without it, we can't survive and thrive in the U.S. It sure is a journey.

There is nothing secretive or mysterious about the process. It's all about laws and regulations, tweaking them, going to courts and fighting, and educating our presidents, congressmen and senators about what's right and wrong about the system. The mainstream media's coverage and portrayal of immigrants within the U.S. is also a source of concern. Much like the other rating-oriented productions of news mongers, immigration reporting can often be narrow, sensationalist, and/or biased, leading to a warped view of immigrants and an incomplete understanding of the immigrant experience amongst the public at large. I always get angry and passionate when I read in the news about how a family from El Salvador, Mexico, or Afghanistan with sad faces and children gets to stay in the U.S., as if it's a handout. The general public needs to know that immigration is not about the poor, the sad and the ugly. It is about our faith in the good (although we also recognize the bad) of America, our survival instincts, our love of this country, and our hope and faith that this country will provide the proper foundation and soil for our families in return as it accepts us into this salad bowl. America will remain a great power in the world well into the future. We will work, pay our fair share of taxes, and we will vote for the best governance because we sacrifice so much for this country. Why would we want this country to fail? If the U.S. fails, we fail, because our dream of coming to the best country in the world would be shattered and we would be too old and tired to start anew in another city or country, now that we have found our home.

It's not impossible to get a green card. Do some soul-searching and assess your strengths: Who am I? What is my level of education? Do I have relatives in the U.S.? Why do I want to stay in the U.S.? Am I the first in my family to come to the U.S.? Am I the first person in my family to graduate from college? If I did not graduate from school, and I was on a student visa to start with, what have I done wrong? The U.S. government will only help save you if you help yourself.

Having learned all I have in the thirty plus years I have been in the United States, through this book I would like to be a form of support for immigrants who often do not have a built-in support system in our newly adopted country. When you think about it, the U.S. born citizens, no matter how poor or unfortunate, usually have their relatives and parents here. So as immigrants, we need to reinvent ourselves, be creative, and be flexible. Do lawful things; this is a different culture than back home. Just because lipstick, candies, fruit, and other goodies for sale are all out in the open in a drug store or grocery store doesn't mean that you can take lipstick and slip it in your purse in the land of the free. This is theft in the U.S. and is a criminal act which may lead to denial of a green card.

Selling a phony iPod, DVD, Louis Vuitton purse, or helping a friend by using your good credit to rent a garage in which phony goods are stored is a criminal act. If you get caught, are convicted, or if you plead no contest or guilty, you may become inadmissible or deportable. You might not be able to get your green card.

Also, try not to buy or carry a gun. There are a lot of laws on owning a gun, with registration and form filling requirements. Different state and federal laws have different regulations about whether an immigrant who is not a U.S. citizen can carry or own a gun. I've seen cases where our clients, unbeknownst to them, violate gun ownership or carry concealed weapons and are deemed deportable.

You should read and learn American culture and history, our daily newspapers, and our books. Why come to the U.S. and not learn English? English is actually easier to learn than most other languages. It is definitely easier than Chinese or the Eastern languages. Cultural peculiarities and manners can be just as important to learn as the national language. For example, don't spit in public. Don't eat with your mouth open and/or make noises (such as slurping your soup). Don't eat bread with a fork sticking it into your mouth. If we learn English and learn about American culture, we will ultimately be happier in the U.S., feel more satisfied, and not feel that U.S. immigration laws are discriminatory (which they are in some ways, but our government is making a concerted effort to make changes). However, as I said earlier, we need to make an honest effort to help ourselves before our adopted country can help us in return.

Don't be afraid of failure and low-level paying jobs. You and I know that in most of our home countries, it's shameful to work in a restaurant if we come from a good family. It's embarrassing to hustle and be out of a job, disgraceful to our family if we cannot pass the English speaking test to go to a better university, work as a home nursing aid to a couple, drive someone, or talk about our emotions and how hard it is to make money in the U.S. Still, we *do* talk about these things in the U.S., and it's OK to have a low-level job and make an honest living for an honest day's work. When I was in the Catskills, NY working as a waitress, I even wrote an article and pushed my father to publish it in his weekly newspaper.

Let's get back to discussing how to get a green card in the U.S. now that we like it here and want to stay. There are two ways to get a green card - by applying and going to an interview overseas in the American Consulate/American Embassy, or by applying for Adjustment and Change of Status in the U.S. The green card you obtain through either method will be the same once you get it. You can apply for U.S. citizenship three or five years afterwards; we will get to the U.S. citizenship issue later.

The next thing to decide is on what basis you should apply for the green card. Do you have a U.S. citizen or green card sponsor, such as parents, or a child over 21 years of age? Do you have a skill that the U.S. needs so that you can go through the employment-based green card process and bring your whole family in? Do you have an advanced degree and a great job offer that you would like to stay with in which your employer can petition for me? Are you a religious worker, and your church or place of worship would like you to help spread the word of Jesus, Buddha, or Allah? Are you an abused spouse? A widower? Are you under 18 years old and deserted by your parents? Did your parents ever become U.S. citizens or did your grandparents ever become U.S. citizens? Are you a renowned artist, musician or a fashion model? Do you have skills, and in what ways are you so special that the U.S. wants you? How do you make yourself important to American society or the U.S. economy? Getting and keeping a green card is not really that difficult – just like everything in life, we need to plan, execute, think macro along parallel tracks, and do what is right for you and the country that you call home. Don't do anything without thinking, and don't get so angry and frustrated that you lose it. Once you have done so, it's hard to make a comeback.

This concept also applies to Americans going overseas. We need to respect their sovereignty and soil; just because we are the big, powerful American people doesn't mean that we can go over other countries and chew gum, walk around with shorts and no shirts and ties, take tourist pictures in churches, temples, and mosques when there is a celebration going on, take drugs into or out of their country, or get medical help from their governments without an emergency medical situation.

b. Five Ways to Get a Green Card

There are only five general grounds on which a person can get the treasured green card in the U.S. – **family-based, employment-based, religious-based, investment-based and refugee and asylum-based**. From these five core ways, exceptions are being created. Children over 21 can get green cards and U.S. citizenship now if they were under 21 at the time of the filing and beginning of the parents' green card process. Passport and citizen rules were also changed in March 2002 to include and further codify how children of U.S. citizens born here or naturalized can become U.S. citizens as long as they were admitted as green card holders before the age of 18.

Immigrant Visa (Green Card) Quotas	
FAMILY-BASED GREEN CARDS	**226,000 (current total quota)**
immediate relatives	None
First: Unmarried Sons and Daughters of Citizens	23,400 plus any numbers not required for fourth preference.
Second: Spouses and Children, and Unmarried Sons and Daughters of Permanent Residents	114,200, plus the number (if any) by which the worldwide family preference level exceeds 226,000, and any unused first preference numbers: A. Spouses and Children: 77% of the overall second preference limitation, of which 75% are exempt from the per-country limit; B. Unmarried Sons and Daughters (21 years of age or older): 23% of the overall second preference limitation.

Third: Married Sons and Daughters of Citizens	23,400, plus any numbers not required by first and second preferences.
Fourth: Brothers and Sisters of Adult Citizens	65,000, plus any numbers not required by first three preferences.
EMPLOYMENT-BASED GREEN CARDS	**140,000 (current total quota)**
First: Priority Workers	28.6% of the worldwide employment-based preference level, plus any numbers not required for fourth and fifth preferences.
Second: Members of the Professions Holding Advanced Degrees or Persons of Exceptional Ability	28.6% of the worldwide employment-based preference level, plus any numbers not required by first preference.
Third: Skilled Workers, Professionals, and Other Workers	28.6% of the worldwide level, plus any numbers not required by first and second preferences, not more than 10,000 of which to "Other Workers".
Fourth: Certain Special Immigrants	7.1% of the worldwide level.
Fifth: Employment Creation	7.1% of the worldwide level, not less than 3,000 of which reserved for investors in a targeted rural or high-unemployment area, and 3,000 set aside for investors in regional centers by Sec. 610 of P.L. 102-395.
DIVERSITY VISA LOTTERY	50,000 (current total quota)
AMNESTY	None
ASYLUM	None
REFUGEES	90,000 (current quota)
NACARA	5,000
TEMPORARY PROTECTED STATUS (TPS)	None
SPECIAL AGRICULTURAL WORKER STATUS	None

Source: State Department Visa Bulletin for August 2009

General Forms Filed by GC Applicants	
I-485	Green Card Application
I-765	Application for Employment Authorization

I-131	Application for Travel Document
I-751	Petition to Remove Conditions of Residence
I-90	Form to replace, correct, or extend a green card
G-325A	Form filed concurrently with I-485 listing biographic information in order for FBI and other security agencies to do a background check before USCIS grants a GC
I-864	Affidavit of Support

The other exception is the widower, where the marriage to the U.S. citizen has to be at least for more than two years before the green card application is filed. As an example, say the U.S. citizen (husband A) marries the immigrant (wife B) on October 1, 1995. They live in Japan after that because B has a child that needs to finish school and she does not want to change schools during the middle of the semester. In June 1996, the whole family travels and the mother and her child move to the U.S. with a visa waiver (90 day visa on a green piece of paper) to see if they like the school system. Two months after the family comes to the U.S., and while staying in A's parents' home, A has a massive heart attack and passes away. B now has to help with the funeral arrangements, invite and notify A's friends and parents, and with a visa waiver she cannot extend or change status - no exceptions. In the olden days, the wife and the child could go to Mexico or Canada and return with a new I-94; they are a contiguous foreign country neighbor. Now, the customs officials there will no longer issue a new I-94 to allow such people to come back with a new 90 day visa. They also cannot file for green cards because B was not married to A for more than two years (marriage date was October 1, 1995 and date of death was August 3, 1996). If A had passed away after October 2, 1997, then the widow and stepchild could have self petitioned for a green card under the widower's benefits.

Let's do another scenario. A and B marry on the date as stated above. A had filed I-130 visa petitions for B and his stepchild. Concurrent with the I-130s, B also filed I-485s plus other attachments for his wife and stepchild. They are patiently waiting for the processing of the green card application and have taken fingerprints as per the instructions of the immigration office. A has a massive heart attack and passes away. They have not had the green card interview yet since the normal processing time is four months to two years. The immigration office's position has always been that unless the green card was approved, the widow and child are out of luck. In the past few weeks and months, USCIS has finally taken notice and said that these are approvable cases as long as USCIS can prove the bona fide status of the marriage and the delay is not caused by the immigrant or the U.S. citizen spouse. What if A did not pass away within two years, but passed away on 11/15/99, no relative petition or green card application was filed by A for B? B and stepchild can still get GC by filing on their own because she's not a "legal widow" under the definition of immigration laws.

The most common way for immigrants to get a green card is the employment-based route. Prior to IMMACT 90, which became effective on November 29, 2001, most, if not all immigrants, needed an employer to sponsor us for a green card. After this long process, we were required to work for the sponsoring employer for up to a year after receiving a green card. This regulation has become less stringent through the years with the changes in labor laws and the global employment situation. Our government realized that immigrants should not be treated as indentured servants, and gradually reduced the 1 year rule to 6 months under AC21. Now, foreign nationals need to work for at least 6 months after the filing of the green card, and/or the 6 months following the green card approval.

Let's give an example here, Immigrant A, a foreign student on F-1 visa status wants to the stay in the US and work for her American employer after obtaining her Ph.D. degree. What steps does she need to stay in the US?

Maintaining legal status in the United States	**Becoming a permanent resident of the United States (getting Green Card)**
1. Entered on F-1	Three years for her to get a green card through the employment-based since the investment, religious worker, and asylum routes would not apply to her.
2. OPT granted for 12 months	1. Do a L/C, then an I-140 and file an I-485 when the quota opens. The L/C used to take about nine months including the advertising time although lately, it has taken longer. During the advertising process, if the employer finds someone more qualified than her, then she would not get the green card.
3. COS to H-1B after 10 months (since working for the university, the 65,000, 20,000 H-1B cap, U.S. earned master's degrees do not apply to her)	2. Does she have enough publications and awards for EB-11 to self-apply?
4. H-1B now good for three years and she can do an additional three year extension for the total of six years	3. Or EB-21 – NIW (National Interest Waiver)?
Question: If she does not get a green card within six years, how can she stay? Answer: Check if the H-1B exception applies to her and/or if she qualifies for an O visa.	4. Or EB-12 – Employer sponsor for outstanding professor or researcher
Note: Each visa extension will cost	5. Or EB-21/EB-11 – Employer

money to file.	sponsor

The immigrant and her employer need to talk about the different ways in which he can keep her here to work in his lab without having to pay filing or extension fees for future extensions, or for potential violations if the law changes. The immigrant's need is different than the employer's, because to be a rising star in the research field, she needs to be able to stand on her own two feet and apply for research grants under her own name (a person without a green card or citizenship cannot be awarded federal grants). Thus, her dreams cannot be realized.

Most employers only need to worry about the left hand side of the table above, so that the immigrant can stay legally and work for them. With today's high unemployment rate and other unfavorable economic conditions, the immigrant would probably not be able to find a good job anyway. The immigrant will need to be concerned about the right side, because the right side will allow her to go unhindered by an employer-specific visa.

Making this process harder, in July 2007 the Department of Labor enacted new regulations stating that for all permanent labor certification filings, the employer has to pay the relevant advertising and legal costs. In today's weak economy, why would any employer in his/her right frame of mind pay these costs unless the worker in question is unquestionably indispensable?

The process to obtain the labor certification and green card involves three steps: the filing and approval of the labor certification, the filing and approval of the I-140, and the filing and approval of the green card. The basic idea is to make sure that the forms are filled out correctly. Any missing pertinent information may result in a Notice of Finding (NOF) or a denial. If the labor certification is denied, we can either do the equivalent of an appeal, or we can do a re-filing. A refiling may require a whole new set of advertisements to open up the job market and if an eligible U.S. worker qualifies for the job, then the labor certification process will fail and the immigrant will be denied the green card.

An important test during the labor certification process is the concept of "prevailing wage." The employer has to fill out the forms correctly, do recruiting with both print and internet advertisements, and create internal job postings to notify in-house employees of the job opening. The public ad should contain the job title, recruiting contact, and salary level. This could be a future prospective job offer, because if the immigrant is not currently working with the employer because she does not have a valid visa, she can't begin to work until she gets the green card sponsored by the employer. At the earliest, the work permit [C-9] would be granted 90 days after the I-485/I-765 is filed.

The new PERM rules started in March 2005 after more than 10 years of deliberation back and forth between Labor Department officials and the legacy immigration office. In earlier days (about August 2005 until September 2007), permanent labor certifications were approved or denied in a matter of days or weeks, or two months at the most. At the time of this writing, some labor certifications had been pending in the Atlanta Labor Certification Department for more than twelve months. Audited cases waiting time now is stretching out to more than 1.5 years. The wait is torture.

The I-140 needs to be filed with one of the four service centers after the labor certification is approved. The employer needs to sign this form, either as an individual or a corporation, then file it along with the filing fee, labor certification approval, and other attachments with USCIS.

Speaking of Service Centers, I still remember a time when we could walk to the local immigration offices in the 1970s, 1980s, and early 1990s. We would speak with the officers about different cases, and because of the many years that we had been doing immigration work, we intuitively knew which cases deserved approval and which cases did not. Now there are only 33 district offices and most adjudicating authorities are being limited

Prior to the creation of the Service Centers and the Regional Center concept, H-1B visas, B-2 visa extensions, reinstatements of student visas, work permits, and advance parole were all granted by the local district office. We could even schedule meetings between the officers and immigrants and have them explain face to face why they had fallen out of status. They would promise that it would not happen again and the request would be granted. I've seen quite a few clients who got back in status this way and became great contributing members of our country as their success grew through the years.

Things in the immigration arena have seriously changed. In the 1970s, when immigration offices caught students or immigrants working illegally, they would admonish the offenders, bring them into the office with their lawyers, and warn them that if they got picked up again, deportation proceedings would start. The illegal workers at that time were so scared that of course they stopped, but somehow time passed and they became citizens. In the 1980s and 1990s, immigrants would be advised by their representation to just plead voluntary departure or tell the judge in deportation proceedings that they would go home, and the deportation order or voluntary departure order would be issued. Nothing would happen to the worker after the order. The immigrant would think that she would have no future in the U.S. since the order had already been given to deport her, and instead of advancing in society, learning English, buying a house, and starting a family, she would despair and go into hiding. Immigration officials in those days did not prioritize the deportation of immigrants, and state and local police databases did not contain the status of immigrants. Although the deportation or voluntary departure order hurt the immigrants psychologically, deportation was not enforced. Thus, the surge in the past 10 years of picking up immigrants and incarcerating them has created a large private jailing industry and totally taken immigrants by surprise. Because of the high cost of legal help, these immigrants are really stuck in a quandary.

Let's get back to the student on the F-1, with a degree in Physics. Here, there are two ways to do it – she can have the employer as a sponsor, or she can self-petition because she's that great. She has to prove that she will continue to work in the field in which she has extraordinary ability (physics). She needs to demonstrate that she has "sustained international acclaim." This could also be of a national nature, e.g. published research in scientific journals. If the scientist has published works, how many? Was she ever invited to judge other people's work? Did she ever sit on committees or have membership and associations in her field that only accept outstanding members (as recognized by peers)? Has she done and/or published any original research? Once she thinks she qualifies, we can file all of the documents with USCIS. USCIS may approve or deny the application, but if it is denied we can appeal to the Appeals Board. USCIS decisions have been reversed quite often because most of the arguments about how good and well known the immigrant is are subjective. Scientists are not the only people who can apply for EB-11 processing. People in the arts, music, dance, education, business, athletics and coaching can also apply. However, we need to be careful when we pursue this route for athletes. Athletes have a short shelf life, and in general by the time they are in their late 20s their professional competition days are over. They must then become coaches and teachers. When we do an I-140 under the EB-11 (now it is harder for players; we'll come to that later) we need to be specific as to whether we are filing as an athlete or coach. We'll need a letter and proof that we will be working in that field in the future. If we file as a player and the client becomes a coach, for example, immigration will not approve the case.

If the foreign born has a bachelor's or master's degree and has not made an impact on his work either globally or in the U.S. she can ask the employer to help do a labor certification and to petition for a green card for her.

Another way that we can look at Immigrant A is with an EB-1B – as an "outstanding professor and/or researcher." The employer will have to be willing to petition for this category. Most colleges and universities have rules which state that if the immigrant is only a part-time or adjunct professor or a postdoctoral fellow, they will not sign the papers (and most colleges and universities are not hiring professors and full-time instructors because of budgetary concerns). Research positions must be permanent, which also creates problems. Most jobs are not research-oriented, and this law requires that at least three such positions exist in the relevant department of a company or institute before a research-based EB-1B can be approved. For a university, the law requires that the university official state unequivocally in a letter that the job title is that of a "permanent researcher." This is tough to achieve because most universities give a one year contract, and so officials can't write a letter in good faith to a government entity and say otherwise.

To qualify for this, the immigrant has to be "outstanding" e.g. has to have received major honors and prizes, authored publications in prestigious journals with high impact levels, or judged other people's work and original research with or without commercial value.

It's always advisable for an immigrant with a foreign degree to obtain an equivalency letter, pass a test, or obtain a university acceptance letter for the next level of education. With this proof, there can be no doubt in the mind of the adjudicator that the immigrant has an advanced degree or an equivalent degree in the U.S. We can't expect USCIS adjudicators to know all the methods of accreditation of foreign universities in such a huge world.

After the I-140 is approved by USCIS, we file the I-485 papers with the approval. The I-485 can also be concurrently filed with the I-140 if the quota is open. With the I-485 filing, you can also file an I-765 to ask for work authorization and an I-131 to ask for Advance Parole (multiple travel documents for one year).

Once a person with status or person without status obtains green card status, she can travel in and out of the country, work, buy a house, and have children born here – it's a load off her mind. Best of all, she will no longer wake up during the night in a cold sweat, worried about police knocking at the door. The worst time of day for a person without status is typically early in the morning, between 6 and 9 a.m. This is when ICE officers go to private homes to search for people. Even worse, officers may pick up other friends, acquaintances and relatives who happen to be there. 5 years after obtaining your GC, you can apply for USC. The US does not allow dual citizenship. On the other hand, the US does not force us to relinquish our prior nationality or citizenship.

If you get U.S. citizenship, you can vote in the U.S. and really have a say about how our country is run. You'll feel very much a part of our society as a whole, although it may take years to feel that you are an "insider."

For one thing, when you are stopped by a police officer because you left your purse at home if the police officer is suspicious about your legal status, you don't have to worry that he could detain you for 72 hours to give an ICE officer time to come to the detention center to interview you.

Certain criminal pleas and convictions can make even lawful residents deportable/removable. Aside from the shame and energy spent fighting over a criminal issue, if you are put in such a situation you need to deal with losing your non-immigrant status or green card, mandatory detention, and the realization that no matter how reformed or rehabilitated your behavior may be, you may not be able to come to the U.S. again. The criminal act may become a permanent bar with no possibilities for a waiver.

Depending on where you live, it takes about six months to two years to complete the procedures required for becoming a U.S. citizen. Believe me, gosh, it feels good to be one. I always tell my husband that the best days of my life were the day I got my citizenship, the day we got married, the days my kids were born, and the day I passed my first bar exam. I took two bars; one in New York in 1976 and one in Ohio in 1977 when I moved here after a failed and abusive relationship. Well, that's another story.

The adoption of foreign-born children by U.S. citizens and their passage into the U.S. has also been of great concern lately. The laws here are very simple if we first try to learn the history behind them.

About 15 years ago, U.S. laws were very specific as to the definition of an orphan. Both of the parents of an adopted child have to be proven dead for the child to be deemed an orphan. This held true even if the adoptive parents were successful in adopting the child overseas (this happened often in countries where rape is a shame, abortion is illegal, couples cannot get divorced, and a girl is forced to admit that there is a living father for her child). For a non-orphan to get a green card, she must have lived with her adoptive parents for two years, but this is obviously difficult or impossible when the adoptive parents live in the U.S.

In the past 10 to 15 years, the definition of orphan has become less constricting. As long as one parent is proven dead and the other is totally incapable of supporting the child, you can get the child a green card as an orphan. This "inability to support" the child must be proven, and in more convincing terms than simple emotional factors, having no job, etc.

The U.S. takes adoption cases very seriously. Under the new Child Citizen Act, after a child gets a green card he can become a U.S. citizen immediately. The child would not be able to sponsor or file papers for his natural parents or natural siblings. However, this does not preclude the natural parents or siblings from finding other ways to immigrate to the U.S.

Another way for a foreign born child in the U.S. to obtain a green card is to be declared a "dependent" of the state by a U.S. juvenile court or probate court and deemed eligible by the court for long term foster care due to neglect, abuse or abandonment. Depending on the State Laws on Juvenile Dependency, the final judgment entered has to be entered and filed with the court before a certain birthday (in Ohio, it's age 18), and then the court can apply for a green card with USCIS. If the child is in the custody or constructive custody of the immigration services and ICE services, then the child needs permission from ICE to seek this juvenile custody. Most of the time, however, ICE will deny it.

As I write about immigration laws, the way our government implements and enforces them, and the reasons behind the government's actions, I try to be objective as possible to avoid creating more controversy over the subject. However, I want our foreign-born residents to persevere in spite of all the good times and bad times while going through this process. It is tough to come to the U.S. with very little, start a new life without a support system nearby, get a job and work, learn the culture and language, get a green card, and finally obtain citizenship – potentially a 10 to 20 year journey. Treat it like an adventure and stick with it. It's a humbling experience, but the rewards are great and we come out of it with many stories to tell. The journey also helps us grow as people, becoming more adaptable and knowledgeable.

The United States is very serious about protecting children. The Adam Walsh Child Protective and Safety Act of 2006 mandates that a U.S. citizen filing a petition for spouses, fiancés and stepchildren must disclose to USCIS any criminal records and offenses against minors, especially those involving violence and sex offenses. USCIS is required to notify the beneficiaries of these offenses. The U.S. citizen petitioner may apply for a waiver, but if the decision is in the negative, the denial of a waiver is final. It cannot be appealed or reviewed by a higher level, whether administratively or by the federal courts. Such offenses include kidnapping, false imprisonment, solicitation to engage in sexual conduct, use in a sexual performance, solicitation to practice prostitution, video voyeurism, or distribution of child pornography. When the Act was put into effect, hundreds of approved I-130 or foreign born fiancés and spouses were left stranded overseas. It caused a lot of havoc in our practice, and now we must ask U.S. citizen petitioners how they met their foreign-born fiancés and if they have any criminal records. U.S. citizens are often taken aback by our prying questions, but they are necessary to avoid complications.

This is one reason why I keep impressing upon our young lawyers, and anybody who wants to be great in a field which they are passionate about, that they must keep reading and finding inspiration from the world around them, listening, learning, and being engaged. It is both personally and professionally beneficial to keep current with the news. The world, and all knowledge in it can be thought of as a circle; we apply what we learn to our own work, and in turn create products, physical and intellectual, for others. For example, whenever a war or persecution starts or countries (re)implement a practice such as female genital mutilation, it is imperative that an immigration lawyer is informed and knows to help a client apply for asylum in the U.S. if the practice is considered oppressive in the U.S.

If one applies for an N400 and becomes a citizen of the U.S., he can only travel using a U.S. passport (containing the correct date of birth and country of birth). Make sure that your English name is the same on plane tickets. You may not be allowed to get on the plane with children when traveling without the other parent, so it is best to carry written permission from your spouse for traveling with the children. This is because there have been quite a few incidences in the past of foreign-born spouses taking their children to live in their home country without the other parent's knowledge. Things have evolved in the last 15 years to a point where now, when applying for a U.S. passport for a newborn USC child, both parents must go together to the U.S. post office. The only exception is if the parents are divorced and the custodial parent goes to the post office with the divorce and the custody papers.

To be approved for a U.S. citizenship application, you first need to take the American history, oral, and written English tests, and pass the fingerprint and security clearance checks of the FBI and other agencies. USCIS will review your A permanent administrative files and put them all together to ensure that your entrance into the U.S. was legal, application for a green card and all information are correct, and that you are a person of good moral character. The last step is that you give the oath in front of a Judge. You need to put on the N400 forms the name that you want to use on the Certificate of Naturalization - be careful about this. About 30 years ago, the adjudication officers were generally kinder and would usually put the name down as we wanted it. Instead of using the given Chinese names, we could use our English names. Now on N400 forms, it specifically asks for the surname four times; the name, the name as stated on the green card, any other names used (such as maiden names), and the name to put on the Naturalization Certificate. The new N400 forms are more specific now in question 16 regarding citations, arrests, indictments, and charges, covering all violations of the law, including parking and driving tickets. USCIS is very serious about tracking membership in any associations that we have joined. My advice to my clients is to put down absolutely everything possible; it's better to put more than less, especially now, when the U.S. government is adding to the list of organizations as "terrorist" organizations and is careful to search people's records for hidden agendas, since our world is changing.

After we obtain a green card, and until we apply for U.S. citizenship, we will need to always file U.S. tax returns as a "resident." This means that even if we are working overseas, and the money is paid to us from overseas, we have to report "worldwide" income and can't take the "foreign income" tax exemption that U.S. citizens use. When we only have a green card and not citizenship, we are not allowed to take the "marital deduction" in our wills and estate planning. When in a foreign country where war breaks out, a U.S. rescue helicopter will save U.S. citizens first, and will not protect a green card holder. Therefore, we always advise green card holders to obtain U.S. citizenship. The inconvenience of having to fill out the forms, the $675 filing fee and going through the process of fingerprinting and testing is less serious than later regretting not being a citizen. As I said, Murphy 's Law – anything that can go wrong, will.

Although U.S. laws do not recognize dual citizenship, the country where the green card holder was born does not necessarily have laws requiring her to relinquish her nationality or citizenship.

A U.S. citizen by naturalization or birth may voluntarily relinquish his U.S. citizenship. There is a whole history of case law here. If a U.S. citizen gives up U.S. citizenship for tax purposes, she can never get U.S. citizenship back. She also would not be allowed a tourist visa on another country's passport to enter the U.S. to visit relatives. When clients ask questions like this, I always, always advise them to think twice before making such an irrevocable decision. I completely disagree with their decision to relinquish citizenship. America is such a great country and there are so many people that want green cards and citizenship; why give that up?

Laws enacted in the last 10 to 15 years have made obtaining a green card increasingly difficult. People who were here illegally for more than 180/360 days are subject to a 3 or 10 year bar from entering the U.S. after leaving this country, there is no recourse for most foreign borns except to wait. Some can do a waiver through immigration services for this bar, but they have to have a U.S. citizen or green card spouse or parents. Even then, the beneficiaries must be able to prove extreme hardship to the spouse or parents to request this waiver. The hardship cannot comprise mere separation and financial reasons; it must encompass a "totality" of circumstance. The most common use of this waiver is for a deportee to come back and take care of a sick spouse. A foreign-born who was married with a spouse from his home country and non-U.S.-born children in the home country would not get this waiver by definition and would not be able to return.

Another situation often faced by deported foreign-borns is the inability to come back to the U.S. within ten years of leaving with a final order of deportation or removal. We would need another waiver for this. If the deported person is not subject to a 3 or 10 year bar waiver, this final order deportation (212) waiver can be filed in the U.S. even before leaving the U.S. If there is a 3/10 year bar (601), both waivers would need to be filed in the American Consulate or Embassy where the alien is applying for the immigrant visa. After the immigrant visa interview, which could take upwards of two years, there is another wait for 4 - 12 months for the waiver approval. The person must usually wait in their home country for at least two to three years while their families are in the U.S.

This is one of the reasons why most out of status foreign borns do not want to leave the U.S. to apply for visas, while Congress and our President have proposed that to obtain a green card, foreign-borns would need to first leave the country.

If you are a U.S. citizen and travel overseas, you may want to go to the American Embassy in that country just to see how long the lines are and how anxious the applicants become. It's worth your wait and the time. Every time I did this (once when I rushed over there after losing my passport), it makes me happy and proud that I am an American. It gives me a sense of joyfulness and accomplishment in knowing that after such a long journey, I and many other foreign-born Americans have made it.

Any time that a non-immigrant visa holder or green card holder gets into criminal trouble, she may lose her visa status. Immigration Services cannot take it away just like that, however. They'll have to begin a deportation/removal procedure and send notice of "intent to revoke." At such times, you need to focus. In spite of whatever criminal mistakes you might have made, you need to fight, request relief, try to keep the green card, and hopefully still get U.S. citizenship down the road.

A lot of our clients have asked why they must go through the green card process again when they have admitted their mistakes in the criminal courts, done their time in jail, rehabbed, and paid full restitution for the criminal act. America cannot deport U.S. citizens, but green card status can be taken away. I personally struggled, and continue to struggle with this issue. American is a land built on laws, is so beautiful, and the people here are kind, generous, and often more naïve than those in most other countries. Do we really want foreign people with criminal records staying and possibly committing more crimes? On the other hand, America is all about redemption - a second chance, a failed relationship, a failed family, a killing because of generations of abuse in a rural country - how can we judge who can be redeemed and who cannot? I admit that I don't know, but I'm a great lawyer and I understand the core of this practice. If I and our firm take on representation of a foreign-born with a criminal record, we will fight for relief and "believe" in her rights to be represented, as well as to keep a green card or whatever lifestyle she has left after the horrible ordeal of going through criminal proceedings.

Family-Based

A family-based green card application is a common way to immigrate to the United States.

There are four main categories of family-based green card applications: immediate relatives of U.S. citizens (i.e. spouses and under 21 year old children); parents, spouse, and children of GC holders and of USC, siblings of USC.

Immediate relatives

Immediate relatives of U.S. citizens are given special treatment in the eyes of US immigration, allowing them to immigrate outside of the quota system (in unlimited numbers). These are spouses of USCs, children of USCs under twenty-one years of age who are unmarried, stepchildren when the natural parent married the USC when child is under the age of 18, and parents of USC over 21 year old children.

USCs' fiancés and fiancés' children under 21 years old from previous relationships can obtain K-1 and K-2 visas, respectively, to enter the United States. These visas are good for 90 days and cannot be extended, nor can the visa holders extend or change status to any other type of visa within the country. The fiancés must marry within the 90 days to the same petitioner and gain permanent residency, or lose their status.

I still remember when I started practicing in the 1970s there was no 90 day requirement or requirement to marry the same petitioner for the fiancé visa. This meant that a USC who was madly in love with a foreign born but could not sponsor her because he may still be legally married to a spouse in America could ask his best friend to sponsor and petition for the lady to immigrate to the US. If things worked out, he could now divorce his spouse and marry the lady.

A K-3 visa allows spouses of USCs to come to the U.S., and K-4 visas are granted to U.S. citizens' spouses' children from previous relationships. K-2 and K-4 children may be able to adjust their status in the U.S. even if the marriage of the step-parent and natural parent occurred when the children were over 18, but need to adjust status prior to that of 21 years old. Otherwise they can't adjust because K visa holders can't get GC even if they marry a USC.

When a foreign born marries a U.S. citizen, the citizen must file a separate I-130 for the spouse and each child and I-485s must be filed concurrently with USCIS. An interview takes place after fingerprinting. During the interview, the couple is separated and asked questions about the bona fide status of their marriage as well as the true purpose of the foreign-born for entering the United States. A green card is approved after the interview only if both the husband and the wife pass the test. The foreign-born must prove that there was no preconceived intention of coming to the U.S. to stay and get a green card; the initial purpose must have been business or pleasure (B-1/B-2) if their mode of entry is for the purpose of touring the U.S.. The green card granted in such cases is a two year contingent green card. If the couple remains married for two years after the green card's date of issuance (not the date of marriage, since it takes six months to two years to get the first green card), they both have to file items and evidence to prove the legitimacy of their marriage once more. This adjustment of status within the U.S. is possible even if an immigrant overstays, although those who leave the country may be subjected to a bar.

The immigrant spouse would need to file an I-751 either 3 months before it expires or immediately after the time of a Final Judgment Entry of Divorce (whichever date happens first). Ironically, there is no way to have a case approved for a 10-year green card if the couple are separated and is trying to reconcile. The foreign-born must either be married and cohabitating or divorced with a Final Judgment Entry.

A new Headquarter Memo was recently issued stating that a 751 could now be filed even if the couple is separated and not cohabitating but not divorced yet. This reverses the long time position of Immigration office policy that 751 cannot be filed if the couple is neither living together nor divorced. If nothing is filed by the green card holder when the two year green card expires, he/she will be considered out of status.

In an effort to protect children from potential abuse, the Adam Walsh Child Protective and Safety Act of 2006 mandates that a U.S. citizen filing a petition for spouses, fiancés and stepchildren must disclose to USCIS any criminal records and offenses against minors, particularly violence and sex offenses. Such offenses include kidnapping, false imprisonment, solicitation to engage in sexual conduct, use in a sexual performance, solicitation to practice prostitution, video voyeurism, or distribution of child pornography. USCIS is required to notify the beneficiaries of these offenses. The U.S. citizen petitioner may apply for a waiver to this requirement, but may not appeal the denial of such a waiver.

<u>Other Relatives</u>

Those who are not immediate relatives of U.S. citizens are divided under four preference categories, with a limited number of visas granted each year to each category:

- First preference (F1) - unmarried adult children of U.S. citizens; 23,400 visas plus any visas not used by the fourth preference category.
- Second preference (F2) - spouses of legal permanent residents and their unmarried, minor children (F2A); unmarried adult children of legal permanent residents (F2B); 114,200 visas plus any unused visas in the first preference category.
- Third preference (F3) - married children of US citizens; 23,400 visas plus any unused visas from the first and second categories.

- Fourth preference (F4) - siblings of adult US citizens; 65,000 visas plus any visas not used by the other three categories.

As an exception from these categories, the V visa allows spouses and children (V-2) of green card holders who had an I-130 filed prior to 12/20/00 to enter or stay in the U.S. with a valid visa (as long as they paid the filing fee and additional filing fees to extend the visa each year), and to work temporarily while they wait to receive their green cards – sometimes taking six to eight years.

Let's look at some more scenarios:
1. LPR A went to India to marry foreign born B in 12/1998. After his return to the U.S., he filed the I-130 on 1/20/99. Foreign born B applied for the B-2 visa at least 3 times, paid the application fee 3 times, and was always denied by the American Consulate because of 214(b) – Immigrant Intent. Foreign born B, upon learning of the new V visa law in 12/2000, applied for and was granted the V-1 on 1/2002 and the child's V-2 on 1/2002, entered U.S. on 4/2003 with the V-1/V-2 stay respectively. BCP granted them a 2 year V-1/V-2 I-94 expiring on 4/2005. F-2A quota opened in 12/2007. Can the V-1/V-2 holder get GC? They did not apply for an extension of the V-1/V-2 visa.

Answer: No. Why? 245(i) states that if a foreign born entered U.S. at any time after 12/20/2000 and is out of status and then no I-130, I-140, LC, 360 filed prior to 1/14/98, she cannot get a GC. The I-130 on this case is not filed until 12/98, this Alien does not have 245(i) and thus cannot get GC.

2. Same scenario, only difference is LPR A got GC through a Labor Certification filed for him in 1995. She obtains her GC in 6/1998. Can V-1/V-2 get GC?

Answer: Yes, since LPR has a Labor Certification and I-140 filed for himself prior to 1/14/98, his 245(i) is "grandfathered" to his "prior acquired" spouse and child, and now in 2007, they qualify for 245(i) and will be able to get GC, if no other unforeseeable circumstances arose.

3. LPR C married foreign born D in the U.S. on 11/12/00. I-130 (F2A) filed 12/1/2000. When new law started in 12/20/00, what does foreign born D need to do to get V visa? Does it make a difference if she is out of status? When quota opens, can she get GC?

Answer: After 12/2000, foreign born D can apply for a change of status to that of a V visa. With the V visa approval, she can apply for a Driver's License and SSN and work. She also has 245(i) because I-130 filed prior to 12/00.

4. Same scenario as 1, V-1/V-2 visa holder extends the visa in a timely manner in 1/2005 and was approved. Can she get GC?

Answer: Yes. She does not need 245(i) because she's legal and was not out of the States.

Our office has had the exact same case as Scenario 1, we applied for a Nunc-Pro-Tunc V-1/V-2 extension after the V-1/V-2 had long been expired and we had to file an APA action to Federal District Court to get it. By then, ICE put our client in deportation and we had to terminate the deportation proceedings to get the green cards for the clients.

When filing for a family-based green card, an I-864 must be attached to the green card (I-485) or Packet ¾ filing. Under the new IIRARA Law of November 1996 (effective as of April 1997), the petitioner must also be a sponsor and able to prove that he/she is a citizen or legal permanent resident of the U.S. with a U.S. birth certificate, passport, naturalization certificate, or green card. The sponsor's income must be a minimum of 125% of the U.S. poverty level to be able to sponsor, and the income must be derived from U.S. sources. This is done by filling out an Affidavit of Support and submitting evidence of the ability to financially support the immigrant. Additionally, both the U.S. citizen sponsor and legal permanent resident sponsor must provide proof of the qualifying relationship, such as a birth certificate, marriage license, etc. The 1997 law makes this a legal, enforceable contract between the sponsored person, the government, and the sponsor. If the sponsor does not make enough money, he/she can try to find a joint sponsor who has to be a green card holder or U.S. citizen. The legal responsibility to sponsor only ends when the green card holder becomes a U.S. citizen or earns a total of 40 qualified quarters (credits) or 10 years of working and paying into social security.

Prior to 2005, there was a problem for children who were under 21 at the time of filing losing preferential treatment as minors due to the lengthy process involved in obtaining permanent residency. This was remedied by the passing of CSPA.

A minor child of an F2A spouse can have derivative beneficiary status from an LPR mother or father and not required a separate F2A petition (although a separate petition may be filed if desired). However, in the case of a child of a green card holder who later becomes a U.S. citizen, both the child and the mother will need separate I-130s to be filed on their behalf by the birth father because the child loses beneficiary status after the mother is upgraded from an F2A to an immediate relative on the I-130. Many LPRs who become citizens so that they may upgrade their spouses' status and expedite the process of bringing them to the U.S. do not know that after the change of status the children would need a separate visa petition.

The new CSPA law granted some relief to families in these situations. It states that even after the father *becomes* a citizen, he may write to the immigration and/or U.S. Embassy office choosing to opt out of upgrading the I-130 for his spouse to that of an immediate relative. If he opts out, the spouse may have to wait for a while, as F2A lines are longer than those for immediate relatives.

Visa Petition for Family-based GC Applicants	
I-130	Petition for Alien Relative (does not connote benefits, status or stay period in the U.S.; approval of form allows alien entrepreneur to apply for a GC)

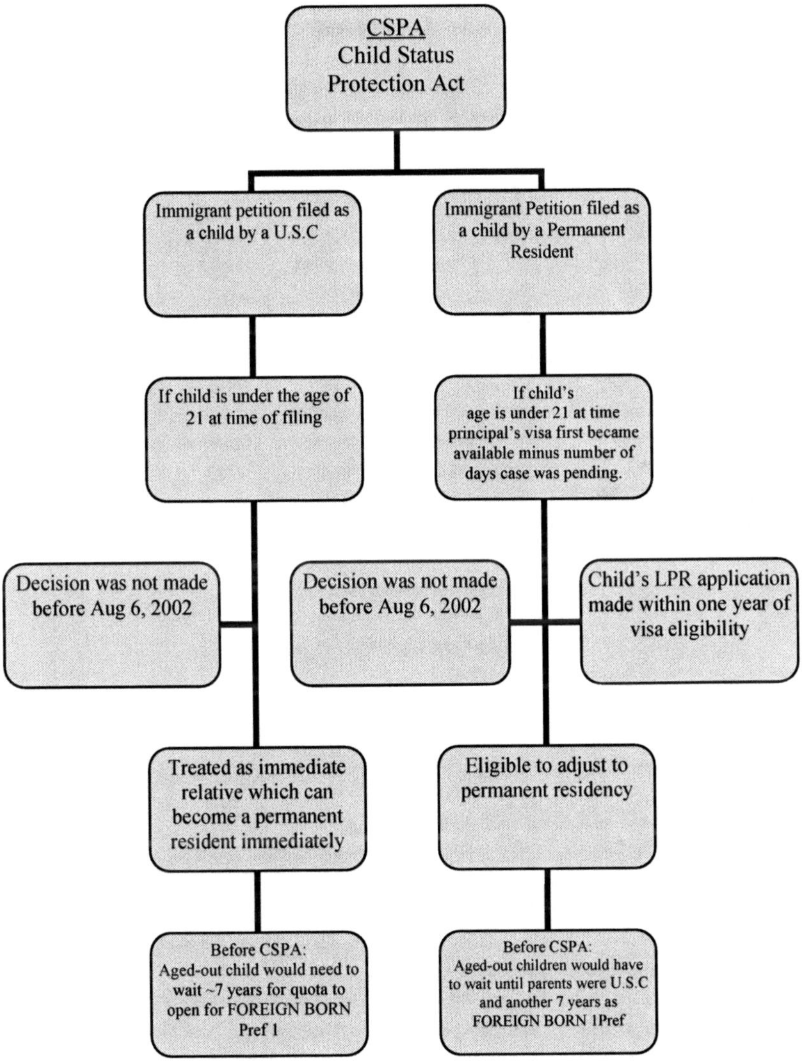
CSPA
Child Status
Protection Act
Immigrant petition filed as a child by a U.S.C
Immigrant Petition filed as a child by a Permanent Resident
If child is under the age of 21 at time of filing
If child's age is under 21 at time principal's visa first became available minus number of days case was pending.
Decision was not made before Aug 6, 2002
Decision was not made before Aug 6, 2002
Child's LPR application made within one year of visa eligibility
Treated as immediate relative which can become a permanent resident immediately
Eligible to adjust to permanent residency
Before CSPA: Aged-out child would need to wait ~7 years for quota to open for FOREIGN BORN Pref 1
Before CSPA: Aged-out children would have to wait until parents were U.S.C and another 7 years as FOREIGN BORN 1Pref

Do not confuse CSPA with President Bush's executive directive allowing 100,000 PR Chinese nationals in the US to obtain green cards after the 6/4/89 Tiananmen Square incident. That directive was also short-term CSPA.

(a) In immigration law, the ages of children are extremely important. Age is determined by the date of birth in the Western calendar.

Age 16	Age 18	Age 21
Final decree of adoption has to have taken place before the age of 16. The only exception is if the adopted parents also adopt a blood-related younger sibling of the 16 year old, and the eldest must be adopted before the age of 18. The relevant age is that of the final adoption judgment.	The registration date of parents' marriage to the step USC parent has to be before the child turns 18. The child can then be petitioned for and sponsored by the U.S.C stepparent to get the green card. If the child is over this age, she has to wait for the natural parent to obtain her green card (after 2 years), then the parent can sponsor her child for F2A/F2B and wait for 8 years to get the green card.	The child reaches maturity. USC children of this age can now sponsor their parents to obtain a green card, and their permanent resident parents can no longer sponsor them. CSPA gave some exceptions here.

(b) Adoption green cards for children: 2 ways – orphans and non-orphans

1. Orphans – either one parent or both parents died
   - If only one parent died, the living parent must be totally incapable of supporting the child and needs to produce a written letter irrevocably relinquishing rights to the child.
   - If the child was adopted abroad, she can come immediately to America with a green card.
   - If both parents died, it's easier to go for an adoption green card. If the child was adopted abroad, she can come to America within a few months. If adoption took place in the U.S. and the child is in the U.S., she has to be admissible to get a GC. For example, if she entered illegally with her living parents, the parents died later, and she was then adopted by another family, she still has to go out of the country to apply for a GC and come back with it if she does not have 245 (i).

2. Non-orphans – both parents living

Final adoption and judgment entry must be before the child turns 16 years old – the only exception is if the child has a younger sibling under 16, and both children can be adopted while the older one is under the age of 18. The children have to live physically with legal custody papers, either through the adoption or guardianship with the adoptive parents for at least two years. After physically living with the parents for two years or after the final decree of adoption, whichever comes later, the adopted parents can file for a green card for the child. The child after the green card approval can no longer sponsor and apply for a GC for her natural parents and natural siblings after getting a GC from her adopted parents. Adoption has to happen before the child turns 16 for this, but the legal living together could happen anytime before she turns 21. The green card should be approved prior to the age of 21. If it isn't, the foreign-born would have to wait at least 4 or 5 years because she would then be over 21 from the adopted parents' I-130 and no longer be an immediate relative (IR), but instead have F-B1 preference.

U.S. immigration law follows the Hague Convention (the international pact governing international adoptions) and is strict in applying them.

The new CSPA law granted some relief to families in these situations. It states that even after the father *becomes* a citizen, he may write to the immigration and/or U.S. Embassy office choosing to opt out of upgrading the I-130 for his spouse to that of an immediate relative.

Abuse

The United States government has created provisions for those who have been physically abused and/or have information about certain forms of criminal activity (T and U visas) and for abused spouses of U.S. citizens. This section has been included in the family-based green card section as spousal abuse stems from marriage-based green cards.

T Visas

To qualify for a T visa, the applicant must be a victim of trafficking, must be present in the U.S., must either have complied with a request for assistance in the investigation and/or prosecution of trafficking acts or be under age 15, and must show that he/she will suffer "extreme hardship involving unusual and severe harm" if deported.

The family members of a victim of trafficking may receive derivative status. If the victim is under 21 years of age, his/her spouse, children, unmarried siblings under the age of 18, and parents can receive derivative status. For a victim who is over age 21, only his/her spouse and children are eligible to receive derivative status. (There are exceptions to this rule if the T application is filed before the applicant is 21 and pending while the applicant turned 21, the applicant is still permitted to file for parents and siblings so long as the sibling is under the age of 18 at time of original T visa was filed).

The parents and unmarried siblings of any of the family members mentioned above can also receive derivative status if the Secretary of Homeland Security agrees they are in danger of reprisal as a result of the victim's cooperation with U.S. law enforcement.

Those with T visas may apply for permanent resident status if they have been continuously present in the U.S. for three years or have been continuously present during a relevant investigation and the prosecution has been completed. The T visa holder must either have complied with the investigation, be able to show that he/she would suffer extreme hardship if forced to leave the U.S., or have been under age 18 at the time of victimization. Only 5,000 victims of trafficking are permitted to receive permanent resident status each year. However, this number only applies to the principal T visa holder. The derivative beneficiaries with T visa status are not counted against this limit.

U Visas

The U visa is available to those who meet four basic requirements: proof of substantial suffering as the result of physical or mental abuse as the victim of certain criminal activity; proof of information about that criminal activity; proof that the person has been, is being, will be, or is likely to be helpful to federal, state, or local authorities; and finally, the criminal activity described must have violated the laws of the U.S. and occurred in the U.S. or in territories of the U.S.

The application must include law enforcement certification, which can be obtained during the investigation or prosecution of the criminal activity. The certification must come from a federal, state, or local law enforcement official, prosecutor, or judge investigating or prosecuting the criminal activity. No official certification form exists, but a letter or other form created by the applicant's representative will be sufficient if signed by the law enforcement official within the six months prior to filing the visa application.

In cases involving substantial physical and/or mental abuse, the applicant should include a personal declaration describing the abuse, photos documenting the abuse, medical reports, declarations by witnesses, law enforcement officials or medical officials, or any other evidence that documents the abuses suffered by the applicant.

There is an annual limit of 10,000 persons who can receive U-1 visa status. Those who are not granted U-1 status as a result of the cap are placed on a waiting list and are notified of their placement on the list; those with older cases receive higher priority.

To avoid inflicting extreme hardship upon victims, the Victims of Trafficking and Violence Protection Act allows for interim relief U status. U visa applicants under the age of 21 may obtain derivate status for their spouses (U-2), children (U-3), parents (U-4), and siblings under 18 (U-5). U visa applicants over 21 may obtain derivative status only for their spouses and children. Applicants for derivative status must procure certification from a government official stating that an investigation or prosecution would be harmed without the assistance of the derivative applicant. Those family members eligible for interim relief U status who are present in the United States must also demonstrate that they would suffer extreme hardship if removed.

If the direct victim is deceased, incapacitated or otherwise incompetent to aid in the investigation and prosecution of the case, the victim's spouse and any children under the age of 21 will be considered victims of criminal activity.

Additionally, if the direct victim is under 21 years of age, his/her parents and unmarried siblings under 18 years of age will also be considered victims.

Those with U status may apply for green cards if certain conditions have been met. The principal beneficiary must have been continuously present in the U.S. for three years and his/her continued presence must be justified based on humanitarian grounds or otherwise be in the national interest of the U.S. Once the principal beneficiary has adjusted status, his/her family members may also adjust status under the same provisions if it is necessary to avoid extreme hardship.

Violence Against Women Act (VAWA)

Passed in 1994 in order to enhance investigation and prosecution of violent crimes against women, VAWA was reauthorized in 2000 and again in 2005. It will come up again for renewal in 2010.

Spousal Abuse

In the majority of family-based green card applications, the U.S. citizen or legal permanent resident petitioner controls when or if the petition is filed. Unfortunately, some petitioners take advantage of their role in this process to threaten and abuse their family members. Many battered women are afraid to turn to the police or other authorities. Recognizing this, the United States government stipulated under the Violence Against Women Act that if a foreign national is the victim of abuse, she may self-petition for an immigrant visa on form I-360.

If a self-petitioner is already the beneficiary of a form I-130 petition filed by an abusive spouse or parent, she will be able to transfer the priority date of the first I-130 petition to the I-360 self-petition. This is extremely important for self-petitioners who must wait for a visa number, as an earlier priority date will result in a shorter waiting time. An applicant who is not the beneficiary of an I-130 may still file an I-360 petition, but will have to wait until a visa number becomes available.

The applicant must have been physically assaulted or subjected to extreme cruelty by a U.S. citizen or lawful permanent resident spouse during the marriage, be the parent of a child who has been abused during the couple's marriage, or be a child abused by a U.S. citizen or legal permanent parent.

If the applicant is a child abused by a U.S. citizen or legal permanent resident parent, the child must be under 21 years of age and unmarried. The child must also submit proof of her relationship to the abusive parent.

Additionally, the abusive spouse or parent must continue to be a U.S. citizen or lawful permanent resident of the United States when the petition is filed and when it is approved. Changes in the abuser's citizenship or lawful permanent resident status after the approval will have no affect on the self-petition.

The victim must also reside in the United States in order to file the petition and must show that she lived with the abuser in the United States in the past. The victim does not have to live with the abuser at the time the application is filed.

Immigration law describes abuse as any act or threatened act of violence, including forceful detention, which results or threatens to result in physical or mental injury. Psychological abuse or sexual abuse or exploitation, including rape, molestation, incest (if the victim is a minor), or forced prostitution are also included in the definition. Other abusive actions may also be considered. The qualifying abuse must have been committed by the citizen or legal permanent resident spouse and must have been perpetrated against the foreign national or his/her child.

The application must include evidence of the abuse, including reports and affidavits from police, judges and other court officials, medical personnel, school officials, clergy, social workers, or other social service agency personnel. If the victim has obtained a restraining order or another sort of order of protection against the abuser, she should submit proof of this as well. Evidence that the abuse victim sought sanctuary in a battered women's shelter or similar refuge should be submitted as well. The victim should submit photographs, if any, of physical injuries sustained due to abuse.

Widows and Widowers

A widow(er) whose spouse was a U.S. citizen may file a self-petition as an immediate relative. To qualify, the immigrant must have been married to the U.S. citizen for at least two years, the applicant must file the relative petition within two years of the spouse's death, the couple must not have been legally separated at the time of death, and the immigrant spouse must not have remarried. To apply, the immigrant must submit proof of the spouse's U.S. citizenship, a valid marriage, and the spouse's death.

A foreign-born widow who was widowed after less than 2 years of marriage and already has a green card does not need to file an I-864, but needs to file an I-751 immediately after the death of her husband. If the widow obtained a green card and her spouse died after more than two years of marriage, she must file an I-360.

Foreign-born widows and widowers whose USC spouses died within the first two years of marriage while the couple awaited approval of the foreign-borns' ten-year green card applications have been automatically denied permanent residency in the past. Because the two-year conditional green cards upon which foreign-born spouses of USCs rely were canceled along with the legal termination of marriages, the unfortunate bereaved have traditionally been prosecuted and deported under this "widow penalty."

Government action to alleviate this legislative oversight recently gained momentum. By early 2009, the First, Sixth and Ninth Circuit Courts ruled that a visa petitioner's death does not end a surviving spouse's eligibility for classification as an immediate relative. USCIS then advised its officers that the widow penalty cannot be applied to cases falling under the jurisdictions of the First, Sixth and Ninth Circuits but should be applied to all other jurisdictions.

In the face of constant criticism regarding the "widow penalty," DHS issued a temporary reprieve for the hundreds of affected widows and widowers. On June 9, 2009, Secretary of Homeland Security Janet Napolitano issued a statement that for two years, all action, including deportation proceedings, would be suspended for foreign nationals whose green card applications were denied because their U.S. citizen spouses passed away during the often-lengthy application process. On June 15, 2009, USCIS Acting Associate Director Donald Neufeld issued a memo clarifying how foreign nationals whose U.S. citizen spouses died before the second anniversary of the marriage can receive deferred action on their case.

The foreign national must file form I-360, with the associated filing fee, at the Vermont Service Center. The applicant should check box 'm' for other purposes of filing the form, and should then explain he/she is filing for deferred action as the surviving spouse of a U.S. citizen married for less than two years. If deferred action is approved, it will be valid for two years. During this time, a foreign national may apply for and receive employment authorization to work in the United States, as well as advanced parole to travel outside of the U.S. Any period of time spent in deferred action does not count as an unlawful presence in the U.S.

Recently, President Barack Obama and some member of Congress have expressed their support for ending the widow penalty. On April 2, 2009, Senator Bill Nelson (D-FL) and Congressman Jim McGovern (D-MA) introduced the Fairness to Surviving Spouses Act of 2009 (S. 815/H.R. 1870) to end the widow penalty. On June 11, 2009, Senator Robert Menendez (D-NJ) introduced the Orphans, Widows and Widowers Protection Act (S. 1247), which addresses surviving relative issues. Department of Homeland Security Appropriations Act of 2010 (H.R. 2892), which eliminates the widow penalty, passed on July 9, 2009. The US Senate deliberated and passed the DHS bill containing the widow penalty relief provisions on October 20, 2009, and will likely be signed by President Obama soon. According to the relief from the widow penalty, there are two remedies accomplished by the new law: (1) allowing all widow(er)s of American citizens and their children to self-petition regardless of whether an I-130 had been filed prior to death, and (2) permitting certain survivors as direct or derivative beneficiaries of petitioners or principal beneficiaries who have died to continue to reside in the U.S.

Self-Petition for Abused-Spouses	
I-360	Petition for Amerasian, Widow(er) or Special Immigrant (does not connote benefits, status or stay period in the U.S.; approval of form allows alien entrepreneur to apply for a GC)

Abandoned Children

Foreign-born children in the U.S. may obtain green cards if declared a "dependent" of the state by a U.S. juvenile court or probate court and deemed eligible by the court for long term foster care due to neglect, abuse or abandonment. The final judgment must be entered and filed with the court before the birthday specified in the relevant state law on juvenile dependency before the court may apply for a green card with USCIS. A child in the custody of immigration services must request permission from ICE to seek juvenile custody. Unfortunately, such requests are most often denied.

Employment-Based

The most frequently used method for immigrants to get a green card is the employment-based route. Like the family-based route, those applying under the basis of employment are separated into several preference levels. These levels include priority workers, those with advanced degrees or exceptional skill, and other skilled workers and professionals. Religious and investment-based applicants constitute the fourth and fifth employment-based preference levels, but are addressed in later sections. Each category has its own quota within the total number allotted each year for employment-based green cards.

EB-1

The EB-1 category is reserved for immigrants holding the highest distinctions, positions, or level of achievement in their fields of endeavor. Those with these exceptional accomplishments are exempt from the labor certification requirement and may apply directly for an I-140, which may save months of processing time. The EB-1 category is partitioned into three subsections. The chart on the following page indicates all qualifications necessary for the EB-1A, EB-1B, and EB-1C.

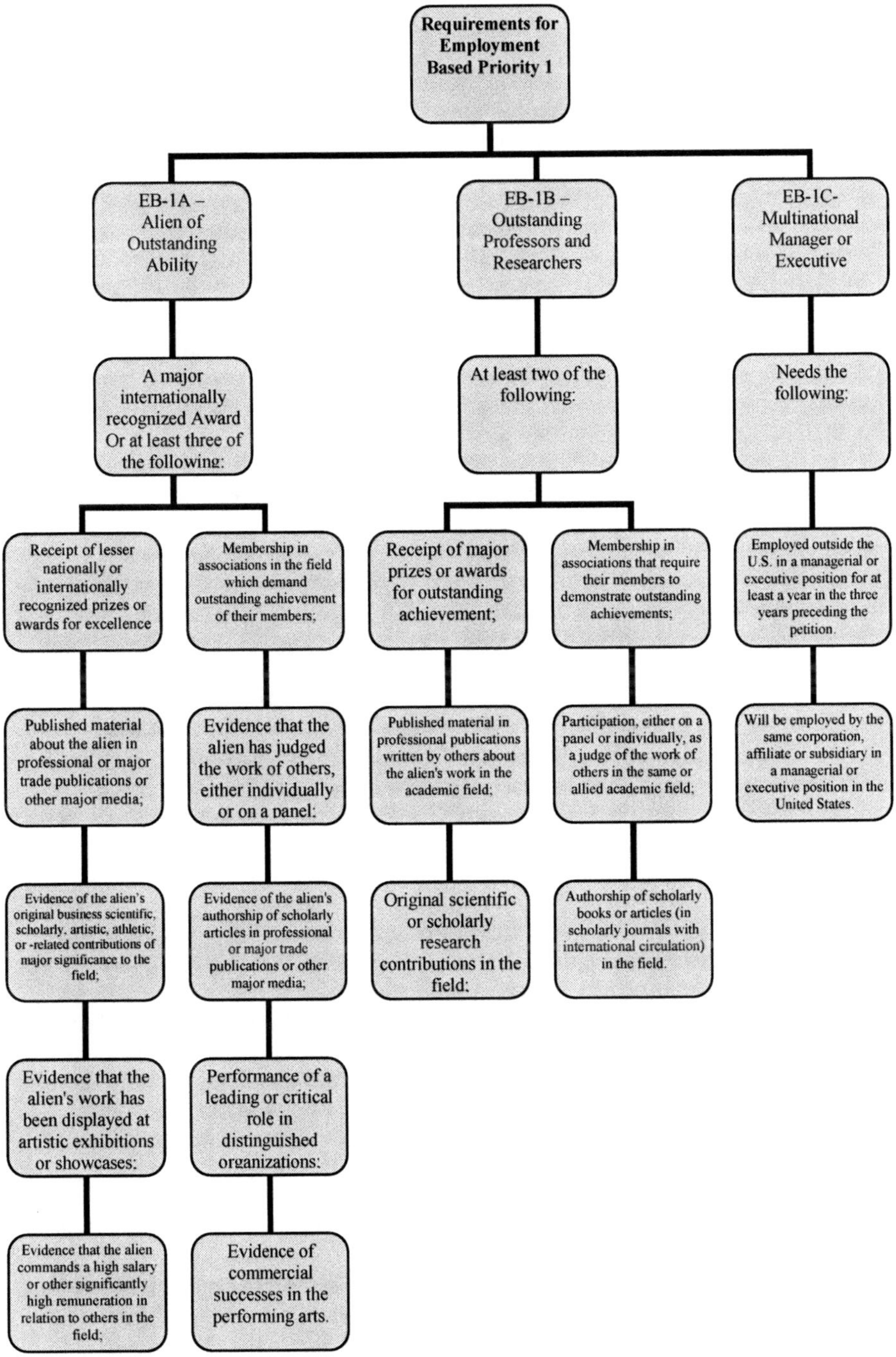
Requirements for Employment Based Priority 1
EB-1A – Alien of Outstanding Ability
EB-1B – Outstanding Professors and Researchers
EB-1C- Multinational Manager or Executive
A major internationally recognized Award Or at least three of the following:
At least two of the following:
Needs the following:
Receipt of lesser nationally or internationally recognized prizes or awards for excellence
Membership in associations in the field which demand outstanding achievement of their members;
Receipt of major prizes or awards for outstanding achievement;
Membership in associations that require their members to demonstrate outstanding achievements;
Employed outside the U.S. in a managerial or executive position for at least a year in the three years preceding the petition.
Published material about the alien in professional or major trade publications or other major media;
Evidence that the alien has judged the work of others, either individually or on a panel;
Published material in professional publications written by others about the alien's work in the academic field;
Participation, either on a panel or individually, as a judge of the work of others in the same or allied academic field;
Will be employed by the same corporation, affiliate or subsidiary in a managerial or executive position in the United States.
Evidence of the alien's original business scientific, scholarly, artistic, athletic, or -related contributions of major significance to the field;
Evidence of the alien's authorship of scholarly articles in professional or major trade publications or other major media;
Original scientific or scholarly research contributions in the field;
Authorship of scholarly books or articles (in scholarly journals with international circulation) in the field.
Evidence that the alien's work has been displayed at artistic exhibitions or showcases;
Performance of a leading or critical role in distinguished organizations;
Evidence that the alien commands a high salary or other significantly high remuneration in relation to others in the field;
Evidence of commercial successes in the performing arts.

EB-1A applicants must be able to prove that they will continue to work in the field in which they have extraordinary ability. They must also have earned "sustained international acclaim." In addition to scientists, individuals in the arts, music, dance, education, business, athletics and coaching may also apply. However, athletes who petition under EB-1A may encounter problems due to the particular nature of their profession. Many athletes change occupations after their professional careers are over, becoming coaches and teachers. Consequently, athletes filing an I-140 under the EB-1A must take special care as to whether they wish to file as athletes or coaches. If an athlete files the application as a professional athlete and later becomes a coach, problems may arise. However, a distinct advantage of the EB-1A is that the applicant may self-petition and does not need an employer sponsor. Furthermore, as a result of the relative subjectivity of many qualifications for an EB-1A, USCIS decisions are often reversed.

The second type of the EB-1, EB-1B, is for "outstanding professors and/or researchers." An employer must petition for the immigrant in this category, making the process relatively difficult compared to that of an EB-1A. Most colleges and universities have rules which stipulate that they will not sponsor potential immigrants who are only part-time or adjunct professors. Research positions must be permanent and the law requires that at least three such positions exist in the relevant department of a company before a research-based EB-1B can be approved. For a university research position, a university official must state unequivocally in a letter that the job title is that of a "permanent researcher." This is frequently difficult to achieve because many universities hire researchers on one year contracts.

There is also an EB-1C category for multinational managers and executives. Those who qualify must have worked at least one year abroad with the same company as a manager or executive out of the three years prior to the EB-1C green card filing.

EB-2

Individuals with advanced degrees or exceptional ability may be able to apply under the EB-2 category. Requirements for an EB-2 differ from those for an EB-1 in that they are generally less stringent but applicants must acquire a labor certification unless they qualify for and obtain a National Interest Waiver (NIW). An NIW is only approved for those whose work in the sciences, arts, or business will be "in the national interest." Because what fulfills this requirement remains largely unspecified, applicants must usually build an inordinately strong case for their intrinsic value to the nation and/or have extraordinary ties to government agencies for an NIW to be granted. The services provided by the immigrant must be of national scope, and it must be proven that accepting the immigrant in question will be of sufficient benefit to the nation to merit the removal of potential competition in the labor certification process.

It is always advisable for an immigrant with a foreign degree to obtain an equivalency letter, pass a test, or obtain a university acceptance letter for the next level of education. With this proof, there can be no doubt in the mind of the adjudicator that the immigrant has an advanced degree or an equivalent degree in the U.S. Doctors, lawyers, engineers with advanced degrees, and MBAs are all in the

EB-2 category. Doctors must pass the U.S.MLE I, II, and III to obtain an H-1B visa unless they are of exceptional merit (EB-1). The U.S.MLE I and II may be sufficient (depending on the State Board of Physician Licensing) for EB-1 doctors to be licensed to practice in their state, but not to obtain an H-1B to work.

EB-3

The EB-3 category applies to "skilled workers, professionals, and other workers." The majority of those who apply for employment-based green cards do so with an EB-3. This category also includes a list of occupations deemed especially desirable by the United States government, designated Schedule A. Schedule A workers, including physical therapists, nurses, and other occupations as needed, are exempt from the labor certification requirement. However, pharmacists, despite their demand in the U.S., must still file for labor certifications.

I'm especially interested in and follow the pharmacist profession. My husband is one. The pharmacists execute the written prescriptions of the white coats (medical doctors) and are held to extremely high standards, and cannot give out pills to addicts. When our family was younger my husband and I would pile our kids into our family car and deliver medications and prescriptions to his patients who were too infirm to drive to his pharmacy. We made a lot of life-long friends through these deliveries.

The Employment-Based Process

An employer can sponsor a foreign-born worker to become a permanent resident and work permanently in the United States. The most common employment-based green card process has three basic steps: labor certification, the immigrant petition (I-140), and the permanent residency application (I-485).

Labor Certification and PERM

The first step in the process is called labor certification, which must be issued by the U.S. Department of Labor. The labor certification process, filed through the Program Electronic Review Management system (PERM), is a market test comprised of a series of recruitment activities. The market test requirements are laid out in federal regulations and are intended to ensure that no qualified U.S. workers able, willing, qualified, and available to accept the job will be displaced by employment of the foreign worker. The foreign worker will be certified only if the employer proves to the Department of Labor that U.S. workers are not available to fill the position.

Prevailing Wage

By sponsoring a foreign-born worker, the employer indicates the intent to hire that worker in a full time position, at a salary equal to or greater than the prevailing wage for the occupation in the area of intended employment, upon completion of the green card process.

Prevailing wage determinations for both the labor certification and H-1B processes are based on the Occupational Employment Statistics (OES) compiled annually by the Department of Labor's Bureau of Labor Statistics. State Workforce Agencies (SWA) make determinations based upon a job's duties, minimum requirements, and geographic location. The job's duties and minimum requirements must be in accordance with industry standards and cannot be unduly restrictive or tailored to the foreign worker's qualifications. All required experience must be quantifiable and measurable.

Recruitment

Since 2007, Department of Labor regulations require the sponsoring employer to pay all related labor certification and recruitment costs.

During the recruitment process, a job order must be placed with the State Workforce Agency (SWA) in the area of intended employment. The SWA will try to locate any U.S. workers who meet the employer's minimum requirements for the position, including education, experience, and training. Other required recruitment activities include print advertisements in a generally circulated newspaper, and internal job postings to notify existing employees.

The employer determines whether any applicant is minimally qualified, and may not discourage U.S. workers from applying or inform them that the recruitment was undertaken solely for labor certification purposes.

If a qualified U.S. worker is found, then the labor certification process stops. However, the process serves only as a test of the relevant labor market, so the employer is not obligated to hire any U.S. worker found through the recruitment process. The employer may choose to restart the labor certification process at a later date.

Filing and Adjudication

If no qualified U.S. workers are found, then the application for labor certification can be filed electronically through the Department of Labor's PERM system. Processing times vary, and have slowed to down considerably over the past year. Some labor certifications remain pending for over 10 months. If the Department of Labor issues an audit for the application, then the processing time may be delayed by an additional 12 months or longer.

If the application for labor certification is denied, the employer can appeal the decision or restart the labor certification process. Note that advertisements are only valid for labor certification purposes for 6 months – since processing times currently exceed that validity period, the employer may be required to repost the job advertisements to restart the process.

Exceptions to Labor Certification

There are several employment-based categories that do not require labor certification. For example, Registered Nurses have been designated as a Schedule A occupation, which means that it is in urgent demand in the U.S. If a Registered Nurse has a valid license and a job offer, he or she can begin the green-card process with the I-140 immigrant petition.

As indicated by the following chart, self-petition applications, intra-company transferees, and outstanding researchers and professors do not require labor certification:

SELF-PETITION *	EMPLOYER SPONSORSHIP REQUIRED
Do not need a petitioning/sponsoring employer/job offer	EB13 – Intra-company transfer
EB11	EB12 – researchers and professors
EB2B—NIW	EB2A
	LC – EB2
	LC – EB3

* Changes in IMMACT90 – purpose is to allow persons in a profession that are frequently free agents themselves to self-sponsor and petition themselves if they have demonstrated an extremely high level of excellence as evidenced by acknowledgements of other experts, newspaper articles, articles written by them in high impact journals

I-140s and I-485s

I-140

Upon approval of the application for labor certification, the sponsoring employer submits an immigrant petition (Form I-140) on behalf of the foreign worker to the U.S. Citizenship and Immigration Services (USCIS). In addition to the required forms, the employer must provide evidence of its ability to pay the prevailing wage since the year that the application for labor certification was filed, and evidence that the sponsored worker meets the position's minimum requirements listed on the labor certification.

Evidence of ability to pay can include copies of the employer's federal tax returns, which should show sufficient earnings and taxable income to support the wages to be paid to the foreign-born worker. If the tax return does not show sufficient earnings, you can check Schedule L of the return and calculate the short term assets less the short term liabilities. The employer can also show that it has been employing the foreign worker at the prevailing wage or higher salary. Evidence of compensation includes paystubs and W-2 forms.

If the employer has more than 100 employees a letter from the company's Chief Financial Officer may be sufficient.

I-485

The last step is for the foreign worker to file the I-485 permanent residence application. The date on which the foreign worker is permitted to file Form I-485 depends on the availability of immigrant visas. If an immigrant visa is immediately available, then Form I-485 may be filed at the same time as Form I-140. However, there are a limited number of immigrant visas available each year, and are backlogged especially for high-volume countries such as China, India, Mexico, and the Philippines. The "priority date," which sets the foreign worker's place in line for a number, is based on the date the application for labor certification was filed with the Department of Labor. After the I-485 is approved, the sponsored worker should receive his or her green card by mail.

Legal Status

Note that neither labor certification nor the I-140 petition provides a foreign-born with legal status in the U.S. Therefore, the foreign-born must maintain legal status until Form I-485 is filed, for example, with nonimmigrant work visas such as H-1B or L visas. However, these work visas are limited in duration. For example, a foreign worker can remain in H-1B status for a maximum of six years, unless he or she qualifies for certain exceptions. Therefore it is important for foreign workers in the U.S., especially those from high-volume countries, to begin the green card process as early as possible.

USCIS recently issued a memorandum regarding Successor-in-Interest Determinations in Adjudicating Form I-140 highlighting three factors which should be considered in evaluating whether a previously-approved labor certification remains valid for I-140 adjudications:

1) whether it is the same job;
2) if the successor has established eligibility for the requested visa classification in all respects; and
3) if the successor has adequately detailed the nature of the transfer of rights, obligations, and ownership of the prior entity.

The points are then outlined for the field as three successor-in-interest factors as follows:

1) the job opportunity offered by the successor must be the same as the job opportunity originally offered on the labor certification;
2) the successor bears the burden of proof to establish eligibility in all respects, including the provision of required evidence from the predecessor entity, such as evidence of the

predecessor's ability to pay the proffered wage, as of the date of filing the labor certification with the Department of Labor; and
3) for a valid successor-in-interest relationship to exist between the successor and the predecessor that filed the labor certification, the petitioner must fully describe and document the transfer and assumption of the ownership of the predecessor by the successor.[227]

Visa Petition for Employment-Based GC Applicants	
I-140 485 Package	Petition for Alien Worker (does not connote benefits, status or stay period in the U.S.; approval of form allows alien beneficiary to apply for a GC)

Things Every US employer/HR person needs to do:

1. Fill in all I-9s correctly. Make sure all the i's are dotted and t's are crossed. All workers, employers, bosses, owners need to fill out this form within three days of hire. The company should designate a bookkeeping person to check all information and to sign correctly.
2. All persons working in your company including USCs, green card holders, legals and illegals should fill out the I-9.
3. Tell the truth. US citizens fill out Part A, green card holders, legal non-immigrant workers and illegals all need to fill out Part B and C. If the worker is illegal, fill it out to the best of your knowledge. The employer will be fined anyway, but at least she is fined for illegal hire and not paperwork violation as well.
4. Do not pay cash to your worker or underpay your workers. Report your payments. You don't want someone to come back and report you.
5. If you hire H-1B workers, when you terminate the employment or when they quit, make sure you inform USCIS that this H-1B is terminated. Once this letter is sent, the H-1B worker cannot come back or report you that you are not paying H-1B prevailing wages.
6. When petitioning for an H-1B visa for a non-immigrant visa worker, you need to pay the required employer filing fee. Don't wiggle out of paying the money and be caught by Immigration and/or DOL. They may do an H-1B audit and drive you nuts. Remember that ICE has a lot of resources and they are the U.S. government. They hire the best people they can afford. You are merely trying to run your business and to earn money for your shareholders.
7. Don't use the word "consultants" or 1099 payment methods to avoid doing I-9s. If under labor law you control the work schedules of the workers, you do need to fill out an I-9. Filling out an I-9 is immigration law. 1099 versus W-2 is tax laws, these laws are interpreted differently by the different agencies.
8. All H-1B visa holders need to be paid by W-2. Once that person gets a green card you can pay them by 1099.

9. Be honest with your legal and/or illegal workforce. Nowadays everybody can sue everybody. Workers have been very empowered. Just because they have no status in America does not mean they cannot report you to the US labor department, CIS, or their labor unions. At the end, they just go home, and you spend thousands of dollars in legal fees defending yourself. Workers today are different from when I came to the U.S. 40 years ago. We didn't have mentors and advisers or friends or the internet to help us navigate the system. We only had the burning desire to become a somebody and not to shame our parents and the people who put their faith in us and loaned us money.
10. Help educate your colleagues and workers. Rules have changed. Years ago organizations were vertical – bosses and workers. Now we are all forming partnerships and moving laterally. Work with your foreign born workers, learn from them and educate them. If you can, get to our heart and gut, we will work hard and jump hoops and die for you because this is our culture. America is a young country, money is important. For most foreign borns, we look at things more long-term. While money is important, other qualities even more so. For example, we believe that good begets good, faith is important, stubbornness is a virtue, and guanzhi (relationships in Chinese) are key. I am always taken aback by the lack of longevity in the American culture. Today this, tomorrow that. America definitely has a very ADD culture in this generation.

Religious-based

Religious-based green cards may also be considered employment-based fourth preference. The religious-based green card category is most often used by R-1 nonimmigrant religious workers who wish to continue their religious profession, ministry, and vocation in the United States on a more permanent basis. There is a limit of 5,000 immigrant visas available annually to religious workers. While the immigrant and nonimmigrant religious worker categories have some similarities, there are also differences.

To apply for a religious-based green card, the religious worker must work for a bona fide, nonprofit, religious organization or an organization that is affiliated with a religious denomination. New religious worker regulations require the employer to sign an attestation as to the validity of the organization and the denomination with which it is affiliated.

Another new feature of the religious worker application is the requirement for on-site inspections of the religious organization, which are conducted by the Department of Homeland Security. According to the government, the site visitation requirement, together with employer attestations, have reduced fraud for both immigrant and nonimmigrant religious worker applications.

Religious workers are categorized into three major classes: ministers, those working in a religious vocation, and those working in a religious occupation. A minister is defined as one who is authorized by religious leaders to conduct worship services and perform other traditional religious functions. A religious vocation is a calling to the religious life with a demonstrable commitment to that life, such as taking vows, which includes monks and nuns. A religious occupation is one that is traditionally part of the work of the denomination, such as religious instructors, missionaries, and liturgical workers. Liturgical workers also include organists. Our firm was one of the first to get a case approved for a Roman Catholic Church Organist back in 1999/2000. This visa does not apply to support staff such as secretaries, janitors, or fund raisers.

Like the nonimmigrant religious worker category, the worker must have been a member of the denomination for at least two years. Unlike the nonimmigrant category, special religious-based green card applicants must have worked for a religious group of the same denomination for at least two years prior to the application. This work may be done either in or out of the U.S.

Prior to June 2009, religious workers seeking permanent residency had to first file their I-360 applications, wait months for an approval, then file their I-485 adjustment of status applications. This led to many problems for applicants, especially those who were nearing the end of their allotted 5 years of nonimmigrant religious worker status. It was also a problem for those who had pending I-360 applications and then had to demonstrate that they had no intention of immigrating to the United States when renewing their nonimmigrant visas. In June 2009, a decision in *Ruiz-Diaz v. United States* significantly changed the application process for special immigrant religious workers by requiring USCIS to allow the concurrent filing of I-360 and I-485 applications for special immigrant religious workers.

There still remains another issue for special immigrant religious workers who are not ministers. While ministers and their counterparts in other religions, such as rabbis, imams, priests etc., can enjoy relatively unfettered immigration to the U.S., the other two classes of special immigrant religious workers are bound by laws which expire if not renewed every three years.

At the time of this writing, the two categories aside from ministers are sunsetting at the end of Sept. 2009 and we are all sitting on pins and needles waiting for the renewal.

This is a tough visa category for us immigration practitioners because of the high perceived fraud level. The required two years of religious work experience is difficult to prove especially when a lot of the vocation requires a vow of poverty (therefore with no filed tax return). Quite a few court cases are filed to seek the determination of whether part-time work of 2 years qualifies for the petition, amongst other concerns.

Visa Petition for Religious-Based GC applicants	
I-360	Petition for Amerasian, Widow(er) or Special Immigrant (does not connote benefits, status or stay period in the U.S.; approval of form allows alien to apply for a GC)

Investment-based

Individuals may also gain a green card through investment; this method is regarded as employment-based fifth preference. This green card category was created under IMMACT 90 to attract foreign capital to the United States and to create jobs for Americans. There is an annual quota of 10,000 for investment-based green card applications. To be eligible for an EB-5, the foreign-born must have invested, or be actively in the process of investing, the required amount of capital into a new business that he/she has established. He/she must further demonstrate how the investment will benefit the U.S. economy and create the required number of full-time jobs in the United States.

To qualify, the investor must invest at least $1,000,000, or at least $500,000 in a targeted employment area (TEA), which is an area where the unemployment rate is at least 150% of the national average unemployment rate or a designated rural area. The investment must also create full-time employment for at least ten qualified individuals. If the investment is made by purchasing or expanding an existing business, the investment must maintain the number of existing employees at no less than the pre-investment level for a period of at least two years,

An applicant whose EB-5 application is approved will then be granted conditional resident status. Similar to certain marriage-based green card applications, this conditional resident status is conferred to ensure that the applicant will fulfill the terms of the permanent resident status. In the case of the investor, he/she must be able to show that the terms of the investment, as outlined in a business plan, have been fulfilled within two years. Six months after an application is approved, the two-year period for the investor to create the required number of full-time jobs begins. Within 90 days of the end of this two-year period, the investor must apply to have the conditional status removed.

Of the 10,000 EB-5 investor visas available annually, 3,000 are set aside for those who apply under a pilot program involving a USCIS-designated "regional center". A regional center is an entity, organization, or agency that has been approved as such by USCIS, focuses on a specific geographical area within the United States, and seeks to promote economic growth through increased export sales, improved regional productivity, the creation of new jobs, and increased domestic capital investment.

Visa Petition for Investment-based GC applicants	
I-526	Immigrant Petition For Alien Entrepreneur (does not connote benefits, status or stay period in the U.S.; approval of form allows alien entrepreneur to apply for a GC)

Regional Centers

As of the time of this writing, Sept. 10, 2009, the following listed Regional Centers were approved. This regional center law was sunsetting at the end of Sept. 2009. As of today, October 23, 2009, this E-B 5 law has not been renewed yet.

Alabama:
Alabama Center for Foreign Investment, LLC
RSA Union Building
100 North Union Street, Suite 682
Montgomery, AL 36104
Tel: 1+ (334) 954-3111
Fax: 1+ (334) 954-3112
Email: info@acfi-alabama.com
www.acfi-alabama.com/alabama.html

California:
California Consortium for Agricultural Export
333 S. Grand Ave., 25th Floor
Los Angeles, CA 90071
Tel: (213) 892-6367
Fax: (213) 892-2267
Email: visa@ccax.com
www.ccax.com/

California Investment Immigration Fund, LLC
c/o Tat Chan
12688 Chapman Ave, #3313
Garden Grove, CA 92840

CMB Export LLC
Corona Professional Center
400 S. Ramona Avenue, Suite 212AA
Corona, CA 91719
Tel: (309) 797-1550
Fax: (309) 797-1655
Email: info@cmbeb5visa.com
www.cmbeb5visa.com

El Monte Regional Center
Jean Lang, Exec. V.P.
10501 Valley Blvd., # 1888
El Monte, CA 91731

Imperial Regional Center
James Lo/Pacificland International Development Inc
c/o Linda Lau, Esq.

150 N. Santa Ana Ave, STE 300
Arcadia, CA 91006

Los Angeles Film Regional Center
CanAm Enterprises, LLC
2029 Century Park East, Suite 1400
Los Angeles, CA90067
Tel: (424) 202-3602
Email: info@losangelesfund.com
http://www.losangelesfund.com

Regional Center Properties
5160 Birch Street, Suite 200
Newport Beach, CA 92660

Southeast Los Angeles Regional Center
David B. Brearley, Esq.
c/o Lincoln Stone
Stone & Grzegorek LLP
800 Wilshire Boulevard, Suite 900
Los Angeles, CA 90017

District of Columbia:
Capitol Area Regional Center
888 16th Street NW - Suite 800
Washington, DC20006
Tel: 1(202)349-9848
Fax: 1(202) 355-1399
Email: info@eb5dc.com
www.eb5dc.com

EB5 America
David Morris
EB-5 Group, LLC
1806 11th Street NW
Washington DC 20001

Florida:
Lake Buena Vista Regional Center
EB5 Management LLC
1725 University Drive, Suite 450
Coral Springs, FL 33071

http://www.eb5greencardusa.com/

Palm Beach Regional Center
Louis Haddad, President
World Trade Center Palm Beach

Phillips Point, West Tower
777 South Flagler Drive, Suite 800
West Palm Beach, FL33401
Tel: (561) 712-1443
Fax: (561) 712-1445
Email: info@wtcpalmbeach.com
http://www.wtcpalmbeach.com

Iowa:
Iowa Department of Economic Development
200 East Grand Avenue
Des Moines, IA50309
Tel: 1(515) 242-4700
Fax: 1(515) 242-4809
Email: info@iowalifechanging.com
http://www.iowalifechanging.com
www.extension.iastate.edu/ag/staff/info/ianewfarmfamily.pdf

Kansas:
Kansas Biofuel Regional Center, LLC
Contact information:
915 Wilshire Blvd., Suite #2050
Los Angeles, CA 90017

Louisiana (& Louisiana/Mississippi):
City of New Orleans Office of Planning and Development
40 Poldras Street, Suite 1000
New Orleans, LA 70112
www.nobleoutreach.com

Gulf Coast Funds Management Regional Center
650 Poydras Street, Suite 2830
New Orleans, LA 70130

Pennsylvania:
Philadelphia Industrial Development Corporation
2600 Centre Square West
1500 Market Street
Philadelphia, PA19102-2126
Tel: (215) 496-8020
Fax: (215) 977-9618
http://www.pidc-pa.org/
www.canamenterprises.com

Pennsylvania Department of Community & Economic Development Regional Center
Harrisburg, PA 17120
www.newPA.com

South Carolina:
Carolina Center for Foreign Investment Regional Center
Allen Ballew/ Jay Rogers
P.O. Box 2487, 101 N. Main St. #1400,
Greenville, SC 29602

South Dakota:
South Dakota International Business Institute
1200 S Jay St.
Aberdeen, SD57401-7198
Tel: (605) 626-3149
Fax: (605) 626-3004
www.sd-exports.org/eb-5

Texas (& Texas/Oklahoma):
Global Century Development Group I, LP
11205 Bellaire Blvd., Suite B-33
Houston, TX 77072-2545

Southwest Biofuels Regional Center, LLC
915 Wilshire Blvd., Suite #2050
Los Angeles, CA 90017

Vermont:
Vermont Agency of Commerce and Community Development
Kevin Dorn, Secretary
NationalLifeBuilding
North, Drawer 20
Montpellier, VT05620-0501
Tel: (802) 828-3211
http://www.dca.state.vt.us
www.eb5greencard.com

Washington:
American Life Ventures, LLC [ALV-Tacoma]
c/o American Life, Inc.
Attn: Ms. Jo Hwang
270 S. Hanford Street, Suite 100
Seattle, WA98134
Tel: (206) 381-1690
Fax: (206) 381-3927
Email: info@americanlifeinc.com
www.amlife.us/visa.html
http://www.amlife.us/tacoma_intro.html

American Life Ventures, LLC [ALV-Everett]
c/o American Life, Inc.
Attn: Ms. Jo Hwang

270 S. Hanford Street, Suite 100
Seattle, WA98134
Tel: (206) 381-1690
Fax: (206) 381-3927
Email: info@americanlifeinc.com
www.amlife.us/visa.html

Whatcom Opportunities Regional Center
1305 11th Street, Suite 304
Bellingham, WA98825
Tel: (360) 201-3933
Email: info@worc.biz
www.worc.biz/

Wisconsin:
Metropolitan Milwaukee Association of Commerce
756 N. Milwaukee Street, Suite 400
Milwaukee, WI53202
Tel: (414) 287-4100
Fax: (414) 271-7753
Email: info@mmac.org
www.mmac.org

Seeking Redesignation

Hawaii:
State of Hawaii, Department of Business,
Economic Development & Tourism
P.O. Box 2359
Honolulu, HI 96804
Tel: (808) 586-2423
Fax: (808) 587-2790
Email: library@dbedt.hawaii.gov
http://hawaii.gov/dbedt

Nevada:
Unibex Global Corporation
1201 Eleanor Avenue
Las Vegas, NV 89106

Washington:
Aero-Space Port International Group
1600 Lind Ave SW, Suite 200
Renton, WA98055
Tel: (425) 264-1000
Fax: (425) 264-1268
www.aspigroup.com

Asylees, Refugees, and Withholding of Removal

The last major category for green card application is the asylum/refugee category. The requirements for refugees and asylees are very similar, the only major difference being that those already present in the United States are classified as asylees, while those outside the U.S. are classified as refugees.

Asylum

Asylum is a form of protection granted to individuals who have been persecuted or fear persecution because of their race, religion, nationality, membership in a particular social group, or political opinion. Asylum provides protection to qualified applicants who are already in the United States or are seeking entry into the United States at a port of entry. Asylum-seekers may apply for asylum regardless of their country of origin and current immigration status.

The U.S. Court of Appeals for the First Circuit provides a useful summation of the asylum standard:

> To establish eligibility for asylum, an alien must prove either past persecution, which gives rise to an inference of future persecution, or establish a well founded fear of future persecution on account of her race, religion, nationality, membership in a social group, or political opinion." Hem v. Mukasey, 514 F.3d 67, 69 (1st Cir. 2008). In contrast, "[t]o qualify for withholding of removal, an alien must show that, more likely than not, he faces persecution on account of one of [these] five protected grounds . . . should he return to his homeland." Pan v. Gonzales, 489 F.3d 80, 85-86 (1st Cir. 2007) (emphasis added); see also 8 U.S.C. § 1101(a)(42)(A); 8 C.F.R. § 1208.16(b)(2). "This 'more likely than not' standard is harder for an alien to satisfy than the 'reasonable possibility' standard for showing a well-founded fear of future persecution in asylum cases." Pan, 489 F.3d at 86.[228]

There used to be an annual quota for asylee grants when U.S. Immigration law allowed the "One Child Policy" under family planning to be one ground for foreign borns to apply for asylee status. It resulted in a long backlog of family members of these asylees to come to America legally. The grant under this way to obtain asylum was termed a conditional grant and until the number opened up the foreign born could not get the "final grant." The line is so long that by the time the number comes up the original finger print is not good because in the meantime they could have had a criminal record. So legacy INS had to send them another fingerprinting appointment and by then the foreign born may have moved and cannot be found.

Without the final grant, the foreign born could not file the I-730 to apply for their family members to come to the U.S. as their beneficiaries. Sometimes the final grant was approved and the foreign born did not even know about it. By the time they find out, two years passed and they could no longer file the I-730.

The 2005 Real ID act changed all this. Now there are no more number limitations on one child policy final grants. This certainly makes our job so much easier. One common scenario is that the spouse may have a final grant but her beneficiary may have already a final order of deportation prior to her being awarded this final grant. Now this principal alien has to file the 730 for her beneficiary and if her children are back home she needs to make sure she files multiple 730s so her children's portion gets sent to the American embassy overseas to be processed for them to enter. The spouse would need his own I-130 approval to do a motion to reopen his own final order of deportation before he can even apply for a green card. In the past few months, as of the time of this writing, I have seen quite a few of these motions denied even though the whole family is allowed to stay. This is another way how immigrants become out of status and there is no rhyme or reason to it, it is absurd. If it were not about true human beings and the reunification of families, then it would be truly comical.

Winning asylum is an uncertain process. As the Society of American Law Teachers (SALT) explains in a 2009 report, there are significant disparities in asylum grant rulings:

> Immigration courts are issuing inconsistent rulings on asylum cases. Immigration court asylum rulings vary based on an asylee's access to counsel, the jurisdiction in which a case is brought, whether or not the asylee is detained, and the gender of the immigration judge. These inconsistencies are evidence that asylum cases are being adjudicated based on aspects that have nothing to do with the merits of the case. . . . In addition, the federal appellate courts are overwhelmed and backlogged . . . Judge Posner, a generally conservative Seventh Circuit Judge, has declared that the adjudication of asylum cases has fallen below the minimum standards of justice. Judge Posner noted that in 2005, forty percent of 136 opinions decided on the merits by immigration courts and affirmed by the Board of Immigration Appeals were reversed by the Seventh Circuit.[229]

There are two main ways of obtaining asylum in the United States: affirmative asylum and defensive asylum.

Affirmative Asylum

In the affirmative asylum process, foreign-borns who are physically present in the United States, regardless of how they arrived or their current immigration status, may apply for asylum on form I-589 with USCIS. Applicants must apply for asylum within one year from the date of last arrival in the United States unless they can show changed circumstances that affect their eligibility or extraordinary circumstances relating to the delay in filing and that they filed within a reasonable amount of time under the circumstances.

Once an application has been received by USCIS, USCIS sends the applicant a notification about his/her asylum interview. Usually, an asylum interview is scheduled within a few months of filing the application, and a decision on the case is received 14 days after the interview. In other cases, getting a decision may take far longer. If an applicant's case is not approved and he/she does not have a valid immigration status, an NTA (Notice to Appear) is issued and the case is referred to an immigration judge at the Executive Office for Immigration Review

(EOIR) to consider the application. Affirmative asylum applicants are free to live in the U.S. pending the completion of the asylum process.

Defensive Asylum

In a defensive asylum case, an applicant requests asylum before an immigration judge as a defense against removal from the United States.

In these cases, the judge hears the applicant's claim and also hears any arguments about the applicant's eligibility made by the U.S. Government, which is represented by an ICE attorney. The judge then makes a decision as to whether asylum should be granted. If the foreign-born's asylum request is denied, the judge determines whether the applicant is eligible for any other forms of relief from removal and, if not, will order the applicant removed from the United States. These decisions can be appealed by either the government or the applicant.

Forms for Asylee/ Refugees	
I-589	Asylum Application
I-730	Refugee/Asylee Relative Petition; needs to be filed within two years of principal's asylum/refugee grant

Refugee Status

Like asylum applicants, those applying for refugee status in the U.S. must show they have been persecuted or fear they will be persecuted because of their race, religion, nationality, membership in a particular social group, or political opinion. Unlike asylum applications, these applicants must be located outside the U.S. and outside their country of origin. Also unlike asylum applications, there is a quota for the number of refugees that may be admitted to the United States each year.

Eligibility for refugee status is determined by many factors. Refugees may be eligible for an interview for resettlement in the United States if the United Nations High Commissioner for Refugees (UNHCR) or the U.S. Embassy refers them to the United States for resettlement, or if they are members of specified groups with special characteristics as determined periodically by the United States government.

An individual who has already been firmly resettled in another country is not eligible for refugee status in the United States. "Firmly resettled" means the person has been offered resident status, citizenship, or some other type of permanent residence. Other instances which may be considered firm resettlement are if a person has dual citizenship with a third country or if he/she is entitled to automatic citizenship in a third country and has no fear of persecution in that third country.

A person seeking entrance as a refugee must also be otherwise admissible to the United States or be granted a waiver of inadmissibility. Certain grounds of inadmissibility do not apply to refugees, such as the likelihood that a person will become a public charge, requirements for labor certification, and documentation requirements. However, criminal or health-related grounds of inadmissibility still apply to refugees.

To apply for refugee status, a foreign-born must contact UNHCR or the nearest U.S. Embassy or Consulate. A representative then contacts the foreign-born to discuss the situation and determine if the person is eligible to apply for refugee status in the United States. If the person is eligible, he/she then must complete a packet of forms, and USCIS then conducts a formal interview and makes a decision. If USCIS determines that the applicant should be resettled as a refugee, the U.S. State Department will complete processing of the application. There are no application fees for refugee status. The applicant's spouse and any unmarried children under the age of 21 may be included as derivatives on the refugee application.

How Asylees and Refugees Can Become Legal Permanent Residents

Refugees are required by law to apply for legal permanent resident status one year after entering the U.S. with refugee status. Asylees become eligible to apply for legal permanent resident status one year after being granted asylum, but are not required to do so.

While the application to adjust status to legal permanent resident is pending, an applicant may travel outside the United States. However, the applicant must have a valid Refugee Travel Document to re-enter the United States. Asylees and refugees may also work in the U.S. and receive their Employment Authorization Documents (EAD) shortly after being granted asylum or arriving in the U.S. as refugees.

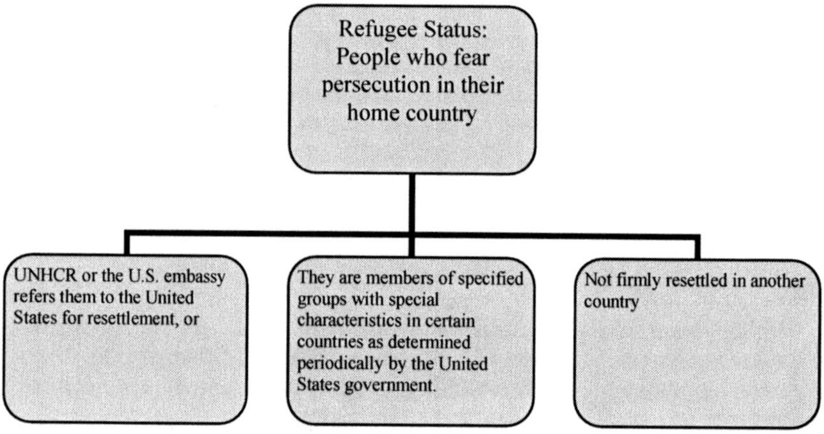

Withholding of Removal

Withholding of removal is a process similar to the defensive asylum process but with some differences. Withholding of removal has a much higher legal standard than asylum. An applicant must show a clear probability that his or her life or freedom will be threatened upon the return to his or her country. As with asylum, the presumption of future persecution also applies where there is a finding of past persecution. Many people apply for asylum and withholding of removal at the same time because withholding does not have a one-year filing deadline as asylum does, and a judge may decide an applicant is eligible for one status and not the other. All withholding of removal claims are decided by EOIR immigration judges during regular removal proceedings.

An order granting withholding of removal prohibits a foreign national's removal to the country where his/her life or freedom would be threatened, but does allow removal to a third country where his/her life or freedom would not be threatened. Withholding of removal does not provide relief for eligible family members in the United States, does not provide the ability to petition to bring eligible family members to the United States, and does not lead to legal permanent residence. Also, those who receive relief under withholding of removal cannot re-enter the United States once they have left. Withholding of removal relief does allow recipients to apply for work authorization.

There are two types of withholding of removal relief: relief under INA 241(b)(3) and relief under the UN Convention Against Torture (CAT).

Relief Under CAT

The UN Convention Against Torture (CAT) is an international treaty provision designed to protect foreign nationals from being returned to countries where they would, more likely than not, face torture. Under CAT torture is defined as severe pain or suffering (physical or mental) that is intentionally inflicted, instigated, or permitted by a public official or other person acting in an official capacity. Under CAT, the United States agrees not to "expel, return, or extradite" foreign nationals to a country where they would be tortured.

To qualify for relief in the U.S. under CAT, an applicant must show that it is more likely than not that he/she would be tortured if removed to a specific country. The torture does not need to be based on one of the five protected grounds (race, religion, nationality, membership in a particular social group, or political opinion), as is required for asylum or withholding of removal under the INA. Further, relief under CAT may be granted to criminals, terrorists, and persecutors, as they cannot be returned to a country where they would face torture. CAT allows for the detention of CAT recipients, where appropriate. It also allows for the removal of CAT recipients to a third country where they would not be tortured.

To apply for withholding of removal relief under CAT, a foreign-born must specifically declare this intent on the application form. An applicant may apply for both forms of relief. During the removal proceedings, the immigration judge will first determine if the applicant qualifies for asylum, then withholding of removal under INA 241(b)(3), and finally withholding of removal under CAT. A person granted CAT relief cannot obtain lawful permanent resident status.

6. GREEN CARD PROCESSING SCENARIOS (including 245(i))

Green cards allow a foreign born to stay, live, travel, and work in the U.S. permanently.

There are certain grounds that render one inadmissible for obtaining a green card. Certain health issues (mental or physical), drug use and addiction, likelihood of becoming a public charge, convictions of crimes of moral turpitude, and prostitution, among other things, can cause one to become ineligible and barred from permanent residency. Certain criminal records are not crimes involving moral turpitude and a person could still get a green card in spite of those acts.

If the foreign born could obtain a criminal record waiver, she is eligible for a green card. Waivers are only available for those who have a USC or LPR parent, spouse or child as a qualifying relative with a showing of extreme hardship to the USC or LPR parent, spouse, or child if inadmissibility would keep the family apart. Those with K-3/K-4 or V-1/V-2 visas can also apply for a waiver.

The green cards granted each year are limited by quotas. All priority dates and quotas are based on place of birth, not nationality. For example, if one was born in Russia, immigrated to Canada at a young age and naturalized to become a Canadian citizen, and now wants to come to the U.S., the Russian quota applies instead of the Canadian quota.

Criminal record waiver (212(h)) is different from material misrepresentation waiver (212(i)). For material misrepresentation waiver you will need either a LPR or USC parent or spouse. A USC child is not enough and would not give you a qualifying relationship. For example, alien entered U.S. with a tourist visa in 1990 and pled guilty to theft of a large TV from a department store in 1996. She married a USC spouse in 1999. Children were not yet born to this marriage. Can she get a green card immediately after marriage? Yes, if the criminal record waiver is approved because of hardship to the USC spouse.

Another scenario: A "foreign-born" came to the U.S. in 1990 without a passport or visa or without being inspected at the airport. The foreign born married a USC spouse in February 2001 and applied for both I-130 and I-485 in March 2001. Can she get a green card? Yes, if she pays a $1000 fine and files a supplemental A together with her 485. Since she never presented herself for inspection she has never made an utterance and thus has never lied to any immigration official. She would not need a 6(c) waiver.

Another scenario: A "foreign-born" came to the U.S. in 1990 with her friend's passport which has a tourist visa inside. She never herself went to the State Dept. to apply for this visa. She married a citizen in March 2001. Can she get a green card? Since she had made a material misrepresentation at the airport (by affirmatively showing her friend's passport to the immigration official) she will need to file for a 212(i) waiver. This waiver could only be approved if her husband would incur extreme hardship if she is being deported to her home country.

I hope you understand the difference between all these types of waivers. This is why it is extremely important for us to spend time with our clients and to really ascertain what they need. Life is harassed, busy, and filled with obligations. If the roadmap for our clients did not start out right correctly, it will take years and years to correct them. I have learned from my own mistakes through the years.

Besides being sponsored by a USC or LPR such as a parent or an over-21 year old child, others with highly desirable skills or advanced degrees and prospective employment within the United States, religious workers, abused spouses, widow(er)s of US citizens, and renowned artists and entertainers are also eligible for permanent residency. Those who have previously stayed in the U.S. illegally for over six months may be barred from making an adjustment of status to that of a legal permanent resident and will be barred from returning to the U.S. after they leave if they are not under 245(i) protection.

With an I-485 filing for one's green card, one may also file an I-765 with the USCIS requesting work authorization under the C(8) category and may also file for an I-131 requesting advance parole (multiple travel documents for travel outside the US for one year). Advance parole is necessary for those whose green card applications are pending but wish to travel outside of the US. She needs to carry her passport with this parole document while travelling. Those who have allowed a lapse in their status, or have not maintained a status for more than 180 days, should not travel on the advance parole documents, even if covered under 245(i), as the act of departing the US would create the bar to adjustment even if the USCIS issued the travel document in error to the applicant.

Legal permanent residents may wish to consider precautions when traveling outside of the United States, as green card holders traveling abroad must return to the United States within 6 months of their date of departure lest immigration officials contest their intentions to retain permanent residency. While the CBP officer can question any entry after any period of absence, there is a rebuttable presumption of abandonment if the green card holder leaves the US for more than 180 days, and it is up to the green card holder as an applicant for admission to prove otherwise with sufficient evidence that the green card holder did not intend to abandon permanent residence. After a year of absence, a green card holder is assumed to have relinquished permanent residency. Consequently, green card holders planning long trips abroad should apply in advance for a reentry permit. Reentry permits allow LPRs to remain out of the country for up to two years, instead of having the automatic abandonment of permanent resident status.

245(i)

245(i) allows an illegal foreign born who had been a beneficiary of a properly filed visa petition and/or labor certification before April 30, 2001 and was physically present in the United States on December 21, 2000 to obtain a GC even though they are not maintaining status. Section 245(i) was first provided under IIRAIRA in 1996, effective April 1, 1997, and the requirements under the previous 245(i) include a person must have been a beneficiary of a properly filed immigrant petition or labor certification on or before January 14, 1998, with no physical presence requirements. This provision also remains as a part of 245(i) to overcome unlawful presence over 180 days or entry without inspection and remains admissible for all other sections. The applicant must pay a fine of $1,000 when applying for a green card under 245(i) and it is still a discretionary adjudication to approve adjustment, but practically speaking the applications to adjust are typically approved unless other reasons of inadmissibility are found.

245(i) also allows the spouse, children and step-children under 21 (if the marriage was before the step-child turned 18) to adjust their status within the U.S. as derivative beneficiaries in a "grandfather clause". The spouse and children of the immigrant as of either January 14, 1998 or April 30, 2001 may adjust their status on any basis at any time prior to an order of removal and will not lose their 245(i) privileges even if divorced, widowed, or no longer under the age of 21. Any spouses or children acquired after a petition filed prior to January 14, 1998 or April 30, 2001 may also obtain green cards under 245(i) if they adjust their status as a derivative of the principal alien, who adjusts status in the United States. Both former and current spouses can get work permits after 90 days when a correctly filed I-485 and I-765 are pending. If a person is in the United States illegally either through entry without admission or over stay of authorized nonimmigrant status of more than 180 days, and never had a visa petition or labor certification filed on his/her behalf before either January 14, 1998 or April 30, 2001, a green card is unobtainable unless the person entered in a valid nonimmigrant status and can classify as an immediate relative. So if a person entered the US illegally, without admission through a port of entry, for example, but is married to a US citizen, he or she will not be able to remain in the US and adjust status to become a lawful permanent resident unless he or she has a 245(i) benefit. Additionally, any misrepresentation of a material fact since or at the time of entry means that the person cannot apply for a green card without a waiver but is not an issue of 245(i).

Misrepresentation and maintaining status are not the same – a 601 waiver is necessary in cases of misrepresentation. To file a 601 waiver, one must have a USC or LPR parent or spouse. In this way, individuals who entered the U.S. with a fraudulent passport or visa may still be able to obtain a green card. It should be noted that a 601 waiver cannot be filed on the basis of having USC children. For example, a Foreign Born enters the US with a fake passport in December 1998. Her parents obtain a green card in 1999 and file an I-130 for her. When the quota opens, she can file an I-485 package (filing fee of $1010) and a supplemental Application with an additional $1,000 filing fee (total $2010) to obtain a Green Card. However, she needs to file a 601 waiver because of the material misrepresentation of showing a phony passport and having lied to the US government at the time of entry, but she does have qualifying relatives because her parents are Legal Permanent Residents and must be able to prove that the parents will suffer extreme hardship if she is not permitted to adjust status. Another example: this same alien who entered on a fake passport is trying to obtain a GC through her employer under a valid labor certification and approved I-140 immigrant petition, but she does not have a USC or LPR parent or spouse. Her spouse is also a foreign born and is not in legal status in the US but they do have a USC-born child. This person, as a beneficiary of an employment based immigrant petition, would not be able to apply for a green card, because the USC child is not a qualifying relative to form the basis of a 601 waiver required for the initial fraudulent entry. She would be deemed inadmissible and the green card application would fail, regardless of when the immigrant petition or labor certification was filed, since this is not an issue of inadmissibility for failing to maintain a lawful status under 245(i), but rather an issue of inadmissibility for fraud or material misrepresentation.

HEALTH RELATED GROUNDS THAT RENDER A PERSON INADMISSIBLE AND INELIGIBLE FOR A GREEN CARD

Communicable Disease of Public Health Significance[230]

1. chancroid
2. gonorrhea
3. granuloma inguinale
4. acquired immune deficiency syndrome (HIV/AIDS) **
5. Hansen's disease (infectious leprosy)
6. lymphogranuloma venereum
7. infectious state syphilis
8. infectious tuberculosis (TB) (clinically active)

Physical or Mental Disorder

1. Current physical or mental disorders, with harmful behavior* associated with the disorder
2. Past physical or mental disorders with associated harmful behavior* likely to recur or lead to other harmful behavior.

*Harmful behavior is behavior that may pose/has posed, a threat to the property, safety or welfare of the applicant or others. A mentally retarded person is no longer inadmissible unless there is a determination that the applicant is exhibiting/has exhibited in the past, associated harmful behavior.

** Communicable diseases of public health significance are determined by the Department of Health and Human Services. Currently, as this book is going to press, HHS has published as a proposed rule in the Federal Register to remove HIV/AIDS from the communicable disease list. Prior to this publication in June 2009, which is not yet a final rule, those who suffer from HIV/AIDS required a qualifying relative for a waiver of inadmissibility and proof of extreme hardship in order to be allowed to adjust.

Green Card Scenarios

We need to think about using my parallel track concept.

Entered and stayed in the U.S. legally	Can get green card – 245(k)
Entered and stayed in the U.S. illegally	Can't get green card – 245(k)
Stayed in the U.S. illegally, entered the U.S. prior to 12/20/00 without misrepresentation	Can get green card as long as an immigrant visa petition or labor certification was filed prior to 4/30/01 – 245(i)
Entered the U.S. at any time after 12/20/00, illegal entry, and illegal stay	Can get green card if immigrant visa petition or labor certification filed prior

	to 1/14/98 – old 245(i)
Entered the U.S. with phony passport or visa	Can get green card if spouse/parent has green card/or is a U.S. citizen and helps file for a I-601 waiver. Children born in the U.S. (citizens) cannot help with a 601 waiver, also need 245(i).
Entered US with I-94. Legal entry, overstay?	Can get GC if spouse/parent is a USC, as immediate relative. No 601 required, unless fraud or material representation found in obtaining visa or entry.

245(i) is an extremely important concept. If a person entered the U.S. illegally and/or is here illegally now, and she has never had any visa petition filed on her behalf, she cannot get a green card. This applies even if she is married to a U.S. citizen. This is another reason why there are so many illegals in the U.S. There is just no way in which we can help them by filing an I-485, because the law states that they are inadmissible.

There was a time that if the filed paperwork does not appear to be prima facially eligible for the benefits, the mailroom in the immigration office would reject the filing and not take the filing fee. Now maybe because CIS does need the money to pay their people, we notice that the mailroom will accept the filing, give us a receipt, but send back a Request for Additional Information asking for additional documents. As of even a few years ago, if they sent the request they would still give us a work permit to give us the benefit of the doubt. Now they will wait until the work permit is granted. If we do not respond to the Request for Evidence, we do not get a work permit. This work permit is precious because we need it to apply for a driver's license, social security number, and to get a job.

If you qualify for 245(i), you need to add Supplement A to green card filing and pay an additional $1000 in filing fees to USCIS. If this I-485 is denied both the fee for I-485 ($1010) and the supplement fee of $1000 is lost. When and if you do a refile or new filing you will have to pay the fees again totaling to $2010.

If you have misrepresented a material fact (or have lied) in order to gain an immigrant benefit since entry or at the time of entry, this is not a 245(i) issue. Lying and out of status are two different things – see above in 245(i) section. To file a 601 waiver, you have to have at least a parent or spouse who is a green card holder or USC who can provide evidence of extreme hardship if the adjustment or admission as lawful permanent resident would not be permitted. There are a lot of our cases where the principal person and his wife came to America and now have children born here, but do not have parents in the United States. These people are now stuck with no qualifying relative and no waiver or relief. These types of immigrants cannot get the green card because they just do not have the basis and the relief. I do not know if our Congress and Senate understood this when they passed this law. They could have added the USC children as a basis because then the system would not separate families, or force USC children to accompany parents to a foreign country.

Since April 1997, the effective date of IIRIRA, the concept of the "3 year/10 year" bar has also been important. If you overstay your authorized stay in the U.S. for more than 180 days but less than 365 days and you leave the U.S. during that time period, you cannot come back to the U.S. for three years absent an exception or waiver of inadmissibility. If you overstay your authorized stay for more than 365 days, you cannot come back for 10 years absent an exception or a waiver of inadmissibility.

1. Immigrant A came to the U.S. with a tourist visa on 8/21/06. The B-1/B-2 visa stamped in her passport is a multiple one, allowing entries up to 5 years, from June 20, 2005-June 20, 2010. (Remember, a visa is only an entry document, that allows a window of time in which to enter the US in that classification, but the amount of time that one is allowed to stay relates only to the I-94 that is issued at the airport, listing a date certain for expiration of stay – the last day in which the person has to leave the US, unless an extension or other petition is filed.) At the airport, she was granted an I-94 valid until 2/21/07, which is a 6 month period of time. She had a round trip ticket leaving the U.S. on 1/4/07. She became sick after the New Year and changed her plane ticket to 1/31/07. One week prior to her scheduled departure date, her boyfriend asked her to stay for a while so that he could convince his mother that she was the right person for him and see if their relationship had further potential. She was so affected by her illness and her boyfriend that she changed her ticket again. She did not file for an extension with the immigration office. The relationship ultimately went nowhere. She left the country on 3/2/07.

In this case, Immigrant A would not have the three year bar from entering the U.S. since she was not out of status for 180 days. But when she does return to a U.S. airport for another trip to visit, her multiple visa will be cancelled by CBP if they notice that she had overstayed her last I-94. CBP will not give her another I-94 to stay in the U.S. and will probably put her on the next flight home.

She will need to go to her embassy or consulate in her home country to apply for a new visa and explain the reason for the previous overstay. She will not need a waiver for the overstay however obtaining another visa that requires a nonimmigrant intent, such as F-1 or B-2, will likely be very difficult.

Anytime a foreign-born leaves with even an hour of overstay, the visa should be considered void – since the CBP officials at the U.S. border will cancel/void visa if the overstay is noticed. This law is different from the 3-year/10-year bar, where the overseas consulate should not issue a visa for any reason, immigrant or nonimmigrant, unless a waiver is obtained, or even if a visa is obtained, the CBP officer should not allow entry for the 3/10 year timeframe unless the visa documents the proper waiver granted.

2. Immigrant A left the U.S. on 9/5/07, but had filed for an extension of her tourist visa on 1/15/07 with USCIS. She left the U.S. without an answer from USCIS (they take about three and a half to six months now to adjudicate the extension). She returns a few months later to the U.S.

She could be denied entry unless she can prove that she had timely filed for an extension prior to expiration of the I-94. All foreign-born non-immigrants carry the burden of proof to evidence prior stay was lawful and that as an applicant for entry, there is no issue of inadmissibility. She should have kept and brought a copy of the Receipt Notice to prove the timely filing of an extension request. If you type the receipt notice number in the USCIS online status website, the result of the filing would be there. If she had kept her receipt notice of the filing, and the case was approved, even after her exit, she should be allowed to enter on the same visa. However, if the case was denied, after her exit, she does not have unlawful presence but the visa can be determined as void since she remained past the initial I-94 expiration.

If she had stayed in America and the visa extension request was denied, then her 180 days of unlawful presence would have started on the date of denial. Even if the extension request was approved, USCIS would have only granted the visa until August 20, 2007, since most requests for visitor stay can only be six months. If she can prove she filed an extension on time and left before USCIS gave her an answer, she would be allowed back into the US provided that she has a valid visa in her passport and she can continue to prove that she has no immigrant intent.

3. Immigrant A with the same entry situation, left on 3/3/08 and never filed an extension.

   She is barred for 10 years because the visa expired on 2/21/07.

4. Immigrant A with the same entry situation, left on 3/3/08, but filed an extension on 1/15/07 and was approved till August 21, 2009.

   She has a total of seven months unlawful presence, resulting in a 3 year bar.

5. Immigrant A never left, fell in love with her U.S. citizen boyfriend, met his family who did not object to the marriage, and married him on March 3, 2008.

She would be able to get a green card so long as there were no other inadmissibility circumstances. He would need to file the I-130 and she would need to file for the I-485 concurrently with USCIS. An interview would take place after the fingerprinting. During the interview, the couple may be separated and asked questions about the bona fide nature of the marriage and the original intent of the foreign-born at the time of entering – what was in her mind when she came through the long line at the airport? Did she want to come here to stay permanently, to work, to marry someone to get a green card, or to go to school? The green card would be approved after the interview only if both of them responded to questions to evidence the *bona fides* of the marriage. The foreign-born must prove that there was no preconceived intention of coming to the U.S. to stay and get a green card; the initial purpose of coming must have been temporary business or pleasure (B-1/B-2).

The green card she would receive would likely be a two year conditional green card, as most interviews and adjudications occur within less than 2 years of marriage for the couple. (If the couple is married for more than two years at the time of the initial adjudication of the application for permanent residence, then a 10 year green card is issued and no condition is made on the permanent residence.) Assuming a conditional green card is granted, the card will be issued for a 2 year period of time. This condition can be removed, if the couple remains married for two years after the date of issue of the green card (not the date of marriage), both of them would have to file a joint I-751 application to remove the conditions and evidence to prove the legitimacy of the marriage once again. An interview of the couple is often requested. If this I-751 is approved, she can get a 10 year green card. The green card itself will expire in 2 years from the date of granting conditional permanent residence, regardless of the status of the marriage. An I-751 filing must be made, otherwise residence is at risk and the foreign born spouse can be placed into removal proceedings. Therefore, if the parties are no longer married when the I-751 is required to be filed, the foreign born person must still file the I-751 in order to prove that the marriage was bona fide upon inception not solely for the purpose of immigration, even if later the marriage fell apart. If the US citizen dies, there are remedies for the foreign born to file alone.

In this case, Immigrant A satisfied the 245(k) requirement of legal entry. Even if she overstayed her visa, as long as she does not leave the country, she can apply for adjustment in the U.S. because the only way a foreign born without 245 (i) can get a green card now with legal entry is via the immediate relative route. However, if she were to leave the country and marry overseas, she would have a difficult time coming back because she overstayed her authorized stay and is subject to a 10 year bar. Consular processing of an immigrant visa for an immediate relative (spouse of USC) would still require a waiver due to the 10 year bar, and there is the potential issue of fraud if she misrepresented herself at the time of entry. This is why a lot of foreign-borns are not willing to go home to legally apply for a green card through the Consulate. Most overseas consulates are perpetually understaffed and bombarded with work and requests, very rarely see extreme hardship in recently acquired marriages, and have a "no" mentality.

Now, 245(i) and the 3 year/10 year bar should not be confused with the 5 year/10 year bar that is imposed when a foreign-born does not leave the U.S. after the judge approves a request for voluntary departure during the deportation hearing. This bar applies if the deportation proceedings had commenced for the foreign-born and she had withdrawn all requests for relief and requested that she go home herself at her own expense, the request was granted by the judge, and the foreign-born did not leave the country within the time allotted (usually 120 days). Under these circumstances, she would not be allowed to adjust her status to that of a green card holder for 10 years if proceedings began after April 1997 (Notice to Appear). She would not be able to obtain a green card for five years if proceedings began before April 1997 (Order to Show Cause). Let's see another example.

6. Immigrant A did not leave the country, her employer was raided by Immigration and Customs Enforcement (ICE) in 2006, she was picked up with 200 other workers, and she was put in jail to be processed by ICE. She was not allowed to make any phone calls and ICE did not interview her until she had been in jail for three days because of their large workload. She called her parents overseas and

waited two weeks while they found a suitable lawyer. The lawyer took another two weeks to get her out of jail with a bond. By that time, she had been in jail for five weeks, and was fed up and ready to go home. However, she couldn't go home yet because a Notice to Appear (NTA) had been issued and she was required to go to a hearing in front of a judge. Once that NTA was issued, USCIS lost jurisdiction over her and she is in the hands of ICE and the court system. The first master hearing was scheduled three months after getting out of jail. During this hearing, she told the judge that she would go home. The judge gave her an order of voluntary departure within 60 days. When she was all ready and packed to go home, her boyfriend proposed (his family had no objections) and they got married within the 60 days.

In this situation, could she get a green card in the U.S.?

The answer is no if she requested voluntary departure but does not leave within the allowed time absent some exception. This would trigger a ten-year bar to adjustment of status and other forms of discretionary relief unless we can argue the bar is not applicable. Now, as lawyers, we would have to review the case and get the I-130 filed. We would be unable to file an I-485 because she had been issued a voluntary departure order and it converts to a removal order if she does not leave within the required time. There is a way around the ten-year bar. Under the new voluntary departure regulations issued in 2009, if she filed a motion to reopen (or a request to withdraw her voluntary departure) prior to the expiration of the voluntary departure period, she would not face the ten-year bar that attaches to an overstay of voluntary departure. Her I-130 would not be approved until 2 to 12 months later. We would need to wait for the Receipt Notice (two and a half to 12 weeks) before filing a Motion to Reopen with the court in order to vacate the voluntary departure. One way to vacate the voluntary departure order is to immediately file the Motion prior to the 60 days and inform the Court that she is married. Still, this is an uphill battle. Thus, even marriage to a U.S. citizen does not solve a lot of immigration issues.

It should also be noted that Immigrant A in this case was extremely fortunate because most judges do not allow bonds and wouldn't have let her out of jail until ICE was ready to deport her. This normally takes quite a few months, as ICE needs to get a travel document from a foreign-born's home country to deport her. In order for a foreign-born's country to issue a travel document, the country's government would have to verify her place of birth, date of birth, parent's names, etc. for security purposes. Why would any country take a person onto their soil not knowing who the person is? Can you imagine Israel accepting someone from an American jail (a foreign born without papers) who gave ICE information that she was born in Jerusalem, although her parents are Palestinian refugees and moved to Jordan after the 1987 war? Every case must be verified before foreign consulates issue travel documents to their nationals.

During the lengthy verification process prior to deportation, most immigrants are simply stuck in jail. The food and conditions in immigration prisons are worse than those in municipal, county, state, and federal detention centers because the immigration prisons lack oversight. Although these private jails are technically accountable to DHS for the illegal aliens' detentions, the U.S. criminal system, and the U.S. detention system (and partially because of it), no agency ultimately enforces the maintenance of living standards within immigration prisons. The New York Times has printed some insightful articles investigating these jails.

7. Immigrant A entered legally, overstayed, and an NTA was issued. She pled voluntary departure, never left, and did not file an appeal since most courts require you to waive the court appeals process before they will entertain a request of voluntary departure. In 2008, she married her U.S. citizen boyfriend.

She is now stuck with a 10 year voluntary departure bar and can't adjust her status to obtain a green card in the U.S. Even if she files the I-130 and returns home to get the green card, she is banned from re-entering the U.S. because of the "3 year/10 year" overstay bar and the final order of deportation. We should not confuse the voluntary departure bar which only applies if she wants to adjust status in the U.S. versus the 3 year/10 year bar which only applies if she leaves the U.S. and wants to come back. If her USC husband can prove extreme hardship --either if she does not come back to the U.S. or if he were to leave the US to be with his wife -- he would suffer extreme hardship, and then he can file for a hardship 601 waiver. She'll also need a 212 waiver because of the final order of deportation. Since she needs both waivers, these packages need to be filed with the American consulate, and are not easily obtained. The standard of extreme hardship goes beyond the normal hardship a family would face due to distance, separation, and financial or economical difficulties.

8. Immigrant M arrives from Mexico illegally in 1995 and has been in the US ever since then. He did not have any employer or family member file for him prior to January 14, 1998 or prior to end of April 2001, so he is not 245(i) eligible. His USC girlfriend has a ten year old USC child with her previous husband. Can the man get a green card and how would he go about it?

Answer: Since he is not 245(i), he cannot adjust status in the U.S. Maybe what can help him is to do a 10 year cancellation case. It will have to be based on hardship to the spouse/child. He will have to marry his girlfriend, but he cannot adjust or get his green card through his US citizen spouse directly while in the US. He would be eligible for a green card if he were in removal proceedings and he could seek cancellation case based on hardship to the spouse or step-child. (The daughter will qualify as his step-child since she is under the age of 18 when his marriage occurs.) If he is granted cancellation, he will get the green card very quickly. Or if proceedings had not been initiated, he could ask his wife to file an I-130 for him, with the knowledge that he would have to go overseas to pursue an immigrant visa but he would need to file for a waiver for both the illegal entry and overstay of more than one year, and the extreme hardship would necessarily be required to be shown only to his spouse, not his step-child.

9. Here is another interesting case our firm just handled. A Chinese client filed for asylum. Asylum was denied. We filed a BIA appeal. This was

dismissed. He was taken into ICE custody. We filed a petition for review with the 6th Circuit along with a motion to stay. The government (OIL – Office of Immigration Litigation) filed a non-opposition response. We faxed a copy of this response to the ICE officer in charge of the case and notified them that the stay was pending. A week later we got a call that our client was on a plane to be deported to China. We called the 6th Circuit to request an emergency ruling on the motion. We called the ICE Office of Chief Counsel and the ICE officer on the plane to discuss the case. The officer on the plane could not do anything because the flight was ready to take off. We found out our client had a layover in Chicago, so we also contacted Customs and Border Patrol and ICE Office of Chief Counsel in Chicago to alert them about the case. We also contacted OIL in Washington D.C. While the client was in flight to Chicago, the 6th Circuit granted the motion to stay the removal. Now, they're bringing him back to Ohio. What a waste of government funds to place the person in custody, accompany him on a plane from Cleveland to Chicago, and try to remove a person that their own government attorney (OIL) had filed a non-opposition to the Motion for a Stay of Removal! In this case, the government's efforts at effectuating the removal order in fact helped the foreign born to receive a stay of removal faster than the 6th Circuit would normally have acted upon the Motion.

10. Immigrant B entered legally on 8/2/06 on a visitor visa and her I-94 expired on 2/1/07. An NTA was issued on 7/1/07, but proceedings were extended a few times. She pled voluntary departure on 6/9/08 and was given 60 days to leave, expiring on 8/8/08. She requested a two month extension on her voluntary departure from ICE (giving her until 10/7/08) and it was granted. She reported to ICE, got a G-146 and airplane ticket, and left the U.S. on 9/6/08. Her U.S. citizen boyfriend went to Mexico to marry her, then returned to the U.S. to file an I-130.

In a situation like this, can we bring her back to the U.S.?

She legally entered and did not work until at least after 90 days, so the adjudicating officer in Juarez, Mexico probably would not charge her with fraudulent entry. The time counted towards her illegal stay in the U.S. She had more than a year of unlawful presence since her plea of voluntary departure on 6/9/08 occurred more than a year after her last authorized stay, 2/1/07. While she left with a G-146 within the voluntary departure time given by the judge and USCIS, she has avoided an order of removal (because a deportation order kicks in when you do not leave within the time frame provided by the judge and ICE for voluntary departure), she remains unable to return immediately without a waiver due to her more than one year presence in the US without an authorized status. She does not have a criminal record, so there is no criminal bar against her. She has no children in the U.S. (or anywhere in the world), so she does not owe child support and won't be barred on those grounds. The 3 and 10 year bar under IIRIRA was passed in 1996 and became effective in April 1997 and really has stumped a lot of Mexican and Canadian nationals who frequently travel back and forth illegally for holidays, celebrations and funerals.

In order to obtain an immigrant visa, she would be required to file for a waiver to evidence extreme hardship to her USC spouse.

Once she gets a green card, we need to see if it is for 2 years or 10 years, based on whether the couple is married for two years when Immigrant B enters the US initially as a permanent residence. If it is a two year conditional green card (i.e. if the entry as a permanent resident happens less than two years after the date of marriage), we will need to file a I-751 within the last three months before it expires. If the marriage does not last those two additional years, then an I-751 needs to be filed immediately after the time of a Final Judgment Entry of Divorce with proof of the *bona fides* of the marriage in order to remove the conditions of residence. If nothing is filed by the green card holder when the two year green card expires, she will be eligible to be placed into removal.

If she remains married and cohabitating with a U.S. citizen spouse, she can apply for U.S. citizenship two years and nine months after the initial entry as a permanent resident or approval of the green card, so long as she meets the residency and other naturalization requirements. If she is no longer married, or is married but not cohabitating with the U.S. citizen, then she can apply for U.S. citizenship after four years and nine months, provided all the residency requirements are met, i.e. she physically resided in the U.S. at least more than half the amount of time required (2 ½ years out of the previous 5), and she meets the other requirements of good moral character and passage of the American civic exam.

11. Immigrant B travels to Mexico and her U.S. citizen boyfriend goes there to marry her. He travels between the U.S., where he works, and Mexico to support this wife until her green card is approved. During the waiting time, she becomes pregnant and gives birth to a baby in Mexico. The baby has a U.S. citizen father and a foreign-born mother.

This child is a USC if the father meets the residency requirements to provide automatic derivative citizenship and the parents can apply for a U.S. passport for their child so that the mother and child can travel together. Immigrant B should be approved for a green card (the total processing time is about 9 months to 1.5 years).

12. Let's assume now that Immigrant B's fiancé is a permanent resident instead of a U.S. citizen, and that he obtained his green card four years ago and will have to wait for one year to apply to naturalize to become a U.S. citizen.

How long must she wait for him to sponsor her, and when can she come to the U.S.? Since the husband is a green card holder, he can file an I-130 family petition. If for whatever reason he can't become a U.S. citizen because of residency requirements – perhaps he's traveling too much to visit her and does not have the mandatory 30 months out of 60 months, or maybe he has criminal CIMT (Crime involving moral turpitude) so that he cannot meet the good moral character finding for naturalization – she would be an F-2A spouse of a green card holder and will have to wait in line after the filing of the I-130 to have her priority date become current. She will probably wait for an immigrant visa number to become available for approximately six (6) years if her permanent resident spouse does not become a

USC (as a foreign person born in Mexico, she has the longest wait according to the immigrant visa bulletin numbers for F2A category - spouses and children under 21 of lawful permanent residents.) Once the immigrant visa number becomes available, she will likely have another 6-12 months of processing for the visa.

13. Immigrant B was pregnant and her husband was still traveling back and forth to Mexico so that he could spend time with her. She gave birth to the baby with him by her side in a Mexican hospital. Her husband became a U.S. citizen in 11/08, three months after the baby was born (8/8/08). The green card interview was held on 12/1/08 in Juarez, Mexico, after the husband (as a new U.S. citizen) had already upgraded the immigrant petition (I-130) to that of an immediate relative (spouse of a U.S. citizen).

Can this baby come to the US as a USC? No, because on the day of the child's, neither of the parents were a US citizen. The naturalization of the father after the birth of the baby does provide an advantage, but it only occurs after the baby enters the US as a lawful permanent resident. Upon admission as a lawful permanent resident, the baby is also automatically considered a US citizen due to the Child Citizenship Act of 2000.

14. Here is another scenario. The husband became a U.S. citizen on 11/8/08. The baby was born in a Mexican hospital on 11/20/08. The mom's green card interview in Mexico was scheduled for 12/29/08.

The baby would be able to travel with the mom because in this case, even though the father was already a U.S. citizen when the baby was born he did not have the requisite 5 years to give the child USC status. The American Embassy has the authority to issue a green card to the baby to travel with the green card mother. After entry, the mother would have to wait three years to get her citizenship (or 5 years if divorced). The child can apply for a U.S. passport right away.

For scenario 12, the mother upon receiving her travel documents should also check to see if the U.S. Consulate or Embassy gave her a green card or K-3 visa. In order to expedite the lengthy process for spouses and children to enter the U.S., the Legal Immigration Family Equity ("LIFE") Act of 2000 created provisions for a V visa and K-3 visa. A V visa allows spouses and children (V-2) of green card holders who had an I-130 filed on or before December 21, 2000 to enter or stay in the U.S. and to work temporarily while they wait to receive their green cards – sometimes waiting six to eight years.

A K-3 allows a spouse of USC to travel to the U.S. and to work during her stay here. But a K-3 is not a green card—she needs to file for a green card as soon as possible. If anything changes in the relationship (divorce or separation), she cannot adjust her status even if she has a job offer, other family members in the US, or a different USC spouse.

When applying for a family-based green card, an I-864 Affidavit of Support needs to be attached to the green card application. Under the new Illegal Immigration Reform and Immigrant Responsibility Act (IIRIRA) of 1996, the petitioner has to be a sponsor. If the petitioner's income does not meet the Federal poverty level guidelines for his or her household size, then the petitioner's assets or the intending immigrant's income or assets can be used in certain situations to meet the requirement. Otherwise, they can try to find a joint sponsor, who has to be a green card holder or U.S. citizen. IIRIRA made the I-864 a legal, enforceable contract between the intending immigrant, the government, and the sponsor(s). The sponsor's legal responsibility ends when the intending immigrant becomes a U.S. citizen or compiles 40 qualifying quarters (i.e. 10 years) of employment and payment into social security.

An I-864 need not be filed unless the matter includes an application for a green card. If a foreign-born is coming to the U.S. on a student visa, or is in the U.S. and is applying to change to student status, an I-134 Affidavit of Support is needed to show that the applicant is unlikely to become a public charge (however, this is more of a moral obligation than a legally enforceable one).

Let's say a U.S. green card holder who moved to Italy married an Italian man. They have a child who never applied for a U.S. passport and was born on Italian soil. Both the father and the child never applied for green cards or U.S. citizenship. Now the child, who is 32 years old, wants to come to the U.S. to begin a new life. His mother had filed an I-130 petition for him years ago and the I-130 quota is now open for him to get a green card. His mother files an I-864 with a U.S.-filed tax return. Her income is from her job in Italy because her spouse and her family remained in Italy. The green card for the son is denied because the income from his sponsor, although more than 125% of the U.S. poverty level, was derived from non-U.S. sources. The U.S. government feels that it has no claim to their earnings.

One extremely important change in the past few years is the American Competitiveness in the 21st Century Act ("AC21"). AC21 allows an employment-based intending immigrant (and his or her family) to remain in the U.S. if immigrant visa quotas are backlogged, through no fault of the alien, even if the alien loses his or her job with the petitioning company, as long as the alien's I-140 immigrant petition was approved, the green card application has been filed and pending for at least 6 months, and the alien's new job is same or similar to the job in the original petition.

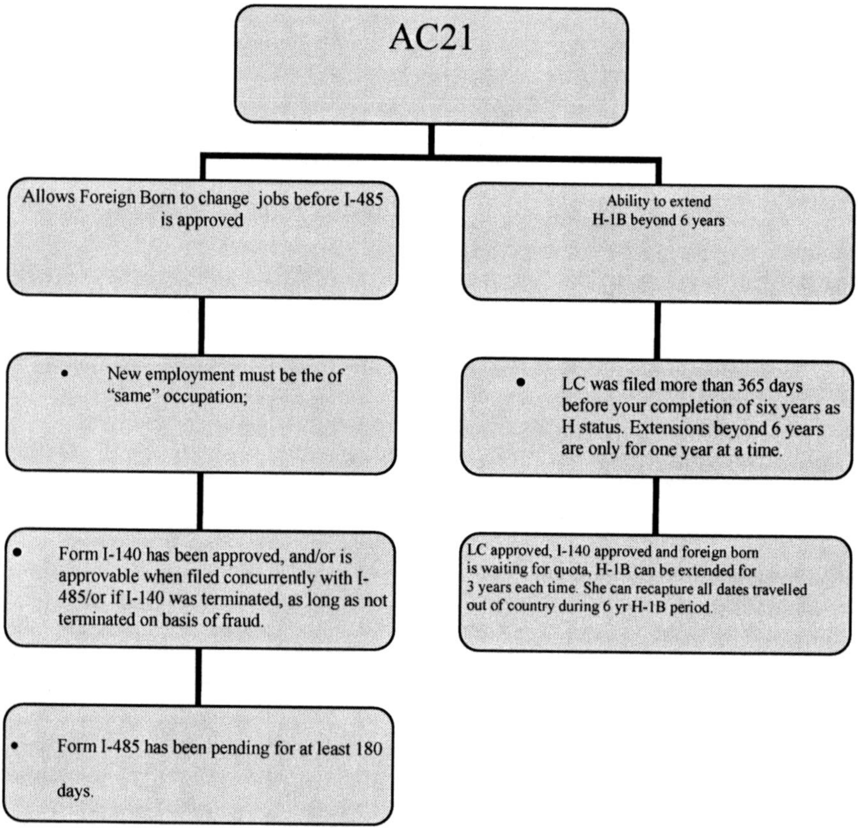

7. U.S. CITIZENSHIP

Those born within the United States or its territories are granted citizenship per the 14th amendment of the U.S. Constitution largely regardless of the status of their parents, with the sole exception of children of diplomats and foreign officials. Others may become U.S. citizens through filing an N600 (for those deriving citizenship from qualifying relatives) or an N400 (for those becoming naturalized citizens).

Children of USCs Born Abroad

Those born outside of the United States may be citizens from birth if both of their married parents are USCs and at least one lived within the U.S. for any length of time prior to the child's birth. Individuals born outside of the United States to one USC parent married to one non-USC parent may be citizens if the USC parent lived within the United States for at least five years prior to the child's birth, with two of those years occurring after the fourteenth birthday. Since 1995, children born to only one USC parent who do not fulfill the above requirements may qualify for expeditious naturalization if a USC grandparent meets the five/two year requirements. Additionally, the Child Citizenship Act of 2000 grants citizenship to LPR children under the age of 18 who are in the legal and physical custody of a USC parent and permanently residing in the United States.

A child born out of wedlock to a USC mother is entitled to citizenship if his/her mother lived in the United States or its territories for one continuous year prior to birth of the child. A child born out of wedlock to a USC father has the same restrictions as that of a child born of one USC parent in wedlock, with the added stipulations, that paternity was established before a consular officer, the father must sign a statement agreeing to provide financial support for the child (and has been providing the same) until the age of 18, and the father must acknowledge his paternity of the child in a written statement.

Citizenship Application for Children or Grandchildren of USCs	
N600	Application for Certificate of Citizenship

Adopted Children of USCs

The adoption of foreign-born children by U.S. citizens and their passage into the U.S. has become an issue of great concern. The Hague Convention of 1993 established guidelines for the adoption of children within signing countries, and its regulations took effect for the United States in April 2008.

The process of adopting a child from a Hague Convention country is slightly different from the procedure followed for children from non-Hague Convention countries. There is also a distinction between children designated Convention adoptees and orphans, with different requirements and restrictions applied to each.

1993 Hague Convention Countries				
Albania	Chile	**Guatemala**	Malta	Romania
Andorra	China (and Hong Kong)	Guinea	Mauritius	San Marino
Armenia	Colombia	Hungary	Mexico	Seychelles
Australia	Costa Rica	Iceland	Moldova	Slovakia
Austria	Cuba	India	Monaco	Slovenia
Azerbaijan	Cyprus	Israel	Mongolia	South Africa
Belarus	Czech Republic	Italy	Netherlands	Spain
Belgium	Denmark	Kenya	New Zealand	Sri Lanka
Belize	Dominican Republic	Latvia	Norway	Sweden
Bolivia	Ecuador	Liechtenstein	Panama	Switzerland
Brazil	El Salvador	Lithuania	Paraguay	Thailand

Bulgaria	Estonia	Luxembourg	Peru	Turkey
Burkina Faso	Finland	Macedonia	Philippines	United Kingdom
Burundi	France	Madagascar	Poland	Uruguay
Cambodia	Georgia	Mali	Portugal	Venezuela
Canada	Germany			

NOTE: The US is not currently (September 14, 2009) processing new adoptions with countries in **bold** above.

Source: http://adoption.state.gov/hague/overview/countries.html

A Convention adoptee is defined as a child living in a Convention country under the age of 16 and unmarried at the time of the visa petition whose parents have relinquished legal custody and issued written consent for the child's adoption and emigration. The child must be adopted within the United States or the Convention country by a married USC couple or a single USC over the age of 25 habitually resident in the United States and deemed suitable for caring for the adoptee by USCIS. All children adopted from a Convention country must meet the requirements for classification as an adoptee.

If both parents are deceased or one parent is deceased and the other is incapable of supporting the child, the child may immigrate as an orphan. A living parent's "inability to support" the child must be proven, however, and in fairly convincing terms. Children must also be adopted before the age of 16 (children under the age of 18 may be adopted along with siblings under the age of 16) to be classified orphans. Orphans must be adopted by married couples or unmarried USCs over the age of 25 to maintain that classification. All children adopted from non-Convention countries must meet the requirements to be designated as an orphan.

Parents seeking to adopt a child from a Hague Convention country must work with an agency approved by the Department of State and the related forms (I-800A and I-800) differ from those for non-Hague Convention countries (I-600A and I-600). Additionally, the visas with which children enter the United States differ.

Hague-Convention adoptees enter the United States with an IH-3 visa (for children adopted overseas) or an IH-4 visa (for children to be adopted within the United States). IH-3 children under the age of 18 acquire citizenship automatically upon entry to the United States, while IH-4 children are LPRs until finalization of the adoption, at which time they gain citizenship.

Non-Hague Convention orphans enter the United States with an issued IR-3 visa (for children who have been adopted overseas) or an IR-4 visa (for children who will be fully and finally adopted within the United States). IR-3 children under the age of 18 acquire citizenship upon entry to the United States, while IR-4 children only obtain green cards. Parents of an IR-4 child must file for citizenship on the child's behalf by the child's 18th birthday using form N-643. If a citizenship application is not filed by that time, the child must become a naturalized citizen of his/her own accord.

Further information regarding adoption may be found at http://adoption.state.gov.

Adoption Forms	
I-800	Petition to Classify Convention Adoptee as an Immediate Relative
I-800A	Application for the Determination of Suitability to Adopt a Child from a Convention Country
I-600	Petition to Classify Orphan as an Immediate Relative
I-600A	Application for Advance Processing of Orphan Petition

One may also become a naturalized citizen five years after obtaining a green card. Exceptions to this include those who have been granted asylum, who may obtain citizenship four years after gaining permanent residency, and spouses of USCs remaining married and cohabitating, who may apply for U.S. citizenship two years and nine months from the date of the Registration of the Marriage Certificate/approval of the green card. If a foreign-born is no longer married, or is married but not cohabitating with the USC spouse, he/she may apply for U.S. citizenship after four years and nine months, provided all the residency requirements are met.

Depending upon one's place of residence, it may take six months to two years for an LPR to complete the required procedures for becoming a U.S. citizen. However, the benefits of becoming a U.S. citizen are significant. For example, LPRs must file U.S. tax returns as a "resident," and LPRs working overseas obtaining foreign income must report "worldwide" income while USCs can avail themselves of a "foreign income" exception. LPRs are also not permitted to use the "marital deduction" in wills and estate planning. It is highly advisable for green card holders to strive for U.S. citizenship.

To be approved for a U.S. citizenship application, one must first take a test on U.S. history and government and both written and oral English tests, then pass fingerprint and security clearance checks of the FBI and other agencies. Those aged 50 or older who have been permanent residents for 20 years or more and those aged 55 or older who have been a permanent resident for 15 years or more may apply for an exemption to the English component of the testing phase, and may take the history test in their native languages. Afterwards, USCIS reviews all relevant files to ensure full legality of the process leading up to citizenship and confirms that the applicant swore allegiance to the United States in front of a Judge. Because USCIS thoroughly scrutinizes applicants' past affiliations, it is advisable to disclose all relevant information on applications.

The Child Citizenship Act of 2000 (CCA) allows some foreign-born children of American citizens to acquire US citizenship. Children who qualify under the CCA are those who did not acquire US citizenship at birth. This includes orphans with a full and final adoption abroad or adoption finalized in the US, biological children, children born out of wedlock (born to parents who are not married) who were legitimated before age 16, certain children born out of wedlock to a mother who naturalizes, and adopted step-children who meet the two-year custody requirement. There are two categories of children that can qualify: those who were born abroad to parents who reside in the US, who can obtain automatic US citizenship, or those who were born abroad to parents who reside outside of the US, who must apply for citizenship in the United States.

To be eligible for automatic US citizenship under the CCA, the child must have at least one American citizen parent by birth or naturalization who lives in the US, be under 18 years of age, live in the custody of the American citizen parent, and get admitted as an immigrant for lawful permanent residence. Additionally, if the child is adopted, the adoption must be full and final. On the date that all of these criteria have been met, the child is automatically granted US citizenship. This means that no formal application needs to be filed in order to obtain the citizenship. However, to obtain proof of the US citizenship, the USC parent must complete Form N-600 on behalf of the child in order to receive a certificate of citizenship.

The children of American citizens who are born and reside abroad must undergo a different process. They must apply to a USCIS district office or sub-office in the United State on Form N-600K and will then have to travel to that office in the US in order to complete the application process. To qualify, at least one parent of the child must be an American citizen by birth or naturalization, the child must be unmarried and under age 18; and the child must get admitted into the United States as a nonimmigrant. Further, the US citizen parent must meet the physical presence requirement. This means that the USC parent must have physically resided in the United States for a total of at least five years, two of which must have been after age 14. In cases when the USC parent does not meet the physical presence requirement, a USC grandparent may satisfy the physical presence requirement if he or she has lived in the US for the required number of years. For example, if the USC parent moved abroad at age 15, he or she does not meet the physical presence requirement. But, if one of the parents of this USC parent moved abroad at age 47, then the grandparent does meet the physical presence requirement and can be included in the child's citizenship application. This does not mean that the USC parent of the child applying is not included on the application; it means that the qualifying grandparent's biological information as well as the information on the grandparent's residence must be included on the citizenship application in addition to the parent's information. Additionally, if a grandparent's US residency is being used to satisfy the physical presence requirement, the grandparent must also go with the USC parent and child to the USCIS office where the N-600K application has been filed. A notable exception to the physical presence requirement applies to the children of some members of the military who are overseas on active duty. In these cases, any period of residence overseas on active duty qualifies as residence in the United States.

In addition to the regulations on obtaining US citizenship, the CCA also provides guidance on how a child who qualifies under the act can obtain an American passport. To apply, the American citizen parent must provide proof of his or her relationship to child, such as a certified copy of the foreign birth certificate or a certified copy of the final adoption decree, and identification documents for the American citizen parent(s). For those who acquire automatic citizenship, the parent must also submit the child's foreign passport containing the I-551 LPR stamp or the child's green card. For those who do not qualify for automatic citizenship, the parent should provide the child's certificate of citizenship.

Naturalization for LPRs	
N400	Application for Naturalization

Dual Citizenship

U.S. laws do not demand that new USCs renounce citizenship in their old countries. However, U.S. officials do not accept the use of passports of other countries for USCs with dual citizenship, and those who become citizens of the U.S. may only travel in and out of the country using U.S. passports.

To Summarize:

Birth on U.S. territory - acquisition at birth
1. Born outside the U.S. when one or both parents are U.S.C – would not need a cert of citizenship
2. Transmitting U.S.C parents must have resided in the U.S. physically for 5 years prior to child's birth, two of which were after the age of 14
3. Other special requirements for child born to unmarried parents

Derivative citizenship – A child born overseas can get citizenship through naturalization or the U.S. birth of one parent. The child has to be admitted to the U.S. with GC status and can get citizenship without the 5 year requisite requirement as long as the child is under the age of 18. The child can obtain a U.S. passport right away.

Naturalization of a GC holder over the age of 18 - If married and cohabitating with a U.S.C spouse, the GC holder can get citizenship in 3 years. If not married to U.S.C, she can get citizenship after 5 years.

Renouncing Citizenship

A U.S. citizen by naturalization or birth may voluntarily relinquish his/her U.S. citizenship. However, if a U.S. citizen gives up U.S. citizenship for purposes such as tax evasion, he/she can never get U.S. citizenship back. The decision to renounce U.S. citizenship should not be taken lightly.

8. ILLEGAL ENTRY/LOSING STATUS, DETENTION, AND DEPORTATION

Detention and Deportation

To put these words in some sort of context, on any given day in 2008, more than 30,000 foreign-borns were in custody under DHS authority in 260 facilities across the country. This is more than three times the number of detainees in 1996.[231] In Fiscal Year 2008, 356,739 foreign-borns were deported from America by DHS, averaging 977 removals per day.

These figures can be quite frightening to an immigrant; the risk of being deported to a place that we struggled so hard to leave, for whatever reason, is no small matter. When I first started practicing immigration law in the 1970s, immigration enforcement was nothing like it is today. We all knew in a way who should be deported, and who shouldn't. It was mostly aliens with serious criminal records that needed to be deported, and this was done quickly. The plane ticket was obtained one or two days after the order was given, the deportees were escorted to the airport, allowed a few minutes to say goodbye to their families, and were put on the plane. These days, ICE puts everybody in detention, including those without criminal records for months before they are removed. This is done secretly, and for security reasons the families and lawyers are not notified. Most of the time, ICE brings the people in the early morning hours or late at night to the airport in prison garb, chains or handcuffs, without money or personal documents, and puts them on a plane to any airport in the country where they were born, irrespective of how far from their hometown that airport is. For example, if a Chinese national's former home is in Guangzhou and he is deported to Beijing, he would need to somehow book another five hour plane ride to the nearest airport in Guangzhou, or a take a 2 or 3 day train ride. Even for someone like me, who has been around a long time as an active practitioner and has "seen it all," I still shake my head in disbelief at such cases and feel terribly for them.

Writing cannot communicate the horror of seeing some child or young adult's parents dragged away from their home in the early morning or in the middle of the night because they have no immigration status in the U.S. Even criminal arrestees have more rights than this. It's difficult for many to understand the emotional turmoil unless they have relatives or close friends in that situation, or are themselves foreign born. Our home is here, our roots are here – it's like a rebirth once we arrive in this country. It's just like someone who lost a child saying to me, "unless you lose a child yourself, you can't know how it feels to lose one."

If deportation occurs, the world seems to stop. Then, the family and the deportee go through the four stages of grief – denial, depression, anger, and acceptance. For immigration lawyers, this is one of the hardest parts of our job; to see families through the grieving and anger and somehow maintain calm so that we can focus on the issues at hand. We have to discuss whether the families want to go overseas and stay there or wait in the U.S., potentially for years, while we see if we can bring the deported person back to the U.S. with a green card. This may require a waiver if there is no permanent bar. If there is a permanent bar, the foreign-born would never be able to return to U.S. soil.

a. Deportation vs. Removal

Prior to April 1, 1997, deportation began with the issuance of an order to show cause (OSC) and notice of hearing by INS. Exclusion proceedings took place when an individual attempted to enter the United States through extralegal means and was arrested at a border or port of entry. The formal "removal" process replaced "exclusion" and "deportation" in 1997. The removal process begins with the issuance of an NTA by ICE and DHS (previously by INS) instead of an OSC. However, NTAs are nearly identical to OSCs and serve a similar purpose. Furthermore, the terms deportation and removal are commonly used interchangeably. One significant difference between the pre-1997 and post-1997 systems is that under the current system, an immigrant is responsible for notifying the government of any changes of address and for appearing at hearings when summoned. Prior to 1997, the burden was on the government to deliver a notification to the immigrant.

Expedited Removal and Deferred Inspection

Expedited removal, formerly proposed under the term "summary exclusion," was also implemented in 1997 and has been expanded to affect foreign-borns caught attempting to enter the country illegally or foreign-borns who have been in the country for less than 2 years and are unable to prove admittance or parole. Those who have had their visas revoked by the government are also subject to expedited removal. Individuals within the country marked for expedited removal are detained without the right to administrative or judicial review, and are deported within two weeks of arrest. Individuals stopped at the border are turned away, and those arriving at a port of entry are sent back to their place of origin via the airline or sea carrier which brought them. However, expedited removal cannot be applied to Canadians or Mexicans without criminal records. The majority of persons fearing persecution if returned to their places of origin are also exempted from expedited removal, although they are held in confinement while adjudication on their case is pending. Although one who is excluded or deported in such a manner are subject to the bar associated with a formal deportation, one may withdraw his/her application for admittance at a border or port of entry, thus voluntarily departing and not subjected to removal proceedings or a bar.

If officials are uncertain as to the legal status of an individual seeking entry into the United States, he/she may be required to report to his/her local ICE office at an appointed date and time to resolve the issue. This is known as deferred inspection, and persons undergoing this procedure do not have a legal status within the United States unless eventually approved by ICE.

Losing Status and Bars of Re-entry

Whenever a foreign-born remains in the country after the expiration of his/her visa, he/she loses legal status. If such a person leaves after even just an hour of overstay, the CBP officials at the U.S. border may void his/her visa and passport. The 180/360 day rule and the 3/10-year bar were promulgated in April 1997. If an individual overstays his/her visa in the U.S. for more than 180 days and thereafter leaves the U.S. (but is not deported), he/she is barred from re-entering the U.S. for three years. If he/she overstays for more than 360 days and leaves (but is not deported), a ten-year bar applies. If he/she overstays for more than 360 days and is deported, a permanent bar applies. It is important to note that the time counted towards illegal stay in the U.S. is frozen when an NTA is issued. There are also exceptions to this rule when certain otherwise illegal immigrants have been given special consideration, such as with 245(i). Some may also apply for a waiver of the bar through immigration services, but such applicants must have a USC or LPR spouse or parents and be able to prove extreme hardship for those persons if separated. Mere separation and financial reasons do not suffice to prove extreme hardship; a "totality" of circumstance is necessary. The most common use of this waiver is with deportees who must return and care for a sick spouse. However, there is no recourse for most deportees except to wait the duration of the bar.

If immigration officials discover that a labor certification or marriage with which an individual obtains his/her green card is fraudulent, the green card may be revoked and the individual put into deportation proceedings.

If deported, an individual is barred from re-entering the United States for a minimum of 5 years. If deported multiple times, an individual is barred from re-entry for 20 years. If the deportee is not subject to a 3/10-year bar or a permanent bar, a waiver for a 5-year bar may be filed even before leaving the U.S. If the 3/10-year bar applies, waivers for both bars must be filed in an American Consulate or Embassy overseas. There also exists a 5/10-year bar for those who overstay for a length of time (but are not deported) after requesting voluntary departure (see section on voluntary departure).

Waiver of Bars of Re-entry	
I-601	"Extreme Hardship" Waiver

b. Criminal Trouble

When a nonimmigrant visa holder or LPR commits a crime, he/she may lose visa/LPR status. In such cases, immigration officials begin a deportation/removal procedure and send notice of their "intent to revoke".

It is wise for non-citizens facing criminal charges to talk to an immigration practitioner to avoid being subjected to deportation after the criminal plea or trial. Although state court judges were previously allowed to issue a state order for "Judicial Recommendation against Deportation," which precluded deportation, they no longer have judicial authority over deportation, as it is a federal matter.

Immigration consequences for person who pled guilty to a crime, convicted after jury or bench trial, or agreed to a criminal diversion because she is a first time offender, can impact on her immigration status. Though the direct consequences of jail time, probation, fines and/or parole may be over with after the plea period, the collateral consequences could be severe and could either result in no waivers, lifetime deportation without hope of ever returning to the U.S., or mandatory detention in ICE custody.

The Federal Anti-Drug Abuse Act of 1988 included only murder, drug-trafficking and weapons trafficking. Now many other offenses, even including misdemeanors, constitute removable offenses.

In 1994, additional offenses were added again to the definition of aggravated felony, including an imposed term of imprisonment of 5 years or longer.

Definitions of aggravated felonies from 1996 Amendments to 2009 have been seriously expanded resulting in mandatory detention and little relief to get green cards. Also, the 1996 Amendments added crimes of violence and revisions to 212 c eligibility.

c. Students Losing Status

Students who come legally can also fall out of status easily. If the country is at war or a recession occurs, students may lose their tuition for a semester of school. These students are rendered immediately out of status and the schools are required to notify SEVIS immediately.

In such a situation, a student must file an I-539, related documents, and the completed form I-20 to show that he/she has been out of status for less than five months. It is important to count months out of status correctly. Because a student need not go to school in the summer, summer months are not counted against a student when considering status.

If the student has indeed been out of status for more than five months, has not been engaged in unauthorized employment, and does not have a record of being a repeat violator, reinstatement of the student's legal status is possible if he/she requests reinstatement promptly and can prove the presence of exceptional circumstances arising from external forces, e.g. illness and serious injury, closure of the school or a natural disaster. Note that this reinstatement only applies to stay in the U.S. and that he/she must stay in the country while awaiting approval. Those who leave will have to explain their situation overseas to the Consulate in order to apply for a visa to return to the U.S.

Although a student may only work on campus while in school as an F-1 (with the exception of the CPT), he/she may apply for off-campus employment work permits after one academic year (nine months) of school if his/her financial source for tuition is lost. The original sponsor must submit a letter to the school stating unforeseen and uncontrollable economic circumstances caused severe economic hardship and thus an inability to pay the student's tuition. With this, the student may be approved for an economic hardship work permit.

If a student becomes ill or suffers injury, he/she must obtain advance permission and blessing from his/her foreign student advisor before he/she can take the semester off or reduce to a course load lower than 12 credit hours. The foreign student must maintain a grade point average equivalent to a "C" or 2.0 GPA.

d. Voluntary Departure

After the issuance of an NTA, the first order of business for a foreign-born should be to check the NTA form for errors. Any mistakes on the form may help in a case, should the individual choose to contest deportation.

The mode of entry of the foreign-born has become extremely important. An individual who entered with a visa and married a U.S. citizen three years later may adjust his/her status in the U.S. to that of a legal permanent resident. A similar individual who entered without a visa on foot from Mexico or Canada cannot. Those who entered with fraudulent passports (arriving aliens) may apply for adjustment of status within the U.S., but must file 601 waivers and provide apologies to the U.S. government.

A foreign-born arrested by a law enforcement officer may not be treated as an arriving alien because he/she is already on U.S. soil, and so cannot adjust status in the U.S. to that of a green card holder.

Those without final orders of deportation may request voluntary departure from the government. A request for voluntary departure is irrevocable. The maximum amount of time for departure allowed under this is 120 days, during which time the immigrant in question may settle his/her affairs and prepare to leave. He/she must pay for a ticket abroad and leave within the allotted time, or will be barred and unable to apply for a green card for 10 years (if proceedings started after April 1997) or 5 years (if they started before). ICE is authorized to extend the time allowed for voluntary departure for another 60 days.

I still remember that a lot of lawyer colleagues in the 1980s and 1990s would bring clients into Immigration and ask for a write-up and to put them into voluntary departure status. In those days this status allowed a foreign born to obtain a work permit and a social security number so they could work. Written extension requests were routinely granted by the immigration officials to allow them to stay. There was a big scandal in Cleveland where some immigration officials were convicted of crimes and went to jail for granting these voluntary departures without permission from their bosses. The work permits in those days were granted in local offices and thus it was easy to get the work permit and voluntary departure the same day. Being a foreign born myself I lucked out because I never brought people in for voluntary departure write-ups because I just knew there was something inherently wrong when it is that easy. By the early 1990s indeed Immigration office began to give people a hard time and also their names and addresses were in their database. They never had the chance to be issued an OSC and to go in front of the judge.

A foreign-born who overstays after pleading voluntary departure cannot obtain legal status or a green card even through marriage to a USC. Such a person cannot obtain a green card overseas and return to the U.S., either, as a 5/10-year bar would apply. Therefore, his/her only recourse would be an extreme hardship waiver.

Voluntary Departure Form	
G-146	Form which needs to be submitted to American Embassy overseas to confirm departure from the U.S.
I-601	"Extreme Hardship" Waiver

e. Taking Your Case to Court

If one does not request voluntary departure, the court schedules master calendar hearings to which attendance is mandatory. If a foreign-born does not appear at a scheduled hearing, the judge will issue an in absentia deportation order. In the event one cannot show up because of illness, incarceration by the criminal system, or a funeral, one must file a motion with the court to request rescheduling. If this motion garners no response, the foreign-born is responsible for appearing, with or without her lawyer.

A green card holder issued an NTA or OSC (Order To Show Cause) because of a criminal issue should seek the advice of both criminal and immigration lawyers. A criminal lawyer's job is very much to avoid a jail term and fines; an immigration attorney's job is to fight deportation and the loss of permanent residency.

Immigration court proceedings are non-jury. The same judges run the same courtrooms with their assistants. The deputies and District Counsels that represent ICE are also often the same people.

After several master calendar hearings, the individual hearing is set. A lawyer should already have taken pleadings and informed the judge of a client's relief in the first or second master. It is the lawyer's responsibility to prep his/her clients well before a hearing, explaining the proceedings of a trial and advising clients to tell the truth. Lawyers may have done these hearings hundreds or thousands of times, but it is the first and only time for a client. It is vital that the clients remember relevant information and that lawyers bring to light relevant information in direct testimony. A separation of witnesses should not be asked for or given unless District Counsel asks for it, because it is beneficial for witnesses to hear what the main parties have testified.

It is also important to have everything on record. Judges have tape recorders in front of them, which they may quietly shut off at certain moments. Lawyers must ensure that the recorders stay on, for in the event of an appeal, the BIA (Board of Immigration Appeals) and the circuit court will be able to hear the judge, and the transcripts will show what the judge and/or District Counsel said. We are lucky to practice in Cleveland because the Judges cannot shut off the recording device without reaching over and we would be able to notice that.

Individual hearings usually last for two to six hours, and sometimes longer. If the foreign-born loses, he/she has thirty days to file an appeal to the BIA. There are no hearing notices issued by the BIA; the appeals proceedings and work are all on paper. Appeals are generally decided 9 months to 2 years after filing. A denial at the BIA level can be appealed to the circuit courts within 30 days.

In cases of particularly high significance, the Attorney General of the U.S. has the power to certify the case to herself and issue a ruling which will become the official interpretation of the law. In *Matter of Compean*, in January 2009, former Attorney General Mukasey issued an opinion stating that aliens in removal proceedings have no right to the assistance of counsel. However, the Attorney General left open the possibility of an alien reopening removal proceedings in extraordinary cases based on lawyer error. This was his 11th hour ruling before he left office and President Obama was sworn in. As of this writing, *Matter of Compean* is no longer law and *Matter of Lozada* came back in full force.

Various circuits may have established different rulings through different precedent-setting cases based on the same situations. Circuits also individually set rules and processing times. For an individual for whom deportation is imminent, it is important to know circuit rules regarding the stay of deportation, as well as local ICE regulations. However, ICE officers have the ability to jail foreign-borns even when a case is pending with circuit courts because a pending case only grants immunity from deportation, not detention.

Although a lawyer may not choose in which circuit court an appealed case is heard after the initial ruling on the case (because appeals must be heard in the circuit with jurisdiction over the state in which the first case was heard), he/she may check local circuit laws prior to the individual hearing and move the case to a circuit with more favorable rulings. The foreign born and their families must have moved their residence and workplace for the court to have jurisdiction. If the rulings on similar cases differ between circuits (a circuit split), lawyers may be able to file cert (certiorari) with the U.S. Supreme Court.

The number of district court and court of appeals immigration cases has increased more than 50% in the past few years, and as such, is now a burgeoning field for immigration practitioners and litigators.

f. Final Orders of Deportation

If a foreign-born loses his/her case in court and all appeals have been exhausted, her deportation will be enforced. When a final order of deportation is entered by an immigration judge, a "bag and baggage" letter ordering the immigrant to pack and report for deportation is sent by ICE. If the foreign-born does not report in accordance with the instructions on the letter, he/she becomes an "absentee" and fugitive of the law. Those in this situation may be able to obtain relief if any of the following apply:

- Kept address current with immigration officials, but did not receive notices for court hearings
- Address on immigration records mistyped
- Translation (if necessary) during court hearings in the wrong language (such as Portuguese vs. Spanish), inadequate or unintelligible
- Circumstances such as serious illness or injury prevented compliance with court orders
- Family would suffer greatly if deported (extreme hardship)

g. Detention

With the rise of controversy concerning illegal immigration, some state police have begun to arrest and detain people without status, and sometimes even LPRs, when in doubt of what action to take.

If an individual is detained, family and/or friends must first find the A (alien) number of the person. If the number is unknown, the date and country of birth must be ascertained. This is because immigration officials file ICE and green card cases under A files. Matters regarding nonimmigrant visas or changes of status are listed under an LIN (short for Lincoln, Nebraska), EAC (Eastern Adjudication Center, in Vermont), WAC (Western Adjudication Center, in California), or SRC (Southern Regional Center, in Texas) number. Without this number, one cannot identify the detainee, or even talk to the officers. One must also research whether or not the detainee has been issued a final order of deportation. If so, he/she will likely be detained for at least 90 days by ICE. After being held for 90 days, ICE review will take place, and if not released at that time, the individual will be subject to a second review 90 days later. Even if one wishes to be deported after spending time in prison, deportation may not occur for weeks or months due to the difficulty of arranging for passports and/or one-way travel documents with his/her country of birth.

Here are some highlights of the Migration Policy Institute's analysis of ICE data on detainees in the system on January 25, 2009:[232]

- Of the 32,000 immigrants in ICE custody, 18,960 had pending removal cases (in other words, they had not received final orders of removal).
- The average length of detention for the 18,960 pre-removal order detainees was 81 days. Seventy-four percent had been detained for less than 90 days, 13 percent for between 90 days and six months, 10 percent for between 6 months and one year; and 3 percent for a year or more.
- 10,873 detainees (or 34 percent) had received "administratively final" orders of removal. The average length of detention *following* receipt of a removal order for 10,771 detainees (those for whom the database provided the *date* of the final removal order) was 72 days.
- A high percentage of detainees (58 percent) did not have criminal records, which is difficult to explain since mandatory detention laws largely apply to criminal aliens; ICE includes persons who have committed immigration-related offenses in its criminal alien nomenclature; and ICE's expanding Secure Communities program, which places arrested and imprisoned noncitizens into removal proceedings, should be feeding large numbers of immigrants into its detention system.
- The "most serious" convictions for nearly 20 percent of criminal aliens in ICE custody were for traffic-related (13 percent) and immigration-related (6 percent) offenses.
- ICE held detainees in 286 facilities which were concentrated in southern and US-Mexico border states
- Nearly 70% of detainees were held in state and local prisons

h. REAL ID Act

The REAL ID Act was enacted on May 11, 2005 in part to improve national security against terrorist actions.[233] To achieve its objectives, the Act imposes certain security, authentication, and issuance procedures standards. The REAL ID Act includes amendments to the INA relating to: burdens of proof and procedure for asylum-seekers and for other forms of relief from removal; the definition and removability provisions for terrorism and terrorist-related activities; and requirements for federally approved identification cards.[234] As a result of the enactment of REAL ID Act, the amended INA has imposed higher burdens and stricter standards of proof for individuals applying for asylum and other related forms of relief. Particularly, it added language on credibility and corroboration, and permits immigration judges to consider even minor inconsistencies when determining credibility of an asylum seeker.[235]

Prior to the enactment of the REAL ID Act, an applicant could be eligible to apply for asylum in the United States as long as an applicant is able to demonstrate that he or she was unwilling or unable to return to his country because of "persecution or a well-founded fear of persecution on account of race, religion, nationality, membership in a particular social group, or political opinion."[236] An applicant "does not bear the unreasonable burden of establishing the exact motivation of a 'persecutor' where different reasons for actions are possible."[237] The Board of Immigration Appeals (BIA) further added that an applicant for asylum must produce evidence, either direct or circumstantial, from which it is reasonable to believe that the harm was or would be motivated in part by an actual or imputed protected ground.[238]

Conversely, as previously noted, the REAL ID Act amended the conditions for granting asylum in several ways including the issues of eligibility requirements, adverse credibility of an asylum seeker and corroboration requirements. The enactment of the REAL ID Act heightens the burden of proving asylum seeker's eligibility. According to INA §208(b)(1)(B)(i):

The burden of proof is on the applicant to establish that the applicant is a refugee, within the meaning of section 101(a)(42)(A).[239] To establish that the applicant is a refugee within the meaning of such section, the applicant must establish that race, religion, nationality, membership in a particular social group, or political opinion was or will be at least one central reason for persecuting the applicant.

Those seeking asylum now must also prove that harm on one of the protected grounds is "at least one central reason for the persecution." In other word, the established harm cannot be merely "incidental or tangential to the persecutor's motivation."[240] An applicant now becomes ineligible to apply for asylum if his or her protected ground is only subordinate to another non-protected reason for the persecution, or an applicant raises a protected ground as only a superficial part of the overall claim.

As a result of the enactment of the REAL ID Act and the following amendment to the INA, courts must now consider a "totality of the circumstances" in determining whether or not applicants for asylum, withholding of removal and CAT relief are credible. This amendment to the INA created a new legal undue burden for asylum seekers because adjudicators can now find applicant's adverse credibility on matters that are irrelevant and that do not go to the heart of the asylum claim.[241] Prior the amendment, any inconsistency had to go to the "heart of claim" to result in an adverse credibility finding. Under the new standard, an adjudicator now could deny a legitimate asylum application if the applicant testified to address inconsistent with his or her application.

With REAL ID Act, an immigration judge is able to ask that the foreign born produce evidence to corroborate otherwise credible testimony, and the foreign born must comply unless he or she does not have the evidence and "cannot reasonably obtain" it.[242] These corroboration requirements are detrimental to applicants with legitimate asylum claims because it is often difficult for applicants to obtain evidence, and adjudicators often require corroboration in such difficult situations. For instance, a Chinese woman seeking asylum after being forced to have an abortion could be required to obtain proof of her abuse from the doctors who performed the procedure.

REAL ID has "heightened the burden of proof for aliens by mandating that a protected ground must serve as "one central reason" for harm. It has therefore increased the already critical need for aliens to establish their credibility."[243]

9. OTHER ISSUES CONCERNING FOREIGN BORNS IN THIS COUNTRY.

a. CHILD STATUS PROTECTION ACT

The 2002 Child Status Protection Act ("CSPA")[244] became effective on August 6, 2002[245] to allow families to remain together during the lengthy process of applying for a green card by permitting children who turn 21 to retain classification as a "child" ("aging out"). Congress's goal in enacting the CSPA was to address the backlog and delays of adjustment of status applications of children. Prior to CSPA, children of foreigners would lose their "child" status upon turning 21. This means that some of these children were not able to emigrate with their parents. The parents needed to file a new I-130 for them and they had to restart at the back of the line, resulting in another 6 to 8 years of wait time. They would have to be left behind in their home country and could not apply for green card status.

Pursuant to enactment of the CSPA, INA § 203(h)(1)[246] provides rules for determining whether certain foreign nationals are "children," as follows:

> In general.--For purposes of subsections (a)(2)(A) and (d), a determination of whether an alien satisfies the age requirement in the matter preceding subparagraph (A) of section 101(b)(1) shall be made using—
>
> (A) the age of the alien on the date on which an immigrant visa number becomes available for such alien (or, in the case of subsection (d), the date on which an immigrant visa number became available for the alien's parent), but only if the alien has sought to acquire the status of an alien lawfully admitted for permanent residence within one year of such availability; reduced by
>
> (B) the number of days in the period during which the applicable petition described in paragraph (2) was pending.

Section 203(h) provides a three-step analysis for determining CSPA eligibility:

The first step is to determine whether a foreign national's situation is covered by the CSPA. Under Section 8, the effective date of the CSPA is August 6, 2002. Therefore if an immigrant petition[247] listing the child was approved on or after August 6, 2002, and the child turned twenty-one (thereby aging-out) on or after August 6, 2002, then the CSPA applies.

The second step, if CSPA applies, is two-tiered. First, the child's "CSPA age" is calculated.[248] The "CSPA age" is determined on the date the child's immigrant visa – or if the child is a derivative beneficiary, the principal beneficiary's immigrant visa – becomes available. The child's actual age on the date the immigrant visa becomes available, minus the number of days that the immigrant visa petition was pending with USCIS[249] is the child's "CSPA age." If the difference is under 21, then the derivative foreign national remains a "child" for purposes of the permanent residence application. The child then becomes eligible to apply for an immigrant visa or adjustment of status.

The foreign national child must also have "sought to acquire the status of an alien lawfully admitted for permanent residence" within one year of the immigrant visa becoming available. Interpretation of the "sought to acquire" language depends on whether the derivative applicant is overseas or in the United States. If both the principal applicant and derivative are in the U.S., then each individual must file an application to adjust to permanent residence (Form

I-485). On the other hand, if the principal is in the U.S. but the derivative is overseas, then the principal must file an Application for Action on an Approved Application or Petition (Form I-824) in order for the derivative to receive an immigrant visa.[250]

If the child's "CSPA age" is not under 21, then the analysis moves on to the third step, as described in INA § 203(h)(3) as follows:

(3) Retention of Priority Date.-

> If the age of an alien is determined under paragraph (1) to be 21 years of age or older for the purposes of subsections (a)(2)(A)[251] and (d),[252] the alien's petition shall automatically be converted to the appropriate category and the alien shall retain the original priority date issued upon receipt of the original petition. (emphasis added)

This provision addresses the aging-out of derivative beneficiaries of parents' family-sponsored and employment-based petitions. According to the statutory language, these derivative beneficiaries automatically convert to the appropriate preference category, and retain their parents' original priority date, if they age-out. However, USCIS has limited this provision to derivatives beneficiaries of the F2A category, and the Service's interpretation was upheld by the decision of the Board of Immigration Appeals in *Matter of Wang*.[253]

When an LPR's child ages out of the second-preference 2A category, after calculating the CSPA age, the child converts to the 2B category. The LPR parent must file a separate I-130 on the child's behalf. The cover letter should make an explicit request to retain the original priority date of the F-2A I-130 so that the CIS does not issue an I-130 receipt with a new priority date.

The BIA also held that CSPA allows for priority date retention when if the LPR parent files a new I-130 for the once-derivative and now aged-out child, where the original petition was an F-4 I-130 sibling petition for the LPR parent.[254]

b. Crime and Moral Turpitude

Even before the issue of national security came to the forefront of Americans' attention, there existed the stereotype that foreign immigrants were more likely to be involved in gangs and criminal activities, which has been in place since colonial times when the arrival of criminals and persons of questionable moral character was an issue of concern. While laws have been passed barring felons and prostitutes from entering the country, the stereotype of new immigrants as more prone to violence and debauchery has been perpetuated by movies glorifying Italian gangsters, Chinese triads, and Russian, Cuban, Japanese, and Columbian organized crime, to name a few. More recently, Mexican immigrants have come under fire for the drug wars which have become increasingly violent and caused much bloodshed in the American Southwest. The highly publicized crackdowns on gang activities in big cities across the country also fuel the theory that poverty-stricken immigrants will tend to resort to crime to supplement their incomes.

Recent scholarly research has proven that the opposite is true. Contrary to popular belief, areas with higher levels of immigration typically have lower crime rates despite the areas being economically disadvantaged.[255] In a study conducted by

Robert J. Sampson, first generation immigrants were 45% less likely than third-generation immigrants to commit a crime. Even in areas where there are significant levels of racial segregation between blacks and whites, immigration within the black population proved to be an inhibiting factor to crime.

This is perhaps because crime does not pay, especially if one is a first-generation immigrant. Whereas the police departments can not deport American citizens who are criminals, the government can and does deport criminals who are nationals of other countries. After all the trouble people go through getting to the United States, they do not want to ruin it over whatever little benefit they may obtain by engaging in illegal activities. Even illegal immigrants must work every day to stay under the radar and avoid encounters with law enforcement officials. There may be other reasons why immigration may be harmful to the United States but increasing the crime rate is not one of them.

c. Media Influence

A large reason these misconceptions about immigrants exist is that the media tends to perpetuate stereotypes through the stories it chooses to cover. There is much more extensive coverage of illegal immigrants than legal immigrants. Refugees are also given more coverage because of their relation to various crises occurring around the globe. This is good business for news outlets because such stories garner high ratings (a large number of viewers).

The media also takes pride in fulfilling its "watchdog" role over government policies. However, the manner in which the media represents illegal immigrants can have a negative effect on all immigrants, regardless of their status. The poorest illegal immigrants are shown arriving on rafts from Cuba, in cargo containers from China, or on foot from Mexico. They are shown sick or starving, despondent or desperate. They are regularly linked to problems with crime and national security, and accused of relying too much on welfare and government health care benefits. By being so one-dimensional in their portrayal of immigration, many media outlets lead the American public to focus only on the negatives that immigration may bring, most points of which remain under contention but are expressed in definitive terms. Most people who are writers and reporters were born in this country or are at least second or third generation descendants of immigrants, so the main body of journalists has not experienced the U.S. visa application process and the subsequent ebb and flow of keeping one's visa status afloat.

Most new immigrants pay taxes dutifully and work to earn their living, despite how hard that may be, but these stories do not get much exposure or circulation. Furthermore, immigrant advocacy groups do not have the audience or influence that general media outlets do, and cannot offset the level of anti-immigration fervor that some news stories generate. Public perception has a key role in influencing public policy, and as the majority of immigrants do not yet have citizenship, the issue of immigration is heavily dependent on the native-born American opinion and vote. Consequently, the media's portrayal of immigrants and immigration has a substantial anti-immigration effect on policy, especially in times of recession. There are some media sources, however, which try to maintain a balanced outlook when addressing the issue of immigration.

Still, there are those stations with a clear left or right-wing bias which tailor their news and opinions to meet the sensibilities of their audiences. These sorts of media organizations are beneficial and necessary for keeping members of the opposite political spectrum honest and for providing more detailed information of a certain political leaning than more moderate outlets are able or willing to provide. However, their coverage of contentious issues can easily devolve into the realm of opinion and the reinforcement of mutually-shared preconceptions with selective data (a problematic process known within the intelligence community as groupthink). It is vital that Americans who watch biased news programming are aware that they may be presented with only one facet of a larger issue, and monitor other sources of information and opinion accordingly in order to formulate their own conclusions. Unfortunately, this is most often not the case. Many citizens make their judgments based on such incomplete information, or worse, readily adopt the opinions of others without individual consideration. Whether pro-immigration or anti-immigration, it is suboptimal to leave one side of an issue underreported.

There may not be a way to change how commercial media reports stories to best suit their interests, but a more informed public may be able to offset these inherent deficiencies in the market economy by being more selective of their news sources. A more educated viewer or reader would assess multiple sources, placing more weight on credible stations or newspapers. In turn, popular media would adjust to better suit the tastes of their audience.

d. The Culture Clash – Different Skin Color

Another source of tension between immigrants and native-born Americans is caused by differences in culture and customs. People are social creatures. It has been proven that those belonging to the same group, even if the connection between its members is tenuous or arbitrary, tend to favor each other over outsiders. As intelligent beings, humans are also judgmental. To better facilitate daily living individuals form opinions about things and store observations and experiences in their memory banks for later use. That is how a person lives and learns, and that is how humans have survived as a species. Unfortunately, many people misapply these types of generalizations when encountering strangers. It is easy to forget that humans are individuals and that each has his/her own personalities and characteristics. When one gets burned by touching a flame as a child, she/he instantly learns not to touch fires again. Every flame can burn; water is always wet. However, seeing a few rich white teenagers driving Hummers does not imply that all white families are wealthy. Yet, dangerous assumptions such as these are made all the time. Every instance of discrimination against an ethnic group has been started by these sorts of prejudices and judgments. It happens when people see others as faceless members of a large group, instead of as individuals. In a way, it is dehumanizing. One must remember that because everyone has a mind of his/her own because people are more unique and less predictable than just about anything else on the face of the planet.

Another problem is that people tend to make illogical connections and assumptions. For example, mastery of the English language might be used as a yardstick for how intelligent a person is. When an immigrant worker does not follow a simple English command, some will automatically attribute the mistake to stupidity instead of a lack in English comprehension. The worker may be extremely intelligent, but not having grown up in an English-speaking environment, will logically have a difficult time following directions that may seem simple to the native speaker.

This causes more difficulty for immigrants hoping to assimilate into American society. It is too easy to avoid finding employment in a workplace requiring English. Or rather, it may be too challenging to get a job requiring English. Many employers would not hire an immigrant, whose English is broken and accent thick, if given a choice between her and a native-born American, if the pay would be the same. Newcomers to this country need environments where they can improve their English, become fluent and become better contributors to society.

e. English-Speaking Ability of Foreign-Borns in the United States (5 Years of Age and Older)

	Estimate
Foreign-Born:	36,914,983
Speak only English	5,817,164
Speak English "very well"	11,762,781
Speak English less than "very well"	19,335,038

Source: U.S. Census Bureau, 2005-2007 American Community Survey

Not only will learning how to speak English help immigrants find better jobs, it may open up cultural and social gateways, as well. America is one of the most diverse countries in the world, and has made tremendous strides towards unity and equality in the past century. There is much to appreciate and enjoy in learning about and befriending other people who share your values. There is also much that others can learn from others different from one self. At first, cultural differences can be estranging, or even intimidating to some people. When isolated in ethnic communities and never learning to speak English, immigrants remain strangers in a foreign land, both in how they feel and the way native-born Americans view them. After an immigrant starts to branch out and associate more with people outside their ethnicities, both they and native-Americans may find that they share more similarities than differences.

f. Educating the Next Generation

On the other side of learning English is the issue for immigrants of retaining their cultural heritage in America and passing that heritage on to their children. Immigrant families in the United States have to consider how to raise their children to succeed in their study of English while staying aware of the roots from which they came. In general, there are three ways of approaching the issue.

The first approach is to abandon all speech in the native language and instruct children with English, exclusively. The pros of this method are that the children will be on a more even footing with their peers when they enter kindergarten and will have an easier time adapting to the all-English environment of school. With only one language to master, children raised in an English-speaking family may have an easier time mastering the English language. This approach also allows the parents to practice their own English, which gives the parents an added incentive to study the language. The cons are that the parents probably do not have perfect English themselves (or may hardly speak any at all), which may still put the children at somewhat of a disadvantage compared to their playmates, and the children lose the opportunity to learn the language of their ancestors in a family setting.

The second method is to speak entirely in the language of the home country. The children may be discouraged from speaking English at home, with the view that they will learn English in school and that the only opportunity for them to learn the language of their home country is at home. The result may be that the child ends up being bilingual, but in their younger years they may have a harder time learning English and interacting with their schoolmates. As seen in the table below, sometimes children who grow up in non-English speaking homes fare worse in their English abilities than other children. However, being bilingual can be a great asset, especially in America, which is not like Europe, where many children grow up speaking two, three, or even four or five languages. As such, people who are fluent in English and a foreign language are highly valued in many jobs in America, as well as having the benefit of being able to more fully understand their cultural backgrounds.

Linguistic Ability of Native-Born Americans (5 Years of Age and Older)

	Estimate
Native:	241,361,740
Speak only English	218,132,417
Speak Spanish:	16,694,180
Speak English "very well"	13,079,962
Speak English less than "very well"	3,614,218
Speak other Indo-European languages:	3,957,784
Speak English "very well"	3,311,671
Speak English less than "very well"	646,113
Speak Asian or Pacific Island languages:	1,711,593
Speak English "very well"	1,372,299
Speak English less than "very well"	339,294
Speak other languages:	865,766
Speak English "very well"	730,893
Speak English less than "very well"	134,873

Source: U.S. Census Bureau, 2005-2007 American Community Survey

The third approach is a mix of the previous two. The children are typically taught the language of their ancestors by attending special language schools for children of their ethnicity once a week. During the week, the children are spoken to with mostly English. This approach has similar results as the first approach. The children will become much more integrated with the American side of their heritage but these weekly classes may be a social setting for children of the same ethnicity. There have been mixed results for children sent to bilingual schools (as opposed to language instruction once a week): while children in these settings may retain some of the spoken language of their ethnicity, it may be detrimental to their English-speaking skills and rarely helps with the reading and writing of the language of their parents

Regardless of which method an immigrant may choose or have chosen for his/her children, an easy way to instill into these children some of their ethnic culture is by celebrating the cultural festivals and holidays at home. There are often summer camps which aim to instill more of their home culture into the children, as well. Children in these settings are able to learn about the culture and history of the land their parents grew up in while experiencing an enjoyable time with other children of their ethnicity. These camps may also be available to and can be equally beneficial to children who are not from the specific ethnicity as the teaching language is usually in English.

g. Incarceration and Deportation

The rate at which illegal immigrants (and some legal immigrants) are being jailed has risen to alarming levels. In the 70s, 80s, and 90s, those who requested voluntary departure were not checked up on, and the rule was generally not enforced. The foreign-borns still had their social security numbers and drivers licenses and kept working, often contributing to the country in the form of income taxes. When their children became 21, they could sponsor their parents.

This changed when the American economy went downhill. For the first time in 30 plus years, families of jailed foreign-borns are seeking help for getting their relatives released by the hundreds each day. After the filing of a mandamus action or an APA action, getting clients out of detention centers falls under the jurisdiction of the District Courts. This mandamus also needs to name, as defendants, the name of the jail that is detaining the foreign-born. This can be very difficult as there is no computerized database or system to track where people are. It can be a stressful process just to locate a detained loved-one.

During the lengthy verification process prior to deportation, most immigrants are simply stuck in jail. Most judges do not allow bonds and do not let immigrants out of jail until ICE is ready to deport them. This normally takes quite a few months, as ICE needs to get a passport from a foreign-born's home country to deport her. In order for a foreign-born's country to issue a passport, the country's government has to verify her place of birth, date of birth, parents' names, etc. for security purposes.

The conditions in which illegal immigrants are detained without recourse or relief are deplorable. Due to the excessive building of jail space in the 1990s and 2000s with the easily obtained tax credits, private jails incarcerate immigrants with DHS paying them more than $100 a night, per person. The food and conditions in immigration prisons are worse than those in municipal, county, state, and federal detention centers because the immigration prisons lack oversight. The jailers may not have guard training and are not federal, state or local government workers. They are typically not paid well and do not understand the difference between immigration and criminal detainees. Although these private jails are technically accountable to DHS, the U.S. criminal system, and the U.S. detention system (and partially because of it), no agency ultimately enforces the maintenance of living standards within immigration prisons. The New York Times has printed many in-depth articles investigating these jails.

The process of deportation proceedings itself may be an ordeal in itself. Today, ICE detains most of those whom they apprehend, sometimes for months before deportation, including those without criminal records. For security reasons, the immigrants' families and lawyers are not notified. After long confinement, ICE officials bring deportees to the airport dressed in prison garb and in chains or handcuffs, sans money or personal documents. Oftentimes, deportation officials place them on planes to any airport in the country where they were born, irrespective of how far from their hometown that airport is. For example, if a Chinese national's former home is in Guangzhou and he is deported to Beijing, he would need to somehow book another five hour plane ride to the nearest airport in Guangzhou, or a take a 3 day train ride.

Criminal arrestees have more rights than these immigrants who may not have committed any crimes. It is difficult for many to understand the emotional turmoil unless they have relatives or close friends in that situation, or are themselves foreign-born. Their homes are in America, their roots have been planted in America – it is like a rebirth when immigrants arrive in this country. This is similar to someone who lost a child says to a friend, "unless you lose a child yourself, you cannot know how it feels to lose one."

h. Other Problems Within the Immigration System

There are numerous issues with the bureaucratic process and stipulations of immigration law which bog down the system and cause humanitarian problems for immigrants. Some of these problems are difficult to prevent, but there is always room for improvement.

One of the problems is that State Department and DHS officials are overworked and underpaid. There may be reasons why the State Department officials overseas grow tired of the games foreign-borns play when they apply for visas. There is a lot of fraud involved; travel agencies which charge exorbitant prices helping to obtain phony documents and bank notes, people stating on visa forms that they are married instead of single, people buying or stealing others' identities (social security numbers), etc., and all for the sole purpose of their desire to enter the U.S. Because of this, burn-out rates for DHS workers are very high. It is a difficult place to work for even the best intentioned and most hardworking people. The field adjudicators, pushed everyday to do dozens of interviews at scheduled time slots, do not have time to read up on new laws although laws, policies, headquarter memos, regulations, field memos and directories change by the day.

There are good reasons for many safeguards and regulations within the immigration system. However, other initiatives taken by policymakers to reform immigration only induce immigrants to make poor life choices or create unnecessary red tape which creates long waiting times and keeps families separated. Workers at immigration headquarters pick up phones readily, but not district offices and ICE. It can be exhausting when dealing with immigration officials. Oftentimes, voicemails take two or three days to be responded to, if at all. The Service Centers with which immigrants file most of their green card applications, naturalization applications, and change of status forms do not have easily navigable systems that a common person without a survival instinct, high energy, tenacity, and passion may use for information.

It is a myth that immigrants are guaranteed a green card if they marry a U.S. citizen. If an individual entered illegally by walking over the border and is not one of the few exceptions, s/he would not be able to get a green card without leaving the country. If the person stayed in the United States for more than 180/360 days they will face a 3/10-year bar from entry into the United States even if his/her spouse lives in America. It is very difficult to obtain waivers in these situations. However, the consensus amongst many would-be immigrants seems to be that the easiest way to get a green card is through marriage to a USC. When immigrants marry for the express purpose of getting a green card and citizenship, they place themselves in situations where they are beholden to their spouse and vulnerable to abuse or exploitation. Large underground industries in mail-order brides and human trafficking have grown to exploit the opportunities presented by imperfections within the American immigration system. On the flip side, U.S. citizens may be used and exploited by immigrants.

While bringing strangers into sham marriages on one end, on the other immigration law can keep loving families separated due to long processing times. Getting a green card through other means, such as with employment-based or other family-based routes, is most often painfully slow. There may be a waiting period of years for families to be reunited while immigration services process filings and applications. There are also some cases in which it is actually better legally for an immigrant to get a divorce than to try to salvage a marriage while separated and working through difficulties, subjecting children to the burdens of having divorced parents.

Other young children are brought to the country illegally and later deported as adults, facing tremendous hardship because they may not be fluent in the language of their country of birth. These people are caught between the stringency of the law and unfortunate circumstance. Allowances on the basis of extreme hardship should be made for these residents, who attended U.S. schools, speak only English, and have joined the American workforce. The United States may condemn those who grew up within the American tradition to poverty in such instances.

Another problem is the system of allocating skilled-immigrant visas through strict quotas by nationality. Herman and Smith highlight the predicament:

> [T]he foundation of the system remains the federal Immigration and Nationality Acts of 1965 and 1952. The 1965 act diversified America by opening immigration to new parts of the world. In a manufacturing era, the act made family reunification an over-arching goal of the system. It gave relatively little attention to the migration of workers. In fact, it imposed rigid nationality quotas on skilled immigrants.[256]

In fact only about 9 percent of immigrant visas are available to high-skill immigrant, with per-country limits on employment visas written into the law. As Herman and Smith explain:

> People from any one nation cannot use more than 7 percent of the visas available that year. This means that workers from large sending countries [e.g. India and China] are forced to wait, sometimes more than 8 years, because their visa allotment has

been "oversubscribed" by their fellow citizens. . . . The 7 percent quota applies equally to every country on Earth, regardless of its size or the potential number of immigrants it sends to America. For example, Malawi, which has a population of 10.5 million people, is allocated the same amount of employment visas as India, which has a population of over 1 billion.[257]

There may not be easy solutions to many of these issues but that should not be a reason to ignore them completely. Only by considering all the factors to U.S. immigration can there be change to improve the process for the good of immigrants, native-born Americans and the United States as a whole. In the mean time, immigrants must make the best of the current situation while native-born Americans learn to accept foreigners different from themselves.

The Society of American Law Teachers (SALT) has issued 8 useful recommendations to the Obama Administration for Immigration Agency Reforms.[258] These are:

- STOP THE CRIMINALIZATION OF IMMIGRANTS.
- REFORM FEDERAL IMMIGRATION ENFORCEMENT INSIDE THE BORDER.
- ELIMINATE LOCAL POLICE ENFORCEMENT OF FEDERAL IMMIGRATION LAWS.
- RECOGNIZE THE RIGHT OF IMMIGRATION DETAINEES TO FAIR TREATMENT, AND INCLUDE ATTENTION TO THE NEEDS OF CHILDREN IN IMMIGRATION CUSTODY.
- TREAT ASYLUM SEEKERS FAIRLY AND RESPECTFULLY.
- END THE PRACTICE OF IDEOLOGICAL EXCLUSION.
- ADDRESS THE IMPACT OF WORKER RIGHTS ISSUES ON IMMIGRATION PATTERNS THROUGH NATIONAL AND INTERNATIONAL INITIATIVES.
- STREAMLINE THE FRAMEWORK FOR COMBATING HUMAN TRAFFICKING.

i. DO'S AND DON'TS FOR FOREIGN BORNS

Do's

- Stay abreast of major changes in immigration law. By staying informed of changes in immigration law, one can prepare herself for overcoming legal obstacles in the future, as well as take full advantage of new avenues for obtaining visas, green cards, or citizenship.

- Inform immigration officials of any changes of address. If a hearing with the Immigration Judge is missed due to one's NTA being sent to an old address, an in absentia order will be issued, leading to detention and deportation.
- Remember important dates, deadlines, and appointments. This includes meetings with immigration officials, court dates, filing deadlines, I-94 dates of departure or expiration, deadlines for voluntary departure, and deadlines for appeals.
- Keep detailed records of employment, residence, tax filings, medical bills, receipts, and other important documents against the event that they are needed.
- Retain all immigration documents and old passports until the acquisition of citizenship. While some lost documents may be replaced through a FOIA (Freedom of Information Act) request, the process is lengthy and recovery of documents is uncertain.
- Dress appropriately and be respectful and attentive when addressing officers and judges. This may make them more receptive to one's testimony.
- Ensure that all personal information on forms, filings, and personal documents/identification is correct.

Don'ts

- Do not overstay. Those who do may be barred from re-entry or unable to adjust their status.
- Do not misrepresent by alleging to be a USC (such as when voting or applying for a job). There may be both criminal and immigration-related repercussions.
- Do not seek benefits from Medicaid or Welfare. Once done, obtaining a green cards or citizenship becomes more difficult.
- Do not work without a valid work permit. Those who work without a work permit for more than 180 days cannot obtain a green card without a waiver.
- Do not lose a record of the A number (Alien number). It is an 8 or 9-digit number which is preceded with the letter A. Those who only file an NIV petition with USCIS or a visa petition are not assigned an A number.
- Do not be late to appointments with immigration officials and judges. Tardiness may hurt the chances of attaining a favorable ruling on a case, and in some instances the case may simply not be heard.

j. IMPORTANT CHANGES TO IMMIGRATION LAW FROM THE 1980s

Immigration Marriage Fraud Amendments of 1986

- Gave a 2-year conditional resident status to foreign-borns married to U.S. citizens if the marriage happened within 2 years before the green card application

- Foreign-borns can start applying after 1 year and 9 months to remove conditions on the green card
- Form I-751 is used and upon approval a 10-year green card will be issued

Immigration Reform and Control Act of 1986

- Unlawful for employers to knowingly hire foreign-borns unauthorized to work
- Sanctioned employers who did not submit valid I-9 forms, a form that proves a person's eligibility to work in the U.S.
- Provided amnesty for foreign-borns who were illegal before January 1, 1982, allowing them to apply to INS for legal resident status by May 4, 1988, as long as certain conditions are met

Immigration Act of 1990

- Began the "battered spouse waiver" in which a "battered spouse" who obtained conditional permanent residency could waive the requirement to remove the condition, and eventually become a legal permanent resident
- Created the diversity lottery system to even out the number of immigrants from nations that were considered to be underrepresented in the U.S.
- Increased number of new immigrants allowed per year to 700,000 from 500,000

Illegal Immigration Reform and Immigrant Responsibility Act of 1996

- Created the Affidavit of Support I-864 requirement for family-sponsored immigrants, requiring minimum income requirements for the sponsor, in an effort to curb unsupported foreign-borns from draining U.S. resources
- Established more controls over U.S. borders while increasing restrictions on immigration

INA & 245(i) in December 1997

- Allows undocumented foreign-borns and foreign-borns who entered illegally to apply for a green card in the United States if a family-based petition or labor certification was filed prior to January 14, 1998

AC21 - The American Competitiveness in the 21st Century Act of October 2000

- Allows foreign borns to begin work with new employer of at the time of filing of H-1B transfer instead of waiting for the H-1B to be approved.
- Foreign born could come under 245(i) from a filed labor certification and/or I-140 even though she is not getting green card from this filing, the same rule does not apply to the foreign born who is being substituted into an approved labor certification owned by the employer who filed; allows the foreign born to use her own

old priority date for a newly filed labor certification and approved I-140.

Legal Immigration and Family Equity Act (LIFE Act) in December 2000 – 245(i)

- Section 245 (i) of the Immigration and Nationality Act allows certain applicants for permanent residency or labor certification to adjust their status in the U.S. without returning to their home country. LIFE temporarily extended the filing deadline under 245(i) from January 14, 1998 until April 30, 2001.

Child Citizen Act of 2000 (CCA)

- Allows some foreign-born children of American citizens to acquire US citizenship. Children who qualify under the CCA are those who did not acquire US citizenship at birth. This includes orphans with a full and final adoption abroad or adoption finalized in the US, biological children, children born out of wedlock (born to parents who are not married) who were legitimated before age 16, certain children born out of wedlock to a mother who naturalizes, and adopted step-children who meet the two-year custody requirement. There are two categories of children that can qualify: those who were born abroad to parents who reside in the US, who can obtain automatic US citizenship, or those who were born abroad to parents who reside outside of the US, who must apply for citizenship in the United States.

Child Status Protection Act (CSPA) in August 2002

- Enacted to provide relief for children who "age out" as a result of petition delays, locking in the age of the child at an earlier date and preserving the status of a "child" for many individuals who otherwise would age out.
- Prior to CSPA, green card applications as direct or derivative beneficiary child would be approved only if adjudicated prior to child turning 21 (after one turns 21, the person ages out and would lose the preferential status of a "child"). CSPA locks in the age at an earlier date, preserving the status as a "child."
- The age of the child locks in on the date that the priority date becomes current, less the number of days the petition is pending, as long as the beneficiary applies for permanent resident status within one year of visa availability date.

Real ID Act in 2005

- Corroboration not necessary, immigration judge may waive credible testimony with other record evidence, "totality of circumstances" on credibility, applicant has to prove at least one of the 5 grounds for asylum was at least one "central reason," removed 1000 cap number on one child policy and 1000 cap number on asylee green cards.

Violence Against Women Act in 2005

- Amended T and U visas, allowed abused men and women to self-petition for green cards, required USC fiancés to provide criminal records.

k. FILING TIPS

- One may call the number on your receipt for the status of cases.
- Premium processing is available for certain visa applications for an additional fee. Petitions filed with premium processing are decided upon within 15 days of receipt.
- All requests to USCIS, ICE and CBP must include the following:
  - Type of petition
  - Alien number of foreign-born –OR-
  - Receipt notice number of the filing –OR-
  - Name of foreign-born, including last name, date of birth and place of birth –AND-
  - Petitioner's full name OR
  - Petitioner's full name and petitioner's A number
- Children under the age of 14 cannot sign their own forms; the parent or legal guardian must sign in their stead.
- Immigration forms require original signatures. Signature stamp and electronic signatures are unacceptable except for applications USCIS allows to be filed online.
- Ensure that all necessary supporting evidence is filed with forms. USCIS may deny a petition if vital information is missing or send a Request for Evidence (RFE) or Notice of Intent to Deny (NOID).
- Obtain tracking information and proof of delivery for applications and documents mailed to government agencies. Be sure to save the tracking receipts.
- The filing fee should not bounce from the Bank.
- Have cover letter and paperclip together with the filing to explain the nature of the case.
- Follow instructions as in the booklet or USCIS website.
- Correct filing fee
- File: Make sure to file with USCIS office or Service Center having jurisdiction over the case.

10. LIST OF ACRONYMS AND ABBREVIATIONS

AC21 – American Competitiveness in the 21st Century Act
BIA – Board of Immigration Appeals
CAT – (UN) Convention Against Torture
CBP – Customs and Borders Protection
CPT – Curriculum Practical Training
CSPA – Child Status Protection Act
DHS – Department of Homeland Security
DOJ – Department of Justice
EAD – Employment Authorization Document
EOIR – Executive Office for Immigration Review
FOIA – Freedom of Information Act
GC – Green Card
ICE – Immigration and Customs Enforcement
IJ – Immigration Judge
IMMACT 90 – Immigration Act of 1990
INS – Immigration and Naturalization Services
LCA – Labor Condition Application
LPR – Legal Permanent Resident
NIV – Non-Immigrant Visa
NIW – National Interest Waiver
NOID – Notice of Intent to Deny
NOF – Notice of Findings
NTA – Notice to Appear
OES - Occupational Employment Statistics
OPT – Optional Practical Training
OSC – Order to Show Cause
PERM - Program Electronic Review Management
RFE – Request for Additional Evidence
SESA - State Employment Service Agency
SEVIS – Student and Exchange Visitor Information System
TEA – Target Employment Area
TPS – Temporary Protected Status
UNHCR – United Nations High Commissioner for Refugees
USC – U.S. Citizen
USCIS – U.S. Citizenship and Immigration Services

11. GLOSSARY AND EXPLANATIONS

Age out children – children who are too old to benefit from the green card status of a relative (as a general rule, over 21 years old)
AOS – Adjustment of status – the process of changing your status to that of a permanent resident.
Asylum – seeking refuge in the United States after one already comes into the country so that one does not have to return to his/her home country where he/she might become persecuted if he/she were to return
CBP – Customs and Borders Protection
Conditional Permanent Resident Status – permanent resident status conferred when PR was obtained either through marriage to a US citizen or as an immigrant investor. The green card is only valid for 2 years. The conditional status must be removed through a request in order to get the 10 year green card.
Deportation – prior to 1996 the proceedings taken to expel foreign-borns who are without legal status who were apprehended in the United States; those in deportation proceeding can not adjust their status
Derivative Beneficiaries – family members of the original visa holder that receive benefits based on their relation to the original visa holder (e.g. a derivative beneficiary of a F-1 student could be a F-2 spouse of said student).
Diversity visa – also known as the "green card lottery", makes available 50,000 immigrant visas for those from countries and regions with low rates of admission to the US.
Documented Aliens – alternative term for legal alien or immigrant with status
Dual nationality – possessing nationality to two countries simultaneously.
Entering US:
Entering with inspection – entering the United States with a US visa at the border or port of entry and having your identification looked at by a customs official; even if it was done with a fake passport it is possible to eventually adjust to permanent residency and United States citizenship
Exclusion – prior to 1996 the proceedings taken to expel arriving aliens or foreign-borns who were apprehended for violations of immigration laws at ports of entry or on boats coming to the United States; those in exclusion proceedings are not barred from adjusting their status
GC – Green Card, the document which proves permanent residency
Green Card holder – permanent resident of the United States, person can reside in the United States without education or employment requirements; only qualification is the person can not be out of the United States for more than 1year without a travel document issued by USCIS (re-entry permit) to ensure admission to the U.S. on re-entry.
I-94 – document filled out upon entry into the U.S. which determines legal status and length of stay in the US
ICE – Immigration and Customs Enforcement – the department in the American government in charge of deportations
IJ – Immigration Judge
Illegal Alien – person living in U.S. without a visa. This word generated a lot of debates in our community. Liberals think that they should be named as

undocumented aliens but the Conservatives think that they should be using this term.
Illegal Entry – entering the country without going through custom's inspection; except for a very few exceptions it becomes impossible to become a permanent resident or U.S. citizen
Illegal Status – in the United States without the auspices of the U.S. government, if caught will undergo deportation proceedings
Illegitimate child – child born out of wedlock, for the purposes of immigration the mother is considered to be the sole parent and for the child to be considered an orphan by U.S. immigration the mother must be unable to provide for the child and relinquish in writing rights to the child
Immigration – the act of migrating into a country from another country
Legacy INS – Immigration and Naturalization Services, the department that was replaced by the USCIS after the creation of the Department of Homeland Security
Legal Status – in the United States under the auspices of the U.S. government
Legitimate child – child born in wedlock, for the purposes of immigration at least one parent of the child must be deceased and the other parent unable to support the child for U.S. immigration to consider the child an orphan
Legitimated child – child born in wedlock but father later acknowledges the child, for the purposes of immigration legitimated children are given the same requirements as legitimate children
National – a person owing allegiance to a country
Naturalized citizen – a U.S. citizen who was born the citizen of another country but became a citizen of the United States later in life, i.e. who did not acquire citizenship based on birth in the U.S.
NIV – Non-Immigrant visa, all visas that do not move you toward immigrating to the United States
NOF – Notice of Findings – issued by Labor Department after the filing of the PERM (LC) by the employer to request additional information or to clarify a certain point. We are allowed 30 days to respond and a "Final Determination" will be issued denying or approving the LC filing.
NOID – notice of intent to deny
NTA – Notice to appear, issued by ICE to begin removal proceedings
OSC – Order to show cause, issued by legacy INS as a means to start the deportation process
Permanent Resident (or Legal Permanent Resident)– a non-citizen who has the right to live and work in the United States and are afforded certain privileges in terms of employment
Principal visa holder – the main visa holder upon whom the visa status depends for the rest of the family members.
Real ID Act – 2005 act in which certain rules and regulations were put on the issuance of driver's licenses, also made obtaining asylum more difficult
Removal – after 1996 all proceedings to expel illegal immigrants both arriving aliens and non-arriving aliens are called removal proceedings. However after 2006 arriving aliens are allowed adjustment of status.
RFE – Request for Evidence that is issued to an applicant after filing a visa

TPS – Temporary protected status for countries designated by the US Attorney General.
Undocumented Aliens – alternative term for illegal alien or immigrant without legal status
Aliens – person living in the U.S. who is not a citizen of the United States
U.S. Circuit Court of Appeals – the intermediate court, after a decision is reached in an U.S. District Court, the party which lost can try to appeal in the Circuit Court of Appeals that oversees the District Court in which the case was lost. There are 13 U.S. Appeals courts in the country.
U.S.C – U.S. Citizen
USCIS – Citizenship and Immigration Services, short for USCIS the department in the American government in charge of benefits associated with immigrating to the United States
U.S. District Court - the lowest court in the federal court system, all federal courts start at a U.S. District Court
U.S. Supreme Court – the highest court in the Federal courts system, it is the last resort for those cases already decided by a U.S. Circuit Court of Appeals, as there is only one U.S. Supreme Court most cases are not selected to be heard at the Supreme Court and so are decided at the Appeals court level
U.S. Worker – U.S. citizens or green card holders that qualify for the job.
FBN (Foreign Born Nationals) citizens who live in the United States but are born in another country and remain a citizen of a country other than the United States
VWP – Visa Waiver program

12. RESOURCES

- USCIS – www.uscis.gov
- State Department – www.state.gov
- AILA (American Immigration Lawyers' Association)
- Federal Bar Association Immigration Law Committee
- American Bar Association
- Your local bar association – check the internet
- NAACP (National Association for the Advancement of Colored People)
- Infopass appointment with your local District Office, scheduled through the web.
- Urban League
- Defense Association
- Public libraries
- NAPABA (North Asian Pacific American Bar Association) Immigration Law Committee

WORKS CITED

---

[1] Public Agenda (Scott Bittle and Jonathan Rochkind), "A Place to Call Home: What Immigrants Say Now About Life in America," available at http://publicagenda.org/pages/immigrants.

[2] Public Agenda (Scott Bittle and Jonathan Rochkind), "A Place to Call Home: What Immigrants Say Now About Life in America," available at http://publicagenda.org/pages/immigrants.

[3] Andrea Nill, *Why Legalizing 12 Million Undocumented Immigrants Would Help U.S. Economy*, Jun. 30, 2009, http://wonkroom.thinkprogress.org/2009/06/30/lamar-smith-immigration.

[4] Andrea Nill, *Why Legalizing 12 Million Undocumented Immigrants Would Help U.S. Economy*, Jun. 30, 2009, http://wonkroom.thinkprogress.org/2009/06/30/lamar-smith-immigration.

[5] Maria E. Enchautegui, "Immigration and wage changes of high school dropouts," Monthly Labor Review, October 1997.

[6] Peter B. Dixon and Maureen T. Rimmer, "Restriction or Legalization? Measuring the Economic Benefits of Immigration Reform," Trade Policy Analysis No. 40, August 13, 2009, available at http://www.freetrade.org/files/pubs/pas/tpa-040.pdf.

[7] Peter B. Dixon and Maureen T. Rimmer, "Restriction or Legalization? Measuring the Economic Benefits of Immigration Reform," Trade Policy Analysis No. 40, August 13, 2009, 1.

[8] Peter B. Dixon and Maureen T. Rimmer, "Restriction or Legalization? Measuring the Economic Benefits of Immigration Reform," Trade Policy Analysis No. 40, August 13, 2009, 1.

[9] Rob Paral and Associates, "The Disparity Between Immigrant Workers and Unemployed Natives: Untying the Knot," Immigration Policy Center Special Report, August 2009, 13.

[10] Rob Paral and Associates, "The Disparity Between Immigrant Workers and Unemployed Natives: Untying the Knot," Immigration Policy Center Special Report, August 2009, 13.

[11] Rob Paral and Associates, "The Disparity Between Immigrant Workers and Unemployed Natives: Untying the Knot," Immigration Policy Center Special Report, August 2009, 13.

[12] "Immigration and Welfare," Wall Street Journal, 24 May 2007: A16.

[13] Adam Liptak, "Justices Opt for Fewer Cases, and Professors and Lawyers Ponder Why," The New York Times, Sept. 29, 2009.

[14] This Timeline is drawn from http://memory.loc.gov/learn//features/immig/timeline.html, http://ocp.hul.harvard.edu/immigration/dates.html, http://www.pbs.org/itvs/thecity/america1.html, Cheryl Shanks, *Immigration and the Politics of American Sovereignty*, 1890-1990 (2001), and E. Willard Miller and Ruby M. Miller, *United States Immigration: A Reference Handbook* (1996).

[15] T.H. Breen and Timothy Hall, *Colonial America in an Atlantic World* (New York: Pearson Education, 2004), 6-13.

[16] T.H. Breen and Timothy Hall, *Colonial America in an Atlantic World* (New York: Pearson Education, 2004), 31-35.
[17] T.H. Breen and Timothy Hall, *Colonial America in an Atlantic World* (New York: Pearson Education, 2004), 31-35.
[18] Alan Taylor, *American Colonies* (New York: Viking Penguin, 2001), 32-37.
[19] Isaac Asimov, *The Shaping of North America* (Boston: Houghton Mifflin Company, 1973), 48-53; T.H. Breen and Timothy Hall, *Colonial America in an Atlantic World* (New York: Pearson Education, 2004), 23.
[20] Silvio Torres-Saillant and Ramona Hernández, The Dominican Americans (Westport, Connecticut: Greenwood Press, 1998), 2.
[21] T.H. Breen and Timothy Hall, *Colonial America in an Atlantic World* (New York: Pearson Education, 2004), 36-41, 49; Isaac Asimov, *The Shaping of North America* (Boston: Houghton Mifflin Company, 1973), 56-60..
[22] T.H. Breen and Timothy Hall, *Colonial America in an Atlantic World* (New York: Pearson Education, 2004), 36-41.
[23] T.H. Breen and Timothy Hall, *Colonial America in an Atlantic World* (New York: Pearson Education, 2004), 180-181.
[24] T.H. Breen and Timothy Hall, *Colonial America in an Atlantic World* (New York: Pearson Education, 2004), 69; Isaac Asimov, *The Shaping of North America* (Boston: Houghton Mifflin Company, 1973), 61-66.
[25] T.H. Breen and Timothy Hall, *Colonial America in an Atlantic World* (New York: Pearson Education, 2004), 69; Isaac Asimov, *The Shaping of North America* (Boston: Houghton Mifflin Company, 1973), 61-66.
[26] Joan Morrison and Charlotte Fox Zabusky, *American Mosaic: The Immigrant Experience in the Words of Those Who Lived It.* University of Pittsburgh Press, Pittsburgh, PA: 1980.
[27] T.H. Breen and Timothy Hall, *Colonial America in an Atlantic World* (New York: Pearson Education, 2004), 23-26.
[28] T.H. Breen and Timothy Hall, *Colonial America in an Atlantic World* (New York: Pearson Education, 2004), 76-77; Richard Middleton, *Colonial America* (Oxford: Blackwell Publishers, 1996), 10-11.
[29] Richard Middleton, *Colonial America* (Oxford: Blackwell Publishers, 1996), 52-53.
[30] T.H. Breen and Timothy Hall, *Colonial America in an Atlantic World* (New York: Pearson Education, 2004), 86-93.
[31] T.H. Breen and Timothy Hall, *Colonial America in an Atlantic World* (New York: Pearson Education, 2004), 100.
[32] Alan Taylor, *American Colonies* (New York: Viking Penguin, 2001), 134, 136; T.H. Breen and Timothy Hall, *Colonial America in an Atlantic World* (New York: Pearson Education, 2004), 96-98.
[33] T.H. Breen and Timothy Hall, *Colonial America in an Atlantic World* (New York: Pearson Education, 2004), 23, 112-113.
[34] T.H. Breen and Timothy Hall, *Colonial America in an Atlantic World* (New York: Pearson Education, 2004), 116-117.

[35] T.H. Breen and Timothy Hall, *Colonial America in an Atlantic World* (New York: Pearson Education, 2004), 119-121.
[36] T.H. Breen and Timothy Hall, *Colonial America in an Atlantic World* (New York: Pearson Education, 2004), 125-130.
[37] Isaac Asimov, *The Shaping of North America* (Boston: Houghton Mifflin Company, 1973), 160-161.
[38] T.H. Breen and Timothy Hall, *Colonial America in an Atlantic World* (New York: Pearson Education, 2004), 123, 131; Isaac Asimov, *The Shaping of North America* (Boston: Houghton Mifflin Company, 1973), 160-161.
[39] Jon Butler, *Becoming America* (Cambridge: Harvard University Press, 2000), 23.
[40] Alan Taylor, *American Colonies* (New York Viking Penguin, 2001), 99.
[41] T.H. Breen and Timothy Hall, *Colonial America in an Atlantic World* (New York: Pearson Education, 2004), 70-71; Isaac Asimov, *The Shaping of North America* (Boston: Houghton Mifflin Company, 1973), 116-119.
[42] Isaac Asimov, *The Shaping of North America* (Boston: Houghton Mifflin Company, 1973), 143-246.
[43] Jon Butler, *Becoming America* (Cambridge, Massachusetts: Harvard University Press, 2000), 29.
[44] T.H. Breen and Timothy Hall, *Colonial America in an Atlantic World* (New York: Pearson Education, 2004), 72.
[45] T.H. Breen and Timothy Hall, *Colonial America in an Atlantic World* (New York: Pearson Education, 2004), 77.
[46] Kenneth M. Stampp, *The Peculiar Institution* (New York: Vintage Books, 1989), 392.
[47] Dorothy Schneider and Carl J. Schneider, *Slavery in America* (New York: Infobase Publishing, 2007), 35.
[48] Gad Heuman and James Walvin, *The Slavery Reader* (New York: Routeledge, 2003), 8; Dorothy Schneider and Carl J. Schneider, *Slavery in America* (New York: Infobase Publishing, 2007), 35.
[49] Betty Wood, *Slavery in Colonial Georgia* (Athens: University of Georgia Press, 1984),), 72-74, 78, 88, 96; Adam Rothman, *Slave Country* (Cambridge, Massachusetts: Harvard University Press, 2005), 2.
[50] Ernest Obadele-Starks, *Freebooters and Smugglers* (Fayetteville: University of Arkansas Press, 2007), 9-10; Kenneth M. Stampp, *The Peculiar Institution* (New York: Vintage Books, 1989), 25, 271-272.
[51] Enrico Dal Lago, *Agrarian Elites* (Baton Rouge: Louisiana State University Press, 2005), 62.
[52] Jean M. West, "King Cotton: The Fiber of Slavery," *Slavery in America*, <http://www.slaveryinamerica.org/history/hs_es_cotton.htm>, access. July 2009.
[53] John B. Boles, *Black Southerners 1619-1869* (Lexington: University Press of Kentucky, 1983), 392; Jean M. West, "King Cotton: The Fiber of Slavery," *Slavery in America*, < http://www.slaveryinamerica.org/history/hs_es_cotton.htm>, access. July 2009.
[54] Kenneth M. Stampp, *The Peculiar Institution* (New York: Vintage Books, 1989), 62-67.

[55] Junius P. Rodriguez, *Encyclopedia of Slave Resistence and Rebellion Volume II* (Westport: Greenwood Press, 2007), 486-491; Jon Butler, *Becoming America* (Cambridge: Harvard University Press, 2000), 46.
[56] Kevin Kenny, *The American Irish* (New York: Pearson Education Inc., 2000), 46, 72, 90,102-103, 113; Jay P. Dolan, *The Irish Americans* (New York: Bloomsbury Press, 2008), 67; Edward Laxton, *The Famine Ships* (New York: Henry Holt and Company, 1996), 24, 27.
[57] Jay P. Dolan, *The Irish Americans* (New York: Bloomsbury Press, 2008), 61, 97-98; Lawrence J. McCaffrey, *The Irish Catholic Diaspora in America* (Washington D.C.: Catholic University of American Press, 1997), 72.
[58] Jay P. Dolan, *The Irish Americans* (New York: Bloomsbury Press, 2008), 61.
[59] Hamilton Holt, ed. *The Life Stories of Undistinguished Americans: As Told by Themselves* (New York: J. Pott & Co., 1906).
[60] Arif Dirlik, *Chinese on the American Frontier* (Lanham, Maryland: Rowman & Littlefield Publishers Inc, 2001), 245-246; Susie Lan Cassel, *The Chinese in America* (Walnut Creek, CA: Altamira Press, 2002), 24; Peter Kwong and Dušanka Miščević, *Chinese America* (New York: The New Press, 2005), 35-36.
[61] Sucheng Chan, *Entry Denied* (Philadelphia: Temple University Press, 1991), 5-6; Peter Kwong and Dušanka Miščević, *Chinese America* (New York: The New Press, 2005), 35-36.
[62] Susie Lan Cassel, *The Chinese in America* (Walnut Creek, CA: Altamira Press, 2002), 91-92; Peter Kwong and Dušanka Miščević, *Chinese America* (New York: The New Press, 2005), 68.
[63] Susie Lan Cassel, *The Chinese in America* (Walnut Creek, CA: Altamira Press, 2002), 91-92.
[64] Peter Kwong and Dušanka Miščević, *Chinese America* (New York: The New Press, 2005), 92; Ronald H. Bayor, *The Columbia Documentary History of Race and Ethnicity in America* (New York: Columbia University Press, 2004), 231.
[65] Sucheng Chan, *Entry Denied* (Philadelphia: Temple University Press, 1991), 26, 31, 60; Peter Kwong and Dušanka Miščević, *Chinese America* (New York: The New Press, 2005), 98, 139..
[66] Joan Morrison and Charlotte Fox Zabusky, *American Mosaic: The Immigrant Experience in the Words of Those Who Lived It.* University of Pittsburgh Press, Pittsburgh, PA: 1980, 196-199.
[67] Ronald H. Bayor, *The Columbia Documentary History of Race and Ethnicity in America* (New York: Columbia University Press, 2004), 228; Roger Daniels, *Coming to America* (New York: Visual Education Corporation, 2002), 146-154.
[68] Roger Daniels, *Coming to America* (New York: Visual Education Corporation, 2002), 146-154.
[69] Odd S. Lovoll, *The Promise of America: A History of the Norwegian-American People* (Minneapolis: University of Minnesota Press, 1984), 14-26; Roger Daniels, *Coming to America* (New York: Visual Education Corporation, 2002), 174.
[70] Lars Ljungmark, *Swedish Exodus*, trans. Kermit B. Westerberg, (London: Swedish Pioneer Historical Society, 1979), 29; Roger Daniels, *Coming to America* (New York: Visual Education Corporation, 2002), 168.

[71] Frederick Hale, *Danes in North America* (Seattle: University of Washington Press, 1984), xi-xx.
[72] Hans Norman and Harold Runblomp, *Transatlantic Connections: Nordic Migration to the New World after 1800* (Oxford: Norwegian University Press, 1988), 85, 189, 88-89.
[73] The Biography of a Bootblack: Rocco Corresca, *Independent*, LIV (Dec. 4, 1902), 2863-67.
[74] Philip di Franco, *The Italian American Experience* (New York: RGA Publishing Group, Inc., 1988), 87; Salvatore J. Lagumina et al., "Anti-Italian Discrimination," *The Italian American Experience* (New York: Garland Publishing, Inc., 2000), 17; Luciano J. Iorizzo and Salvatore Mondello, *The Italian Americans* (Boston: Twayne Publishers, 1980), 76, 104.
[75] Philip di Franco, *The Italian American Experience* (New York: RGA Publishing Group, Inc., 1988), 72-74, 76-81; Luciano J. Iorizzo and Salvatore Mondello, *The Italian Americans* (Boston: Twayne Publishers, 1980), 60, 64.
[76] Luciano J. Iorizzo and Salvatore Mondello, *The Italian Americans* (Boston: Twayne Publishers, 1980), 57-59, 63.
[77] Salvatore J. Lagumina et al., "Anti-Italian Discrimination," *The Italian American Experience* (New York: RGA Publishing Group, Inc., 1988), 17-18, 405; Patrick J. Gallo, *Old Bread, New Wine* (Chicago: Nelson-Hall Inc. Publishers, 1981), 183-190; Philip di Franco, *The Italian American Experience* (New York: RGA Publishing Group, Inc., 1988), 85; Luciano J. Iorizzo and Salvatore Mondello, *The Italian Americans* (Boston: Twayne Publishers, 1980), 81.
[78] Charles C. Moskos, *Greek Americans: Struggle and Success* (New Brunswick, New Jersey: Transaction Publishers, 1989), 8-30.
[79] Steven Bela Vardy, *The Hungarian-Americans* (Boston: Twayne Publishers, 1985), 18-20.
[80] Roger Daniels, *Coming to America* (New York: Visual Education Corporation, 2002), 232-235.
[81] Myron B. Kuropas, *The Ukranian Americans* (Toronto: University of Toronto Press, 1991), 20-39.
[82] Joan Morrison and Charlotte Fox Zabusky, *American Mosaic: The Immigrant Experience in the Words of Those Who Lived It.* University of Pittsburgh Press, Pittsburgh, PA: 1980, 154-161.
[83] Joan Morrison and Charlotte Fox Zabusky, *American Mosaic: The Immigrant Experience in the Words of Those Who Lived It.* University of Pittsburgh Press, Pittsburgh, PA: 1980, 161-169.
[84] Roger Daniels, *Coming to America* (New York: Visual Education Corporation, 2002), 215, 219.
[85] Helena Znanieka Lopata, *Polish Americans* (New Brunswick: Transaction Publishers, 1994), 17-49.
[86] Joan Morrison and Charlotte Fox Zabusky, *American Mosaic: The Immigrant Experience in the Words of Those Who Lived It.* University of Pittsburgh Press, Pittsburgh, PA: 1980, 137-141.
[87] James McBride, *The Color of Water* (New York: Penguin, 2006), 1-2, 16.

[88] Roger Daniels, *Coming to America* (New York, Visual Education Corporation, 2002), 224-225; Rudolf Glanz, *The Jewish Women of America* (New York: Ktav Publishing House, 1976), 1.
[89] Roger Daniels, *Coming to America* (New York: Visual Education Corporation, 2002), 226-228.
[90] Gerald Sorin, *A Time for Building* (Baltimore: The John Hopkins University Press, 1992), 1-56.
[91] Joan Morrison and Charlotte Fox Zabusky, *American Mosaic: The Immigrant Experience in the Words of Those Who Lived It*. University of Pittsburgh Press, Pittsburgh, PA: 1980, 32-35.
[92] June Namias. *First Generation: In the Words of Twentieth-Century American Immigrants*. Beacon Press, Boston: 1978, 79-85.
[93] Gary Y. Okihiro, *The Columbia Guide to Asian American History* (New York: Columbia University Press, 2001), 179, 182; David J. O'Brien and Stephen S. Fugita, *The Japanese American Experience* (Bloomington: Indiana University Press, 2001), 10-12; Robert A. Wilson and Bill Hosokawa, *East to America* (New York: William Morrow and Company, Inc., 1980), 17, 28; Paul R. Spickard, *Japanese Americans* (New York: Twayne Publishers, 1996), 21.
[94] Steve Boisson, *Immigrants: The Last Time America Sent Her Own Packing*, American History Magazine, Sept. 2006, available at http://www.historynet.com/immigrants-the-last-time-america-sent-her-own-packing.htm.
[95] Francisco Balderrama and Raymond Rodriguez, *Decades of Betrayal*, in Steve Boisson, *Immigrants: The Last Time America Sent Her Own Packing*, American History Magazine Sept. 2006, available at http://www.historynet.com/immigrants-the-last-time-america-sent-her-own-packing.htm.
[96] Steve Boisson, *Immigrants: The Last Time America Sent Her Own Packing*, American History Magazine, Sept. 2006, available at http://www.historynet.com/immigrants-the-last-time-america-sent-her-own-packing.htm.
[97] Gregory Rodrigues, *Mongrels, Bastards, Orphans, and Vagabonds* (New York: Pantheon Books, 2007), 93-94, 132, 133, 135; Matt S. Meir and Feliciano Ribera, *Mexican Americans/American Mexicans* (Hill and Wang, 1993), 104-105; Manuel G. Gonzales, *Mexicanos* (Bloomington: Indiana University, 1999), 157.
[98] Gregory Rodrigues, *Mongrels, Bastards, Orphans, and Vagabonds* (New York: Pantheon Books, 2007), 106, 112, 128-136.
[99] Patrick J. Gallo, *Old Bread, New Wine* (Chicago: Nelson-Hall Inc. Publishers, 1981), 42.
[100] Roger Daniels, *Coming to America* (New York: Visual Education Corporation, 2002), 258-264.
[101] Christopher Capozzola, *Uncle Sam Wants You* (Oxford: Oxford University Press, 2008), 61.
[102] H.C. Peterson and Gilbert C. Fite, *Opponents of War* (Seattle: University of Washington Press, 1999), 194-207.

[103] Christopher Capozzola, *Uncle Sam Wants You* (Oxford: Oxford University Press, 2008), 173, 177, 179-180, 204.
[104] H.C. Peterson and Gilbert C. Fite, *Opponents of War* (Seattle: University of Washington Press, 1999), 194-207; Arnoldo De León and Richard Griswold del Castillo, *North Aztlán* (Wheeling, Illinois: Harland Davidson, Inc., 2006), 88; Christopher Capozzola, *Uncle Sam Wants You* (Oxford: Oxford University Press, 2008), 32.
[105] H.C. Peterson and Gilbert C. Fite, *Opponents of War* (Seattle: University of Washington Press, 1999), 97-100.
[106] H.C. Peterson and Gilbert C. Fite, *Opponents of War* (Seattle: University of Washington Press, 1999), 8-9, 24, 47, 76.
[107] Frederick Lewis Allen, *Only Yesterday* (New York: Harper & Row Publishers, 1957), 56-57; H.C. Peterson and Gilbert C. Fite, *Opponents of War* (Seattle: University of Washington Press, 1999), 285-296.
[108] Gregory Rodrigues, *Mongrels, Bastards, Orphans, and Vagabonds* (New York: Pantheon Books, 2007), 130-132.
[109] Isaac Asimov, *From Harding to Hiroshima* (New York: Dembner Books, 1988), 24.
[110] David M. Kennedy, *Freedom from Fear* (New York: Oxford University Press, 1999), 14; Carlos B. Cordova, *The Salvadoran Americans* (Westport, Connecticut: Greenwood Press, 1998), 55-58, 74, 75.
[111] David M. Kennedy, *Freedom from Fear* (New York: Oxford University Press, 1999), 162-163, 166, 288.
[112] David M. Kennedy, *Freedom from Fear* (New York: Oxford University Press, 1999), 15.
[113] Ronald H. Bayor, *The Columbia Documentary History of Race and Ethnicity in America* (New York: Columbia University Press, 2004), 607; F. Acuña, *Occupied America* (Harrisonbury: R.R. Donelly and Sons Company, 2007), 169; Rodolfo F. Acuña, *Occupied America* (Harrisonbury: R.R. Donelly and Sons Company, 2007), 194.
[114] Henry L. Feingold, *A Time for Search* (Baltimore: The John Hopkins University Press, 1992), 29, 221; David M. Kennedy, *Freedom from Fear* (New York: Oxford University Press, 1999), 416-417.
[115] Gary Y. Okihiro, *The Columbia Guide to Asian American History* (New York: Columbia University Press, 2001), 105-106.
[116] David M. Kennedy, *Freedom from Fear* (New York: Oxford University Press, 1999), 754.
[117] Andrew E. Taslitz, Stories Of Fourth Amendment Disrespect: From Elian To The Internment, 70 Fordham L. Rev. 2257, 2306-2307 (2002),.
[118] Salvatore J. Lagumina et al., "World War II Internment and Prisoners of War," *The Italian American Experience* (New York: RGA Publishing Group, Inc., 1988), 702-705.
[119] Roger Daniels, *Coming to America* (New York: Visual Education Corporation, 2002), 305-306.

[120] Roger Daniels, *Coming to America* (New York: Visual Education Corporation, 2002), 235.
[121] Gregory Rodrigues, *Mongrels, Bastards, Orphans, and Vagabonds* (New York: Pantheon Books, 2007), 192-193.
[122] Gregory Rodrigues, *Mongrels, Bastards, Orphans, and Vagabonds* (New York: Pantheon Books, 2007), 197.
[123] Matt S. Meir and Feliciano Ribera, *Mexican Americans/American Mexicans* (Hill and Wang, 1993), 184.
[124] Roger Daniels, *Coming to America* (New York: Visual Education Corporation, 2002), 232, 359; Barbara M. Posadas, *The Filipino Americans* (Westport, Connecticut: Greenwood Press: 1999), 38-39; Alex Antón and Roger E. Herández, *Cubans in America* (New York: Kensington Books, 2009), 149.
[125] Randa A. Kayyali, *The Arab Americans* (Westport, Connecticut: Greenwood Press, 2006) 27-43.
[126] Gregory Orfalea, *Arab Americans: A History* (Northhampton, Massachusetts: Olive Branch Press, 2006), 152, 300-312.
[127] Roger Daniels, *Coming to America* (New York: Visual Education Corporation, 2002), 360-361.
[128] Karen Isaksen Leonard, *The South Asian Americans* (Westport, Connecticut, Greenwood Press, 1998), 68.
[129] Roger Daniels, *Coming to America* (New York: Visual Education Corporation, 2002), 363.
[130] Susan Bibler Coutin, Migrants' Complex Affiliations, SPRING 2009, Volume XXIV, Number 2, http://www.abanet.org/publiced/focus/FocusSpring2009.pdf.
[131] Carlos B. Cordova, *The Salvadoran Americans* (Westport, Connecticut, Greenwood Press, 1998), 55-58, 74, 75.
[132] David G. Gutierrez, *The Columbia History of Latinos in the United States Since 1960* (New York, Columbia University Press, 2004,) 191-214.
[133] Alex Antón and Roger E. Herández, *Cubans in America* (New York: Kensington Books, 2009), 149; Miguel Gonzalez-Pando, *The Cuban Americans* (Westport, Connecticut: Greenwood Press, 1998), 10-19.
[134] Silvio Torres-Saillant and Ramona Hernández, The Dominican Americans (Westport, Connecticut: Greenwood Press, 1998), 29-31.
[135] Silvio Torres-Saillant and Ramona Hernández, The Dominican Americans (Westport, Connecticut: Greenwood Press, 1998), 9, 33-60.
[136] Flore Zéphir, *The Haitian Americans* (Westport, Connecticut, Greenwood Press, 1998), 17, 48-57, 67-75.
[137] David M. Reimers, Other Immigrants: The Global Origins of the American People (New York: New York University Press, 2005), 74, 233-234, 250.
[138] Central Intelligence Agency, CIA World Factbook: Jamaica, https://www.cia.gov/library/publications/the-world-factbook/geos/jm.html, 29 July 2009; Freedom House, Freedom House Country Report: Jamaica http://www.freedomhouse.org/template.cfm?page=22&year=2009&country=7632, 29 July 2009.

[139] Patricia J. F. Rosof, *Ethnic and immigration groups: The United States, Canada, and England* (Haworth Press, 1983), 54; Central Intelligence Agency, CIA World Factbook: Jamaica, https://www.cia.gov/library/publications/the-world-factbook/geos/jm.html, 29 July 2009; Freedom House, Freedom House Country Report: Jamaica
http://www.freedomhouse.org/template.cfm?page=22&year=2009&country=7632, 29 July 2009; United Nations, U.N. Public Administration Network, http://unpan1.un.org/intradoc/groups/public/documents/APCITY/UNPAN022370.pdf, 29 July 2009.
[140] Roger Daniels, *Coming to America* (New York: Visual Education Corporation, 2002), 366.
[141] Ilpyóng J. Kim, *Korean Americans: Past, Present, and Future* (New York: Hollym International Corporation, 2004), 17, 28-31.
[142] Roger Daniels, *Coming to America* (New York: Visual Education Corporation, 2002), 365.
[143] María E. Pérez y González, *Puerto Ricans in the United States* (Westport, Connecticut: Greenwood Press, 2000), 26-39.
[144] Juan Gonzalez, *Harvest of Empire* (Newyork: Viking Penguis, 2000), 149, 158; David G. Gutierrez, *The Columbia History of Latinos in the United States Since 1960* (New York, Columbia University Press, 2004), 262, 268.
[145] David G. Gutierrez, *The Columbia History of Latinos in the United States Since 1960* (New York, Columbia University Press, 2004), 259-274.
[146] Roger Daniels, *Coming to America* (New York: Visual Education Corporation, 2002), 345; Hien Duc Do, *The Vietnamese Americans* (Westport, Connecticut: Greenwood Press, 1999), 26-47.
[147] John A. Arthur, INVISIBLE SOJOURNERS: AFRICAN IMMIGRANT DIASPORA IN THE UNITED STATES 1 (2000).
[148] *Id.*
[149] *Id.* at 2.
[150] *Id.*
[151] http://www.census.gov/population/cen2000/stp-159/STP-159-africa.pdf
[152] http://www.migrationinformation.org/usfocus/display.cfm?ID=147
[153] Wilson, Jill. 2003. "African-born Residents of the United States." Migration Policy Institute. http://www.migrationinformation.org/USFocus/display.cfm?ID=147
[154] Ibid.
[155] Ibid.
[156] Halter, Marilyn. "Africa: West." *The New Americans: A Guide to Immigration Since 1965*. Ed. Mary C. Waters and Reed Ueda. Harvard University Press: Cambridge, 2007. pg. 283.
[157] Wilson, Jill. 2003. "African-born Residents of the United States." Migration Policy Institute. http://www.migrationinformation.org/USFocus/display.cfm?ID=147
[158] Monger, Randall. 2010. "U.S. Legal Permanent Residents." U.S. Department of Homeland Security, Office of Immigration Statistics.
http://www.dhs.gov/xlibrary/assets/statistics/publications/lpr_fr_2009.pdf

[159] Wilson, Jill. 2003. "African-born Residents of the United States." Migration Policy Institute. http://www.migrationinformation.org/USFocus/display.cfm?ID=147
[160] Martin, Daniel C. 2010. "Refugees and Asylees: 2009." U.S. Department of Homeland Security, Office of Immigration Statistics. http://www.dhs.gov/xlibrary/assets/statistics/publications/ois_rfa_fr_2009.pdf
[161] Ibid.
[162] Ibid.
[163] Ibid.
[164] http://www.migrationinformation.org/usfocus/display.cfm?ID=147#3
[165] *Id.*
[166] John A. Arthur, at 2-3.
[167] *Id.* at 17, 20.
[168] *Id.* at 20.
[169] http://www.migrationinformation.org/usfocus/display.cfm?ID=147#3
[170] http://www.state.gov/r/pa/ei/bgn/2836.htm
[171] http://www.everyculture.com/multi/Le-Pa/Nigerian-Americans.html
[172] *Id.*
[173] *Id.*
[174] *Id.*
[175] http://www.census.gov/population/cen2000/stp-159/STP-159-nigeria.pdf
[176] http://www.state.gov/r/pa/ei/bgn/2860.htm
[177] http://www.migrationinformation.org/usfocus/display.cfm?ID=147#3
[178] http://www.everyculture.com/multi/Du-Ha/Ghanaian-Americans.html
[179] http://www.state.gov/r/pa/ei/bgn/2860.htm
[180] http://www.state.gov/r/pa/ei/bgn/2860.htm
[181] http://www.state.gov/r/pa/ei/bgn/2860.htm
[182] http://www.everyculture.com/multi/Du-Ha/Ghanaian-Americans.html
[183] *Id.*
[184] http://www.unhcr.org/4922d41a0.html
[185] *Id.*
[186] http://www.everyculture.com/multi/Le-Pa/Liberian-Americans.html
[187] http://www.everyculture.com/multi/Le-Pa/Liberian-Americans.html
[188] http://www.everyculture.com/multi/Le-Pa/Liberian-Americans.html
[189] http://migration.ucdavis.edu/mn/more.php?id=2204_0_2_0
[190] MARK BIXLER, THE LOST BOYS OF SUDAN xiv (2005).
[191] http://www.lsga.org/Programs/refugee/Sudanese.htm
[192] 2010 UNHCR Country Profile. http://www.unhcr.org/pages/49e483ad6.html
[193] http://www.migrationinformation.org/usfocus/display.cfm?ID=585
[194] *From Horror to Homelessness*, Human Rights Watch report, available at http://www.hrw.org/node/81794 (documenting the extortion, detention, violence, and deportation at the hands of the Kenyan police faced by a record number of Somalis entering Kenya. The new refugees are joining over a quarter of a million fellow refugees struggling to survive in camps designed for one-third that number.)
[195] http://www.lsga.org/Programs/refugee/Somalis.htm

[196] http://www.lsga.org/Programs/Refugee/Som_Bantu.htm

[197] Department of Homeland Security. *2009 Yearbook of Immigration Statistics.* Table 3. http://www.dhs.gov/files/statistics/publications/yearbook.shtm
[198] Ibid.
[199] Department of Homeland Security. *2009 Yearbook of Immigration Statistics.* Table 17. http://www.dhs.gov/files/statistics/publications/yearbook.shtm
[200] Marrow, Helen B. "Africa: South Africa and Zimbabwe." *The New Americans: A Guide to Immigration Since 1965*. Ed. Mary C. Waters and Reed Ueda. Harvard University Press: Cambridge, 2007. pg. 307
[201] Marrow, Helen B. "Africa: South Africa and Zimbabwe." *The New Americans: A Guide to Immigration Since 1965*. Ed. Mary C. Waters and Reed Ueda. Harvard University Press: Cambridge, 2007. pg. 308
[202] Marrow, Helen B. pg. 313.
[203] Marrow, Helen B. pg. 314
[204] Marrow, Helen B. pg. 309
[205] Marrow, Helen B. pg. 313
[206] Lefko-Everett, Kate. 2004. "Botswana's Changing Migration Patterns." Migration Policy Institute. http://www.migrationinformation.org/Feature/display.cfm?id=246
[207] Kusow, A. (2007). Africa: East. In M. C. Waters, R. Ueda, & H. B. Marrow (Eds.), *The New Americans: A Guide to Immigration Since 1965* (pp. 295-306). Cambridge, Massachusetts: Harvard University Press.

[208] "Though Obama Had to Leave to Find Himself, It is Hawaii That Made His Rise Possible (2008, August 24). *The Washington Post*. Pg. A22.
[209] Kusow, 2007.
[210] Ibid.
[211] U.S. Department of State. (2010, May 12). *Background Note: Kenya.* Retrieved from http://www.state.gov/r/pa/ei/bgn/2962.htm
[212] Terrazas, A. M. (2007, June). *Beyond Regional Circularity: The Emergence of an Ethiopian Diaspora* . Retrieved from Migration Information Source: http://www.migrationinformation.org/Profiles/display.cfm?ID=604

[213] Kobel, P. S. (2007). *Ethiopian Americans.* Retrieved from Countries and Their Cultures: http://www.everyculture.com/multi/Du-Ha/Ethiopian-Americans.html

[214] Terrazas, 2007.
[215] Terrazas, 2007.
[216] Roberts, M. A. (1982, Spring). The U.S. and Refugees: The Refugee Act of 1980. *Issue: A Journal of Opinion, 12*(1/2), 4-6.

[217] Kobel, 2007.
[218] Ibid.
[219] Ibid.
[220] Keatley, P. (2003, August 18). *Obituary: Idi Amin.* Retrieved from The Guardian: http://www.guardian.co/uk/news/2003/aug/18/guardianobituaries

[221] Kusow, 2007.
[222] Miller, O. (n.d.). *Ugandan Americans.* Retrieved from Countries and Their Cultures: http://www.everyculture.com/multi/Sr-Z/Ugandan-Americans.html

[223] Roger Daniels, *Coming to America* (New York: Visual Education Corporation, 2002), 359.
[224] Roger Daniels, *Coming to America* (New York: Visual Education Corporation, 2002), 347; Alex Antón and Roger E. Herández, *Cubans in America* (New York: Kensington Books, 2009), 207.
[225] Martha Donkor, *Sudanese Refugees in the United States* (Lewiston, The Edwin Mellen Press, 2008), 85.
[226] USCIS, Temporary Benefits Employment Categories and Required Documentation, http://www.uscis.gov/portal/site/uscis/menuitem.5af9bb95919f35e66f614176543f6d1a/?vgnextoid=229c6138f898d010VgnVCM10000048f3d6a1RCRD&vgnextchannel=91919c7755cb9010VgnVCM10000045f3d6a1RCRD, 3 June 2009.
[227] Thomson Reuters Interpreter Release, *USCIS Issues Memorandum Instructing on Successor-in-Interest Determinations in Adjudicating Form I-140*, September 4, 2009, 86 No. 34 Interpreter Releases 2198-2199.
[228] *Lumataw v. Holder*, No. 08-1757, On Petition For Review Of An Order Of The Board Of Immigration, Decided September 9, 2009, US COA 1st Circuit.
[229] Society of American Law Teachers (SALT), Recommendations to the Administration for Immigration Agency Reforms, June 16, 2009, http://www.saltlaw.org/userfiles/6-09immigrationstatement.pdf, p. 19.
[230] These regulations are in 42 CFR 34.2(b). Two new disease categories were added in 2008. See CDC Updates to Medical Examinations of Aliens, http://travel.state.gov/visa/laws/telegrams/telegrams_4388.html and http://www.cdc.gov/ncidod/dq/ifr_main.htm.
[231] Amnesty International, Jailed without Justice: Immigration Detention in the U.S.A, 6, March.
[232] Donald Kerwin and Serena Yi-Ying Lin, *Immigration Detention: Can ICE Meet Its Legal Imperatives and Case Management Responsibilities?*, Migration Policy Institute, September 2009, *available at* http://www.migrationpolicy.org/pubs/detentionreportSept1009.pdf.
[233] See REAL ID Act and Persecution and Torture Claims Three Years Later, Thomas Hutchins, Esq., prepared for AILA panel REAL ID Act and Persecution and Torture Claims Three Years Later, Vancouver, Canada, June 28, 2008 (citing CRS

Report RL32754, Immigration: Analysis of the Major Provisions of the REAL ID Act of 2005, by Michael John Garcia, Margaret Mikyung Lee, and Todd Tatelman (May 25, 2005), at 1-3).

[234] See Judicial Review Provisions of the Real ID Act, AILF Legal Action Center, American Immigration Law Foundation, June 7, 2005.

[235] See REAL ID Act and Persecution and Torture Claims Three Years Later, Thomas Hutchins, Esq., prepared for AILA panel REAL ID Act and Persecution and Torture Claims Three Years Later, Vancouver, Canada, June 28, 2008 (citing CRS Report RL32754, Immigration: Analysis of the Major Provisions of the REAL ID Act of 2005, by Michael John Garcia, Margaret Mikyung Lee, and Todd Tatelman (May 25, 2005), at 1-3).

[236] Id.; see *Matter of Mogharrabi*, 19 I&N Dec. 439 (BIA 1987).

[237] *Matter of J-B-N- & S-M-*, 24 I&N Dec. 208, 211 (BIA 2007) (quoting *Matter of Fuentes*, 19 I&N Dec. 658, 662 (BIA 1988)).

[238] Id. (quoting *Matter of S-P-*, 21 I&N Dec. at 494).

[239] Refers to definition of "refugee."

[240] H.R. Rep. No. 109-72, at 163 (quoting Asylum and Withholding Definitions, 65 Fed. Reg. 76,588, 76,592 (Dec. 7, 2000)); cited in *Matter of J-B-N- & S-M-*, 24 I&N Dec. 208, 213 (BIA 2007).

[241] *Matter of J-Y-C-*, 24 I&N Dec. 260 (BIA 2007).

[242] See REAL ID Act and Persecution and Torture Claims Three Years Later, Thomas Hutchins, Esq., prepared for AILA panel REAL ID Act and Persecution and Torture Claims Three Years Later, Vancouver, Canada, June 28, 2008 at page 16.

[243] James Feroli, Immigration Briefings June 2009, Credibility, Burden of Proof, and Corroboration Under the Real ID Act, pg. 1.

[244] PL 107-208, 116 Stat. 927 (Aug. 6, 2002).

[245] Pub. L. No. 107-208, 116 Stat. 927 (2002)

[246] 8 U.S.C. § 1153(h)(1).

[247] For classification under INA § 204, 8 USC 1154.

[248] INA § 203(h)(1)(A)-(B).

[249] The number of days the petition was pending, from the filing date to the approval date, represents the amount of time it took USCIS to adjudicate the petition.

[250] The "sought to acquire" language and one-year requirement of INA § 203(h)(1)(A) have been the subject of some debate, particularly in the situation where the derivative is overseas. The State Department has issued a cable memorandum advising that the "sought to acquire" language can only mean when the immigrant visa first becomes available for the principal applicant. Department of State, Cable Memorandum, Child Status Protection Act: ALDAC #2, 03 State 015049 (January 17, 2003). The cable memorandum recognizes that Form I-824 can be filed at the same time as when an application to adjust to permanent residence is filed by the principal, and states that the one-year "sought to acquire" requirement can only be met if the I-824 is filed within the one year when the immigrant visa becomes available to the parent. However, this advisory memorandum fails to recognize that having an immigrant visa number available to the parent does not mean that the application for permanent residence has been reviewed or approved, nor does it mean

that an immigrant visa is available to the derivative. An immigrant visa cannot be available to an overseas derivative until the underlying application to adjust status of the principal is approved. Therefore, a true reading of the CSPA language is that a derivative is entitled to CSPA benefits so long as he or she had sought to acquire permanent residence through his or her principal parent filing an I-824, so long as it was filed within one year of the approval of the principal's application to for permanent residence. This interpretation recognizes the title of the Form I-824, Application for Action on an Approved Application or Petition, which cannot be approved or acted upon until the principal's permanent residence application is approved. Congress could rectify the erroneous interpretation of the CSPA both in terms of clarifying "sought to acquire" to mean when parents' I-485 applications are approved, and also to confirm language already in CSPA to allow retention of priority dates.

[251] Subsection (a)(2)(A) refers to INA § 203(a)(2)(A) which provides the statutory authority to issue visas to sons and daughters of lawful permanent residents.

[252] Subsection (d) refers to INA § 203(d) which provides the statutory authority to issue visas to derivative beneficiaries, i.e. spouses and children, to immigrate with the principal beneficiary.

[253] 25 I&N Dec. 28 (BIA 2009).

[254] Matter of Garcia, A 79 001 587 (BIA June 16, 2006).

[255] Robert J. Sampson, "Rethinking Crime and Immigration" February 2008, Vol. 7, No. 1, Pages 28–33 ,
Posted online on February 7, 2008.

[256] Richard T. Herman and Robert L. Smith, Immigrant, Inc.: Why Immigrant Entrepreneurs Are Driving the New Economy (and How They Will Save the American Worker), John Wiley & Sons, 2010, 167.

[257] Richard T. Herman and Robert L. Smith, Immigrant, Inc.: Why Immigrant Entrepreneurs Are Driving the New Economy (and How They Will Save the American Worker), John Wiley & Sons, 2010, 170.

[258] Society of American Law Teachers (SALT), Recommendations to the Administration for Immigration Agency Reforms, June 16, 2009, http://www.saltlaw.org/userfiles/6-09immigrationstatement.pdf.

CONTACT MARGARET W. WONG & ASSOC. CO., LPA

Cleveland Office:
3150 Chester Avenue
Cleveland, OH 44114
Phone: (216) 566-9908
Fax: (216) 566-1125

Columbus Office:
By appointment only
470 Olde Worthington Road Suite 200
Westerville, OH 43082
Phone: (614) 221-8892

Detroit Office:
By appointment only
Detroit City Airport Signature Building
11201 Conner Ave.
Detroit, MI 48213
Phone: (313) 527-9989

Atlanta Office:
5425 Peachtree Parkway
Norcross, GA 30092
Phone: (678) 906-4061

New York Office:
401 Broadway,
Suite 1620
New York, NY 10013
Phone: (212) 226-7011